Fundamentals of Business Law I

Roger LeRoy Miller | Gaylord A. Jentz

CENGAGE
Learning™

Australia • Brazil • Japan • Korea • Mexico • Singapore • Spain • United Kingdom • United States

CENGAGE
Learning™

Fundamentals of Business Law I

Roger LeRoy Miller | Gaylord A. Jentz

Executive Editors:
Maureen Staudt
Michael Stranz

Senior Project Development Manager:
Linda de Stefano

Marketing Specialist:
Sara Mercurio

Production/Manufacturing Manager:
Donna M. Brown

PreMedia Supervisor:
Joel Brennecke

Rights & Permissions Specialist:
Kalina Hintz
Todd Osborne

Cover Image:
Getty Images*

* Unless otherwise noted, all cover images used by Custom Solutions, a part of Cengage Learning, have been supplied courtesy of Getty Images with the exception of the Earthview cover image, which has been supplied by the National Aeronautics and Space Administration (NASA).

For product information and technology assistance, contact us at
Cengage Learning Customer & Sales Support, 1-800-354-9706

For permission to use material from this text or product,
submit all requests online at **cengage.com/permissions**
Further permissions questions can be emailed to
permissionrequest@cengage.com

ISBN-13: 978-1-111-07076-2

ISBN-10: 1-111-07076-8

Cengage Learning
5191 Natorp Boulevard
Mason, Ohio 45040
USA

Cengage Learning is a leading provider of customized learning solutions with office locations around the globe, including Singapore, the United Kingdom, Australia, Mexico, Brazil, and Japan. Locate your local office at:
international.cengage.com/region

Cengage Learning products are represented in Canada by Nelson Education, Ltd.

For your lifelong learning solutions, visit **www.cengage.com/custom**

Visit our corporate website at **www.cengage.com**

Printed in the United States of America

Acknowledgements

The content of this text has been adapted from the following product(s):

Fundamentals of Business Law: Summarized Cases
Miller/Jentz ISBN-10: (0-324-59573-5)
ISBN-13: (978-0-324-59573-4)

Table Of Contents

1

The Legal and Constitutional Environment of Business

LEARNING OBJECTIVES

AFTER READING THIS CHAPTER, YOU SHOULD BE ABLE TO ANSWER THE FOLLOWING QUESTIONS:

1 What is the Uniform Commercial Code?

2 What is the common law tradition?

3 What is a precedent? When might a court depart from precedent?

4 What are some important differences between civil law and criminal law?

5 How does the U.S. Constitution affect business activities in the United States?

T he law is of interest to all persons, not just to lawyers. Those entering the world of business will find themselves subject to numerous laws and government regulations. A basic knowledge of these laws and regulations is beneficial— if not essential—to anyone contemplating a successful career in today's business world.

Although the law has had and will continue to have different definitions, they all are based on the general observation that, at a minimum, **law** consists of *enforceable rules governing relationships among individuals and between individuals and their society.* These "enforceable rules" may consist of unwritten principles of behavior established by a nomadic tribe. They may be set forth in an ancient or a contemporary law code. They may consist of written laws and court decisions created by modern legislative and judicial bodies, as in the United States. Regardless of how such rules are created, they all have one thing in common: they establish rights, duties, and privileges that are consistent with the values and beliefs of their society or its ruling group.

In this introductory chapter, we first look at an important question for any student reading this text: How does the legal environment affect business decision making? We next describe the basic sources of American law, the common law tradition, and some general classifications of law. We conclude the chapter with a discussion of the U.S. Constitution as it affects business.

BUSINESS ACTIVITIES AND THE LEGAL ENVIRONMENT

As those entering the world of business will learn, laws and government regulations affect virtually all business activities—hiring and firing decisions, workplace safety, the manufacturing and marketing of products, and business financing, to name just a few. To make good business decisions, a basic knowledge of the laws and regulations governing these activities is beneficial, if not essential. In today's world, though, a knowledge of "black-letter" law is not enough. Businesspersons are also pressured to make ethical decisions. Thus, the study of business law necessarily involves an ethical dimension.

Many Different Laws May Affect a Single Business Transaction

As you will note, each chapter in this text covers a specific area of the law and shows how the legal rules in that area affect business activities. Although compartmentalizing the law in this fashion facilitates learning, it does not indicate the extent to which many different laws may apply to just one transaction. **■EXAMPLE 1.1** Suppose that you are the president of NetSys, Inc., a company that creates and maintains computer network systems for its clients, including business firms. NetSys also markets software for customers who require an internal computer network. One day, Janet Hernandez, an operations officer for Southwest Distribution Corporation (SDC), contacts you by e-mail about a possible contract involving SDC's computer network. In deciding whether to enter into a contract with SDC, you need to consider, among other things, the legal requirements for an enforceable contract. Are the requirements different for a contract for services and a contract for products? What are your options if SDC **breaches** (breaks, or fails to perform) the contract? The answers to these questions are part of contract law and sales law.

Other questions might concern payment under the contract. How can you guarantee that NetSys will be paid? For example, if SDC pays with a check that is returned for insufficient funds, what are your options? Answers to these questions can be found in the laws that relate to negotiable instruments (such as checks) and creditors' rights. Also, a dispute may arise over the rights to NetSys's software, or there may be a question of liability if the software is defective. There may be an issue as to whether you and Hernandez had the authority to make the deal in the first place, or an accountant's evaluation of the contract may lead to a dispute. Resolutions of these questions may be found in the laws that relate to intellectual property, e-commerce, torts, product liability, agency, business organizations, or professional liability. ◼

Finally, if any dispute cannot be resolved amicably, then the laws and the rules concerning courts and court procedures spell out the steps of a lawsuit. Exhibit 1–1 illustrates the various areas of the law that may influence business decision making.

To prevent potential legal disputes, businesspersons need to be aware of the many different laws that may apply to a single business transaction. It is equally important for businesspersons to understand enough about the law to know when to turn to an expert for advice.

Ethics and Business Decision Making

Merely knowing the areas of law that may affect a business decision is not sufficient in today's business world. Businesspersons must also take ethics into account. As you will learn in Chapter 3, *ethics* is generally defined as the study of what constitutes right or wrong behavior. Today, business decision makers need to consider not just whether a decision is legal, but also whether it is ethical.

EXHIBIT 1–1 Areas of the Law That May Affect Business Decision Making

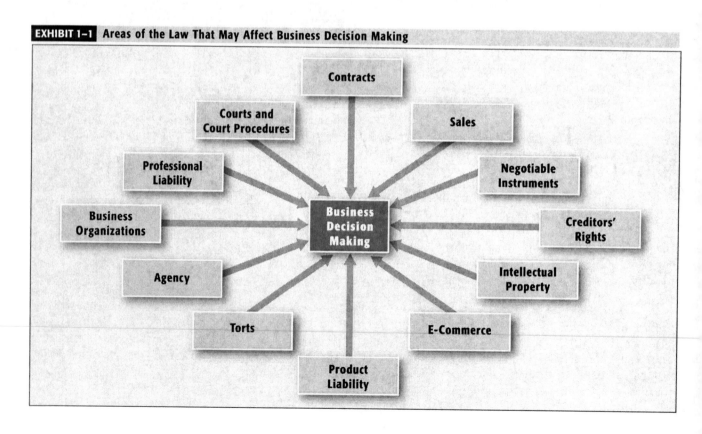

Throughout this text, you will learn about the relationship between the law and ethics, as well as about some of the types of ethical questions that often arise in the business context. Not only is Chapter 3 devoted solely to an examination of the importance of ethical considerations in business decision making, but various other elements in every chapter of this text are designed to help you become aware of the ethical aspects of questions that businesspersons may face. For example, the *Ethical Consideration* questions that follow selected cases in this text explore the ethical dimensions of the case. In addition, the case problems at the end of each chapter include *A Question of Ethics* designed to introduce you to the ethical aspects of a specific case involving a real-life situation.

SOURCES OF AMERICAN LAW

There are numerous sources of American law. **Primary sources of law,** or sources that establish the law, include the following:

1 The U.S. Constitution and the constitutions of the various states.

2 Statutes, or laws, passed by Congress and by state legislatures.

3 Regulations created by administrative agencies, such as the federal Food and Drug Administration.

4 Case law (court decisions).

We describe each of these important primary sources of law in the following pages. (See the appendix at the end of this chapter for a discussion of how to find statutes, regulations, and case law.)

Secondary sources of law are books and articles that summarize and clarify the primary sources of law. Legal encyclopedias, compilations (such as *Restatements of the Law,* which summarize court decisions on a particular topic), official comments to statutes, treatises, articles in law reviews published by law schools, and articles in other legal journals are examples of secondary sources of law. Courts often refer to secondary sources of law for guidance in interpreting and applying the primary sources of law discussed here.

Constitutional Law

The federal government and the states have separate written constitutions that set forth the general organization, powers, and limits of their respective governments. **Constitutional law** is the law as expressed in these constitutions.

The U.S. Constitution is the supreme law of the land. As such, it is the basis of all law in the United States. A law in violation of the Constitution, if challenged, will be declared unconstitutional and will not be enforced no matter what its source. Because of its paramount importance in the American legal system, we discuss the U.S. Constitution at length later in this chapter and present the complete text of the Constitution in Appendix B.

The Tenth Amendment to the U.S. Constitution reserves to the states all powers not granted to the federal government. Each state in the union has its own constitution.

Statutory Law

Laws enacted by legislative bodies at any level of government, such as the statutes passed by Congress or by state legislatures, make up the body of law generally referred to as **statutory law.** When a legislature passes a statute, that statute ultimately is included in the federal code of laws or the relevant state code of laws. Whenever a particular statute is mentioned in this text, we usually provide a footnote showing its **citation** (a reference to a publication in which a legal authority—such as a statute or a court decision—or other source can be found). In the appendix following this chapter, we explain how you can use these citations to find statutory law.

Statutory law also includes local **ordinances**—statutes (laws, rules, or orders) passed by municipal or county governing units to govern matters not covered by federal or state law. Ordinances commonly have to do with city or county land use (zoning ordinances), building and safety codes, and other matters affecting the local governing unit.

A federal statute, of course, applies to all states. A state statute, in contrast, applies only within the state's borders. State laws thus may vary from state to state. No federal statute may violate the U.S. Constitution, and no state statute or local ordinance may violate the U.S. Constitution or the relevant state constitution.

Uniform Laws During the 1800s, the differences among state laws frequently created difficulties for businesspersons conducting trade and commerce among the states. To counter these problems, a group of legal scholars, judges, and lawyers formed the National Conference of Commissioners on Uniform State Laws (NCCUSL) in 1892 to draft **uniform laws** ("model statutes") for the states to consider adopting. The NCCUSL still exists today and continues to issue new uniform laws and periodic revisions of earlier laws.

Each state has the option of adopting or rejecting a uniform law. *Only if a state legislature adopts a uniform law does that law become part of the statutory law of that state.* Note that a state legislature may adopt all or part of a uniform law as it is written, or the legislature may rewrite the law however the legislature wishes. Hence, even though many states may have adopted a uniform law, those states' laws may not be entirely "uniform."

The earliest uniform law, the Uniform Negotiable Instruments Law, was completed by 1896 and was adopted in every state by the early 1920s (although not all states used exactly the same wording). Over the following decades, other acts were drawn up in a similar manner. In all, the NCCUSL has issued more than two hundred uniform acts since its inception. The most ambitious uniform act of all, however, was the Uniform Commercial Code.

The Uniform Commercial Code (UCC) The Uniform Commercial Code (UCC), which was created through the joint efforts of the NCCUSL and the American Law Institute,[1] was first issued in 1952. The UCC has been adopted in all fifty states,[2] the District of Columbia, and the Virgin Islands. The UCC facilitates commerce among the states by providing a uniform, yet flexible, set of rules governing commercial transactions. The UCC assures businesspersons that their contracts, if validly entered into, normally will be enforced. Because of its importance in the area of commercial law, we cite the UCC frequently in this text. We also present excerpts of the UCC in Appendix C.

Administrative Law

An increasingly important source of American law is **administrative law**, which consists of the rules, orders, and decisions of administrative agencies. An **administrative agency** is a federal, state, or local government agency established to perform a specific function. Rules issued by various administrative agencies now affect virtually every aspect of a business's operations, including the firm's capital structure and financing, its hiring and firing procedures, its relations with employees and unions, and the way it manufactures and markets its products.

Federal Agencies At the national level, numerous **executive agencies** exist within the cabinet departments of the executive branch. For example, the Food and Drug Administration is within the U.S. Department of Health and Human Services. Executive agencies are subject to the authority of the president, who has the power to appoint and remove officers of federal agencies. There are also many **independent regulatory agencies** at the federal level, including the Federal Trade Commission, the Securities and Exchange Commission, and the Federal Communications Commission. The president's power is less pronounced in

regard to independent agencies, whose officers serve for fixed terms and cannot be removed without just cause.

State and Local Agencies There are administrative agencies at the state and local levels as well. Commonly, a state agency (such as a state pollution-control agency) is created as a parallel to a federal agency (such as the Environmental Protection Agency). Just as federal statutes take precedence over conflicting state statutes, so do federal agency regulations take precedence over conflicting state regulations. Because the rules of state and local agencies vary widely, we focus here exclusively on federal administrative law.

Agency Creation Because Congress cannot possibly oversee the actual implementation of all the laws it enacts, it must delegate such tasks to agencies, especially when the legislation involves highly technical matters, such as air and water pollution. Congress creates an administrative agency by enacting **enabling legislation,** which specifies the name, composition, purpose, and powers of the agency being created.

■EXAMPLE 1.2 The Federal Trade Commission (FTC) was created in 1914 by the Federal Trade Commission Act.[3] This act prohibits unfair and deceptive trade practices. It also describes the procedures the agency must follow to charge persons or organizations with violations of the act, and it provides for judicial review (review by the courts) of agency orders. Other portions of the act grant the agency powers to "make rules and regulations for the purpose of carrying out the Act," to conduct investigations of business practices, to obtain reports from interstate corporations concerning their business practices, to investigate possible violations of the act, to publish findings of its investigations, and to recommend new legislation. The act also empowers the FTC to hold trial-like hearings and to **adjudicate** (resolve judicially) certain kinds of disputes that involve FTC regulations. ■

Note that the powers granted to the FTC incorporate functions associated with the legislative branch of government (rulemaking), the executive branch (investigation and enforcement), and the judicial branch (adjudication). Taken together, these functions constitute **administrative process,** which is the administration of law by administrative agencies.

Case Law and Common Law Doctrines

The rules of law announced in court decisions constitute another basic source of American law. These rules of law include interpretations of constitutional provisions, of statutes enacted by legislatures, and of regulations created by administrative agencies. Today, this body of judge-made law is referred to as **case law.** Case law—the doctrines and principles

---

1. This institute was formed in the 1920s and consists of practicing attorneys, legal scholars, and judges.
2. Louisiana has adopted only Articles 1, 3, 4, 5, 7, 8, and 9.

3. 15 U.S.C. Sections 45–58.

announced in cases—governs all areas not covered by statutory law or administrative law and is part of our common law tradition. We look at the origins and characteristics of the common law tradition in some detail in the pages that follow.

THE COMMON LAW TRADITION

Because of our colonial heritage, much of American law is based on the English legal system. A knowledge of this tradition is crucial to understanding our legal system today because judges in the United States still apply common law principles when deciding cases.

Early English Courts

After the Normans conquered England in 1066, William the Conqueror and his successors began the process of unifying the country under their rule. One of the means they used to do this was the establishment of the king's courts, or *curiae regis*. Before the Norman Conquest, disputes had been settled according to the local legal customs and traditions in various regions of the country. The king's courts sought to establish a uniform set of rules for the country as a whole. What evolved in these courts was the beginning of the **common law**—a body of general rules that applied throughout the entire English realm. Eventually, the common law tradition became part of the heritage of all nations that were once British colonies, including the United States.

Courts developed the common law rules from the principles underlying judges' decisions in actual legal controversies. Judges attempted to be consistent, and whenever possible, they based their decisions on the principles suggested by earlier cases. They sought to decide similar cases in a similar way and considered new cases with care, because they knew that their decisions would make new law. Each interpretation became part of the law on the subject and served as a legal **precedent**—that is, a decision that furnished an example or authority for deciding subsequent cases involving similar legal principles or facts.

In the early years of the common law, there was no single place or publication where court opinions, or written decisions, could be found. Beginning in the late thirteenth and early fourteenth centuries, however, each year portions of significant decisions of that year were gathered together and recorded in *Year Books*. The *Year Books* were useful references for lawyers and judges. In the sixteenth century, the *Year Books* were discontinued, and other reports of cases became available. (See the appendix to this chapter for a discussion of how cases are reported, or published, in the United States today.)

Stare Decisis

The practice of deciding new cases with reference to former decisions, or precedents, eventually became a cornerstone of the English and U.S. judicial systems. The practice forms a doctrine called *stare decisis*[4] ("to stand on decided cases").

The Importance of Precedents in Judicial Decision Making   Under the doctrine of *stare decisis*, once a court has set forth a principle of law as being applicable to a certain set of facts, that court and courts of lower rank must adhere to that principle and apply it in future cases involving similar fact patterns. *Stare decisis* has two aspects: first, that decisions made by a higher court are binding on lower courts; and second, that a court should not overturn its own precedents unless there is a strong reason to do so.

Controlling precedents in a *jurisdiction* (an area in which a court or courts have the power to apply the law—see Chapter 2) are referred to as binding authorities. A **binding authority** is any source of law that a court must follow when deciding a case. Binding authorities include constitutions, statutes, and regulations that govern the issue being decided, as well as court decisions that are controlling precedents within the jurisdiction. United States Supreme Court case decisions, no matter how old, remain controlling until they are overruled by a subsequent decision of the Supreme Court, by a constitutional amendment, or by congressional legislation.

Stare Decisis and Legal Stability   The doctrine of *stare decisis* helps the courts to be more efficient because if other courts have carefully reasoned through a similar case, their legal reasoning and opinions can serve as guides. *Stare decisis* also makes the law more stable and predictable. If the law on a given subject is well settled, someone bringing a case to court can usually rely on the court to make a decision based on what the law has been.

Departures from Precedent   Although courts are obligated to follow precedents, sometimes a court will depart from the rule of precedent if it decides that a given precedent should no longer be followed. If a court decides that a precedent is simply incorrect or that technological or social changes have rendered the precedent inapplicable, the court might rule contrary to the precedent. Cases that overturn precedent often receive a great deal of publicity.

■EXAMPLE 1.3   In *Brown v. Board of Education of Topeka*,[5] the United States Supreme Court expressly overturned precedent when it concluded that separate educational facilities for

---

4. Pronounced *stahr-ee dih-si*-sis.
5. 347 U.S. 483, 74 S.Ct. 686, 98 L.Ed. 873 (1954). See the appendix at the end of this chapter for an explanation of how to read legal citations.

whites and blacks, which had been upheld as constitutional in numerous previous cases,[6] were inherently unequal. The Supreme Court's departure from precedent in *Brown* received a tremendous amount of publicity as people began to realize the ramifications of this change in the law. ∎

When There Is No Precedent   At times, a court hears a case for which there are no precedents within its jurisdiction on which to base its decision. When hearing such cases, called "cases of first impression," courts often look at precedents established in other jurisdictions for guidance. Precedents from other jurisdictions, because they are not binding on the court, are referred to as **persuasive authorities**. A court may also consider various other factors, including legal principles and policies underlying previous court decisions or existing statutes, fairness, social values and customs, public policy, and data and concepts drawn from the social sciences.

Can a court consider unpublished decisions as persuasive precedent? See this chapter's *Adapting the Law to the Online Environment* feature on the following page for a discussion of this issue.

Equitable Remedies and Courts of Equity

A **remedy** is the means given to a party to enforce a right or to compensate for the violation of a right. ∎**EXAMPLE 1.4** If Shem is injured because of Rowan's wrongdoing, a court may order Rowan to compensate Shem for the harm by paying him a certain amount. ∎

In the early king's courts of England, the kinds of remedies that could be granted were severely restricted. If one person wronged another, the king's courts could award as compensation either money or property, including land. These courts became known as *courts of law*, and the remedies were called *remedies at law*. Even though this system introduced uniformity in the settling of disputes, when plaintiffs wanted a remedy other than economic compensation, the courts of law could do nothing, so "no remedy, no right."

Remedies in Equity   *Equity* refers to a branch of the law, founded in justice and fair dealing, that seeks to supply a fair and adequate remedy when no remedy is available at law. In medieval England, when individuals could not obtain an adequate remedy in a court of law, they petitioned the king for relief. Most of these petitions were decided by an adviser to the king called the *chancellor*. The chancellor was said to be the "keeper of the king's conscience." When the chancellor thought that the claim was a fair one, new and unique

remedies were granted. In this way, a new body of rules and remedies came into being, and eventually formal *chancery courts*, or *courts of equity*, were established. The remedies granted by these courts were called *remedies in equity*. Thus, two distinct court systems were created, each having its own set of judges and its own set of remedies.

Plaintiffs (those bringing lawsuits) had to specify whether they were bringing an "action at law" or an "action in equity," and they chose their courts accordingly. ∎**EXAMPLE 1.5** A plaintiff might ask a court of equity to order a **defendant** (a person against whom a lawsuit is brought) to perform within the terms of a contract. A court of law could not issue such an order because its remedies were limited to payment of money as compensation for damages. A court of equity, however, could issue a decree for *specific performance*—an order to perform what was promised. A court of equity could also issue an *injunction*, directing a party to do or refrain from doing a particular act. In certain cases, a court of equity could allow for the *rescission* (cancellation) of the contract, thereby returning the parties to the positions that they held prior to the contract's formation. ∎ Equitable remedies will be discussed in greater detail in Chapter 12.

The Merging of Law and Equity   Today, in most states, the courts of law and equity have merged, and thus the distinction between the two courts has largely disappeared. A plaintiff may now request both legal and equitable remedies in the same action, and the trial court judge may grant either form—or both forms—of relief. The merging of law and equity, however, does not diminish the importance of distinguishing legal remedies from equitable remedies. To request the proper remedy, a businessperson (or her or his attorney) must know what remedies are available for the specific kinds of harms suffered. Today, as a rule, courts will grant an equitable remedy only when the remedy at law (money damages) is inadequate. Exhibit 1–2 on page 9 summarizes the procedural differences (applicable in most states) between an action at law and an action in equity.

CLASSIFICATIONS OF LAW

The huge body of the law may be broken down according to several classification systems. For example, one classification system divides law into **substantive law** (all laws that define, describe, regulate, and create legal rights and obligations) and **procedural law** (all laws that establish the methods of enforcing the rights established by substantive law). Other classification systems divide law into federal law and state law or private law (dealing with relationships between persons) and public law (addressing the relationship between persons and their governments).

---

6. See *Plessy v. Ferguson*, 163 U.S. 537, 16 S.Ct. 1138, 41 L.Ed. 256 (1896).

ADAPTING THE LAW TO THE ONLINE ENVIRONMENT   How the Internet Is Expanding Precedent

The notion that courts should rely on precedents to decide the outcome of similar cases has long been a cornerstone of U.S. law. Nevertheless, the availability of "unpublished opinions" over the Internet is changing what the law considers to be precedent. An *unpublished opinion* is a decision made by an appellate court that is not intended for publication in a reporter (the bound books that contain court opinions).[a] Courts traditionally have not considered unpublished opinions to be "precedent," binding or persuasive, and attorneys were often not allowed to refer to these decisions in their arguments.

An Increasing Number of Decisions Are Not Published in Case Reporters but Are Available Online

The number of court decisions not published in printed books has risen dramatically in recent years. By some estimates, nearly 80 percent of the decisions of the federal appellate courts are unpublished. The number is equally high in some state court systems. California's intermediate appellate courts, for example, publish only about 7 percent of their decisions.

Even though certain decisions are not intended for publication, they are posted ("published") almost immediately on online legal databases, such as Westlaw and Lexis. With the proliferation of free legal databases and court Web sites, the general public also has almost instant access to the unpublished decisions of most courts. This situation has caused a substantial amount of debate over whether unpublished opinions should be given the same precedential effect as published opinions.

Should Unpublished Decisions Establish Precedent?

Prior to the Internet, one might have been able to justify not considering unpublished decisions to be precedent on the grounds of fairness. How could courts and lawyers be expected to consider the reasoning in unpublished decisions if they were not printed in the case reporters? Now that opin-

ions are so readily available on the Web, however, this justification is no longer valid. Moreover, it now seems unfair not to consider these decisions as precedent to some extent because they are so publicly accessible.

Another argument against allowing unpublished decisions to be precedent concerns the quality of the legal reasoning set forth in these decisions. Staff attorneys and law clerks frequently write unpublished opinions so that judges can spend more time on the opinions intended for publication. Consequently, some claim that allowing unpublished decisions to establish precedent could result in bad precedents because the reasoning may not be up to par. If the decision is regarded merely as persuasive precedent, however, then judges who disagree with the reasoning are free to reject the conclusion.

The United States Supreme Court Changes Federal Rules on Unpublished Opinions as of 2007

In spite of objections from several hundred judges and lawyers, the United States Supreme Court made history in 2006 when it announced that it would allow lawyers to refer to (cite) unpublished decisions in all federal courts. The new rule, Rule 32.1 of the Federal Rules of Appellate Procedure, states that federal courts may not prohibit or restrict the citation of federal judicial opinions that have been designated as "not for publication," "non-precedential," or "not precedent." The rule applies only to federal courts and only to unpublished opinions issued after January 1, 2007. It does not specify the effect that a court must give to one of its unpublished opinions or to an unpublished opinion from another court. Basically, the rule simply makes all the federal courts follow a uniform rule that allows attorneys to cite—and judges to consider as persuasive precedent—unpublished decisions beginning in 2007.

The impact of this new rule remains to be seen. At present, the majority of states do not allow their state courts to consider the rulings in unpublished cases as persuasive precedent, and this rule does not affect the states. The Supreme Court's decision, however, provides an example of how technology—the availability of unpublished opinions over the Internet—has affected the law.

FOR CRITICAL ANALYSIS *Now that the Supreme Court is allowing unpublished decisions to be used as persuasive precedent in federal courts, should state courts follow? Why or why not?*

---

a. Recently decided cases that are not yet published are also sometimes called *unpublished opinions,* but because these decisions will eventually be printed in reporters, we do not include them here.

EXHIBIT 1–2	Procedural Differences between an Action at Law and an Action in Equity	
PROCEDURE	**ACTION AT LAW**	**ACTION IN EQUITY**
Initiation of lawsuit	By filing a complaint.	By filing a petition.
Decision	By jury or judge.	By judge (no jury).
Result	Judgment.	Decree.
Remedy	Monetary damages.	Injunction, specific performance, or rescission.

Frequently, people use the term **cyberlaw** to refer to the emerging body of law that governs transactions conducted via the Internet. Cyberlaw is not really a classification of law, nor is it a new *type* of law. Rather, it is an informal term used to describe traditional legal principles that have been modified and adapted to fit situations that are unique to the online world. Of course, in some areas new statutes have been enacted, at both the federal and the state levels, to cover specific types of problems stemming from online communications. Throughout this book, you will read how the law in a given area is evolving to govern specific legal issues that arise in the online context.

Civil Law and Criminal Law

Civil law spells out the rights and duties that exist between persons and between persons and their governments, and the relief available when a person's rights are violated. Typically, in a civil case, a private party sues another private party (although the government can also sue a party for a civil law violation) to make that other party comply with a duty or pay for the damage caused by the failure to comply with a duty. **■EXAMPLE 1.6** If a seller fails to perform a contract with a buyer, the buyer may bring a lawsuit against the seller. The purpose of the lawsuit will be either to compel the seller to perform as promised or, more commonly, to obtain money damages for the seller's failure to perform. ■

Much of the law that we discuss in this text is civil law. Contract law, for example, which we discuss in Chapters 7 through 13, is civil law. The whole body of tort law (see Chapter 4) is civil law. Note that *civil law* is not the same as a *civil law system*. As you will read shortly, a **civil law system** is a legal system based on a written code of laws.

Criminal law has to do with wrongs committed against society for which society demands redress. Criminal acts are proscribed by local, state, or federal government statutes. Thus, criminal defendants are prosecuted by public officials, such as a district attorney (D.A.), on behalf of the state, not by their victims or other private parties. Whereas in a civil case the object is to obtain remedies (such as money damages) to compensate the injured party, in a

criminal case the object is to punish the wrongdoer in an attempt to deter others from similar actions. Penalties for violations of criminal statutes consist of fines and/or imprisonment—and, in some cases, death. We will discuss the differences between civil and criminal law in greater detail in Chapter 6.

National and International Law

Although the focus of this book is U.S. business law, increasingly businesspersons in this country engage in transactions that extend beyond our national borders. In these situations, the laws of other nations or the laws governing relationships among nations may come into play. For this reason, those who pursue a career in business today should have an understanding of the global legal environment.

National Law   The law of a particular nation, such as the United States or Sweden, is **national law.** National law, of course, varies from country to country because each country's law reflects the interests, customs, activities, and values that are unique to that nation's culture. Even though the laws and legal systems of various countries differ substantially, broad similarities do exist.

Two types of legal systems predominate around the globe today. One is the common law system of England and the United States, which we have already discussed. The other system is based on Roman civil law, or "code law."[7] The term *civil law*, as used here, refers not to civil as opposed to criminal law but to codified law—an ordered grouping of legal principles enacted into law by a legislature or governing body. In a civil law system, the primary source of law is a statutory code, and case precedents are not judicially binding, as they normally are in a common law system. Although judges in a civil law system commonly refer to

---

7. A third, less prevalent, legal system is common in Islamic countries, where the law is often influenced by *sharia*, the religious law of Islam. Although *sharia* affects the legal codes of many Muslim countries, the extent of its impact and its interpretation vary widely.

previous decisions as sources of legal guidance, they are not bound by precedent; in other words, the doctrine of *stare decisis* does not apply. Exhibit 1–3 lists some countries that today follow either the common law system or the civil law system.

International Law In contrast to national law, international law applies to more than one nation. **International law** can be defined as a body of written and unwritten laws observed by independent nations and governing the acts of individuals as well as governments. International law is an intermingling of rules and constraints derived from a variety of sources, including the laws of individual nations, the customs that have evolved among nations in their relations with one another, and treaties and international organizations. In essence, international law is the result of centuries-old attempts to reconcile the traditional need of each nation to be the final authority over its own affairs with the desire of nations to benefit economically from trade and harmonious relations with one another.

The key difference between national law and international law is that government authorities can enforce national law. If a nation violates an international law, however, the most that other countries or international organizations can do (if persuasive tactics fail) is to resort to coercive actions against the violating nation. (See Chapter 32 for a more detailed treatment of international law.)

THE CONSTITUTION AS IT AFFECTS BUSINESS

Each of the sources of law discussed earlier helps to frame the legal environment of business. Because laws that govern business have their origin in the lawmaking authority granted by the U.S. Constitution, we examine that document more closely here. We focus on two areas of the Constitution of particular concern to business—the commerce clause and the Bill of Rights. As mentioned earlier, the Constitution pro-

vides the legal basis for both state and federal (national) powers. It is the supreme law in this country, and any law that conflicts with the Constitution, if challenged in court, will be declared invalid by the court.

The Commerce Clause

To prevent states from establishing laws and regulations that would interfere with trade and commerce among the states, the Constitution expressly delegated to the national government the power to regulate interstate commerce. Article I, Section 8, of the U.S. Constitution expressly permits Congress "[t]o regulate Commerce with foreign Nations, and among the several States, and with the Indian Tribes." This clause, referred to as the **commerce clause,** has had a greater impact on business than any other provision in the Constitution.

Initially, the commerce power was interpreted as being limited to *interstate* commerce (commerce among the states) and not applicable to *intrastate* commerce (commerce within a state). In 1824, however, in the landmark case *Gibbons v. Ogden,*[8] the United States Supreme Court held that commerce within a state could also be regulated by the national government as long as the commerce *substantially affected* commerce involving more than one state.

The Commerce Clause and the Expansion of National Powers In *Gibbons v. Ogden,* the commerce clause was expanded to regulate activities that "substantially affect interstate commerce." As the nation grew and faced new kinds of problems, the commerce clause became a vehicle for the additional expansion of the national government's regulatory powers. Even activities that seemed purely local came under the regulatory reach of the national government if those activities were deemed to substantially affect interstate commerce. ■EXAMPLE 1.7 In 1942, in *Wickard v. Filburn,*[9] the

---

8. 22 U.S. (9 Wheat.) 1, 6 L.Ed. 23 (1824).
9. 317 U.S. 111, 63 S.Ct. 82, 87 L.Ed. 122 (1942).

EXHIBIT 1–3 The Legal Systems of Selected Nations			
CIVIL LAW		**COMMON LAW**	
Argentina	Indonesia	Australia	Nigeria
Austria	Iran	Bangladesh	Singapore
Brazil	Italy	Canada	United Kingdom
Chile	Japan	Ghana	United States
China	Mexico	India	Zambia
Egypt	Poland	Israel	
Finland	South Korea	Jamaica	
France	Sweden	Kenya	
Germany	Tunisia	Malaysia	
Greece	Venezuela	New Zealand	

Code book to make ruling

Precedents and case Law

Supreme Court held that wheat production by an individual farmer intended wholly for consumption on his own farm was subject to federal regulation. The Court reasoned that the home consumption of wheat reduced the market demand for wheat and thus could have a substantial effect on interstate commerce. ◼

The following landmark case involved a challenge to the scope of the national government's constitutional authority to regulate local activities.

CASE 1.1 Heart of Atlanta Motel v. United States

LANDMARK AND CLASSIC CASES

Supreme Court of the United States, 379 U.S. 241, 85 S.Ct. 348, 13 L.Ed.2d 258 (1964).
www.findlaw.com/casecode/supreme.html [a]

FACTS The owner of the Heart of Atlanta Motel, in violation of the Civil Rights Act of 1964, refused to rent rooms to African Americans. The motel owner brought an action in a federal district court to have the Civil Rights Act declared unconstitutional, alleging that Congress had exceeded its constitutional authority to regulate commerce by enacting the act. The owner argued that his motel was not engaged in interstate commerce but was "of a purely local character." The motel, however, was accessible to state and interstate highways. The owner advertised nationally, maintained billboards throughout the state, and accepted convention trade from outside the state (75 percent of the guests were residents of other states). The court ruled that the act did not violate the Constitution and enjoined (prohibited) the owner from discriminating on the basis of race. The owner appealed. The case ultimately went to the United States Supreme Court.

ISSUE Did Congress exceed its constitutional power to regulate interstate commerce by enacting the Civil Rights Act of 1964?

DECISION No. The United States Supreme Court upheld the constitutionality of the act.

REASON The Court noted that the act was passed to correct "the deprivation of personal dignity" accompanying the denial of equal access to "public establishments." Testimony before

Congress leading to the passage of the act indicated that African Americans in particular experienced substantial discrimination in attempting to secure lodging while traveling. This discrimination impeded interstate travel and thus impeded interstate commerce. As for the owner's argument that his motel was "of a purely local character," the Court said that even if this was true, the motel affected interstate commerce. According to the Court, "if it is interstate commerce that feels the pinch, it does not matter how local the operation that applies the squeeze." Therefore, under the commerce clause, "the power of Congress to promote interstate commerce also includes the power to regulate the local incidents thereof, including local activities."

IMPACT OF THIS CASE ON TODAY'S LAW *If the United States Supreme Court had invalidated the Civil Rights Act of 1964, the legal landscape of the United States would be much different today. The act prohibits discrimination based on race, color, national origin, religion, or gender in all "public accommodations," including hotels and restaurants. The act also prohibits discrimination in employment based on these criteria. Although state laws now prohibit many of these forms of discrimination as well, the protections available vary from state to state—and it is not certain when (and if) such laws would have been passed had the 1964 federal Civil Rights Act been deemed unconstitutional.*

RELEVANT WEB SITES *To locate information on the Web concerning the* Heart of Atlanta Motel *decision, go to this text's Web site at* **www.cengage.com/blaw/fbl**, *select "Chapter 1," and click on "URLs for Landmarks."*

a. Under "Citation Search," type in "379" before "U.S." and then "241." Click "Search" to access this court opinion.

◼

The Commerce Power Today   Today, at least theoretically, the power over commerce authorizes the national government to regulate every commercial enterprise in the United States. Federal (national) legislation governs virtually every major activity conducted by businesses—from hiring and firing decisions to workplace safety, competitive practices, and financing. In the last fifteen years, however, the Supreme

Court has begun to curb somewhat the national government's regulatory authority under the commerce clause. In 1995, the Court held—for the first time in sixty years—that Congress had exceeded its regulatory authority under the commerce clause. The Court struck down an act that banned the possession of guns within one thousand feet of any school because the act attempted to regulate an area that

[handwritten margin note: negative—states cannot regulate interstate commerce]

had "nothing to do with commerce."[10] Subsequently, the Court invalidated key portions of two other federal acts on the ground that they exceeded Congress's commerce clause authority.[11]

In one notable case, however, the Supreme Court did allow the federal government to regulate noncommercial activities taking place wholly within a state's borders. **■EXAMPLE 1.8** Eleven states, including California, have adopted "medical marijuana" laws that legalize marijuana for medical purposes. Marijuana possession, however, is illegal under the federal Controlled Substances Act (CSA).[12] After the federal government seized the marijuana that two seriously ill California women were using on the advice of their physicians, the women argued that it was unconstitutional for the federal act to prohibit them from using marijuana for medical purposes that were legal within the state. In 2003, the U.S. Court of Appeals for the Ninth Circuit agreed, deciding the case on commerce clause grounds. In 2005, however, the United States Supreme Court held that Congress has the authority to prohibit the *intra*state possession and noncommercial cultivation of marijuana as part of a larger regulatory scheme (the CSA).[13] In other words, state medical marijuana laws do not pose barriers to federal drug enforcement. ■

The Regulatory Powers of the States   As part of their inherent sovereignty, state governments have the authority to regulate affairs within their borders. This authority stems in part from the Tenth Amendment to the Constitution, which reserves to the states all powers not delegated to the national government. State regulatory powers are often referred to as **police powers.** The term encompasses not only the enforcement of criminal law but also the right of state governments to regulate private activities to protect or promote the public order, health, safety, morals, and general welfare. Fire and building codes, antidiscrimination laws, parking regulations, zoning restrictions, licensing requirements, and thousands of other state statutes covering virtually every aspect of life have been enacted pursuant to a state's police powers. Local governments, including cities, also exercise police powers. Generally, state laws enacted pursuant to a state's police powers carry a strong presumption of validity.

The "Dormant" Commerce Clause   The United States Supreme Court has interpreted the commerce clause to mean that the national government has the *exclusive* authority to regulate commerce that substantially affects trade and commerce among the states. This express grant of authority to the national government, which is often referred to as the "positive" aspect of the commerce clause, implies a negative aspect—that the states do *not* have the authority to regulate interstate commerce. This negative aspect of the commerce clause is often referred to as the "dormant" (implied) commerce clause.

The dormant commerce clause comes into play when state regulations affect interstate commerce. In this situation, the courts normally weigh the state's interest in regulating a certain matter against the burden that the state's regulation imposes on interstate commerce. Because courts balance the interests involved, it can be extremely difficult to predict the outcome in a particular case. **■EXAMPLE 1.9** At one time, many states regulated the sale of alcoholic beverages, including wine, through a "three-tier" system. This system required separate licenses for producers, wholesalers, and retailers, subject to a complex set of overlapping regulations that effectively banned direct sales to consumers from out-of-state wineries. In-state wineries, in contrast, could obtain a license for direct sales to consumers. In 2005, the United States Supreme Court ruled that these laws violated the dormant commerce clause. The Court reasoned that by mandating different treatment of in-state and out-of-state economic interests, these laws deprived "citizens of their right to have access to the markets of other states on equal terms."[14] ■

Business and the Bill of Rights

The importance of having a written declaration of the rights of individuals eventually caused the first Congress of the United States to enact twelve amendments to the Constitution and submit them to the states for approval. The first ten of these amendments, commonly known as the **Bill of Rights,** were adopted in 1791 and embody a series of protections for the individual against various types of interference by the federal government.[15] Some constitutional protections apply to business entities as well. For example, corporations exist as separate legal entities, or legal persons, and enjoy many of the same rights and privileges as natural persons do. Summarized here are the protections guaranteed

---

10. The United States Supreme Court held the Gun-Free School Zones Act of 1990 to be unconstitutional in *United States v. Lopez,* 514 U.S. 549, 115 S.Ct. 1624, 131 L.Ed.2d 626 (1995).

11. See, for example, *Printz v. United States,* 521 U.S. 898, 117 S.Ct. 2365, 138 L.Ed.2d 914 (1997), involving the Brady Handgun Violence Prevention Act of 1993; and *United States v. Morrison,* 529 U.S. 598, 120 S.Ct. 1740, 146 L.Ed.2d 658 (2000), concerning the federal Violence Against Women Act of 1994.

12. 21 U.S.C. Sections 801 *et seq.*

13. *Gonzales v. Raich,* 545 U.S. 1, 125 S.Ct. 2195, 162 L.Ed.2d 1 (2005).

14. *Granholm v. Heald,* 544 U.S. 460, 125 S.Ct. 1885, 161 L.Ed.2d 796 (2005); see also *Cherry Hill Vineyard, LLC v. Baldacci,* 505 F.3d 28 (1st Cir. 2007).

15. One of these proposed amendments was ratified more than two hundred years later (in 1992) and became the Twenty-seventh Amendment to the U.S. Constitution. See Appendix B.

by these ten amendments (see the Constitution in Appendix B for the complete text of each amendment):

1 The First Amendment guarantees the freedoms of religion, speech, and the press and the rights to assemble peaceably and to petition the government.

2 The Second Amendment concerns a well-regulated militia and the right of the people to keep and bear arms.

3 The Third Amendment prohibits, in peacetime, the lodging of soldiers in any house without the owner's consent.

4 The Fourth Amendment prohibits unreasonable searches and seizures of persons or property.

5 The Fifth Amendment guarantees the rights to *indictment*[16] (formal accusation—see Chapter 6) by grand jury, to due process of law, and to fair payment when private property is taken for public use. The Fifth Amendment also prohibits compulsory self-incrimination and double jeopardy (trial for the same crime twice).

6 The Sixth Amendment guarantees the accused in a criminal case the right to a speedy and public trial by an impartial jury and with counsel. The accused has the right to cross-examine witnesses against him or her and to solicit testimony from witnesses in his or her favor.

7 The Seventh Amendment guarantees the right to a trial by jury in a civil (noncriminal) case involving at least twenty dollars.[17]

8 The Eighth Amendment prohibits excessive bail and fines, as well as cruel and unusual punishment.

9 The Ninth Amendment establishes that the people have rights in addition to those specified in the Constitution.

10 The Tenth Amendment establishes that those powers neither delegated to the federal government nor denied to the states are reserved for the states.

As originally intended, the Bill of Rights limited only the powers of the national government. Over time, however, the Supreme Court "incorporated" most of these rights into the protections against state actions afforded by the Fourteenth Amendment to the Constitution. That amendment, passed in 1868 after the Civil War, provides in part that "[n]o State shall . . . deprive any person of life, liberty, or property, without due process of law." Starting in 1925, the Supreme Court began to define various rights and liberties guaranteed in the national Constitution as constituting "due process of law," which was required of state

governments under the Fourteenth Amendment. Today, most of the rights and liberties set forth in the Bill of Rights apply to state governments as well as the national government.

We will look closely at several of the amendments in the above list in Chapter 6, in the context of criminal law and procedures. Here, we examine two important guarantees of the First Amendment—freedom of speech and freedom of religion—and the Fourth Amendment's prohibition of *unreasonable* searches and seizures. These protections have all been applied to the states through the due process clause of the Fourteenth Amendment. As you read through the following pages, keep in mind that none of these (or other) constitutional freedoms confers an absolute right. Ultimately, it is the United States Supreme Court, as the final interpreter of the Constitution, that gives meaning to these rights and determines their boundaries.

The First Amendment—Freedom of Speech Freedom of speech is the most prized freedom that Americans have. Indeed, it is essential to our democratic form of government, which could not exist if people were not allowed to express their political opinions freely and criticize government actions or policies. Because of its importance, the courts traditionally have protected this right to the fullest extent possible.

Speech often includes not only what we say, but also what we do to express our political, social, and religious views. The courts generally protect **symbolic speech**—gestures, movements, articles of clothing, and other forms of nonverbal expressive conduct. **■EXAMPLE 1.10** The burning of the American flag to protest government policies is a constitutionally protected form of expression. Similarly, participating in a hunger strike or wearing a black armband would be protected as symbolic speech. **■**

Reasonable Restrictions. Expression—oral, written, or symbolized by conduct—is subject to reasonable restrictions. A balance must be struck between a government's obligation to protect its citizens and those citizens' exercise of their rights. Reasonableness is analyzed on a case-by-case basis. If a restriction imposed by the government is content neutral, then a court may allow it. To be content neutral, the restriction must be aimed at combating some societal problem, such as crime, and not be aimed at suppressing the expressive conduct or its message. **■EXAMPLE 1.11** Courts have often protected nude dancing as a form of symbolic expression. Nevertheless, the courts have also allowed content-neutral laws that ban all public nudity, not just erotic dancing.[18] **■**

---

16. Pronounced in-*dyte*-ment.

17. Twenty dollars was forty days' pay for the average person when the Bill of Rights was written.

18. See, for example, *Rameses, Inc. v. County of Orange*, 481 F.Supp.2d 1305 (M.D.Fla. 2007); and *City of Erie v. Pap's A.M.*, 529 U.S. 277, 120 S.Ct. 1382, 146 L.Ed.2d 265 (2000).

The United States Supreme Court has also held that schools may restrict students' free speech rights at school events. **■EXAMPLE 1.12** In 2007, the Court heard a case involving a high school student who had held up a banner saying "Bong Hits 4 Jesus" at an off-campus but school-sanctioned event. In a split decision, the majority of the Court ruled that school officials did not violate the student's free speech rights when they confiscated the banner and suspended the student for ten days. Because the banner could reasonably be interpreted as promoting the use of marijuana, and because the school had a written policy against illegal drugs, the majority concluded that the school's actions were justified. Several justices disagreed, however, noting that the majority's holding creates a special exception that will allow schools to censor any student speech that mentions drugs.[19] ■

ultimate significant

Corporate Political Speech. Political speech by corporations also falls within the protection of the First Amendment. Many years ago, the United States Supreme Court ruled that a Massachusetts statute, which prohibited corporations from making political contributions or expenditures that individuals were permitted to make, was unconstitutional.[20] Although the Supreme Court has reversed this trend somewhat,[21] corporate political speech continues to be given significant protection under the First Amendment. **■EXAMPLE 1.13** In 2003 and again in 2007, the Supreme Court struck down portions of bipartisan campaign-finance reform laws as unconstitu-

tional. The Court found that these provisions constituted unlawful restraints on corporate political speech.[22] ■

Substantial

Commercial Speech. The courts also give substantial protection to "commercial" speech, which consists of communications—primarily advertising and marketing—made by business firms that involve only their commercial interests. The protection given to commercial speech under the First Amendment is not as extensive as that afforded to noncommercial speech, however. A state may restrict certain kinds of advertising, for example, in the interest of protecting consumers from being misled by the advertising practices. States also have a legitimate interest in the beautification of roadsides, and this interest allows states to place restraints on billboard advertising. **■EXAMPLE 1.14** Café Erotica, a nude-dancing establishment, sued the state after being denied a permit to erect a billboard along an interstate highway in Florida. The state appellate court decided that because the law directly advanced a substantial government interest in highway beautification and safety, it was not an unconstitutional restraint on commercial speech.[23] ■

Generally, a restriction on commercial speech will be considered valid as long as it meets three criteria: (1) it must seek to implement a substantial government interest, (2) it must directly advance that interest, and (3) it must go no further than necessary to accomplish its objective. At issue in the following case was whether a government agency had unconstitutionally restricted commercial speech when it prohibited the inclusion of a certain illustration on beer labels.

19. *Morse v. Frederick*, ___ U.S. ___, 127 S.Ct. 2618, 168 L.Ed.2d 290 (2007).
20. *First National Bank of Boston v. Bellotti*, 435 U.S. 765, 98 S.Ct. 1407, 55 L.Ed.2d 707 (1978).
21. See *Austin v. Michigan Chamber of Commerce*, 494 U.S. 652, 110 S.Ct. 1391, 108 L.Ed.2d 652 (1990), in which the Supreme Court upheld a state law prohibiting corporations from using general corporate funds for independent expenditures in state political campaigns.

22. *McConnell v. Federal Election Commission*, 540 U.S. 93, 124 S.Ct. 619, 157 L.Ed.2d 491 (2003); and *Federal Election Commission v. Wisconsin Right to Life, Inc.*, ___U.S. ___, 127 S.Ct. 2652, 168 L.Ed.2d 329 (2007).
23. *Café Erotica v. Florida Department of Transportation*, 830 So.2d 181 (Fla.App. 1 Dist. 2002); review denied, *Café Erotica/We Dare to Bare v. Florida Department of Transportation*, 845 So.2d 888 (Fla. 2003).

CASE 1.2   Bad Frog Brewery, Inc. v. New York State Liquor Authority

United States Court of Appeals, Second Circuit, 134 F.3d 87 (1998).
www.findlaw.com/casecode/index.html[a]

FACTS Bad Frog Brewery, Inc., makes and sells alcoholic beverages. Some of the beverages feature labels that display a drawing of a frog making the gesture generally known as "giving the finger." Bad Frog's authorized New York distributor, Renaissance Beer Company, applied to the New York State

Liquor Authority (NYSLA) for brand label approval, as required by state law before the beer could be sold in New York. The NYSLA denied the application, in part, because "the label could appear in grocery and convenience stores, with obvious exposure on the shelf to children of tender age." Bad Frog filed a suit in a federal district court against the NYSLA, asking for, among other things, an injunction against the denial of the application. The court granted summary judgment in favor of the NYSLA. Bad Frog appealed to the U.S. Court of Appeals for the Second Circuit.

a. Under the heading "US Court of Appeals," click on "2nd." Enter "Bad Frog Brewery" in the "Party Name Search" box and click on "search." On the resulting page, click on the case name to access the opinion.

CASE 1.2—Continued

ISSUE Was the New York State Liquor Authority's ban of Bad Frog's beer labels a reasonable restriction on commercial speech?

DECISION No. The U.S. Court of Appeals for the Second Circuit reversed the judgment of the district court and remanded the case for judgment to be entered in favor of Bad Frog.

REASON The appellate court held that the NYSLA's denial of Bad Frog's application violated the First Amendment. The ban on the use of the labels lacked a "reasonable fit" with the state's interest in shielding minors from vulgarity, and the NYSLA did not adequately consider alternatives to the ban. The court acknowledged that the NYSLA's interest "in protecting children from vulgar and profane advertising" was "substantial." The question was whether banning Bad Frog's labels "directly advanced" that interest. "In view of the wide currency of vulgar displays throughout contemporary society, including comic books targeted directly at children, barring

such displays from labels for alcoholic beverages cannot realistically be expected to reduce children's exposure to such displays to any significant degree." The court concluded that a "commercial speech limitation" must be "part of a substantial effort to advance a valid state interest, not merely the removal of a few grains of offensive sand from a beach of vulgarity." Finally, as to whether the ban on the labels was more extensive than necessary to serve this interest, the court pointed out that there were "numerous less intrusive alternatives." For example, the NYSLA's "concern could be less intrusively dealt with by placing restrictions on the permissible locations where the appellant's products may be displayed within * * * stores."

WHAT IF THE FACTS WERE DIFFERENT? *If Bad Frog had sought to use the offensive label to market toys instead of beer, would the court's ruling likely have been the same? Explain your answer.*

■

Unprotected Speech. The United States Supreme Court has made it clear that certain types of speech will not be given any protection under the First Amendment. Speech that harms the good reputation of another, or defamatory speech (see Chapter 4), will not be protected. Speech that violates criminal laws (such as threatening speech) is not constitutionally protected. Other unprotected speech includes "fighting words," or words that are likely to incite others to respond violently.

The First Amendment, as interpreted by the Supreme Court, also does not protect obscene speech. Establishing an objective definition of obscene speech has proved difficult, however, and the Court has grappled from time to time with this problem. In a 1973 case, *Miller v. California,*[24] the Supreme Court created a test for legal obscenity, which involved a set of requirements that must be met for material to be legally obscene. Under this test, material is obscene if (1) the average person finds that it violates contemporary community standards; (2) the work taken as a whole appeals to a prurient (arousing or obsessive) interest in sex; (3) the work shows patently offensive sexual conduct; and (4) the work lacks serious redeeming literary, artistic, political, or scientific merit.

Because community standards vary widely, the *Miller* test has had inconsistent application, and obscenity remains a constitutionally unsettled issue. Numerous state and federal

statutes make it a crime to disseminate obscene materials, however, and the Supreme Court has often upheld such laws, including laws prohibiting the sale and possession of child pornography.

Online Obscenity. Congress first attempted to protect minors from pornographic materials on the Internet by passing the Communications Decency Act (CDA) of 1996. The CDA declared it a crime to make available to minors online any "obscene or indecent" message that "depicts or describes, in terms patently offensive as measured by contemporary community standards, sexual or excretory activities or organs."[25] Civil rights groups challenged the act, and ultimately the United States Supreme Court ruled that portions of the act were unconstitutional. The Court held that the terms *indecent* and *patently offensive* covered large amounts of nonpornographic material with serious educational or other value.[26]

A second attempt to protect children from online obscenity, the Child Online Protection Act (COPA) of 1998,[27] met with a similar fate. Although the COPA was more narrowly tailored than its predecessor, the CDA, it still used "contemporary community standards" to define which material was obscene

---

24. 413 U.S. 15, 93 S.Ct. 2607, 37 L.Ed.2d 419 (1973).

25. 47 U.S.C. Section 223(a)(1)(B)(ii).
26. *Reno v. American Civil Liberties Union,* 521 U.S. 844, 117 S.Ct. 2329, 138 L.Ed.2d 874 (1997).
27. 47 U.S.C. Section 231.

and harmful to minors. In 2004, the United States Supreme Court concluded that it was likely that the COPA did violate the right to free speech and prevented enforcement of the act.[28]

In 2000, Congress enacted the Children's Internet Protection Act (CIPA),[29] which requires public schools and libraries to block adult content from access by children by installing **filtering software.** Such software is designed to prevent persons from viewing certain Web sites by responding to a site's Internet address or its meta tags, or key words. The CIPA was also challenged on constitutional grounds, but in 2003 the Supreme Court held that the act did not violate the First Amendment. The Court concluded that because libraries can disable the filters for any patrons who ask, the system is reasonably flexible and does not burden free speech to an unconstitutional extent.[30]

Because of the difficulties of policing the Internet as well as the constitutional complexities of prohibiting online obscenity through legislation, obscenity on the Internet is a continuing problem in the United States (and worldwide). In 2005, the Federal Bureau of Investigation established an anti-porn squad to target and prosecute companies that distribute child pornography in cyberspace. The Federal Communications Commission has also passed new obscenity regulations for television networks.

The First Amendment—Freedom of Religion The First Amendment states that the government may neither establish any religion nor prohibit the free exercise of religious practices. The first part of this constitutional provision is referred to as the **establishment clause,** and the second part is known as the **free exercise clause.** Government action, both federal and state, must be consistent with this constitutional mandate.

The Establishment Clause. The establishment clause prohibits the government from establishing a state-sponsored religion, as well as from passing laws that promote (aid or endorse) religion or that show a preference for one religion over another. The establishment clause does not require a complete separation of church and state, though. On the contrary, it requires the government to accommodate religions. *The govert must he equal to all religions.*

The establishment clause covers all conflicts about such matters as the legality of state and local government support for a particular religion, government aid to religious organizations and schools, the government's allowing or requiring school prayers, and the teaching of evolution versus fundamentalist theories of creation. For a government law or policy to be constitutional, it must not have the primary effect of advancing or inhibiting religion. Generally, federal or state regulation that does not promote religion or place a significant burden on religion is constitutional even if it has some impact on religion.

Religious displays on public property have often been challenged as violating the establishment clause, and the United States Supreme Court has ruled on a number of such cases. Generally, the Court has focused on the proximity of the religious display to nonreligious symbols, such as reindeer and candy canes, or to symbols from different religions, such as a menorah (a nine-branched candelabrum used in celebrating Hanukkah). **■EXAMPLE 1.15** In 2005, however, the Supreme Court took a slightly different approach. The dispute involved a six-foot-tall monument of the Ten Commandments on the Texas state capitol grounds. The Court held that the monument did not violate the establishment clause because the Ten Commandments had historical as well as religious significance.[31] ■

The Free Exercise Clause. The free exercise clause guarantees that a person can hold any religious belief that she or he wants or can choose to have no religious belief. When religious *practices* work against public policy and the public welfare, however, the government can act. For example, regardless of a child's or parent's religious beliefs, the government can require certain types of vaccinations. Similarly, although children of Jehovah's Witnesses are not required to say the Pledge of Allegiance at school, their parents cannot prevent them from accepting medical treatment (such as blood transfusions) if their lives are in danger. Additionally, public school students can be required to study from textbooks chosen by school authorities.

For business firms, an important issue involves the accommodation that businesses must make for the religious beliefs of their employees. Federal employment laws require business firms to accommodate employees' religious beliefs. If an employee's religion prohibits him or her from working on a certain day of the week or at a certain type of job, the employer must make a reasonable attempt to accommodate these religious requirements. Employers must reasonably accommodate an employee's religious beliefs even if the beliefs are not based on the tenets or dogma of a particular church, sect, or denom-

← child curot muke a choice, havemut invenes.

---

28. *American Civil Liberties Union v. Ashcroft,* 542 U.S. 656, 124 S.Ct. 2783, 159 L.Ed.2d 690 (2004). See also *Ashcroft v. American Civil Liberties Union,* 535 U.S. 564, 122 S.Ct. 1700, 152 L.Ed.2d 771 (2002); and *American Civil Liberties Union v. Ashcroft,* 322 F.3d 240 (3d Cir. 2003).

29. 17 U.S.C. Sections 1701–1741.

30. *United States v. American Library Association,* 539 U.S. 194, 123 S.Ct. 2297, 156 L.Ed.2d 221 (2003).

31. *Van Orden v. Perry,* 545 U.S. 677, 125 S.Ct. 2854, 162 L.Ed.2d 607 (2005).

ination. The only requirement is that the belief be religious in nature and sincerely held by the employee.

Fourth Amendment—Searches and Seizures The Fourth Amendment protects the "right of the people to be secure in their persons, houses, papers, and effects." Before searching or seizing private property, law enforcement officers must usually obtain a **search warrant**—an order from a judge or other public official authorizing the search or seizure.

Search Warrants and Probable Cause. To obtain a search warrant, law enforcement officers must convince a judge that they have reasonable grounds, or probable cause, to believe a search will reveal evidence of a specific illegality. To establish *probable cause*, the officers must have trustworthy evidence that would convince a reasonable person that the proposed search or seizure is more likely justified than not. Furthermore, the Fourth Amendment prohibits *general* warrants. It requires a particular description of whatever is to be searched or seized. General searches through a person's belongings are impermissible. The search cannot extend beyond what is described in the warrant.

The requirement for a search warrant has several exceptions. One exception applies when the items sought are likely to be removed before a warrant can be obtained. **■EXAMPLE 1.16** During a routine traffic stop, a police officer sees evidence that the car is being used to transport illegal drugs. If the officer has probable cause to believe that an automobile contains evidence of a crime and that the vehicle will likely be unavailable by the time a warrant is

obtained, the officer can search the vehicle without a warrant. ■

Searches and Seizures in the Business Context. Constitutional protection against unreasonable searches and seizures is important to businesses and professionals. Equally important is the government's interest in ensuring compliance with federal and state regulations, especially rules meant to protect the safety of employees and the public.

Because of the strong governmental interest in protecting the public, a warrant normally is not required for the seizure of spoiled or contaminated food. In addition, warrants are not required for searches of businesses in such highly regulated industries as liquor, guns, and strip mining. General manufacturing is not considered to be one of these highly regulated industries, however.

Generally, government inspectors do not have the right to search business premises without a warrant, although the standard of probable cause is not the same as that required in nonbusiness contexts. The existence of a general and neutral enforcement plan normally will justify issuance of the warrant. Lawyers and accountants frequently possess the business records of their clients, and inspecting these documents while they are out of the hands of their true owners also requires a warrant.

In the following case, after receiving a report of suspected health-care fraud, state officials entered and searched the office of a licensed physician without obtaining a warrant. The physician claimed that the search was unreasonable and improper.

CASE 1.3   United States v. Moon

United States Court of Appeals, Sixth Circuit, 513 F.3d 527 (2008).
www.ca6.uscourts.gov[a]

FACTS Young Moon was a licensed physician, specializing in oncology and hematology. Moon operated a medical practice in Crossville, Tennessee. As part of her practice, Moon contracted with the state of Tennessee to provide medical treatment to patients pursuant to a state and federally funded health benefit program for the uninsured known as "TennCare." Moon routinely utilized chemotherapy medications in her treatment of cancer patients insured under the program. In March 2001, the Tennessee Bureau of Investigation (TBI) received a complaint from one of Moon's employees alleging that she had administered partial doses of chemotherapy

medication while billing the insurance program for full doses. In January 2002, investigating agents conducted an on-site review at Moon's office. The agents identified themselves, informed Moon of a general complaint against her, and requested permission to "scan" particular patient records. Moon agreed. She also provided the agents with a location where they could scan the requested files. Later, Moon attempted to suppress the evidence, arguing that it was obtained without a search warrant. The federal district court sentenced Moon to 188 months in prison, followed by two years of supervised release. She was also ordered to pay restitution of $432,000. She appealed her conviction and sentence to the U.S. Court of Appeals for the Sixth Circuit.

a. Click on "Opinions Search" and in the "Short Title contains" box, type in "Moon." Click on "Submit Query." Under "Published Opinions," select the link to "08a0031p.06" to access the opinion.

CASE 1.3–Continues next page

CASE 1.3—Continued

ISSUE Can state officials scan a physician's business records without a warrant if the physician agreed to allow the search?

DECISION Yes. The U.S. Court of Appeals for the Sixth Circuit affirmed the district court's decision.

REASON The appellate court acknowledged that the Fourth Amendment prohibits the government from conducting unreasonable searches and seizures, but found that in this case an exception applied. "The well-delineated exception at issue here is consent. If an officer obtains consent to search, a warrantless search does not offend the Constitution." Further, "consent is voluntary when it is unequivocal, specific, and intelligently given, uncontaminated by duress or coercion." Moon clearly stated that it would be acceptable for agents to access requested files and that they could "scan whatever they needed to." Because Moon voluntarily allowed the agents to examine her files and to scan them, the resulting evidence did not have to be suppressed. A search warrant was not necessary.

WHAT IF THE FACTS WERE DIFFERENT? *Assume that Moon had proved that using partial doses of the chemotherapy drugs did not affect the "cure" rate for her cancer patients. Would the court have ruled differently? Why or why not?*

■

Due Process Both the Fifth and the Fourteenth Amendments provide that no person shall be deprived "of life, liberty, or property, without due process of law." The due process clause of each of these constitutional amendments has two aspects—procedural and substantive. Note that the due process clause applies to "legal persons," such as corporations, as well as to individuals.

Procedural Due Process. Procedural due process requires that any government decision to take life, liberty, or property must be made fairly—that is, the government must give a person proper notice and an opportunity to be heard. Fair procedures must be used in determining whether a person will be subjected to punishment or have some burden imposed on him or her. Fair procedure has been interpreted as requiring that the person have at least an opportunity to object to a proposed action before a fair, neutral decision maker (which need not be a judge). In most states, a driver's license is construed as a property interest. Therefore, the state must provide some sort of opportunity for the driver to object before suspending or terminating the license.

PREVENTING LEGAL DISPUTES Many of the constitutional protections discussed in this chapter have become part of our culture in the United States. Due process, especially procedural due process, has become synonymous with what Americans consider "fair." For this reason, businesspersons seeking to avoid legal disputes should consider giving due process to anyone who might object to some business decision or action, whether that person is an employee, a partner, an affiliate, or a customer. For instance, giving ample notice of new policies to all affected persons is a prudent move, as is giving them at least an opportunity to express their opinions on the matter. Providing an opportunity to be heard is often the ideal way to make people feel that they are being treated fairly. If people believe that a businessperson or firm is fair and listens to both sides of an issue, they are less likely to sue that businessperson or firm.

■

Substantive Due Process. Substantive due process protects an individual's life, liberty, or property against certain government actions regardless of the fairness of the procedures used to implement them. Substantive due process limits what the government may do in its legislative and executive capacities. Legislation must be fair and reasonable in content and must further a legitimate governmental objective. Only when state conduct is arbitrary, or shocks the conscience, however, will it rise to the level of violating substantive due process.[32]

If a law or other governmental action limits a fundamental right, the state must have a legitimate and compelling interest to justify its action. Fundamental rights include interstate travel, privacy, voting, marriage and family, and all First Amendment rights. Thus, a state must have substantial reason for taking any action that infringes on a person's free speech rights. In situations not involving fundamental rights, a law or action does not violate substantive due process if it rationally relates to any legitimate government purpose. Under this test, virtually any business regulation will be upheld as reasonable. The United States Supreme Court has sustained insurance regulations, price and wage controls, banking limitations, and restrictions on unfair com-

---

32. See, for example, *Breen v. Texas A&M University*, 485 F.3d 325 (5th Cir. 2007).

petition and trade practices against substantive due process challenges.

■EXAMPLE 1.17 If a state legislature enacted a law imposing a fifteen-year term of imprisonment without a trial on all businesspersons who appeared in their own television commercials, the law would be unconstitutional on both substantive and procedural grounds. Substantive review would invalidate the legislation because it infringes on freedom of speech. Procedurally, the law is unfair because it imposes the penalty without giving the accused a chance to defend her or his actions. ■

REVIEWING The Legal and Constitutional Environment of Business

Suppose that the California legislature passes a law that severely restricts carbon dioxide emissions from automobiles in that state. A group of automobile manufacturers files a suit against the state of California to prevent the enforcement of the law. The automakers claim that a federal law already sets fuel economy standards nationwide and that these standards are essentially the same as carbon dioxide emission standards. According to the automobile manufacturers, it is unfair to allow California to impose more stringent regulations than those set by the

federal law. Using the information presented in the chapter, answer the following questions.

1 Who are the parties (the plaintiffs and the defendant) in this lawsuit?

2 Are the plaintiffs seeking a legal remedy or an equitable remedy? Why?

3 What is the primary source of the law that is at issue here?

4 Read through the appendix that follows this chapter, and then answer the following question: Where would you look to find the relevant California and federal laws?

TERMS AND CONCEPTS

adjudicate 5
administrative agency 5
administrative law 5
administrative process 5
Bill of Rights 12
binding authority 6
breach 3
case law 5
citation 4
civil law 9
civil law system 9
commerce clause 10
common law 6
constitutional law 4

criminal law 9
cyberlaw 9
defendant 7
due process clause 18
enabling legislation 5
establishment clause 16
executive agency 5
filtering software 16
free exercise clause 16
independent regulatory agency 5
international law 10
law 2
national law 9
ordinance 4

persuasive authority 7
plaintiff 7
police powers 12
precedent 6
primary source of law 4
procedural law 7
remedy 7
search warrant 17
secondary source of law 4
stare decisis 6
statutory law 4
substantive law 7
symbolic speech 13
uniform law 4

CHAPTER SUMMARY The Legal and Constitutional Environment of Business

Sources of American Law
(See pages 4–6.)

1. *Constitutional law*—The law as expressed in the U.S. Constitution and the various state constitutions. The U.S. Constitution is the supreme law of the land. State constitutions are supreme within state borders to the extent that they do not violate the U.S. Constitution or a federal law.

(Continued)

CHAPTER SUMMARY	The Legal and Constitutional Environment of Business—Continued
Sources of American Law— Continued	2. *Statutory law*—Laws or ordinances created by federal, state, and local legislatures and governing bodies. None of these laws can violate the U.S. Constitution or the relevant state constitutions. Uniform laws, when adopted by a state legislature, become statutory law in that state.
	3. *Administrative law*—The rules, orders, and decisions of federal or state government administrative agencies. Federal administrative agencies are created by enabling legislation enacted by the U.S. Congress. Agency functions include rulemaking, investigation and enforcement, and adjudication.
	4. *Case law and common law doctrines*—Judge-made law, including interpretations of constitutional provisions, of statutes enacted by legislatures, and of regulations created by administrative agencies. The common law—the doctrines and principles embodied in case law—governs all areas not covered by statutory law (or agency regulations issued to implement various statutes).
The Common Law Tradition (See pages 6–7.)	1. *Common law*—Law that originated in medieval England with the creation of the king's courts, or *curiae regis,* and the development of a body of rules that were common to (or applied throughout) the land.
	2. *Stare decisis*—A doctrine under which judges "stand on decided cases"—or follow the rule of precedent—in deciding cases. *Stare decisis* is the cornerstone of the common law tradition.
	3. *Remedies*—
	a. Remedies at law—Money or something else of value.
	b. Remedies in equity—Remedies that are granted when the remedies at law are unavailable or inadequate. Equitable remedies include specific performance, an injunction, and contract rescission (cancellation).
Classifications of Law (See pages 7–10.)	The law may be broken down according to several classification systems, such as substantive or procedural law, federal or state law, and private or public law. Two broad classifications are civil and criminal law, and national and international law. Cyberlaw is not really a classification of law but a term that is used for the growing body of case law and statutory law that applies to Internet transactions.
The Constitution as It Affects Business (See pages 10–19.)	1. *Commerce clause*—Expressly permits Congress to regulate commerce. That power authorizes the national government, at least theoretically, to regulate every commercial enterprise in the United States. Under their police powers, state governments may regulate private activities to protect or promote the public order, health, safety, morals, and general welfare.
	2. *Bill of Rights*—The first ten amendments to the U.S. Constitution. They embody a series of protections for individuals—and in some cases, business entities—against various types of interference by the federal government. One of the freedoms guaranteed by the Bill of Rights that affects businesses is the freedom of speech guaranteed by the First Amendment. Also important are the protections of the Fifth and the Fourteenth Amendments, which provide that no person shall be deprived of "life, liberty, or property, without due process of law."

FOR REVIEW

Answers for the even-numbered questions in this **For Review** *section can be found on this text's accompanying Web site at* **www.cengage.com/blaw/fbl**. *Select "Chapter 1" and click on "For Review."*

1 What is the Uniform Commercial Code?

2 What is the common law tradition?

3 What is a precedent? When might a court depart from precedent?

4 What are some important differences between civil law and criminal law?

5 How does the U.S. Constitution affect business activities in the United States?

QUESTIONS AND CASE PROBLEMS

HYPOTHETICAL SCENARIOS AND CASE PROBLEMS

1.1 Binding versus Persuasive Authority. A county court in Illinois is deciding a case involving an issue that has never been addressed before in that state's courts. The Iowa Supreme Court, however, recently decided a case involving a very similar fact pattern. Is the Illinois court obligated to follow the Iowa Supreme Court's decision on the issue? If the United States Supreme Court had decided a similar case, would that decision be binding on the Illinois court? Explain.

1.2 Hypothetical Question with Sample Answer. This chapter discussed a number of sources of American law. Which source of law takes priority in each of the following situations, and why?

1 A federal statute conflicts with the U.S. Constitution.

2 A federal statute conflicts with a state constitution.

3 A state statute conflicts with the common law of that state.

4 A state constitutional amendment conflicts with the U.S. Constitution.

5 A federal administrative regulation conflicts with a state constitution.

For a sample answer to Question 1.2, go to Appendix E at the end of this text.

1.3 Commerce Clause. Suppose that Georgia enacts a law requiring the use of contoured rear-fender mudguards on trucks and trailers operating within its state lines. The statute further makes it illegal for trucks and trailers to use straight mudguards. In thirty-five other states, straight mudguards are legal. Moreover, in the neighboring state of Florida, straight mudguards are explicitly required by law. There is some evidence suggesting that contoured mudguards might be a little safer than straight mudguards. Discuss whether this Georgia statute would violate the commerce clause of the U.S. Constitution.

(margin handwriting: Yes because Tollens is protected by F. R Law and her company must respect her religion and accommodate her beliefs.)

1.4 Freedom of Religion. A business has a backlog of orders, and to meet its deadlines, management decides to run the firm seven days a week, eight hours a day. One of the employees, Marjorie Tollens, refuses to work on Saturday on religious grounds. Her refusal to work means that the firm may not meet its production deadlines and may therefore suffer a loss of future business. The firm fires Tollens and replaces her with an employee who is willing to work seven days a week. Tollens claims that in terminating her employment, her employer violated her constitutional right to the free exercise of her religion. Do you agree? Why or why not?

1.5 Reading Citations. Assume that you want to read the court's entire opinion in the case of *Buell-Wilson v. Ford Motor Co.,* 160 Cal.App.4th 1107, 73 Cal.Rptr.3d 277 (2008). The case focuses on whether a punitive damages award was excessive. (Note that this case will be presented in Chapter 4 of this text

as Case 4.1.) Read the section entitled "Finding Case Law" in the appendix that follows this chapter, and then explain specifically where you would find the court's opinion.

1.6 Stare Decisis. In the text of this chapter, we stated that the doctrine of *stare decisis* "became a cornerstone of the English and U.S. judicial systems." What does *stare decisis* mean, and why has this doctrine been so fundamental to the development of our legal tradition?

1.7 Case Problem with Sample Answer. For decades, New York City has had to deal with the vandalism and defacement of public property caused by unauthorized graffiti. Among other attempts to stop the damage, in December 2005 the city banned the sale of aerosol spray-paint cans and broad-tipped indelible markers to persons under twenty-one years of age and prohibited them from possessing such items on property other than their own. By May 1, 2006, five people—all under age twenty-one—had been cited for violations of these regulations, while 871 individuals had been arrested for actually making graffiti. Artists who wished to create graffiti on legal surfaces, such as canvas, wood, and clothing, included college student Lindsey Vincenty, who was studying visual arts. Unable to buy her supplies in the city or to carry them in the city if she bought them elsewhere, Vincenty, with others, filed a suit in a federal district court on behalf of themselves and other young artists against Michael Bloomberg, the city's mayor, and others. The plaintiffs claimed that, among other things, the new rules violated their right to freedom of speech. They asked the court to enjoin the enforcement of the rules. Should the court grant this request? Why or why not? [*Vincenty v. Bloomberg,* 476 F.3d 74 (2d Cir. 2007)]

After you have answered Problem 1.7, compare your answer with the sample answer given on the Web site that accompanies this text. Go to www.cengage.com/blaw/fbl, select "Chapter 1," and click on "Case Problem with Sample Answer."

1.8   A Question of Ethics. *Aric Toll owns and manages the Balboa Island Village Inn, a restaurant and bar in Newport Beach, California. Anne Lemen owns "Island Cottage," a residence across an alley from the Inn. Lemen often complained to the authorities about excessive noise and the behavior of the Inn's customers, whom she called "drunks" and "whores." Lemen referred to Theresa Toll, Aric's wife, as "Madam Whore." Lemen told the Inn's bartender Ewa Cook that Cook "worked for Satan," was "Satan's wife," and was "going to have Satan's children." She told the Inn's neighbors that it was "a whorehouse" with "prostitution going on inside" and that it sold illegal drugs, sold alcohol to minors, made "sex videos," was involved in child pornography, had "Mafia connections," encouraged "lesbian activity," and stayed open until 6:00 A.M. Lemen also voiced her complaints to potential customers, and* *the Inn's sales dropped more than 20 percent. The Inn filed a suit in a California state court against Lemen, asserting defamation and other claims. [Balboa Island Village Inn, Inc. v. Lemen, 40 Cal.4th 1141, 156 P.3d 339 (2007)]*

1 Are Lemen's statements about the Inn's owners and activities protected by the Constitution? Should they be protected? In whose favor should the court rule? Why?

2 Did Lemen behave unethically in this case? Explain.

CRITICAL THINKING AND WRITING ASSIGNMENTS

1.9   Critical Legal Thinking. John's company is involved in a lawsuit with a customer, Beth. John argues that for fifty years, in cases involving circumstances similar to this case, judges have ruled in a way that indicates that the judge in this case should rule in favor of John's company. Is this a valid argument? If so, must the judge in this case rule as those other judges have? What argument could Beth use to counter John's reasoning?

1.10 Critical Thinking and Writing Assignment for Business. The commerce clause was originally interpreted to regulate only

interstate commerce. Over time, however, the United States Supreme Court has made it clear that the commerce clause also applies to commerce that is purely intrastate. Today, the federal government has the power to regulate every commercial enterprise in the United States. What does this mean for commercial businesses that operate only within the borders of one state? Does it promote or discourage intrastate commerce?

ACCESSING THE INTERNET

Today, business law professors and students can go online to access information on almost every topic covered in this text. A good point of departure for online legal research is this text's Web site at

www.cengage.com/blaw/fbl

There, you will find numerous materials relevant to this text and to business law generally, including links to various legal resources on the Web. Additionally, every chapter in this text ends with an *Accessing the Internet* feature that contains selected Web addresses.

You can access many of the sources of law discussed in this chapter at the FindLaw Web site, which is probably the most comprehensive source of free legal information on the Internet. Go to

www.findlaw.com

The Legal Information Institute at Cornell Law School, which offers extensive information about U.S. law, is also a good starting point for legal research. The URL for this site is

www.law.cornell.edu

The Library of Congress offers extensive links to state and federal government resources at

www.loc.gov

For an online version of the U.S. Constitution that provides hypertext links to amendments and other changes, go to

www.law.cornell.edu/constitution/constitution.overview.html

For discussions of current issues involving the rights and liberties contained in the Bill of Rights, go to the Web site of the American Civil Liberties Union at

www.aclu.org

Summaries and the full texts of constitutional law decisions by the United States Supreme Court are included at the Oyez site, which also features audio clips of arguments before the Court. Go to

www.oyez.org

PRACTICAL INTERNET EXERCISES

Go to this text's Web site at **www.cengage.com/blaw/fbl**, select "Chapter 1," and click on "Practical Internet Exercises." There you will find the following Internet research exercises that you can perform to learn more about the topics covered in this chapter.

PRACTICAL INTERNET EXERCISE 1-1   LEGAL PERSPECTIVE—Internet Sources of Law

PRACTICAL INTERNET EXERCISE 1-2   MANAGEMENT PERSPECTIVE—Online Assistance from Government Agencies

PRACTICAL INTERNET EXERCISE 1-3   MANAGEMENT PERSPECTIVE—Commercial Speech

BEFORE THE TEST

Go to this text's Web site at **www.cengage.com/blaw/fbl**, select "Chapter 1," and click on "Interactive Quizzes." You will find a number of interactive questions relating to this chapter.

APPENDIX TO CHAPTER 1

The statutes, agency regulations, and case law referred to in this text establish the rights and duties of businesspersons engaged in various types of activities. The cases presented in the following chapters provide you with concise, real-life illustrations of how the courts interpret and apply these laws. Because of the importance of knowing how to find statutory, administrative, and case law, this appendix offers a brief introduction to how these laws are published and to the legal "shorthand" employed in referencing these legal sources.

FINDING STATUTORY AND ADMINISTRATIVE LAW

When Congress passes laws, they are collected in a publication titled *United States Statutes at Large*. When state legislatures pass laws, they are collected in similar state publications. Most frequently, however, laws are referred to in their codified form—that is, the form in which they appear in the federal and state codes. In these codes, laws are compiled by subject.

United States Code

The *United States Code* (U.S.C.) arranges all existing federal laws of a public and permanent nature by subject. Each of the fifty subjects into which the U.S.C. arranges the laws is given a title and a title number. For example, laws relating to commerce and trade are collected in "Title 15, Commerce and Trade." Titles are subdivided by sections. A citation to the U.S.C. includes title and section numbers. Thus, a reference to "15 U.S.C. Section 1" means that the statute can be found in Section 1 of Title 15. ("Section" may also be designated by the symbol §, and "Sections" by §§.)

Sometimes, a citation includes the abbreviation *et seq.*— as in "15 U.S.C. Sections 1 *et seq.*" The term is an abbreviated form of *et sequitur*, which is Latin for "and the following"; when used in a citation, it refers to sections that concern the same subject as the numbered section and follow it in sequence.

Commercial publications of these laws and regulations are available and are widely used. For example, West Group publishes the *United States Code Annotated* (U.S.C.A.). The U.S.C.A. contains the complete text of laws included in the U.S.C., notes of court decisions that interpret and apply specific sections of the statutes, and the text of presidential proclamations and executive orders. The U.S.C.A. also includes research aids, such as cross-references to related statutes, historical notes, and library references. A citation to the U.S.C.A. is similar to a citation to the U.S.C.: "15 U.S.C.A. Section 1."

State Codes

State codes follow the U.S.C. pattern of arranging law by subject. The state codes may be called codes, revisions, compilations, consolidations, general statutes, or statutes, depending on the preferences of the states. In some codes, subjects are designated by number. In others, they are designated by name. For example, "13 Pennsylvania Consolidated Statutes Section 1101" means that the statute can be found in Title 13, Section 1101, of the Pennsylvania code. "California Commercial Code Section 1101" means the statute can be found in Section 1101 under the subject heading "Commercial Code" of the California code. Abbreviations may be used. For example, "13 Pennsylvania Consolidated Statutes Section 1101" may be abbreviated "13 Pa. C.S. § 1101," and "California Commercial Code Section 1101" may be abbreviated "Cal. Com. Code § 1101."

Administrative Rules

Rules and regulations adopted by federal administrative agencies are compiled in the *Code of Federal Regulations* (C.F.R.). Like the U.S.C., the C.F.R. is divided into fifty titles. Rules within each title are assigned section numbers. A full citation to the C.F.R. includes title and section numbers. For example, a reference to "17 C.F.R. Section 230.504" means that the rule can be found in Section 230.504 of Title 17.

FINDING CASE LAW

Before discussing the case reporting system, we need to look briefly at the court system (which will be discussed in detail in Chapter 2). There are two types of courts in the United States, federal courts and state courts. Both the federal and the state court systems consist of several levels, or tiers, of courts. *Trial courts*, in which evidence is presented and testimony given, are on the bottom tier (which also includes lower courts handling specialized issues). Decisions from a trial court can be appealed to a higher court, which commonly would be an intermediate *court of appeals*, or an *appellate court*. Decisions from these intermediate courts of appeals may be appealed to an even higher court, such as a state supreme court or the United States Supreme Court.

State Court Decisions

Most state trial court decisions are not published. Except in New York and a few other states that publish selected opinions of their trial courts, decisions from state trial courts are merely filed in the office of the clerk of the court, where the decisions are available for public inspection. (Sometimes, they can be found online as well.) Written decisions of the appellate, or reviewing, courts, however, are published and distributed. As you will note, most of the state court cases presented in this book are from state appellate courts. The reported appellate decisions are published in volumes called *reports* or *reporters*, which are numbered consecutively. State appellate court decisions are found in the state reporters of that particular state.

Additionally, state court opinions appear in regional units of the *National Reporter System*, published by West Group. Most lawyers and libraries have the West reporters because they report cases more quickly and are distributed more widely than the state-published reports. In fact, many states have eliminated their own reporters in favor of West's National Reporter System. The National Reporter System divides the states into the following geographic areas: *Atlantic* (A. or A.2d), *North Eastern* (N.E. or N.E.2d), *North Western* (N.W. or N.W.2d), *Pacific* (P., P.2d, or P.3d), *South Eastern* (S.E. or S.E.2d), *South Western* (S.W., S.W.2d, or S.W.3d), and *Southern* (So. or So.2d). (The *2d* and *3d* in the abbreviations refer to *Second Series* and *Third Series*, respectively.) The states included in each of these regional divisions are indicated in Exhibit 1A–1 on the following page, which illustrates West's National Reporter System.

After appellate decisions have been published, they are normally referred to (cited) by the name of the case; the volume, name, and page number of the state's official reporter (if different from West's National Reporter System); the volume, name, and page number of the *National Reporter*; and the volume, name, and page number of any other selected reporter. This information is included in the *citation*. (Citing a reporter by volume number, name, and page number, in that order, is common to all citations.) When more than one reporter is cited for the same case, each reference is called a *parallel citation*. Note that some states have adopted a "public domain citation system" that uses a somewhat different format for the citation. For example, in Wisconsin, a Wisconsin Supreme Court decision might be designated "2008 WI 40," meaning that the case was decided in the year 2008 by the Wisconsin Supreme Court and was the fortieth decision issued by that court during that year. Parallel citations to the *Wisconsin Reports* and West's *North Western Reporter* are still included after the public domain citation.

Consider the following case citation: *Ramirez v. Health Net of Northeast, Inc.*, 285 Conn. 1, 938 A.2d 576 (2008). We see that the opinion in this case can be found in Volume 285 of the official *Connecticut Reports*, which reports only the decisions of the Supreme Court of Connecticut, on page 1. The parallel citation is to Volume 938 of the *Atlantic Reporter, Second Series*, page 576. In presenting opinions in this text, in addition to the reporter, we give the name of the court hearing the case and the year of the court's decision. Sample citations to state court decisions are explained in Exhibit 1A–2 on pages 27–29.

Federal Court Decisions

Federal district court decisions are published unofficially in West's *Federal Supplement* (F.Supp. or F.Supp.2d), and opinions from the circuit courts of appeals (federal reviewing courts) are reported unofficially in West's *Federal Reporter* (F., F.2d, or F.3d). Cases concerning federal bankruptcy law are published unofficially in West's *Bankruptcy Reporter* (Bankr.). The official edition of United States Supreme Court decisions is the *United States Reports* (U.S.), which is published by the federal government. Unofficial editions of Supreme Court cases include West's *Supreme Court Reporter* (S.Ct.) and the *Lawyers' Edition of the Supreme Court Reports* (L.Ed. or L.Ed.2d). Sample citations for federal court decisions are also listed and explained in Exhibit 1A–2.

Unpublished Opinions and Old Cases

Many court opinions that are not yet published or that are not intended for publication can be accessed through Westlaw® (abbreviated in citations as "WL"), an online legal database maintained by Thomson Reuters/West. When no citation to a published reporter is available for cases cited in this text, we give the WL citation (see Exhibit 1A–2 for an example).

On a few occasions, this text cites opinions from old, classic cases dating to the nineteenth century or earlier; some of these are from the English courts. The citations to these cases may not conform to the descriptions given above because the reporters in which they were published have since been replaced.

READING AND UNDERSTANDING CASE LAW

The cases in this text have been condensed from the full text of the courts' opinions. For those wishing to review court cases for future research projects or to gain additional legal information, the following sections will provide useful insights into how to read and understand case law.

Case Titles and Terminology

The title of a case, such as *Adams v. Jones*, indicates the names of the parties to the lawsuit. The *v.* in the case title stands for *versus*, which means "against." In the trial court,

EXHIBIT 1A–1   West's National Reporter System—Regional/Federal

Regional Reporters	Coverage Beginning	Coverage
Atlantic Reporter (A. or A.2d)	1885	Connecticut, Delaware, District of Columbia, Maine, Maryland, New Hampshire, New Jersey, Pennsylvania, Rhode Island, and Vermont.
North Eastern Reporter (N.E. or N.E.2d)	1885	Illinois, Indiana, Massachusetts, New York, and Ohio.
North Western Reporter (N.W. or N.W.2d)	1879	Iowa, Michigan, Minnesota, Nebraska, North Dakota, South Dakota, and Wisconsin.
Pacific Reporter (P., P.2d, or P.3d)	1883	Alaska, Arizona, California, Colorado, Hawaii, Idaho, Kansas, Montana, Nevada, New Mexico, Oklahoma, Oregon, Utah, Washington, and Wyoming.
South Eastern Reporter (S.E. or S.E.2d)	1887	Georgia, North Carolina, South Carolina, Virginia, and West Virginia.
South Western Reporter (S.W., S.W.2d, or S.W.3d)	1886	Arkansas, Kentucky, Missouri, Tennessee, and Texas.
Southern Reporter (So. or So.2d)	1887	Alabama, Florida, Louisiana, and Mississippi.

Federal Reporters		
Federal Reporter (F., F.2d, or F.3d)	1880	U.S. Circuit Courts from 1880 to 1912; U.S. Commerce Court from 1911 to 1913; U.S. District Courts from 1880 to 1932; U.S. Court of Claims (now called U.S. Court of Federal Claims) from 1929 to 1932 and since 1960; U.S. Courts of Appeals since 1891; U.S. Court of Customs and Patent Appeals since 1929; U.S. Emergency Court of Appeals since 1943.
Federal Supplement (F.Supp. or F.Supp.2d)	1932	U.S. Court of Claims from 1932 to 1960; U.S. District Courts since 1932; U.S. Customs Court since 1956.
Federal Rules Decisions (F.R.D.)	1939	U.S. District Courts involving the Federal Rules of Civil Procedure since 1939 and Federal Rules of Criminal Procedure since 1946.
Supreme Court Reporter (S.Ct.)	1882	United States Supreme Court since the October term of 1882.
Bankruptcy Reporter (Bankr.)	1980	Bankruptcy decisions of U.S. Bankruptcy Courts, U.S. District Courts, U.S. Courts of Appeals, and the United States Supreme Court.
Military Justice Reporter (M.J.)	1978	U.S. Court of Military Appeals and Courts of Military Review for the Army, Navy, Air Force, and Coast Guard.

NATIONAL REPORTER SYSTEM MAP

EXHIBIT 1A-2 **How to Read Citations**

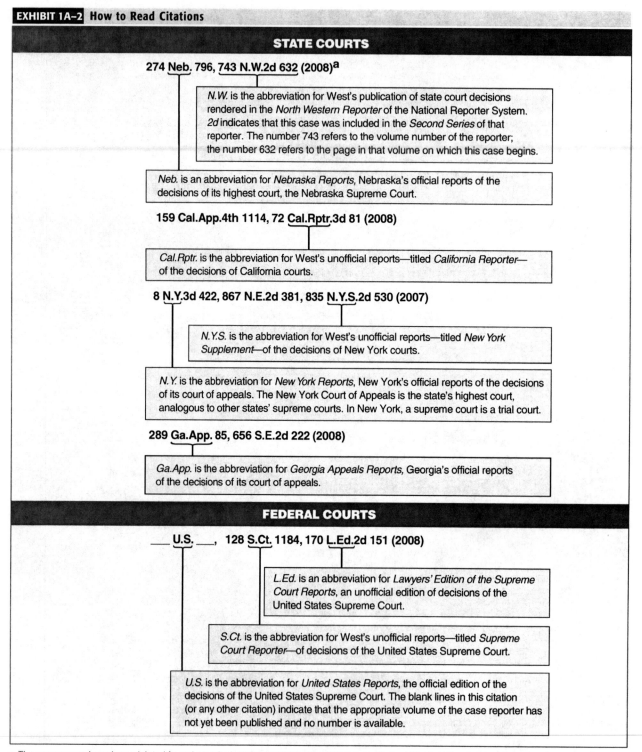

STATE COURTS

274 Neb. 796, 743 N.W.2d 632 (2008)[a]

> *N.W.* is the abbreviation for West's publication of state court decisions rendered in the *North Western Reporter* of the National Reporter System. *2d* indicates that this case was included in the *Second Series* of that reporter. The number 743 refers to the volume number of the reporter; the number 632 refers to the page in that volume on which this case begins.

> *Neb.* is an abbreviation for *Nebraska Reports,* Nebraska's official reports of the decisions of its highest court, the Nebraska Supreme Court.

159 Cal.App.4th 1114, 72 Cal.Rptr.3d 81 (2008)

> *Cal.Rptr.* is the abbreviation for West's unofficial reports—titled *California Reporter*—of the decisions of California courts.

8 N.Y.3d 422, 867 N.E.2d 381, 835 N.Y.S.2d 530 (2007)

> *N.Y.S.* is the abbreviation for West's unofficial reports—titled *New York Supplement*—of the decisions of New York courts.

> *N.Y.* is the abbreviation for *New York Reports*, New York's official reports of the decisions of its court of appeals. The New York Court of Appeals is the state's highest court, analogous to other states' supreme courts. In New York, a supreme court is a trial court.

289 Ga.App. 85, 656 S.E.2d 222 (2008)

> *Ga.App.* is the abbreviation for *Georgia Appeals Reports,* Georgia's official reports of the decisions of its court of appeals.

FEDERAL COURTS

___ U.S. ___, 128 S.Ct. 1184, 170 L.Ed.2d 151 (2008)

> *L.Ed.* is an abbreviation for *Lawyers' Edition of the Supreme Court Reports,* an unofficial edition of decisions of the United States Supreme Court.

> *S.Ct.* is the abbreviation for West's unofficial reports—titled *Supreme Court Reporter*—of decisions of the United States Supreme Court.

> *U.S.* is the abbreviation for *United States Reports,* the official edition of the decisions of the United States Supreme Court. The blank lines in this citation (or any other citation) indicate that the appropriate volume of the case reporter has not yet been published and no number is available.

a. The case names have been deleted from these citations to emphasize the publications. It should be kept in mind, however, that the name of a case is as important as the specific page numbers in the volumes in which it is found. If a citation is incorrect, the correct citation may be found in a publication's index of case names. In addition to providing a check on errors in citations, the date of a case is important because the value of a recent case as an authority is likely to be greater than that of older cases from the same court.

(Continued)

EXHIBIT 1A–2 How to Read Citations—Continued

FEDERAL COURTS (Continued)

512 F.3d 582 (9th Cir. 2008)

> *9th Cir.* is an abbreviation denoting that this case was decided in the U.S. Court of Appeals for the Ninth Circuit.

533 F.Supp.2d 740 (W.D.Mich. 2008)

> *W.D.Mich.* is an abbreviation indicating that the U.S. District Court for the Western District of Michigan decided this case.

ENGLISH COURTS

9 Exch. 341, 156 Eng.Rep. 145 (1854)

> *Eng.Rep.* is an abbreviation for *English Reports, Full Reprint,* a series of reports containing selected decisions made in English courts between 1378 and 1865.

> *Exch.* is an abbreviation for *English Exchequer Reports,* which includes the original reports of cases decided in England's Court of Exchequer.

STATUTORY AND OTHER CITATIONS

18 U.S.C. Section 1961(1)(A)

> *U.S.C.* denotes *United States Code,* the codification of *United States Statutes at Large.* The number 18 refers to the statute's U.S.C. title number and 1961 to its section number within that title. The number 1 in parentheses refers to a subsection within the section, and the letter A in parentheses to a subdivision within the subsection.

UCC 2–206(1)(b)

> *UCC* is an abbreviation for *Uniform Commercial Code.* The first number 2 is a reference to an article of the UCC, and 206 to a section within that article. The number 1 in parentheses refers to a subsection within the section, and the letter b in parentheses to a subdivision within the subsection.

***Restatement (Second) of Torts,* Section 568**

> *Restatement (Second) of Torts* refers to the second edition of the American Law Institute's *Restatement of the Law of Torts.* The number 568 refers to a specific section.

17 C.F.R. Section 230.505

> *C.F.R.* is an abbreviation for *Code of Federal Regulations,* a compilation of federal administrative regulations. The number 17 designates the regulation's title number, and 230.505 designates a specific section within that title.

EXHIBIT 1A–2 How to Read Citations—Continued

WESTLAW CITATIONS[b]

2008 WL 427478

WL is an abbreviation for Westlaw. The number 2008 is the year of the document that can be found with this citation in the Westlaw database. The number 427478 is a number assigned to a specific document. A higher number indicates that a document was added to the Westlaw database later in the year.

UNIFORM RESOURCE LOCATORS (URLs)

http://www.westlaw.com[c]

The suffix *com* is the top level domain (TLD) for this Web site. The TLD *com* is an abbreviation for "commercial," which usually means that a for-profit entity hosts (maintains or supports) this Web site.

westlaw is the host name—the part of the domain name selected by the organization that registered the name. In this case, West Group registered the name. This Internet site is the Westlaw database on the Web.

www is an abbreviation for "World Wide Web." The Web is a system of Internet servers that support documents formatted in *HTML* (hypertext markup language). HTML supports links to text, graphics, and audio and video files.

http://www.uscourts.gov

This is "The Federal Judiciary Home Page." The host is the Administrative Office of the U.S. Courts. The TLD *gov* is an abbreviation for "government." This Web site includes information and links from, and about, the federal courts.

http://www.law.cornell.edu/index.html

This part of a URL points to a Web page or file at a specific location within the host's domain. This page is a menu with links to documents within the domain and to other Internet resources.

This is the host name for a Web site that contains the Internet publications of the Legal Information Institute (LII), which is a part of Cornell Law School. The LII site includes a variety of legal materials and links to other legal resources on the Internet. The TLD *edu* is an abbreviation for "educational institution" (a school or a university).

http://www.ipl.org/div/news

This part of the Web site points to a static *news* page at this Web site, which provides links to online newspapers from around the world.

div is an abbreviation for "division," which is the way that the Internet Public Library tags the content on its Web site as relating to a specific topic.

ipl is an abbreviation for "Internet Public Library," which is an online service that provides reference resources and links to other information services on the Web. The IPL is supported chiefly by the School of Information at the University of Michigan. The TLD *org* is an abbreviation for "organization" (normally nonprofit).

b. Many court decisions that are not yet published or that are not intended for publication can be accessed through Westlaw, an online legal database.

c. The basic form for a URL is "service://hostname/path." The Internet service for all of the URLs in this text is *http* (hypertext transfer protocol). Because most Web browsers add this prefix automatically when a user enters a host name or a hostname/path, we have omitted the http:// from the URLs listed in this text.

Adams was the plaintiff—the person who filed the suit. Jones was the defendant. If the case is appealed, however, the appellate court will sometimes place the name of the party appealing the decision first, so the case may be called *Jones v. Adams*. Because some reviewing courts retain the trial court order of names, it is often impossible to distinguish the plaintiff from the defendant in the title of a reported appellate court decision. You must carefully read the facts of each case to identify the parties.

The following terms and phrases are frequently encountered in court opinions and legal publications. Because it is important to understand what these terms and phrases mean, we define and discuss them here.

Plaintiffs and Defendants As mentioned in Chapter 1, the plaintiff in a lawsuit is the party that initiates the action. The defendant is the party against which a lawsuit is brought. Lawsuits frequently involve more than one plaintiff and/or defendant.

Appellants and Appellees The *appellant* is the party that appeals a case to another court or jurisdiction from the court or jurisdiction in which the case was originally brought. Sometimes, an appellant is referred to as the *petitioner*. The *appellee* is the party against which the appeal is taken. Sometimes, the appellee is referred to as the *respondent*.

Judges and Justices The terms *judge* and *justice* are usually synonymous and represent two designations given to judges in various courts. All members of the United States Supreme Court, for example, are referred to as justices. And justice is the formal title usually given to judges of appellate courts, although this is not always the case. In New York, a justice is a judge of the trial court (which is called the Supreme Court), and a member of the Court of Appeals (the state's highest court) is called a judge. The term *justice* is commonly abbreviated to J., and *justices* to JJ. A Supreme Court case might refer to Justice Ginsburg as Ginsburg, J., or to Chief Justice Roberts as Roberts, C.J.

Decisions and Opinions Most decisions reached by reviewing, or appellate, courts are explained in written *opinions*. The opinion contains the court's reasons for its decision, the rules of law that apply, and the judgment. When all judges or justices unanimously agree on an opinion, the opinion is written for the entire court and can be deemed a *unanimous opinion*. When there is not unanimous agreement, a *majority opinion* is written, outlining the views of the majority of the judges or justices deciding the case.

Often, a judge or justice who feels strongly about making or emphasizing a point that was not made or emphasized in the unanimous or majority opinion will write a *concurring opinion*. That means the judge or justice agrees (concurs) with the judgment given in the unanimous or majority opinion but for different reasons. When there is not a unanimous opinion, a *dissenting opinion* is usually written by a judge or justice who does not agree with the majority. (See the *Extended Case Study* following Chapter 3 on pages 77 and 78 for an example of a dissenting opinion.) The dissenting opinion is important because it may form the basis of the arguments used years later in overruling the precedential majority opinion. Occasionally, a court issues a *per curiam* (Latin for "of the court") opinion, which does not indicate which judge or justice authored the opinion.

A Sample Court Case

Knowing how to read and analyze a court opinion is an essential step in undertaking accurate legal research. A further step involves "briefing" the case. Legal researchers routinely brief cases by summarizing and reducing the texts of the opinions to their essential elements. (For instructions on how to brief a case, go to Appendix A at the end of this text.) The cases contained within the chapters of this text have already been analyzed and partially briefed by the authors, and the essential aspects of each case are presented in a convenient format consisting of four basic sections: *Facts, Issue, Decision,* and *Reason*. Each case is followed by either a brief *For Critical Analysis* section, which presents a question regarding some issue raised by the case; a *Why Is This Case Important?* section, which explains the significance of the case; or a *What If the Facts Were Different?* question, which alters the facts slightly and asks you to consider how this would change the outcome. A section entitled *Impact of This Case on Today's Law* concludes the *Landmark and Classic Cases* that appear throughout the text to indicate the significance of the case for today's legal landscape.

To illustrate the elements in a court opinion, we present an annotated opinion in Exhibit 1A–3 on pages 31 and 32. The opinion is from an actual case that the U.S. Court of Appeals for the Ninth Circuit decided in 2008.

You will note that triple asterisks (* * *) frequently appear in the quoted portions of the opinion. The triple asterisks indicate that we have deleted a few words or sentences from the opinion for the sake of readability or brevity. Additionally, when the opinion cites another case or legal source, the citation to the case or other source has been omitted to save space and to improve the flow of the text. These editorial practices are continued in the other court opinions presented in this book. In addition, whenever we present a court opinion that includes a term or phrase that may not be readily understandable, a bracketed definition or paraphrase has been added.

EXHIBIT 1A–3 A Sample Court Case

This section contains the citation—the name of the case, the name of the court that heard the case, the year of the decision, and the reporter in which the court's opinion can be found.

BERGER v. CITY OF SEATTLE
U.S. Court of Appeals, Ninth Circuit, 512 F.3d 582 (2008).

This section identifies the parties and describes the events leading up to the trial and its appeal. The decision of the lower court is included, as well as the issue to be decided by the U.S. Court of Appeals for the Ninth Circuit.

FACTS In the heart of the city of Seattle, Washington, is the Seattle Center, an entertainment zone covering eighty acres of land. Within this area, the city requires that all street performers follow the so-called Campus Rules. One such rule, Rule F.1, requires a permit for street performers and requires badges to be worn during street performances. Michael Berger, a street performer, has been performing there since the 1980s. After the Campus Rules were enacted in 2002, Berger obtained a permit. Thereafter, Seattle Center authorities received numerous publicly filed complaints alleging that Berger had exhibited threatening behavior. Also, the Seattle Center staff reported several rule violations. In 2003, Berger filed a **complaint** seeking damages and **injunctive relief**, alleging that the Campus Rules violated the **First Amendment** to the U.S. Constitution. In 2005, a federal district court granted **summary judgment** to Berger. The city appealed the district court's order of summary judgment to the U.S. Court of Appeals for the Ninth Circuit and sought a reversal with instructions to enter summary judgment in its favor.

A document that, when filed with a court, initiates a lawsuit.

A court decree ordering a person to do or refrain from doing a certain act.

The First Amendment to the Constitution guarantees, among other freedoms, the right of free speech—to express one's views without governmental restrictions.

A judgment that a court enters without beginning or continuing a trial. It can be entered only if no facts are in dispute and the only question is how the law applies.

This section presents the central issue (or issues) to be decided by the court. In this case, the U.S. Court of Appeals for the Ninth Circuit considered whether certain rules imposed on street performers by local government authorities satisfied the requirements for valid restrictions on speech under the First Amendment to the U.S. Constitution.

ISSUE Did the rules issued by the Seattle Center under the city's authority meet the requirements for valid restrictions on speech under the First Amendment?

This section contains the court's decision on the issue or issues before it. An appellate court's decision is often phrased with reference to the decision of the lower court from which the case was appealed. For example, an appellate court may "affirm" or "reverse" (as it did in this case) a lower court's ruling.

DECISION Yes. The U.S. Court of Appeals for the Ninth Circuit reversed the decision of the lower court and **remanded** the case for further proceedings. "Such content neutral and narrowly tailored rules * * * must be upheld."

Sent back.

(Continued)

EXHIBIT 1A-3 A Sample Court Case—Continued

This section indicates the relevant laws and legal principles that the court applied in coming to its conclusion in the case. The relevant law in the *Berger* case included the requirements under the First Amendment for evaluating the purpose and effect of government regulation with respect to expression. This section also explains the court's application of the law to the facts in this case.

REASON The appellate court looked at the rules requiring permits and badges to determine if they were "content neutral." Time, place, and manner restrictions do not violate the First Amendment if they burden all expression equally and do not allow officials to treat messages differently. The court found that the rules in this case met this requirement and did not discriminate based on content. The court also concluded that the rules were "narrowly tailored" to "promote a substantial government interest that would be achieved less effectively" otherwise. With the rules, the city was trying to "reduce territorial disputes among performers, deter patron harassment, and facilitate the identification and apprehension of offending performers." This was pursuant to the valid governmental objective of protecting the safety and convenience of the other performers and the public generally. The public's complaints about Berger and others showed that unregulated street performances posed a threat to the city's interest in maintaining order at the Seattle Center. The court was "satisfied that the city's permit scheme was designed to further valid governmental objectives."

2

Nature and Classification

AFTER READING THIS CHAPTER, YOU SHOULD BE ABLE TO ANSWER THE FOLLOWING QUESTIONS:

1 What is a contract? What is the objective theory of contracts?

2 What are the four basic elements necessary to the formation of a valid contract?

3 What is the difference between an implied-in-fact contract and an implied-in-law contract (quasi contract)?

4 How does a void contract differ from a voidable contract? What is an unenforceable contract?

5 Why have plain language laws been enacted? What rules guide the courts in interpreting contracts?

C ontract law deals with, among other things, the formation and keeping of promises. **A promise** is an assertion that something either will or will not happen in the future.

Like other types of law, contract law reflects our social values, interests, and expectations at a given point in time. It shows, for example, what kinds of promises our society thinks should be legally binding. It distinguishes between promises that create only *moral* obligations (such as a promise to take a friend to lunch) and promises that are legally binding (such as a promise to pay for merchandise purchased). Contract law also demonstrates what excuses our society accepts for breaking certain types of promises. In addition, it shows what promises are considered to be contrary to public policy—against the interests of society as a whole—and therefore legally invalid. When the person making a promise is a child or is mentally incompetent, for example, a question will arise as to whether the promise should be enforced. Resolving such questions is the essence of contract law.

AN OVERVIEW OF CONTRACT LAW

Before we look at the numerous rules that courts use to determine whether a particular promise will be enforced, it is necessary to understand some fundamental concepts of contract law. In this section, we describe the sources and general function of contract law. We also provide the definition of a contract and introduce the objective theory of contracts.

Sources of Contract Law

The common law governs all contracts except when it has been modified or replaced by statutory law, such as the Uniform Commercial Code (UCC),[1] or by administrative agency regulations. Contracts relating to services, real estate, employment, and insurance, for example, generally are governed by the common law of contracts.

Contracts for the sale and lease of goods, however, are governed by the UCC—to the extent that the UCC has modified general contract law. The relationship between general contract law and the law governing sales and leases of goods will be explored in detail in Chapter 14. In this unit covering the common law of contracts (Chapters 7 through 13), we indicate briefly in footnotes the areas in which the UCC has significantly altered common law contract principles.

---

1. See Chapter 1 and Chapter 14 for further discussions of the significance and coverage of the Uniform Commercial Code (UCC). Excerpts from the UCC are presented in Appendix C at the end of this book.

The Function of Contracts

No aspect of modern life is entirely free of contractual relationships. You acquire rights and obligations, for example, when you borrow funds, when you buy or lease a house, when you obtain insurance, when you form a business, and when you purchase goods or services. Contract law is designed to provide stability and predictability for both buyers and sellers in the marketplace.

Contract law assures the parties to private agreements that the promises they make will be enforceable. Clearly, many promises are kept because the parties involved feel a moral obligation to do so or because keeping a promise is in their mutual self-interest. The **promisor** (the person making the promise) and the **promisee** (the person to whom the promise is made) may decide to honor their agreement for other reasons. Nevertheless, the rules of contract law are often followed in business agreements to avoid potential problems.

By supplying procedures for enforcing private agreements, contract law provides an essential condition for the existence of a market economy. Without a legal framework of reasonably assured expectations within which to plan and venture, businesspersons would be able to rely only on the good faith of others. Duty and good faith are usually sufficient, but when dramatic price changes or adverse economic conditions make it costly to comply with a promise, these elements may not be enough. Contract law is necessary to ensure compliance with a promise or to entitle the innocent party to some form of relief.

Definition of a Contract

A **contract** is an agreement that can be enforced in court. It is formed by two or more parties who agree to perform or to refrain from performing some act now or in the future. Generally, contract disputes arise when there is a promise of future performance. If the contractual promise is not fulfilled, the party who made it is subject to the sanctions of a court (see Chapter 12). That party may be required to pay monetary damages for failing to perform the contractual promise; in limited instances, the party may be required to perform the promised act.

The Objective Theory of Contracts

In determining whether a contract has been formed, the element of intent is of prime importance. In contract law, intent is determined by what is referred to as the **objective theory of contracts,** not by the personal or subjective intent, or belief, of a party. The theory is that a party's intention to enter into a contract is judged by outward, objective facts as interpreted by a *reasonable person,* rather than by the party's own secret, sub-jective intentions. Objective facts include (1) what the party said when entering into the contract, (2) how the party acted or appeared, and (3) the circumstances surrounding the transaction. As will be discussed later in this chapter, in the section on express versus implied contracts, intent to form a contract may be manifested by conduct, as well as by words, oral or written.

Freedom of Contract and Freedom from Contract

As a general rule, the law recognizes everyone's ability to enter freely into contractual arrangements. This recognition is called *freedom of contract,* a freedom protected by the U.S. Constitution in Article I, Section 10. Because freedom of contract is a fundamental public policy of the United States, courts rarely interfere with contracts that have been voluntarily made.

Of course, as in other areas of the law, there are many exceptions to the general rule that contracts voluntarily negotiated will be enforced. For example, illegal bargains, agreements that unreasonably restrain trade, and certain unfair contracts made between one party with a great amount of bargaining power and another with little power are generally not enforced. In addition, as you will read in Chapter 10, certain contracts and clauses may not be enforceable if they are contrary to public policy, fairness, and justice. These exceptions provide *freedom from contract* for persons who may have been pressured into making contracts unfavorable to themselves.

ELEMENTS OF A CONTRACT

The many topics that will be discussed in the following chapters on contract law require an understanding of the basic elements of a valid contract and the way in which the contract was created. The topics to be covered in this unit on contracts also require an understanding of the types of circumstances in which even legally valid contracts will not be enforced.

Requirements of a Valid Contract

The following list briefly describes the four requirements that must be met for a valid contract to exist. If any of these elements is lacking, no contract will have been formed. (Each item will be explained more fully in subsequent chapters.)

1 *Agreement.* An agreement to form a contract includes an *offer* and an *acceptance.* One party must offer to enter into a legal agreement, and another party must accept the terms of the offer (see Chapter 8).

2 *Consideration.* Any promises made by parties must be supported by legally sufficient and bargained-for consideration (something of value received or promised to convince a person to make a deal) (see Chapter 8).

3 *Contractual capacity.* Both parties entering into the contract must have the contractual capacity to do so; the law must recognize them as possessing characteristics that qualify them as competent parties (see Chapter 9).

4 *Legality.* The contract's purpose must be to accomplish some goal that is legal and not against public policy (see Chapter 9).

Defenses to the Enforceability of a Contract

Even if all of the elements of a valid contract are present, a contract may be unenforceable if the following requirements are not met.

1 *Genuineness of assent, or voluntary consent.* The consent of both parties must be genuine. For example, if a contract was formed as a result of fraud, mistake, or duress, the contract may not be enforceable.

2 *Form.* The contract must be in whatever form the law requires; for example, some contracts must be in writing to be enforceable.

The failure to fulfill either requirement may be raised as a *defense* to the enforceability of an otherwise valid contract. Both requirements will be explained in more detail in Chapter 10.

TYPES OF CONTRACTS

There are numerous types of contracts. They are categorized based on legal distinctions as to their formation, performance, and enforceability.

Contract Formation

As you can see in Exhibit 7–1, three classifications, or categories, of contracts are based on how and when a contract is formed. The best way to explain each type of contract is to compare one type with another, as we do in the following pages.

Bilateral versus Unilateral Contracts Every contract involves at least two parties. The **offeror** is the party making the offer. The **offeree** is the party to whom the offer is made. The offeror always promises to do or not to do something and thus is also a promisor. Whether the contract is classified as *bilateral* or *unilateral* depends on what the offeree must do to accept the offer and bind the offeror to a contract.

Bilateral Contracts. If the offeree can accept the offer simply by promising to perform, the contract is a **bilateral contract.** Hence, a bilateral contract is a "promise for a promise." An example of a bilateral contract is a contract in which one person agrees to buy another person's automobile for a specified price. No performance, such as the payment of funds or delivery of goods, need take place for a bilateral contract to be formed. The contract comes into existence at the moment the promises are exchanged.

    ■EXAMPLE 7.1 Jeff offers to buy Ann's digital camera for $200. Jeff tells Ann that he will give her the cash for the camera on the following Friday when he gets paid. Ann accepts Jeff's offer and promises to give him the camera when he pays her on Friday. Jeff and Ann have formed a bilateral contract. **■**

Unilateral Contracts. If the offer is phrased so that the offeree can accept only by completing the contract performance, the contract is a **unilateral contract.** Hence, a unilateral contract is a "promise for an act." In other words, the

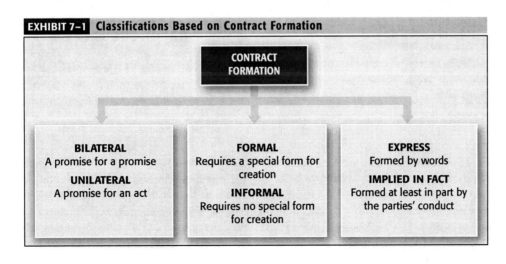

EXHIBIT 7–1	**Classifications Based on Contract Formation**

CONTRACT FORMATION

| **BILATERAL**
A promise for a promise
UNILATERAL
A promise for an act | **FORMAL**
Requires a special form for creation
INFORMAL
Requires no special form for creation | **EXPRESS**
Formed by words
IMPLIED IN FACT
Formed at least in part by the parties' conduct |

contract is formed not at the moment when promises are exchanged but rather when the contract is *performed*. **■EXAMPLE 7.2** Reese says to Celia, "If you drive my car from New York to Los Angeles, I'll give you $1,000." Only on Celia's completion of the act—bringing the car to Los Angeles—does she fully accept Reese's offer to pay $1,000. If she chooses not to accept the offer to drive the car to Los Angeles, there are no legal consequences. ■

Contests, lotteries, and other competitions offering prizes are also examples of offers for unilateral contracts. If a person complies with the rules of the contest—such as by submitting the right lottery number at the right place and time—a unilateral contract is formed, binding the organization offering the prize to a contract to perform as promised in the offer.

Can a school's, or an employer's, letter of tentative acceptance to a prospective student, or a possible employee, qualify as a unilateral contract? That was the issue in the following case.

CASE 7.1   Ardito v. City of Providence

United States District Court, District of Rhode Island, 263 F.Supp.2d 358 (2003).

FACTS In 2001, the city of Providence, Rhode Island, decided to begin hiring police officers to fill vacancies in its police department. Because only individuals who had graduated from the Providence Police Academy were eligible, the city also decided to conduct two training sessions, the "60th and 61st Police Academies." To be admitted, an applicant had to pass a series of tests and be deemed qualified by members of the department after an interview. The applicants judged most qualified were sent a letter informing them that they had been selected to attend the academy if they successfully completed a medical checkup and a psychological examination. The letter for the applicants to the 61st Academy, dated October 15, stated that it was "a conditional offer of employment." Meanwhile, a new chief of police, Dean Esserman, decided to revise the selection process, which caused some of those who had received the letter to be rejected. Derek Ardito and thirteen other newly rejected applicants filed a suit in a federal district court against the city, seeking a halt to the 61st Academy unless they were allowed to attend. They alleged, among other things, that the city was in breach of contract.

ISSUE Was the October 15 letter a unilateral offer that the plaintiffs had accepted by passing the required medical and psychological examinations?

DECISION Yes. The court issued an injunction to prohibit the city from conducting the 61st Police Academy unless the plaintiffs were included.

REASON The court found the October 15 letter to be "a classic example of an offer to enter into a unilateral contract. The October 15 letter expressly stated that it was a 'conditional offer of employment' and the message that it conveyed was that the recipient would be admitted into the 61st Academy if he or she successfully completed the medical and psychological examinations." The court contrasted the letter with "notices sent to applicants by the City at earlier stages of the selection process. Those notices merely informed applicants that they had completed a step in the process and remained eligible to be considered for admission into the Academy. Unlike the October 15 letter, the prior notices did not purport to extend a 'conditional offer' of admission." The court concluded that "[t]he plaintiffs accepted the City's offer of admission into the Academy by satisfying the specified conditions. Each of the plaintiffs submitted to and passed lengthy and intrusive medical and psychological examinations."

 WHAT IF THE FACTS WERE DIFFERENT? *Suppose that the October 15 letter had used the phrase* potential offer of employment *rather than the word* conditional. *Would the court in this case still have considered the letter to be a unilateral contract?*

■

Revocation of Offers for Unilateral Contracts. A problem arises in unilateral contracts when the promisor attempts to *revoke* (cancel) the offer after the promisee has begun performance but before the act has been completed. **■EXAMPLE 7.3** Roberta offers to buy Ed's sailboat, moored in San Francisco, on delivery of the boat to Roberta's dock in Newport Beach, three hundred miles south of San Francisco. Ed rigs the boat and sets sail. Shortly before his arrival at Newport Beach, Ed receives a radio message from Roberta withdrawing her offer. Roberta's offer is to form a unilateral contract, and only Ed's delivery of the sailboat at her dock is an acceptance. ■

In contract law, offers are normally *revocable* (capable of being taken back, or canceled) until accepted. Under the traditional view of unilateral contracts, Roberta's revocation would terminate the offer. Because of the harsh effect on the offeree of the revocation of an offer to form a unilateral contract, the modern-day view is that once performance has been *substantially* undertaken, the offeror cannot revoke the offer. Thus, in our example, even though Ed has not yet accepted the offer by complete performance, Roberta is prohibited from revoking it. Ed can deliver the boat and bind Roberta to the contract.

Formal versus Informal Contracts Another classification system divides contracts into formal contracts and informal contracts. **Formal contracts** are contracts that require a special form or method of creation (formation) to be enforceable.[2] *Contracts under seal* are a type of formal contract that involves a formalized writing with a special seal attached.[3] In the past, the seals were often made of wax and impressed on the paper document. Today, the significance of the seal in contract law has lessened, though standard-form contracts still sometimes include a place for a seal next to the signature lines. Letters of credit, which are frequently used in international sales contracts, are another type of formal contract. As will be discussed in Chapter 32, letters of credit are agreements to pay contingent on the purchaser's receipt of invoices and bills of lading (documents evidencing receipt of, and title to, goods shipped).

Informal contracts (also called *simple contracts*) include all other contracts. No special form is required (except for certain types of contracts that must be in writing), as the contracts are usually based on their substance rather than their form. Typically, businesspersons put their contracts in writing to ensure that there is some proof of a contract's existence should problems arise.

Express versus Implied Contracts Contracts may also be formed and categorized as express or implied by the conduct of the parties. We look here at the differences between these two types of contracts.

Express Contracts. In an **express contract,** the terms of the agreement are fully and explicitly stated in words, oral or written. A signed lease for an apartment or a house is an express written contract. If a classmate accepts your offer to sell your textbooks from last semester for $300, an express oral contract has been made.

Implied Contracts. A contract that is implied from the conduct of the parties is called an **implied-in-fact contract,** or an implied contract. This type of contract differs from an express contract in that the *conduct* of the parties, rather than their words, creates and defines at least some of the terms of the contract.

Requirements for an Implied-in-Fact Contract. For an implied-in-fact contract to arise, certain requirements must be met. Normally, if the following conditions exist, a court will hold that an implied contract was formed:

1 The plaintiff furnished some service or property.

2 The plaintiff expected to be paid for that service or property, and the defendant knew or should have known that payment was expected (by using the objective-theory-of-contracts test discussed on page 153).

3 The defendant had a chance to reject the services or property and did not.

■EXAMPLE 7.4 Suppose that you need an accountant to fill out your tax return this year. You look through the Yellow Pages and find an accounting firm located in your neighborhood. You drop by the firm's office, explain your problem to an accountant, and learn what fees will be charged. The next day you return and give the receptionist all of the necessary information and documents, such as canceled checks and W-2 forms. Then you walk out the door without saying anything expressly to the accountant.

In this situation, you have entered into an implied-in-fact contract to pay the accountant the usual and reasonable fees for her accounting services. The contract is implied by your conduct and by hers. She expects to be paid for completing your tax return. By bringing in the records she will need to do the work, you have implied an intent to pay for her services. ■

Note that a contract can be a mixture of an express contract and an implied-in-fact contract. In other words, a contract may contain some express terms, while others are implied. During the construction of a home, the homeowner often requests that the builder make changes in the original specifications. When do these changes form part of an implied-in-fact contract that makes the homeowner liable to the builder for any extra expenses? That was the issue in the following case.

---

2. See *Restatement (Second) of Contracts*, Section 6, which explains that formal contracts include (1) contracts under seal, (2) recognizances, (3) negotiable instruments, and (4) letters of credit. As mentioned in Chapter 1, *Restatements of the Law* are books that summarize court decisions on a particular topic and that courts often refer to for guidance.

3. A seal may be actual (made of wax or some other durable substance), impressed on the paper, or indicated simply by the word *seal* or the letters *L.S.* at the end of the document. *L.S.* stands for *locus sigilli*, which means "the place for the seal."

CASE 7.2 Uhrhahn Construction & Design, Inc. v. Hopkins

Court of Appeals of Utah, 179 P.3d 808 (2008).

FACTS Uhrhahn Construction was hired by Lamar Hopkins (Hopkins) and his wife, Joan, for several projects in the building of their home. Each project was based on a cost estimate and specifications. Each of the proposals accepted by Hopkins said that any changes in the signed contracts would be made only "upon written orders." When work was in progress, Hopkins made several requests for changes. There was no written record of these changes, but Uhrhahn performed the work and Hopkins paid for it. A dispute arose after Hopkins requested that Uhrhahn use Durisol blocks rather than cinder blocks in some construction. The original proposal specified cinder blocks, but Hopkins told Uhrhahn that the change should be made because Durisol was "easier to install than traditional cinder block and would take half the time." Hopkins said the total cost would be the same. Uhrhahn orally agreed to the change, but demanded extra payment after discovering that Durisol blocks were more complicated to use than cinder blocks. Hopkins refused to pay, claiming that the cost should be the same. Uhrhahn sued. The trial court held for Uhrhahn, finding that the Durisol blocks were more costly to install. The homeowners appealed.

ISSUE Did the homeowners and the builder have an implied-in-fact contract regarding the substitution of Durisol blocks for the cinder blocks specified in the contract?

DECISION Yes. The Utah appeals court affirmed the decision of the trial court, finding that there was a valid

contract between the parties and that both parties had agreed to oral changes in the contract. The changes created an implied-in-fact contract by which the builder agreed to provide extra work in exchange for additional compensation from the homeowners.

REASON The court found that the elements of a contract were present—offer and acceptance, competent parties, and consideration. The terms were clearly specified in the proposals accepted by Hopkins. Uhrhahn promised to perform work in exchange for payment. Although the contract stated that any changes would be in writing, both parties waived that term in the contract when they orally agreed on some changes in the work performed. As often happens in construction, changes were requested that were outside the contract. The builder did the work, and the buyer accepted the work. Such oral modification of the original contract creates an enforceable contract, and payment is due for the extra work. This is an implied-in-fact contract. Hopkins requested Uhrhahn to perform certain work. Uhrhahn expected to be compensated for the work, and Hopkins knew or should have known that Uhrhahn would expect to be paid for work that was outside the specifications of the original contract.

 FOR CRITICAL ANALYSIS—Technological Consideration *Would the outcome of this case have been different if the parties had communicated by e-mail for all details regarding changes in the work performed? Why or why not?*

Contract Performance

Contracts are also classified according to their state of performance. A contract that has been fully performed on both sides is called an **executed contract**. A contract that has not been fully performed on either side is called an **executory contract**. If one party has fully performed but the other has not, the contract is said to be executed on the one side and executory on the other, but the contract is still classified as executory.

■EXAMPLE 7.5 Assume that you agree to buy ten tons of coal from Western Coal Company. Further assume that Western has delivered the coal to your steel mill, where it is now being burned. At this point, the contract is an executory contract—it is executed on the part of Western and executory on your part. After you pay Western for the coal, the contract will be executed on both sides. ■

Contract Enforceability

A **valid contract** has the four elements necessary for contract formation: (1) an agreement (offer and acceptance) (2) supported by legally sufficient consideration (3) for a legal purpose and (4) made by parties who have the legal capacity to enter into the contract. As mentioned, we will discuss each of these elements in the following chapters. As you can see in Exhibit 7–2 on the next page, valid contracts may be enforceable, voidable, or unenforceable. Additionally, a contract may be referred to as a *void contract*. We look next at the meaning of the terms *voidable, unenforceable,* and *void* in relation to contract enforceability.

Voidable Contracts   A **voidable contract** is a *valid* contract but one that can be avoided at the option of one or both of

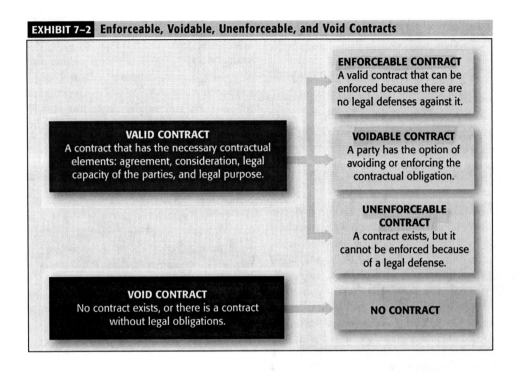

EXHIBIT 7-2 Enforceable, Voidable, Unenforceable, and Void Contracts

VALID CONTRACT
A contract that has the necessary contractual elements: agreement, consideration, legal capacity of the parties, and legal purpose.

ENFORCEABLE CONTRACT
A valid contract that can be enforced because there are no legal defenses against it.

VOIDABLE CONTRACT
A party has the option of avoiding or enforcing the contractual obligation.

UNENFORCEABLE CONTRACT
A contract exists, but it cannot be enforced because of a legal defense.

VOID CONTRACT
No contract exists, or there is a contract without legal obligations.

NO CONTRACT

the parties. The party having the option can elect either to avoid any duty to perform or to *ratify* (make valid) the contract. If the contract is avoided, both parties are released from it. If it is ratified, both parties must fully perform their respective legal obligations.

As you will read in Chapter 9, contracts made by minors, insane persons, and intoxicated persons may be voidable. As a general rule, for example, contracts made by minors are voidable at the option of the minor. Additionally, contracts entered into under fraudulent conditions are voidable at the option of the defrauded party. Contracts entered into under legally defined duress or undue influence are voidable (see Chapter 10).

Unenforceable Contracts An **unenforceable contract** is one that cannot be enforced because of certain legal defenses against it. It is not unenforceable because a party failed to satisfy a legal requirement of the contract; rather, it is a valid contract rendered unenforceable by some statute or law. For example, some contracts must be in writing (see Chapter 10), and if they are not, they will not be enforceable except in certain exceptional circumstances.

Void Contracts A **void contract** is no contract at all. The terms *void* and *contract* are contradictory. None of the parties has any legal obligations if a contract is void. A contract can be void because, for example, one of the parties was previously determined by a court to be legally insane (and thus

lacked the legal capacity to enter into a contract) or because the purpose of the contract was illegal.

QUASI CONTRACTS

Quasi contracts, or contracts *implied in law,* are wholly different from actual contracts. Express contracts and implied-in-fact contracts are actual or true contracts formed by the words or actions of the parties. The word *quasi* is Latin for "as if" or "analogous to." Quasi contracts are not true contracts because they do not arise from any agreement, express or implied, between the parties themselves. Rather, quasi contracts are fictional contracts that courts can impose on the parties "as if" the parties had entered into an actual contract. They are equitable rather than legal contracts. Usually, quasi contracts are imposed to avoid the *unjust enrichment* of one party at the expense of another. The doctrine of unjust enrichment is based on the theory that individuals should not be allowed to profit or enrich themselves inequitably at the expense of others.

EXAMPLE 7.6 A vacationing physician is driving down the highway and finds Emerson lying unconscious on the side of the road. The physician renders medical aid that saves Emerson's life. Although the injured, unconscious Emerson did not solicit the medical aid and was not aware that the aid had been rendered, Emerson received a valuable benefit, and the requirements for a quasi contract were fulfilled. In such a situation, the law normally will impose a quasi contract, and Emerson will have to pay the physician for the reasonable value of the medical services provided. ■

Limitations on Quasi-Contractual Recovery

Although quasi contracts exist to prevent unjust enrichment, the party who obtains a benefit is not liable for the fair value in some situations. Basically, a party who has conferred a benefit on someone else unnecessarily or as a result of misconduct or negligence cannot invoke the doctrine of quasi contract. The enrichment in those situations will not be considered "unjust."

■EXAMPLE 7.7 You take your car to the local car wash and ask to have it run through the washer and to have the gas tank filled. While your car is being washed, you go to a nearby shopping center for two hours. In the meantime, one of the workers at the car wash mistakenly assumes that your car is the one that he is supposed to hand wax. When you come back, you are presented with a bill for a full tank of gas, a wash job, and a hand wax. Clearly, a benefit has been conferred on you. But this benefit occurred because of a mistake by the car wash employee. You have not been *unjustly* enriched under these circumstances. People normally cannot be forced to pay for benefits "thrust" on them. ■

When an Actual Contract Exists

The doctrine of quasi contract generally cannot be used when an actual contract covers the area in controversy. This is because a remedy already exists if a party is unjustly enriched as a result of a breach of contract: the nonbreaching party can sue the breaching party for breach of contract. In this instance, a court does not need to impose a quasi contract to achieve justice. **■EXAMPLE 7.8** Fung contracts with Cameron to deliver a furnace to a building owned by Bateman. Fung delivers the furnace, but Cameron never pays Fung. Bateman has been unjustly enriched in this situation, to be sure. Nevertheless, Fung cannot recover from Bateman in quasi contract because Fung had an actual contract with Cameron. Fung already has a remedy—he can sue for breach of contract to recover the price of the furnace from Cameron. No quasi contract need be imposed by the court in this situation to achieve justice. ■

INTERPRETATION OF CONTRACTS

Sometimes, parties agree that a contract has been formed but disagree on its meaning or legal effect. One reason that this may happen is that one of the parties is not familiar with the legal terminology used in the contract. To an extent, *plain language laws* have helped to avoid this difficulty. Sometimes, though, a dispute may still arise over the meaning of a contract simply because the rights or obligations under the contract are not expressed clearly—no matter how "plain" the language used.

In this section, we look at some common law rules of contract interpretation. These rules, including the *plain meaning rule* and various other rules that have evolved over time, provide the courts with guidelines for deciding disputes over how contract terms or provisions should be interpreted. Exhibit 7–3 provides a brief graphic summary of how these rules are applied.

PREVENTING LEGAL DISPUTES

To avoid disputes over contract interpretation, make sure that your intentions are clearly expressed in the contracts. Careful drafting of contracts not only helps prevent potential disputes over the meaning of certain

---

EXHIBIT 7–3 Rules of Contract Interpretation

WRITTEN CONTRACT

PLAIN MEANING RULE
If a court determines that the terms of the contract are clear from the written document alone, the plain meaning rule will apply, and the contract will be enforced according to what it clearly states.

OTHER RULES OF INTERPRETATION
If a court finds that there is a need to determine the parties' intentions from the terms of the contract, the court will apply a number of well-established rules of interpretation. For example, one rule of interpretation states that specific wording will be given greater weight than general wording.

Nature and Classification

terms but may also be crucial if your firm brings or needs to defend against a lawsuit for breach of contract. By using simple, clear language and avoiding legalese, you take a major step toward avoiding contract disputes.

■

Plain Language Laws

Today, the federal government and a majority of the states have enacted plain language laws to regulate legal writing. All federal agencies are required to use plain language in most of their forms and written communications. Plain language requirements have been extended to agency rulemaking as well.

At the state level, plain language laws frequently apply to consumer contracts that are primarily for personal, family, or household purposes. For example, a New York law requires residential leases and other consumer contracts to be (1) "written in a clear and coherent manner using words with common and everyday meanings" and (2) "appropriately divided and captioned by [the] various sections."[4] If a party to a contract, such as an insurance company, violates a plain language statute, a consumer can sue that party for damages if she or he suffers harm (unless the party can show that it

4. New York General Obligations Law Section 5-702.

made a good faith effort to comply with the statute). Some state statutes even allow parties to submit proposed contracts to the state attorney general, whose approval then eliminates any liability for damages because of a supposed violation of the plain language statute.

The legal profession is also moving toward plain English, and court rules in many jurisdictions require attorneys to use plain language in court documents. At times, judges have refused to accept motions that are incoherent due to their highly technical legal language. A number of states have also rewritten their jury instructions. Generally, the revised instructions are phrased in simpler language, use the active voice more often, and avoid "legalese" to the extent that it is possible to do so.

The Plain Meaning Rule

When a contract's writing is clear and unequivocal, a court will enforce it according to its obvious terms. The meaning of the terms must be determined from the *face of the instrument*—from the written document alone. This is sometimes referred to as the *plain meaning rule*.

Under this rule, if a contract's words appear to be clear and unambiguous, a court cannot consider *extrinsic evidence*, which is any evidence not contained in the document itself. Admissibility of extrinsic evidence can significantly affect how a court interprets ambiguous contractual provisions and thus can affect the outcome of litigation. The following case illustrates these points.

CASE 7.3 **Wagner v. Columbia Pictures Industries, Inc.**

California Court of Appeal, Second District, 146 Cal.App.4th 586, 52 Cal.Rptr.3d 898 (2007).

FACTS Actor Robert Wagner entered into an agreement with Spelling-Goldberg Productions (SGP) "relating to Charlie's Angels (herein called the 'series')." The contract entitled Wagner to 50 percent of the net profits that SGP received "for the right to exhibit photoplays of the series and from the exploitation of all ancillary, music and subsidiary rights in connection therewith." SGP hired Ivan Goff and Ben Roberts to write the series, under a contract subject to the Writers Guild of America Minimum Basic Agreement (MBA).[a] The MBA stipulates that the writer of a television show retains the right to make and market films based on the material, subject to the producer's right to buy this right if the writer decides to sell it within five years. The first "Charlie's Angels" episode

a. The Writers Guild of America is an association of screen and television writers that negotiates industrywide agreements with motion picture and television producers to cover the rights of its members.

aired in 1976. In 1982, SGP sold its rights to the series to Columbia Pictures Industries, Inc. Thirteen years later, Columbia bought the movie rights to the material from Goff's and Roberts's heirs. In 2000 and 2003, Columbia produced and distributed two "Charlie's Angels" films. Wagner filed a suit in a California state court against Columbia, claiming a share of the profits from the films. The court granted Columbia's motion for summary judgment. Wagner appealed to a state intermediate appellate court.

ISSUE Does the language of the Wagner contract with SGP entitle Columbia to all of the profits from the two "Charlie's Angels" films?

DECISION Yes. The state intermediate appellate court affirmed the lower court's judgment. The contract "unambiguously" stated the conditions under which the

CASE 7.3—Continued

parties were to share the films' profits, and those conditions had not occurred.

REASON Wagner offered evidence to show that a previous contract with SGP had been intended to give him half of the net profits from a property titled "Love Song" that were received from all sources without limitation as to source or time. Wagner argued that the "Charlie's Angels" agreement used identical language in its profits provision, which thus should be interpreted to give him the same share. The court stated that an "agreement is the writing itself." Extrinsic evidence is not admissible "to show intention independent of an unambiguous written instrument." In this case, even if the parties intended Wagner to share in the profits from all sources, "they did not say so in their contract." Under the language of the contract, Wagner was entitled to share in the

profits from the exercise of the movie rights to "Charlie's Angels" if those rights were exploited as "ancillary" or "subsidiary" to the primary "right to exhibit photoplays of the series," but not if those rights were acquired separately. SGP's contract with Goff and Roberts was subject to the MBA, under which the writers kept the movie rights, which the producer could buy if the writers opted to sell them within five years. SGP did not acquire the movie rights to "Charlie's Angels" by exercising this right within the five-year period. Columbia obtained those rights independently more than five years later.

 FOR CRITICAL ANALYSIS—Legal Consideration *How might the result in this case have been different if the court had allowed Wagner's extrinsic evidence of the prior contract regarding "Love Song" to be used as evidence in this dispute?*

■

Other Rules of Interpretation

Generally, a court will interpret the language to give effect to the parties' intent *as expressed in their contract.* This is the primary purpose of the rules of interpretation—to determine the parties' intent from the language used in their agreement and to give effect to that intent. A court normally will not make or remake a contract, nor will it normally interpret the language according to what the parties *claim* their intent was when they made the contract.[5] The courts use the following rules in interpreting contractual terms:

1 Insofar as possible, a reasonable, lawful, and effective meaning will be given to all of a contract's terms.

2 A contract will be interpreted as a whole; individual, specific clauses will be considered subordinate to the contract's general intent. All writings that are a part of the same transaction will be interpreted together.

3 Terms that were the subject of separate negotiation will be given greater consideration than standardized terms and terms that were not negotiated separately.

4 A word will be given its ordinary, commonly accepted meaning, and a technical word or term will be given its technical meaning, unless the parties clearly intended something else.

5 Specific and exact wording will be given greater consideration than general language.

6 Written or typewritten terms prevail over preprinted terms.

7 Because a contract should be drafted in clear and unambiguous language, a party that uses ambiguous expressions is held to be responsible for the ambiguities. Thus, when the language has more than one meaning, it will be interpreted *against* the party that drafted the contract.

8 Evidence of *trade usage, prior dealing,* and *course of performance* may be admitted to clarify the meaning of an ambiguously worded contract. (We define and discuss these terms in Chapter 14.) What each of the parties does pursuant to the contract will be interpreted as consistent with what the other does and with any relevant usage of trade and course of dealing or performance. Express terms (terms expressly stated in the contract) are given the greatest weight, followed by course of performance, course of dealing, and custom and usage of trade—in that order. When considering custom and usage, a court will look at the trade customs and usage common to the particular business or industry and to the locale in which the contract was made or is to be performed.

---

5. Nevertheless, if a court finds that, even after applying the rules of interpretation, the terms is susceptible to more than one meaning, the court may permit extrinsic evidence to prove what the parties intended. See, for example, *Langdon v. United Restaurants, Inc.,* 105 S.W.3d 882 (Mo.Ct.App. 2003).

Nature and Classification

 Grant Borman, who was engaged in a construction project, leased a crane from Allied Equipment and hired Crosstown Trucking Company to deliver the crane to the construction site. Crosstown, while the crane was in its possession and without permission from either Borman or Allied Equipment, used the crane to install a transformer for a utility company, which paid Crosstown for the job. Crosstown then delivered the crane to Borman's construction site at the appointed time of delivery. When Allied Equipment learned of the unauthorized use of the crane by Crosstown, it sued Crosstown for damages, seeking to recover the rental value of Crosstown's use of the crane. Using the information presented in the chapter, answer the following questions.

1 What are the four requirements of a valid contract?

2 Did Crosstown have a valid contract with Borman concerning the use of the crane? If so, was it a bilateral or unilateral contract? Explain.

3 Can Allied Equipment obtain damages from Crosstown based on an implied-in-fact contract? Why or why not?

4 Should a court impose a quasi contract on the parties in this situation to allow Allied to recover damages from Crosstown? Why or why not?

TERMS AND CONCEPTS

bilateral contract 154
contract 153
executed contract 157
executory contract 157
express contract 156
formal contract 156
implied-in-fact contract 156

informal contract 156
objective theory of contracts 153
offeree 154
offeror 154
promise 152
promisee 153
promisor 153

quasi contract 158
unenforceable contract 158
unilateral contract 154
valid contract 157
void contract 158
voidable contract 157

CHAPTER SUMMARY Nature and Classification

An Overview of Contract Law (See pages 152–153.)	1. *Sources of contract law*—The common law governs all contracts except when it has been modified or replaced by statutory law, such as the Uniform Commercial Code (UCC), or by administrative agency regulations. The UCC governs contracts for the sale or lease of goods (see Chapter 14).
	2. *The function of contracts*—Contract law establishes what kinds of promises will be legally binding and supplies procedures for enforcing legally binding promises, or agreements.
	3. *The definition of a contract*—A contract is an agreement that can be enforced in court. It is formed by two or more competent parties who agree to perform or to refrain from performing some act now or in the future.
	4. *Objective theory of contracts*—In contract law, intent is determined by objective facts, not by the personal or subjective intent, or belief, of a party.
Elements of a Contract (See pages 153–154.)	1. *Requirements of a valid contract*—The four requirements of a valid contract are agreement, consideration, contractual capacity, and legality.
	2. *Defenses to the enforceability of a contract*—Even if the four requirements of a valid contract are met, a contract may be unenforceable if it lacks genuineness of assent or is not in the required form.
Types of Contracts (See pages 154–158.)	1. *Bilateral*—A promise for a promise.
	2. *Unilateral*—A promise for an act (acceptance is the completed—or substantial—performance of the contract by the offeree).

CHAPTER SUMMARY Nature and Classification—Continued

Types of Contracts—Continued

3. *Formal*—Requires a special form for contract formation.
4. *Informal*—Requires no special form for contract formation.
5. *Express*—Formed by words (oral, written, or a combination).
6. *Implied in fact*—Formed at least in part by the conduct of the parties.
7. *Executed*—A fully performed contract.
8. *Executory*—A contract not yet fully performed.
9. *Valid*—A contract that has the necessary contractual elements of offer and acceptance, consideration, parties with legal capacity, and a legal purpose.
10. *Voidable*—A contract that a party has the option of avoiding or enforcing.
11. *Unenforceable*—A valid contract that cannot be enforced because of a legal defense.
12. *Void*—No contract exists, or there is a contract without legal obligations.

Quasi Contracts
(See pages 158–159.)

A quasi contract, or a contract implied in law, is a contract that is imposed by law to prevent unjust enrichment.

Interpretation of Contracts
(See pages 159–161.)

Increasingly, plain language laws are requiring private contracts to be written in plain language so that the terms are clear and understandable to the parties. Under the plain meaning rule, a court will enforce the contract according to its plain terms, the meaning of which must be determined from the written document alone. Other rules applied by the courts when interpreting contracts include the following:

1. A reasonable, lawful, and effective meaning will be given to all contract terms.
2. A contract will be interpreted as a whole, specific clauses will be considered subordinate to the contract's general intent, and all writings that are a part of the same transaction will be interpreted together.
3. Terms that were negotiated separately will be given greater consideration than standardized terms and terms not negotiated separately.
4. Words will be given their commonly accepted meanings and technical words their technical meanings, unless the parties clearly intended otherwise.
5. Specific wording will be given greater consideration than general language.
6. Written or typewritten terms prevail over preprinted terms.
7. A party that uses ambiguous expressions is held to be responsible for the ambiguities.
8. Evidence of prior dealing, course of performance, or usage of trade is admissible to clarify an ambiguously worded contract.

FOR REVIEW

Answers for the even-numbered questions in this **For Review** *section can be found on this text's accompanying Web site at* **www.cengage.com/blaw/fbl**. *Select "Chapter 7" and click on "For Review."*

1 What is a contract? What is the objective theory of contracts?
2 What are the four basic elements necessary to the formation of a valid contract?
3 What is the difference between an implied-in-fact contract and an implied-in-law contract (quasi contract)?
4 How does a void contract differ from a voidable contract? What is an unenforceable contract?
5 Why have plain language laws been enacted? What rules guide the courts in interpreting contracts?

HYPOTHETICAL SCENARIOS AND CASE PROBLEMS

7.1 Express versus Implied Contracts. Suppose that a local businessperson, McDougal, is a good friend of Krunch, the owner of a local candy store. Every day on his lunch hour McDougal goes into Krunch's candy store and spends about five minutes looking at the candy. After examining Krunch's candy and talking with Krunch, McDougal usually buys one or two candy bars. One afternoon, McDougal goes into Krunch's candy shop, looks at the candy, and picks up a $1 candy bar. Seeing that Krunch is very busy, he catches Krunch's eye, waves the candy bar at Krunch without saying a word, and walks out. Is there a contract? If so, classify it within the categories presented in this chapter.

7.2 Hypothetical Question with Sample Answer. Janine was hospitalized with severe abdominal pain and placed in an intensive care unit. Her doctor told the hospital personnel to order around-the-clock nursing care for Janine. At the hospital's request, a nursing services firm, Nursing Services Unlimited, provided two weeks of in-hospital care and, after Janine was sent home, an additional two weeks of at-home care. During the at-home period of care, Janine was fully aware that she was receiving the benefit of the nursing services. Nursing Services later billed Janine $4,000 for the nursing care, but Janine refused to pay on the ground that she had never contracted for the services, either orally or in writing. In view of the fact that no express contract was ever formed, can Nursing Services recover the $4,000 from Janine? If so, under what legal theory? Discuss.

For a sample answer to Question 7.2, go to Appendix E at the end of this text.

7.3 Contract Classification. High-Flying Advertising, Inc., contracted with Big Burger Restaurants to fly an advertisement above the Connecticut beaches. The advertisement offered $5,000 to any person who could swim from the Connecticut beaches to Long Island across the Long Island Sound in less than a day. McElfresh saw the streamer and accepted the challenge. He started his marathon swim that same day at 10 A.M. After he had been swimming for four hours and was about halfway across the sound, McElfresh saw another plane pulling a streamer that read, "Big Burger revokes." Is there a contract between McElfresh and Big Burger? If there is a contract, what type(s) of contract is (are) formed?

7.4 Implied Contract. Thomas Rinks and Joseph Shields developed Psycho Chihuahua, a caricature of a Chihuahua dog with a "do-not-back-down" attitude. They promoted and marketed the character through their company, Wrench, L.L.C. Ed Alfaro and Rudy Pollak, representatives of Taco Bell Corp., learned of Psycho Chihuahua and met with Rinks and Shields to talk about using the character as a Taco Bell "icon." Wrench sent

artwork, merchandise, and marketing ideas to Alfaro, who promoted the character within Taco Bell. Alfaro asked Wrench to propose terms for Taco Bell's use of Psycho Chihuahua. Taco Bell did not accept Wrench's terms, but Alfaro continued to promote the character within the company. Meanwhile, Taco Bell hired a new advertising agency, which proposed an advertising campaign involving a Chihuahua. When Alfaro learned of this proposal, he sent the Psycho Chihuahua materials to the agency. Taco Bell made a Chihuahua the focus of its marketing but paid nothing to Wrench. Wrench filed a suit against Taco Bell in a federal district court, claiming in part that it had an implied contract with Taco Bell, which the latter breached. Do these facts satisfy the requirements for an implied contract? Why or why not? [*Wrench, L.L.C. v. Taco Bell Corp.*, 256 F.3d 446 (6th Cir.2001), *cert. denied*, 534 U.S. 1114, 122 S.Ct. 921, 151 L.Ed.2d 885 (2002)]

7.5 Interpretation of Contracts. East Mill Associates (EMA) was developing residential "units" in East Brunswick, New Jersey, within the service area of the East Brunswick Sewerage Authority (EBSA). The sewer system required an upgrade to the Ryder's Lane Pumping Station to accommodate the new units. EMA agreed to pay "fifty-five percent (55%) of the total cost" of the upgrade. At the time, the estimated cost to EMA was $150,000 to $200,000. Impediments to the project arose, however, substantially increasing the cost. Among other things, the pumping station had to be moved to accommodate a widened road nearby. The upgrade was delayed for almost three years. When it was completed, EBSA asked EMA for $340,022.12, which represented 55 percent of the total cost. EMA did not pay. EBSA filed a suit in a New Jersey state court against EMA for breach of contract. What rule should the court apply to interpret the parties' contract? How should that rule be applied? Why? [*East Brunswick Sewerage Authority v. East Mill Associates, Inc.*, 365 N.J.Super. 120, 838 A.2d 494 (A.D. 2004)]

7.6 Case Problem with Sample Answer. In December 2000, Nextel South Corp., a communications firm, contacted R. A. Clark Consulting, Ltd., an executive search firm, about finding an employment manager for Nextel's call center in Atlanta, Georgia. Over the next six months, Clark screened, evaluated, and interviewed more than three hundred candidates. Clark provided Nextel with more than fifteen candidate summaries, including one for Dan Sax. Nextel hired Sax for the position at an annual salary of $75,000. Sax started work on June 25, 2001, took two weeks' vacation, and quit on July 31 in the middle of a project. Clark spent the next six weeks looking for a replacement, until Nextel asked Clark to stop. Clark billed Nextel for its service, but Nextel refused to pay, asserting in part that the parties had not signed an agreement. Nextel's typical agreement specified payment to an employment agency of 20 percent of an employee's salary. Clark filed a suit in a Georgia state court against Nextel to recover the reasonable value of its services. What is a quasi contract? What would Clark have to show to recover on this basis? Should the court rule in Clark's favor? Explain. [*Nextel South Corp. v. R. A. Clark Consulting, Ltd.*, 266 Ga.App. 85, 596 S.E.2d 416 (2004)]

 After you have answered Problem 7.6, compare your answer with the sample answer given on the Web site that accompanies this text. Go to www.cengage.com/blaw/fbl, select "Chapter 7," and click on "Case Problem with Sample Answer."

7.7 Contract Enforceability. California's Subdivision Map Act (SMA) prohibits the sale of real property until a map of its subdivision is filed with, and approved by, the appropriate state agency. In 2004, Black Hills Investments, Inc., entered into two contracts with Albertson's, Inc., to buy two parcels of property in a shopping center development. Each contract required that "all governmental approvals relating to any lot split [or] subdivision" be obtained before the sale but permitted Albertson's to waive this condition. Black Hills made a $133,000 deposit on the purchase. A few weeks later, before the sales were complete, Albertson's filed with a local state agency a map that subdivided the shopping center into four parcels, including the two that Black Hills had agreed to buy. In 2005, Black Hills objected to concessions that Albertson's had made to a buyer of one of the other parcels, terminated its deal, and asked for its deposit. Albertson's refused. Black Hills filed a suit against Albertson's, arguing that the contracts were void. Are these contracts valid, voidable, unenforceable, or void? Explain. [*Black Hills Investments, Inc. v. Albertson's, Inc.*, 146 Cal.App.4th 883, 53 Cal.Rptr.3d 263 (4 Dist. 2007)]

7.8 🌐 **A Question of Ethics.** *International Business Machines Corp.* (IBM) hired Niels Jensen as a software sales rep-

resentative. In 2001, IBM presented a new "Software Sales Incentive Plan" (SIP) at a conference for its sales employees. A brochure stated, "[T]here are no caps to your earnings; the more you sell, . . . the more earnings for you." The brochure outlined how the plan worked and referred the employees to the "Sales Incentives" section of IBM's corporate intranet for more details. Jensen was given a "quota letter" that said he would be paid $75,000 as a base salary and, if he attained his quota, an additional $75,000 as incentive pay. In September, Jensen closed a deal with the U.S. Department of the Treasury's Internal Revenue Service worth more than $24 million to IBM. Relying on the SIP brochure, Jensen estimated his commission to be $2.6 million. IBM paid him less than $500,000, however. Jensen filed a suit against IBM, contending the SIP brochure and quota letter constituted a unilateral offer that became a binding contract when Jensen closed the sale. Consider the following questions. [Jensen v. International Business Machines Corp., 454 F.3d 382 (4th Cir. 2006)]

1 Is it fair to the employer to hold that the SIP brochure and quota letter created a unilateral contract if IBM did not *intend* to create such a contract? Is it fair to the employee to hold that *no* contract was created? Explain.

2 The "Sales Incentives" section of IBM's intranet included a clause providing that "[m]anagement will decide if an adjustment to the payment is appropriate" when an employee closes a large transaction. Jensen's quota letter stated, "[The SIP] program does not constitute a promise by IBM to make any distributions under it. IBM reserves the right to adjust the program terms or to cancel or otherwise modify the program at any time." How do these statements affect your answers to the above questions? From an ethical perspective, would it be fair to hold that a contract exists despite these statements?

🗿 CRITICAL THINKING AND WRITING ASSIGNMENTS

7.9 Critical Legal Thinking. Review the list of basic requirements for contract formation. Then analyze the relationship entered into when a student enrolls in a college or university. Has a bilateral contract or a unilateral contract been formed? Discuss.

7.10 📹 **Video Question.** Go to this text's Web site at **www.cengage.com/blaw/fbl** and select "Chapter 7." Click on "Video Questions" and view the video titled *Bowfinger*. Then answer the following questions.

1 In the video, Renfro (Robert Downey, Jr.) says to Bowfinger (Steve Martin), "You bring me this script and

Kit Ramsey and you've got yourself a 'go' picture." Assume that their agreement is a contract. Is the contract bilateral or unilateral? Is it express or implied? Is it formal or informal? Is it executed or executory? Explain.

2 What criteria would a court rely on to interpret the terms of the contract?

3 Recall from the video that the contract between Bowfinger and the producer was oral. Suppose that a statute requires contracts of this type to be in writing. In that situation would the contract be void, voidable, or unenforceable? Explain.

ACCESSING THE INTERNET

For updated links to resources available on the Web, as well as a variety of other materials, visit this text's Web site at

www.cengage.com/blaw/fbl

The 'Lectric Law Library provides information on contract law, including a definition of a contract and the elements required for a contract. Go to

www.lectlaw.com/lay.html

and scroll down to "Contracts."

For easy-to-understand definitions of legal terms and concepts, including terms and concepts relating to contract law, go to the following Web site and key in a term, such as *contract* or *consideration:*

dictionary.law.com

PRACTICAL INTERNET EXERCISES

Go to this text's Web site at **www.cengage.com/blaw/fbl**, select "Chapter 7," and click on "Practical Internet Exercises." There you will find the following Internet research exercises that you can perform to learn more about the topics covered in this chapter.

PRACTICAL INTERNET EXERCISE 7–1 LEGAL PERSPECTIVE—Contracts and Contract Provisions

PRACTICAL INTERNET EXERCISE 7–2 MANAGEMENT PERSPECTIVE—Implied Employment Contracts

PRACTICAL INTERNET EXERCISE 7–3 HISTORICAL PERSPECTIVE—Contracts in Ancient Mesopotamia

BEFORE THE TEST

Go to this text's Web site at **www.cengage.com/blaw/fbl**, select "Chapter 7," and click on "Interactive Quizzes." You will find a number of interactive questions relating to this chapter.

3

Agreement and Consideration

LEARNING OBJECTIVES

AFTER READING THIS CHAPTER, YOU SHOULD BE ABLE TO ANSWER THE FOLLOWING QUESTIONS:

1 What elements are necessary for an effective offer? What are some examples of nonoffers?

2 In what circumstances will an offer be irrevocable?

3 What are the elements that are necessary for an effective acceptance?

4 What is consideration? What is required for consideration to be legally sufficient?

5 In what circumstances might a promise be enforced despite a lack of consideration?

In Chapter 7, we pointed out that promises and agreements, and the knowledge that some of those promises and agreements will be legally enforced, are essential to civilized society. The homes we live in, the food we eat, the clothes we wear, the cars we drive, the books we read, the concerts and professional sporting events we attend—all of these have been purchased through contractual agreements. Contract law developed over time, through the common law tradition, to meet society's need to know with certainty what kinds of promises, or contracts, will be enforced and the point at which a valid and binding contract is formed.

For a contract to be considered valid and enforceable, the requirements listed in Chapter 7 must be met. In this chapter, we look closely at two of these requirements, *agreement* and *consideration*. As you read through this chapter, keep in mind that the requirements of agreement and consideration apply to all contracts, regardless of how they are formed. Many contracts continue to be formed in the traditional way—through the exchange of paper documents. Increasingly, though, contracts are also being formed online—through the exchange of electronic messages or documents. We discuss online contracts to a limited extent in this chapter and will look at them more closely in Chapter 13.

AGREEMENT

An essential element for contract formation is **agreement**— the parties must agree on the terms of the contract. Ordinarily, agreement is evidenced by two events: an *offer* and an *acceptance*. One party offers a certain bargain to another party, who then accepts that bargain.

Because words often fail to convey the precise meaning intended, the law of contracts generally adheres to the *objective theory of contracts*, as discussed in Chapter 7. Under this theory, a party's words and conduct are held to mean whatever a reasonable person in the offeree's position would think they meant.

Requirements of the Offer

An **offer** is a promise or commitment to perform or refrain from performing some specified act in the future. As discussed in Chapter 7, the party making an offer is called the *offeror*, and the party to whom the offer is made is called the *offeree*.

Three elements are necessary for an offer to be effective:

1 There must be a serious, objective intention by the offeror.

2 The terms of the offer must be reasonably certain, or definite, so that the parties and the court can ascertain the terms of the contract.

3 The offer must be communicated to the offeree.

Once an effective offer has been made, the offeree's acceptance of that offer creates a legally binding contract (providing the other essential elements for a valid and enforceable contract are present).

In today's e-commerce world, offers are frequently made online. Essentially, the requirements for traditional offers apply to online offers as well, as you will read in Chapter 13.

Intention   The first requirement for an effective offer to exist is a serious, objective intention on the part of the offeror. Intent is not determined by the *subjective* intentions, beliefs, or assumptions of the offeror. Rather, it is determined by what a reasonable person in the offeree's position would conclude the offeror's words and actions meant. Offers made in obvious anger, jest, or undue excitement do not meet the serious-and-objective-intent test. Because these offers are not effective, an offeree's acceptance does not create an agreement.

■**EXAMPLE 8.1**   You and three classmates ride to school each day in Julio's new automobile, which has a market value of $18,000. One cold morning, the four of you get into the car, but Julio cannot get it started. He yells in anger, "I'll sell this car to anyone for $500!" You drop $500 in his lap. A reasonable person, taking into consideration Julio's frustration and the obvious difference in value between the car's market price and the purchase price, would declare that Julio's offer was not made with serious and objective intent and that you do not have an agreement. ■

In the subsections that follow, we examine the concept of intention further as we look at the distinctions between offers and nonoffers. In the following classic case in the area of contractual agreement, the court had to decide whether an offer was intended when boasts, brags, and dares "after a few drinks" resulted in a contract to sell certain property.

CASE 8.1   **Lucy v. Zehmer**

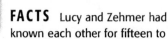

LANDMARK AND CLASSIC CASES

Supreme Court of Appeals of Virginia, 196 Va. 493, 84 S.E.2d 516 (1954).

FACTS   Lucy and Zehmer had known each other for fifteen to twenty years. For some time, Lucy had been wanting to buy Zehmer's farm. Zehmer had always told Lucy that he was not interested in selling. One night, Lucy stopped in to visit with the Zehmers at a restaurant they operated. Lucy said to Zehmer, "I bet you wouldn't take $50,000 for that place." Zehmer replied, "Yes, I would, too; you wouldn't give fifty." Throughout the evening, the conversation returned to the sale of the farm. At the same time, the parties were drinking whiskey. Eventually, Zehmer wrote up an agreement, on the back of a restaurant check, for the sale of the farm, and he asked his wife to sign it—which she did. When Lucy brought an action in a Virginia state court to enforce the agreement, Zehmer argued that he had been "high as a Georgia pine" at the time and that the offer had been made in jest: "two doggoned drunks bluffing to see who could talk the biggest and say the most." Lucy claimed that he had not been intoxicated and did not think Zehmer had been, either, given the way Zehmer handled the transaction. The trial court ruled in favor of the Zehmers, and Lucy appealed.

ISSUE   Can the agreement between the parties be avoided on the basis of intoxication?

DECISION   No. The agreement to sell the farm was binding.

REASON   The court held that the evidence given about the nature of the conversation, the appearance and completeness of the agreement, and the signing all tended to show that a serious business transaction, not a casual jest, was intended. The court had to look into the objective meaning of the words and acts of the Zehmers: "An agreement or mutual assent is of course essential to a valid contract, but the law imputes to a person an intention corresponding to the reasonable meaning of his words and acts. If his words and acts, judged by a reasonable standard, manifest an intention to agree, it is immaterial what may be the real but unexpressed state of mind."

 WHAT IF THE FACTS WERE DIFFERENT?   *Suppose that the day after Lucy signed the real estate sales agreement, he decided that he did not want the farm after all, and Zehmer sued Lucy to perform the contract. Would this change in the facts alter the court's decision that Lucy and Zehmer had created an enforceable contract? Why or why not?*

IMPACT OF THIS CASE ON TODAY'S LAW   *This is a classic case in contract law because it so clearly illustrates the objective theory of contracts with respect to determining*

CASE 8.1—Continued

whether an offer was intended. Today, the objective theory of contracts continues to be applied by the courts, and Lucy v. Zehmer *is routinely cited as a significant precedent in this area.*

RELEVANT WEB SITES *To locate information on the Web concerning the* Lucy v. Zehmer *decision, go to this text's Web site at* **www.cengage.com/blaw/fbl**, *select "Chapter 8," and click on "URLs for Landmarks."*

■

Expressions of Opinion. An expression of opinion is not an offer. It does not demonstrate an intention to enter into a binding agreement. **■EXAMPLE 8.2** In *Hawkins v. McGee*,[1] Hawkins took his son to McGee, a physician, and asked McGee to operate on the son's hand. McGee said that the boy would be in the hospital three or four days and that the hand would *probably* heal a few days later. The son's hand did not heal for a month, but nonetheless the father did not win a suit for breach of contract. The court held that McGee did not make an offer to heal the son's hand in three or four days. He merely expressed an opinion as to when the hand would heal. ■

Statements of Future Intent. A statement of an *intention* to do something in the future is not an offer. **■EXAMPLE 8.3** If Ari says, "I *plan* to sell my stock in Novation, Inc., for $150 per share," a contract is not created if John "accepts" and tenders $150 per share for the stock. Ari has merely expressed his intention to enter into a future contract for the sale of the stock. If John accepts and tenders the $150 per share, no contract is formed, because a reasonable person would conclude that Ari was only *thinking about* selling his stock, not promising to sell it. ■

Preliminary Negotiations. A request or invitation to negotiate is not an offer; it only expresses a willingness to discuss the possibility of entering into a contract. Examples are statements such as "Will you sell Forest Acres?" and "I wouldn't sell my car for less than $8,000." A reasonable person in the offeree's position would not conclude that such a statement indicated an intention to enter into a binding obligation. Likewise, when the government and private firms need to have construction work done, they invite contractors to submit bids. The *invitation* to submit bids is not an offer, and a contractor does not bind the government or private firm by submitting a bid. (The bids that the contractors submit are offers, however, and the government or private firm can bind the contractor by accepting the bid.)

Advertisements, Catalogues, and Circulars. In general, advertisements, mail-order catalogues, price lists, and circular letters (meant for the general public) are treated as invitations to negotiate, not as offers to form a contract.[2] **■EXAMPLE 8.4** You put an ad in the classified section of your local newspaper offering to sell your guitar for $275. Seven people call and "accept" your "offer" before you can remove the ad from the newspaper. If the ad were truly an offer, you would be bound by seven contracts to sell your guitar. Because *initial* advertisements are treated as *invitations* to make offers rather than offers, however, you will have seven offers to choose from, and you can accept the best one without incurring any liability for the six you reject. ■ On some occasions, though, courts have construed advertisements to be offers because the ads contained definite terms that invited acceptance (such as an ad offering a reward for the return of a lost dog).[3]

Price lists are another form of invitation to negotiate or trade. A seller's price list is not an offer to sell at that price; it merely invites the buyer to offer to buy at that price. In fact, the seller usually puts "prices subject to change" on the price list. Only in rare circumstances will a price quotation be construed as an offer.

Auctions. In an auction, a seller "offers" goods for sale through an auctioneer, but this is not an offer to form a contract. Rather, it is an invitation asking bidders to submit offers. In the context of an auction, a bidder is the offeror, and the auctioneer is the offeree. The offer is accepted when the auctioneer strikes the hammer. Before the fall of the hammer, a bidder may revoke (take back) her or his bid, or the auctioneer may reject that bid or all bids. Typically, an auctioneer will reject a bid that is below the price the seller is willing to accept.

When the auctioneer accepts a higher bid, he or she rejects all previous bids. Because rejection terminates an offer (as will be discussed later), those bids represent offers that have been terminated. Thus, if the highest bidder withdraws his or her bid before the hammer falls, none of the previous bids is reinstated. If the bid is not withdrawn or rejected, the contract is formed when the auctioneer announces, "Going once, going twice, sold!" (or something similar) and lets the hammer fall.

---

1. 84 N.H. 114, 146 A. 641 (1929).

2. *Restatement (Second) of Contracts*, Section 26, Comment b.
3. The classic example is *Lefkowitz v. Great Minneapolis Surplus Store, Inc.*, 251 Minn. 188, 86 N.W.2d 689 (1957).

Traditionally, auctions have been either "with reserve" or "without reserve." In an auction with reserve, the seller (through the auctioneer) may withdraw the goods at any time before the auctioneer closes the sale by announcement or by the fall of the hammer. All auctions are assumed to be auctions with reserve unless the terms of the auction are explicitly stated to be *without reserve*. In an auction without reserve, the goods cannot be withdrawn by the seller and must be sold to the highest bidder. In auctions with reserve, the seller may reserve the right to confirm or reject the sale even after "the hammer has fallen." In this situation, the seller is obligated to notify those attending the auction that sales of goods made during the auction are not final until confirmed by the seller.

Agreements to Agree.   Traditionally, agreements to agree—that is, agreements to agree to the material terms of a contract at some future date—were not considered to be binding contracts. The modern view, however, is that agreements to agree may be enforceable agreements (contracts) if it is clear that the parties intend to be bound by the agreements. In other words, under the modern view the emphasis is on the parties' intent rather than on form.

■EXAMPLE 8.5   After a patron was injured and nearly drowned on a water ride at Six Flags Amusement Park, Six Flags, Inc., filed a lawsuit against the manufacturer that had designed the ride. The defendant manufacturer claimed that there was no binding contract between the parties, only preliminary negotiations that were never formalized into a contract to construct the ride. The court, however, held that a faxed document specifying the details of the water ride, along with the parties' subsequent actions (beginning construction and handwriting notes on the fax), was sufficient to show an intent to be bound. Because of the court's finding, the manufacturer was required to provide insurance for the water ride at Six Flags, and its insurer was required to defend Six Flags in the personal-injury lawsuit that arose out of the incident.[4] ■

Increasingly, the courts are holding that a preliminary agreement constitutes a binding contract if the parties have agreed on all essential terms and no disputed issues remain to be resolved.[5] In contrast, if the parties agree on certain major terms but leave other terms open for further negotiation, a preliminary agreement is binding only in the sense that the parties have committed themselves to negotiate the undecided terms in good faith in an effort to reach a final agreement.[6]

In the following case, the dispute was over an agreement to settle a case during a trial. One party claimed that the agreement formed via e-mail was binding, and the other party claimed it was merely an agreement to agree or to work out the terms of a settlement in the future. Can an exchange of e-mails create a complete and unambiguous agreement?

---

4. *Six Flags, Inc. v. Steadfast Insurance Co.*, 474 F.Supp.2d 201 (D.Mass. 2007).
5. See, for example, *Tractebel Energy Marketing, Inc. v. AEP Power Marketing, Inc.*, 487 F.3d 89 (2d Cir. 2007); and *Fluorine On Call, Ltd. v. Fluorogas Limited*, No. 01-CV-186 (W.D.Tex. 2002), contract issue affirmed on appeal at 380 F.3d 849 (5th Cir. 2004).
6. See, for example, *MBH, Inc. v. John Otte Oil & Propane, Inc.*, 727 N.W.2d 238 (Neb.App. 2007); and *Barrand v. Whataburger, Inc.*, 214 S.W.3d 122 (Tex.App.—Corpus Christi 2006).

CASE 8.2   Basis Technology Corp. v. Amazon.com, Inc.

Appeals Court of Massachusetts, 71 Mass.App.Ct. 29, 878 N.E.2d 952 (2008).
www.malawyersweekly.com/macoa.cfm[a]

FACTS Basis Technology Corporation created software and provided technical services for Amazon.com, Inc.'s, Japanese-language Web site. The agreement between the two companies allowed for separately negotiated contracts for additional services that Basis might provide to Amazon. At the end of 1999, Basis and Amazon entered into stock-purchase agreements. Later, Amazon objected to certain actions related to the securities that Basis sold. Basis sued Amazon for various claims involving these securities and for failing to pay for services performed by Basis that were not included in the original agreement. During the trial, the two parties appeared to reach an agreement to settle out of court via a series of e-mail exchanges outlining the settlement. When Amazon reneged, Basis served a motion to enforce the proposed settlement. The trial judge entered a judgment against Amazon, which appealed.

ISSUE Was the agreement that was entered into via e-mail by the two parties involved in the litigation a binding settlement contract?

DECISION Yes. The Appeals Court of Massachusetts affirmed the trial court's finding that Amazon intended to be bound by the terms of the e-mail exchanges.

REASON The court examined the evidence consisting of e-mails between the two parties. It pointed out that in open court and on the record, counsel "reported the result of the

---

a. In the search box on the right, enter "71 Mass.App.Ct. 29," and click on "Search." On the resulting page, click on the case name.

CASE 8.2—Continued

settlement without specification of the terms." Amazon claimed that the e-mail terms were not complete and definite enough to form an agreement. The court noted, nonetheless, that "provisions are not ambiguous simply because the parties have developed different interpretations of them." In the exchange of e-mails, the essential business terms were indeed resolved. Afterwards, the parties were simply proceeding to record the settlement terms, not to create them. The e-mails

constituted a complete and unambiguous statement of the parties' desire to be bound by the settlement terms.

 WHAT IF THE FACTS WERE DIFFERENT?
Assume that the attorneys for both sides had simply had a phone conversation that included all of the terms to which they actually agreed in their e-mail exchanges. Would the court have ruled differently? Why or why not?

[handwritten: Offer Revocation is effective when the offeree gets the relation. (recieved)]

Definiteness   The second requirement for an effective offer involves the definiteness of its terms. An offer must have reasonably definite terms so that a court can determine if a breach has occurred and give an appropriate remedy.[7]

An offer may invite an acceptance to be worded in such specific terms that the contract is made definite. **■EXAMPLE 8.6** Marcus Business Machines contacts your corporation and offers to sell "from one to ten MacCool copying machines for $1,600 each; state number desired in acceptance." Your corporation agrees to buy two copiers. Because the quantity is specified in the acceptance, the terms are definite, and the contract is enforceable. ■

Communication   A third requirement for an effective offer is communication—the offer must be communicated to the offeree. **■EXAMPLE 8.7** Tolson advertises a reward for the return of her lost cat. Dirlik, not knowing of the reward, finds the cat and returns it to Tolson. Ordinarily, Dirlik cannot recover the reward because an essential element of a reward contract is that the one who claims the reward must have known it was offered. A few states would allow recovery of the reward, but not on contract principles—Dirlik would be allowed to recover on the basis that it would be unfair to deny him the reward just because he did not know about it. ■

Termination of the Offer

The communication of an effective offer to an offeree gives the offeree the power to transform the offer into a binding, legal obligation (a contract) by an acceptance. This power of acceptance does not continue forever, though. It can be terminated by action of the parties or by operation of law.

Termination by Action of the Parties   An offer can be terminated by the action of the parties in any of three ways: by revocation, by rejection, or by counteroffer.

Revocation of the Offer.   The offeror's act of withdrawing an offer is referred to as **revocation.** Unless an offer is irrevocable, the offeror usually can revoke the offer (even if he or she has promised to keep the offer open), as long as the revocation is communicated to the offeree before the offeree accepts. Revocation may be accomplished by an express repudiation of the offer (for example, with a statement such as "I withdraw my previous offer of October 17") or by the performance of acts that are inconsistent with the existence of the offer and that are made known to the offeree.

■EXAMPLE 8.8 Geraldine offers to sell some land to Gary. A week passes, and Gary, who has not yet accepted the offer, learns from his friend Konstantine that Geraldine has in the meantime sold the property to Nunan. Gary's knowledge of Geraldine's sale of the land to Nunan, even though he learned of it through a third party, effectively revokes Geraldine's offer to sell the land to Gary. Geraldine's sale of the land to Nunan is inconsistent with the continued existence of the offer to Gary, and thus the offer to Gary is revoked. ■

The general rule followed by most states is that a revocation becomes effective when the offeree or the offeree's agent (a person who acts on behalf of another) actually receives it. Therefore, a letter of revocation mailed on April 1 and delivered at the offeree's residence or place of business on April 3 becomes effective on April 3.

An offer made to the general public can be revoked in the same manner in which the offer was originally communicated. **■EXAMPLE 8.9** A department store offers a $10,000 reward to anyone providing information leading to the apprehension of the persons who burglarized its downtown store. The offer is published in three local papers and in four papers in neighboring communities. To revoke the offer, the store must publish the revocation in all seven papers for the same number of days it published the offer. The revocation is then accessible to the general public, and the offer is revoked even if some particular offeree does not know about the revocation. ■

Irrevocable Offers.   Although most offers are revocable, some can be made irrevocable. Increasingly, courts refuse to allow an

---

7. *Restatement (Second) of Contracts,* Section 33. The Uniform Commercial Code (UCC) has relaxed the requirements regarding the definiteness of terms in contracts for the sale of goods. See UCC 2–204(3).

offeror to revoke an offer when the offeree has changed position because of justifiable reliance on the offer (under the doctrine of *detrimental reliance*, or *promissory estoppel*, discussed later in this chapter). In some circumstances, "firm offers" made by merchants may also be considered irrevocable. We will discuss these offers in Chapter 14.

Another form of irrevocable offer is an option contract. An **option contract** is created when an offeror promises to hold an offer open for a specified period of time in return for a payment (consideration) given by the offeree. An option contract takes away the offeror's power to revoke an offer for the period of time specified in the option. If no time is specified, then a reasonable period of time is implied. **■EXAMPLE 8.10** Suppose that you are in the business of writing movie scripts. Your agent contacts the head of development at New Line Cinema and offers to sell New Line your new movie script. New Line likes your script and agrees to pay you $25,000 for a six-month option. In this situation, you (through your agent) are the offeror, and New Line is the offeree. You cannot revoke your offer to sell New Line your script for the next six months. After six months, if no contract has been formed, New Line loses the $25,000, and you are free to sell your script to another movie studio. ■

Option contracts are also frequently used in conjunction with the sale of real estate. **■EXAMPLE 8.11** You agree with a landowner to lease a house and include in the lease contract a clause stating that you will pay $15,000 for an option to purchase the property within a specified period of time. If you decide not to purchase the home after the specified period has lapsed, you lose the $15,000, and the landlord is free to sell the property to another buyer. ■

offeree

Rejection of the Offer by the Offeree. If the offeree rejects the offer, the offer is terminated. Any subsequent attempt by the offeree to accept will be construed as a new offer, giving the original offeror (now the offeree) the power of acceptance. A rejection is ordinarily accomplished by words or by conduct indicating an intent not to accept the offer.

As with a revocation, a rejection of an offer is effective only when it is actually received by the offeror or the offeror's agent. **■EXAMPLE 8.12** Growgood Farms mails a letter to Smith Soup Company offering to sell carrots at ten cents a pound. (Of course, today, such offers tend to be sent electronically rather than by mail, as will be discussed in Chapter 13.) Smith Soup Company could reject the offer either by sending or faxing a letter to Growgood Farms expressly rejecting the offer or by mailing the offer back to Growgood, indicating an intent to reject it. Alternatively, Smith could offer to buy the carrots at eight cents per pound (a counteroffer), necessarily rejecting the original offer. ■

Merely inquiring about an offer does not constitute rejection. **■EXAMPLE 8.13** A friend offers to buy your DVD movie collection for $300. You respond, "Is this your best offer?" or "Will you pay me $375 for it?" A reasonable person would conclude that you did not reject the offer but merely made an inquiry for further consideration of the offer. You can still accept and bind your friend to the $300 purchase price. When the offeree merely inquires as to the firmness of the offer, there is no reason to presume that she or he intends to reject it. ■

Counteroffer by the Offeree. A **counteroffer** is a rejection of the original offer and the simultaneous making of a new offer. **■EXAMPLE 8.14** Burke offers to sell his home to Lang for $270,000. Lang responds, "Your price is too high. I'll offer to purchase your house for $250,000." Lang's response is called a counteroffer because it rejects Burke's offer to sell at $270,000 and creates a new offer by Lang to purchase the home at a price of $250,000. ■

At common law, the **mirror image rule** requires that the offeree's acceptance match the offeror's offer exactly. In other words, the terms of the acceptance must "mirror" those of the offer. If the acceptance materially changes or adds to the terms of the original offer, it will be considered not an acceptance but a counteroffer—which, of course, need not be accepted. The original offeror can, however, accept the terms of the counteroffer and create a valid contract.[8]

Termination by Operation of Law The offeree's power to transform an offer into a binding, legal obligation can be terminated by operation of law if any of four conditions occur: lapse of time, destruction of the specific subject matter, death or incompetence of the offeror or offeree, or supervening illegality of the proposed contract.

Lapse of Time. An offer terminates automatically by law when the period of time *specified in the offer* has passed. If the offer states that it will be left open until a particular date, then the offer will terminate at midnight on that day. If the offer states that it will be left open for a number of days, such as ten days, this time period normally begins to run when the offer is actually received by the offeree, not when it is formed or sent. When the offer is delayed (through the misdelivery of mail, for example), the period begins to run from the date the offeree would have received the offer, but only if the offeree knows or should know that the offer is delayed.[9]

---

8. The mirror image rule has been greatly modified in regard to sales contracts. Section 2–207 of the UCC provides that a contract is formed if the offeree makes a definite expression of acceptance (such as signing the form in the appropriate location), even though the terms of the acceptance modify or add to the terms of the original offer (see Chapter 14).

9. *Restatement (Second) of Contracts*, Section 49.

EXAMPLE 8.15 Beth offers to sell her boat to Jonah, stating that the offer will remain open until May 20. Unless Jonah accepts the offer by midnight on May 20, the offer will lapse (terminate). Now suppose that Beth writes a letter to Jonah, offering to sell him her boat if Jonah accepts the offer within twenty days of the letter's date, which is May 1. Jonah must accept within twenty days after May 1, or the offer will terminate. Suppose that instead of including the date May 1 in her letter, Beth had simply written to Jonah offering to sell him her boat if Jonah accepted within twenty days. In this instance, Jonah must accept within twenty days of receiving the letter. The same rule would apply if Beth used insufficient postage and Jonah received the letter ten days late without knowing that it had been delayed. If, however, Jonah knew that the letter was delayed, the offer would lapse twenty days after the day he ordinarily would have received the offer had Beth used sufficient postage. ■

If the offer does not specify a time for acceptance, the offer terminates at the end of a *reasonable* period of time. A reasonable period of time is determined by the subject matter of the contract, business and market conditions, and other relevant circumstances. An offer to sell farm produce, for example, will terminate sooner than an offer to sell farm equipment because farm produce is perishable and subject to greater fluctuations in market value.

Destruction of the Subject Matter. An offer is automatically terminated if the specific subject matter of the offer is destroyed before the offer is accepted. For example, if Bekins offers to sell his prize cow to Yatsen, but the cow is struck by lightning and dies before Yatsen can accept, the offer is automatically terminated. (Note that if Yatsen accepted the offer just before lightning struck the cow, a contract would have been formed, but, because of the cow's death, a court would likely excuse Bekins's obligation to perform the contract on the basis of impossibility of performance—see Chapter 11.)

Death or Incompetence of the Offeror or Offeree. An offeree's power of acceptance is terminated when the offeror or offeree dies or is deprived of legal capacity to enter into the proposed contract, *unless the offer is irrevocable.*[10] A revocable offer is personal to both parties and normally cannot pass to a decedent's heirs or estate or to the guardian of a mentally incompetent person. This rule applies whether or not one party had notice of the death or incompetence of the other party. **EXAMPLE 8.16** Kapola, who is quite ill, writes to her friend Amanda, offering to sell Amanda her grand piano for

only $400. That night, Kapola dies. The next day, Amanda, not knowing of Kapola's death, writes a letter to Kapola, accepting the offer and enclosing a check for $400. Is there a contract? No. There is no contract because the offer automatically terminated on Kapola's death. ■

Supervening Illegality of the Proposed Contract. A statute or court decision that makes an offer illegal automatically terminates the offer. **EXAMPLE 8.17** Acme Finance Corporation offers to lend Jack $20,000 at 15 percent interest annually, but before Jack can accept, the state legislature enacts a statute prohibiting loans at interest rates greater than 12 percent. In this situation, the offer is automatically terminated. (If the statute is enacted after Jack accepts the offer, a valid contract is formed, but the contract may still be unenforceable—see Chapter 9.) ■

Acceptance

An **acceptance** is a voluntary act by the offeree that shows assent, or agreement, to the terms of an offer. The offeree's act may consist of words or conduct. The acceptance must be unequivocal and must be communicated to the offeror.

Who Can Accept? Generally, a third person cannot substitute for the offeree and effectively accept the offer. After all, the identity of the offeree is as much a condition of a bargaining offer as any other term contained therein. Thus, except in special circumstances, only the person to whom the offer is made or that person's agent can accept the offer and create a binding contract. For example, Lottie makes an offer to Paul. Paul is not interested, but his friend José accepts the offer. No contract is formed.

Unequivocal Acceptance To exercise the power of acceptance effectively, the offeree must accept unequivocally. This is the *mirror image rule* previously discussed. If the acceptance is subject to new conditions or if the terms of the acceptance materially change the original offer, the acceptance may be deemed a counteroffer that implicitly rejects the original offer.

Certain terms, when added to an acceptance, will not qualify the acceptance sufficiently to constitute rejection of the offer. **EXAMPLE 8.18** Suppose that in response to a person offering to sell a painting by a well-known artist, the offeree replies, "I accept; please send a written contract." The offeree is requesting a written contract but is not making it a condition for acceptance. Therefore, the acceptance is effective without the written contract. In contrast, if the offeree replies, "I accept *if* you send a written contract," the acceptance is expressly conditioned on the request for a writing, and the

---

10. *Restatement (Second) of Contracts*, Section 48. If the offer is irrevocable, it is not terminated when the offeror dies.

statement is not an acceptance but a counteroffer. (Notice how important each word is!)[11] ■

Silence as Acceptance   Ordinarily, silence cannot constitute acceptance, even if the offeror states, "By your silence and inaction, you will be deemed to have accepted this offer." This general rule applies because an offeree should not be put under a burden of liability to act affirmatively in order to reject an offer. No consideration—that is, nothing of value—has passed to the offeree to impose such a liability.

In some instances, however, the offeree does have a duty to speak; if so, his or her silence or inaction will operate as an acceptance. Silence may be an acceptance when an offeree takes the benefit of offered services even though he or she had an opportunity to reject them and knew that they were offered with the expectation of compensation. **■EXAMPLE 8.19** Suppose that John, a college student who earns extra income by washing store windows, taps on the window of a store and catches the attention of the store's manager. John points to the window and raises his cleaner, signaling that he will be washing the window. The manager does nothing to stop him. Here, the store manager's silence constitutes an acceptance, and an implied-in-fact contract is created. The store is bound to pay a reasonable value for John's work. ■

Silence can also operate as an acceptance when the offeree has had prior dealings with the offeror. If a merchant, for example, routinely receives shipments from a supplier and in the past has always notified the supplier when defective goods are rejected, then silence constitutes acceptance. Also, if a buyer solicits an offer specifying that certain terms and conditions are acceptable, and the seller makes the offer in response to the solicitation, the buyer has a duty to reject—that is, a duty to tell the seller that the offer is not acceptable. Failure to reject (silence) will operate as an acceptance.

Communication of Acceptance   Whether the offeror must be notified of the acceptance depends on the nature of the contract. In a bilateral contract, communication of acceptance is necessary because acceptance is in the form of a promise (not performance), and the contract is formed when the promise is made (rather than when the act is performed). Communication of acceptance is not necessary, however, if the offer dispenses with the requirement. Also, if the offer can be accepted by silence, no communication is necessary.

Because a unilateral contract calls for the full performance of some act, acceptance is usually evident, and notification is unnecessary. Nevertheless, exceptions do exist, such as when

the offeror requests notice of acceptance or has no way of determining whether the requested act has been performed. In addition, sometimes the law (such as Article 2 of the Uniform Commercial Code—UCC) requires notice of acceptance, and thus notice is necessary.

Mode and Timeliness of Acceptance   Acceptance in bilateral contracts must be timely. The general rule is that acceptance in a bilateral contract is timely if it is made before the offer is terminated. Problems may arise, though, when the parties involved are not dealing face to face. In such situations, the offeree should use an authorized mode of communication.

The Mailbox Rule.   Acceptance takes effect, thus completing formation of the contract, at the time the offeree sends or delivers the communication via the mode expressly or impliedly authorized by the offeror. This is the so-called **mailbox rule,** also called the *deposited acceptance rule,* which the majority of courts uphold. Under this rule, if the authorized mode of communication is the mail, then an acceptance becomes valid when it is dispatched (placed in the control of the U.S. Postal Service)—*not* when it is received by the offeror.

The mailbox rule was formed to prevent the confusion that arises when an offeror sends a letter of revocation but, before it arrives, the offeree sends a letter of acceptance. Thus, whereas a revocation becomes effective only when it is *received* by the offeree, an acceptance becomes effective on *dispatch* (when sent, even if it is never received), provided that an *authorized* means of communication is used.

The mailbox rule does not apply to instantaneous forms of communication, such as when the parties are dealing face to face, by telephone, or by fax. There is still some uncertainty in the courts as to whether e-mail should be considered an instantaneous form of communication to which the mailbox rule does not apply. If the parties have agreed to conduct transactions electronically and if the Uniform Electronic Transactions Act (to be discussed in Chapter 13) applies, then e-mail is considered sent when it either leaves the control of the sender or is received by the recipient. This rule takes the place of the mailbox rule when the Uniform Electronic Transactions Act applies but essentially allows an e-mail acceptance to become effective when sent (as it would if sent by U.S. mail).

Authorized Means of Acceptance.   A means of communicating acceptance can be expressly authorized by the offeror or impliedly authorized by the surrounding facts and circumstances. If an offer stipulates an authorized mode of acceptance (such as by overnight delivery), then the contract is formed at the moment the offeree accepts the offer using the authorized means. **■EXAMPLE 8.20** Sam Perkins, a dealer in Massachusetts, offers to sell a container of antiques to Leaham's Antiques in Colorado. The offer states that

---

11. As noted in footnote 8, in regard to sales contracts, the UCC provides that an acceptance may still be effective even if some terms are added. The new terms are simply treated as proposals for additions to the contract, unless both parties are merchants. If the parties are merchants, the additional terms (with some exceptions) become part of the contract [UCC 2–207(2)].

Leaham's must accept the offer via FedEx overnight delivery. The acceptance is effective (and a binding contract is formed) the moment that Leaham's gives the overnight envelope containing the acceptance to the FedEx driver. ■

If the offeror does not expressly authorize a certain mode of acceptance, then acceptance can be made by any reasonable means. Courts look at the prevailing business usages and the surrounding circumstances in determining whether the mode of acceptance used was reasonable. Usually, the offeror's choice of a particular means in making the offer implies that the offeree can use the *same or a faster* means for acceptance. Thus, if the offer is made via priority mail, it would be reasonable to accept the offer via priority mail or by a faster method, such as by fax.

If the offeror authorizes a particular method of acceptance, but the offeree accepts by a different means, the acceptance may still be effective if the substituted method serves the same purpose as the authorized means. The use of a substitute method of acceptance is not effective on dispatch, though, and no contract will be formed until the acceptance is received by the offeror. Thus, if an offer specifies FedEx overnight delivery but the offeree accepts by overnight delivery from another carrier, such as UPS or DHL, the acceptance will still be effective, but not until the offeror receives it.

 **PREVENTING LEGAL DISPUTES** **An effective way to avoid legal disputes over contracts is to communicate your intentions clearly to the other party and express every detail in writing, even when a written contract is not legally required. If you are the offeror, be explicit in your offer about how long the offer will remain open and stipulate the authorized means of communicating the acceptance. If you are the offeree, make sure that the language you use for any counteroffer, negotiation, or acceptance is absolutely clear and unambiguous. A simple "I accept" is best in most situations. Communicate your acceptance by the means authorized by the offeror or, if none is authorized, by the same method used to convey the offer. This can lessen the potential for problems arising due to revocation or lost communications.**

■

CONSIDERATION AND ITS REQUIREMENTS

In every legal system, some promises will be enforced, and other promises will not be enforced. The simple fact that a party has made a promise, then, does not mean the promise is enforceable. Under the common law, a primary basis for the enforcement of promises is consideration. **Consideration** is usually defined as the value given in return for a promise. We look here at the basic elements of consideration and then at some other contract doctrines relating to consideration.

Elements of Consideration

Often, consideration is broken down into two parts: (1) something of *legally sufficient value* must be given in exchange for the promise, and (2) there must be a *bargained-for exchange*.

Legal Value The "something of legally sufficient value" may consist of (1) a promise to do something that one has no prior legal duty to do (to pay on receipt of certain goods, for example), (2) the performance of an action that one is otherwise not obligated to undertake (such as providing accounting services), or (3) the refraining from an action that one has a legal right to undertake (called a **forbearance**).

Consideration in bilateral contracts normally consists of a promise in return for a promise, as explained in Chapter 7. **■EXAMPLE 8.21** In a contract for the sale of goods, the seller promises to ship specific goods to the buyer, and the buyer promises to pay for those goods when they are received. Each of these promises constitutes consideration for the contract. ■ In contrast, unilateral contracts involve a promise in return for a performance. **■EXAMPLE 8.22** Anita says to her neighbor, "If you paint my garage, I will pay you $800." Anita's neighbor paints the garage. The act of painting the garage is the consideration that creates Anita's contractual obligation to pay her neighbor $800. ■

What if, in return for a promise to pay, a person refrains from pursuing harmful habits, such as the use of tobacco and alcohol? Does such forbearance create consideration for the contract? Normally yes, refraining from doing what one has a legal right to do can constitute consideration.

Bargained-for Exchange The second element of consideration is that it must provide the basis for the bargain struck between the contracting parties. The promise given by the promisor must induce the promisee to incur a legal detriment either now or in the future, and the detriment incurred must induce the promisor to make the promise. This element of bargained-for exchange distinguishes contracts from gifts.

■EXAMPLE 8.23 Roberto says to his son, "In consideration of the fact that you are not as wealthy as your brothers, I will pay you $5,000." This promise is not enforceable because Roberto's son has not given any return consideration for the $5,000 promised. The son (the promisee) incurs no legal detriment; he does not have to promise anything or undertake (or refrain from undertaking) any action to receive the $5,000. Here, Roberto has simply stated his motive for giving his son a gift. The fact that the word *consideration* is used does not, by itself, mean that consideration has been given. ■

Legal Sufficiency and Adequacy of Consideration

Legal sufficiency of consideration involves the requirement that consideration be something of value in the eyes of the law. Adequacy of consideration involves "how much" consideration is given. Essentially, adequacy of consideration concerns the fairness of the bargain. On the surface, fairness would appear to be an issue when the items exchanged are of unequal value. In general, however, courts do not question the adequacy of consideration if the consideration is legally sufficient. Under the doctrine of freedom of contract, parties are usually free to bargain as they wish. If people could sue merely because they had entered into an unwise contract, the courts would be overloaded with frivolous suits.

Nevertheless, in rare situations a court will consider whether the amount or value of the consideration is adequate. This is because apparently inadequate consideration can indicate that fraud, duress, or undue influence was involved (if an elderly person sells her $50,000 car to her neighbor for $5,000, for example). When the consideration is grossly inadequate, a court may declare the contract unenforceable on the ground that it is *unconscionable*,[12] meaning that, generally speaking, it is so one sided under the circumstances as to be clearly unfair. (*Unconscionability* will be discussed further in Chapter 9.)

The determination of whether consideration exists does not depend on the comparative value of the things exchanged. Something need not be of direct economic or financial value to be considered legally sufficient consideration. In many situations, the exchange of promises and potential benefits is deemed sufficient as consideration.

AGREEMENTS THAT LACK CONSIDERATION

Sometimes, one or both of the parties to a contract may think that they have exchanged consideration when in fact they have not. Here we look at some situations in which the parties' promises or actions do not qualify as contractual consideration.

Preexisting Duty

Under most circumstances, a promise to do what one already has a legal duty to do does not constitute legally sufficient consideration because no legal detriment is incurred. The preexisting legal duty may be imposed by law or may arise out of a previous contract. A sheriff, for example, cannot collect a reward for information leading to the capture of a criminal if the sheriff already has a legal duty to capture the criminal. Likewise, if a party is already bound by contract to perform a

certain duty, that duty cannot serve as consideration for a second contract.

■EXAMPLE 8.24 Bauman-Bache, Inc., begins construction on a seven-story office building and after three months demands an extra $75,000 on its contract. If the extra $75,000 is not paid, the firm will stop working. The owner of the land, finding no one else to complete construction, agrees to pay the extra $75,000. The agreement is not enforceable because it is not supported by legally sufficient consideration; Bauman-Bache had a preexisting contractual duty to complete the building. **■**

Unforeseen Difficulties The rule regarding preexisting duty is meant to prevent extortion and the so-called holdup game. What happens, though, when an honest contractor, who has contracted with a landowner to build a house, runs into extraordinary difficulties that were totally unforeseen at the time the contract was formed? In the interests of fairness and equity, the courts sometimes allow exceptions to the preexisting duty rule. In the example just mentioned, if the landowner agrees to pay extra compensation to the contractor for overcoming the unforeseen difficulties (such as having to use dynamite and special equipment to remove an unexpected rock formation to excavate for a basement), the court may refrain from applying the preexisting duty rule and enforce the agreement. When the "unforeseen difficulties" that give rise to a contract modification are the types of risks ordinarily assumed in business, however, the courts will usually assert the preexisting duty rule.[13]

Rescission and New Contract The law recognizes that two parties can mutually agree to rescind their contract, at least to the extent that it is executory (still to be carried out). Rescission[14] is the unmaking of a contract so as to return the parties to the positions they occupied before the contract was made. Sometimes, parties rescind a contract and make a new contract at the same time. When this occurs, it is often difficult to determine whether there was consideration for the new contract or whether the parties had a preexisting duty under the previous contract. If a court finds there was a preexisting duty, then the new contract will be invalid because there was no consideration.

Past Consideration

Promises made in return for actions or events that have already taken place are unenforceable. These promises lack consideration in that the element of bargained-for exchange is missing. In short, you can bargain for something to take place

---

12. Pronounced un-*kon*-shun-uh-bul.

13. Note that under the UCC, any agreement modifying a contract within Article 2 on sales needs no consideration to be binding. See UCC 2–209(1).
14. Pronounced reh-*sih*-zhen.

now or in the future but not for something that has already taken place. Therefore, **past consideration** is no consideration.

EXAMPLE 8.25 Elsie, a real estate agent, does her friend Judy a favor by selling Judy's house and not charging any commission. Later, Judy says to Elsie, "In return for your generous act, I will pay you $6,000." This promise is made in return for past consideration and is thus unenforceable; in effect, Judy is stating her intention to give Elsie a gift. ◼

An employer will often ask an employee to sign a noncompete agreement, also called a covenant not to compete, by which the employee agrees not to work for competitors of the employer for a certain period of time after the employment relationship ends. (*Noncompete agreements* will be discussed further in Chapter 9.) In the following case, the court had to decide if continued employment constituted valid consideration for a noncompete ageement or if it was past consideration.

CASE 8.3 **Access Organics, Inc. v. Hernandez**

Supreme Court of Montana, 341 Mont. 73, 175 P.3d 899 (2008).

FACTS Bonnie Poux hired Andy Hernandez to sell organic produce for her sole proprietorship, Access Organics, Inc. Four months later, he was promoted to sales manager. Soon after, he signed a noncompete agreement in which he agreed "not to directly or indirectly compete with the business . . . for a period of two years following termination of employment." Later, the business encountered financial difficulties. Hernandez left and went into business with another former employee to compete with Access Organics in the sale of produce in the same part of Montana. Poux then sued to enforce the noncompete agreement. The trial court found that Hernandez was in direct competition with Access Organics and was contacting former customers. That was held to be a violation of the noncompete agreement. The agreement was upheld as valid because it was supported by consideration, which was continued employment at Access Organics at the time the agreement was signed. The court ordered Hernandez not to compete directly with Access Organics for the two-year period called for in the agreement. Hernandez appealed.

ISSUE Is continued employment valid consideration to support a noncompete agreement that an employee signed shortly after being hired by an employer?

DECISION No. Montana's highest court held that the noncompete agreement between the employer and the employee was invalid because it was not supported by consideration. Because no contract had been formed, the court reversed the trial court's order that enforced the agreement.

REASON The court noted that although covenants not to compete are restraints of trade and therefore disfavored, they are upheld in some circumstances if supported by consideration. Consideration exists if the employee enters into the noncompete agreement at the time of hiring because then the agreement is part of a bargained-for exchange. In this case, however, Hernandez signed the agreement more than four months after accepting his initial employment. Hernandez was simply told to sign the agreement when he was already working for Access Organics. His prior employment was not consideration because past consideration is insufficient to support a promise. This was an "afterthought agreement" that could have been valid had it been supported by a pay increase or some other new benefit, but it was not. Because the agreement was unsupported by consideration, it did not create an enforceable contract.

 FOR CRITICAL ANALYSIS—Ethical Consideration *How could Access Organics have obtained a noncompete agreement from Hernandez that would have been enforced?*

◼

Illusory Promises

If the terms of the contract express such uncertainty of performance that the promisor has not definitely promised to do anything, the promise is said to be *illusory*—without consideration and unenforceable. **EXAMPLE 8.26** The president of Tuscan Corporation says to his employees, "All of you have worked hard, and if profits remain high, a 10 percent bonus at the end of the year will be given—if management thinks it is

warranted." This is an *illusory promise*, or no promise at all, because performance depends solely on the discretion of the president (the management). There is no bargained-for consideration. The statement declares merely that management may or may not do something in the future. ◼

Option-to-cancel clauses in contracts for specified time periods sometimes present problems in regard to consideration. **EXAMPLE 8.27** Abe contracts to hire Chris for one year at $5,000 per month, reserving the right to cancel the contract at any time. On close examination of these words, you can see that Abe has not actually agreed to hire Chris, as Abe could cancel without liability before Chris started performance. Abe has not given up the opportunity of hiring someone else. This contract is therefore illusory. Now suppose that Abe contracts to hire Chris for a one-year period at $5,000 per month, reserving the right to cancel the contract at any time after Chris has begun performance by giving Chris thirty days' notice. Abe, by saying that he will give Chris thirty days' notice, is relinquishing the opportunity (legal right) to hire someone else instead of Chris for a thirty-day period. If Chris works for one month, at the end of which Abe gives him thirty days' notice, Chris has a valid and enforceable contractual claim for $10,000 in salary. ■

SETTLEMENT OF CLAIMS

Businesspersons or others can settle legal claims in several ways. It is important to understand the nature of the consideration given in these settlement agreements, or contracts. Claims are commonly settled through an *accord and satisfaction*, in which a debtor offers to pay a lesser amount than the creditor purports is owed. Two other methods that are also often used to settle claims are the *release* and the *covenant not to sue*.

Accord and Satisfaction

[handwritten: 1) agreement to recent 2) payment]

In an **accord and satisfaction,** a debtor offers to pay, and a creditor accepts, a lesser amount than the creditor originally claimed was owed. Thus, in an accord and satisfaction, the debtor attempts to terminate an existing obligation. The *accord* is the settlement agreement. In an accord, the debtor offers to give or perform something less than the parties originally agreed on, and the creditor accepts that offer in satisfaction of the claim. *Satisfaction* is the performance (usually payment), which takes place after the accord is executed. A basic rule is that there can be no satisfaction unless there is first an accord.

For accord and satisfaction to occur, the amount of the debt *must be in dispute.* If it is a **liquidated debt,** then accord and satisfaction cannot take place. A debt is liquidated if its amount has been ascertained, fixed, agreed on, settled, or exactly determined. An example of a liquidated debt is a loan contract in which the borrower agrees to pay a stipulated amount every month until the amount of the loan is paid. In the majority of states, acceptance of (an accord for) a lesser sum than the entire amount of a liquidated debt is not satisfaction, and the balance of the debt is still legally owed. The rationale for this rule is that the debtor has given no consider-

ation to satisfy the obligation of paying the balance to the creditor—because the debtor has a preexisting legal obligation to pay the entire debt.

An *unliquidated debt* is the opposite of a liquidated debt. Here, reasonable persons may differ over the amount owed. It is *not* settled, fixed, agreed on, ascertained, or determined. In these circumstances, acceptance of payment of the lesser sum operates as a satisfaction, or discharge, of the debt. One argument to support this rule is that the parties give up a legal right to contest the amount in dispute, and thus consideration is given.

Release

A **release** is a contract in which one party forfeits the right to pursue a legal claim against the other party. Releases will generally be binding if they are (1) given in good faith, (2) stated in a signed writing (required by many states), and (3) accompanied by consideration.[15] Clearly, parties are better off if they know the extent of their injuries or damages before signing releases.

■EXAMPLE 8.28 Suppose that you are involved in an automobile accident caused by Raoul's negligence. Raoul offers to give you $2,000 if you will release him from further liability resulting from the accident. You believe that this amount will cover your damage, so you agree to and sign the release. Later you discover that the repairs to your car will cost $4,200. Can you collect the balance from Raoul? The answer is normally no; you are limited to the $2,000 in the release. Why? The reason is that a valid contract existed. You and Raoul both assented to the bargain (hence, agreement existed), and sufficient consideration was present. Your consideration for the contract was the legal detriment you suffered (by releasing Raoul from liability, you forfeited your right to sue to recover damages, should they be more than $2,000). This legal detriment was induced by Raoul's promise to give you the $2,000. Raoul's promise was, in turn, induced by your promise not to pursue your legal right to sue him for damages. ■

Covenant Not to Sue

Unlike a release, a **covenant not to sue** does not always bar further recovery. The parties simply substitute a contractual obligation for some other type of legal action based on a valid claim. Suppose (following the earlier example) that you agree with Raoul not to sue for damages in a tort action if he will pay for the damage to your car. If Raoul fails to pay, you can bring an action for breach of contract.

---

15. Under the UCC, a written, signed waiver or renunciation by an aggrieved party discharges any further liability for a breach, even without consideration [UCC 1–107].

PROMISSORY ESTOPPEL

Sometimes, individuals rely on promises, and such reliance may form a basis for contract rights and duties. Under the doctrine of **promissory estoppel** (also called *detrimental reliance*), a person who has reasonably relied on the promise of another can often obtain some measure of recovery. When the doctrine of promissory estoppel is applied, the promisor (the offeror) is **estopped** (barred or impeded) from revoking the promise. For the doctrine of promissory estoppel to be applied, the following elements are required:

1 There must be a clear and definite promise.

2 The promisee must justifiably rely on the promise.

3 The reliance normally must be of a substantial and definite character.

4 Justice will be better served by the enforcement of the promise.

■**EXAMPLE 8.29** Your uncle tells you, "I'll pay you $1,500 a week so that you won't have to work anymore." In reliance on your uncle's promise, you quit your job, but your uncle refuses to pay you. Under the doctrine of promissory estoppel, you may be able to enforce his promise.[16] Now your uncle makes a promise to give you $20,000 to buy a car. If you buy the car with your own funds and he does not pay you, you may once again be able to enforce the promise under this doctrine. ■

---

16. A classic example is *Ricketts v. Scothorn*, 57 Neb. 51, 77 N.W. 365 (1898).

REVIEWING Agreement and Consideration

Shane Durbin wanted to have a recording studio custom built in his home. He sent invitations to a number of local contractors to submit bids on the project. Rory Amstel submitted the lowest bid, which was $20,000 less than any of the other bids Durbin received. Durbin then called Amstel to ascertain the type and quality of the materials that were included in the bid and to find out if he could substitute a superior brand of acoustic tiles for the same bid price. Amstel said he would have to check into the price difference. The parties also discussed a possible start date for construction. Two weeks later, Durbin changed his mind and decided not to go forward with his plan to build a recording studio. Amstel filed a suit against Durbin for breach of contract. Using the information presented in the chapter, answer the following questions.

1 Did Amstel's bid meet the requirements of an offer? Explain.

2 Was there an acceptance of the offer? Why or why not?

3 Suppose that the court determines that the parties did not reach an agreement. Further suppose that Amstel, in anticipation of building Durbin's studio, had purchased materials and refused other jobs so that he would have time in his schedule for Durbin's project. Under what theory discussed in the chapter might Amstel attempt to recover these costs?

4 Now suppose that Durbin had gone forward with his plan to build the studio and immediately accepted Amstel's bid without discussing the type or quality of materials. After Amstel began construction, Durbin asked Amstel to substitute a superior brand of acoustic tiles for the tiles that Amstel had intended to use at the time that he bid on the project. Amstel installed the tiles, then asked Durbin to pay the difference in price, but Durbin refused. Can Amstel sue to obtain the price differential from Durbin in this situation? Why or why not?

TERMS AND CONCEPTS

acceptance 173
accord and satisfaction 178
agreement 167
consideration 175
counteroffer 172
covenant not to sue 178

estopped 179
forbearance 175
liquidated debt 178
mailbox rule 174
mirror image rule 172
offer 167

option contract 172
past consideration 177
promissory estoppel 179
release 178
rescission 176
revocation 171

CHAPTER SUMMARY   Agreement and Consideration

Requirements of the Offer (See pages 167–171.)	1. *Intent*—There must be a serious, objective intention by the offeror to become bound by the offer. Nonoffer situations include (a) expressions of opinion; (b) statements of intention; (c) preliminary negotiations; (d) generally, advertisements, catalogues, price lists, and circulars; (e) solicitations for bids made by an auctioneer; and (f) traditionally, agreements to agree in the future. 2. *Definiteness*—The terms of the offer must be sufficiently definite to be ascertainable by the parties or by a court. 3. *Communication*—The offer must be communicated to the offeree.

Termination of the Offer (See pages 171–173.)	1. *By action of the parties*—
	
	   a. Revocation—Unless the offer is irrevocable, it can be revoked at any time before acceptance without liability. Revocation is not effective until received by the offeree or the offeree's agent. Some offers, such as a merchant's firm offer and option contracts, are irrevocable.
	
	   b. Rejection—Accomplished by words or actions that demonstrate a clear intent not to accept the offer; not effective until received by the offeror or the offeror's agent.
	
	   c. Counteroffer—A rejection of the original offer and the making of a new offer.
	
	2. *By operation of law*—
	
	   a. Lapse of time—The offer terminates (1) at the end of the time period specified in the offer or (2) if no time period is stated in the offer, at the end of a reasonable time period.
	
	   b. Destruction of the specific subject matter of the offer—Automatically terminates the offer.
	
	   c. Death or incompetence of the offeror or offeree—Terminates the offer unless the offer is irrevocable.
	
	   d. Illegality—Supervening illegality terminates the offer.

Acceptance (See pages 173–175.)	1. Can be made only by the offeree or the offeree's agent.
	
	2. Must be unequivocal. Under the common law (mirror image rule), if new terms or conditions are added to the acceptance, it will be considered a counteroffer.
	
	3. Acceptance of a unilateral offer is effective on full performance of the requested act. Generally, no communication is necessary.
	
	4. Acceptance of a bilateral offer can be communicated by the offeree by any authorized mode of communication and is effective on dispatch. Unless the offeror expressly specifies the mode of communication, the following methods are impliedly authorized:
	
	   a. The same mode used by the offeror or a faster mode.
	
	   b. Mail, when the two parties are at a distance.
	
	   c. In sales contracts, by any reasonable medium.

Elements of Consideration (See page 175.)	Consideration is broken down into two parts: (1) something of *legally sufficient value* must be given in exchange for the promise, and (2) there must be a *bargained-for exchange*.
Legal Sufficiency and Adequacy of Consideration (See page 176.)	Legal sufficiency of consideration relates to the first element of consideration—something of legal value must be given in exchange for a promise. Adequacy of consideration relates to "how much" consideration is given and whether a fair bargain was reached. Courts will inquire into the adequacy of consideration (whether the consideration is legally sufficient) only when fraud, undue influence, duress, or unconscionability may be involved.

CHAPTER SUMMARY	Agreement and Consideration—Continued
Agreements That Lack Consideration (See pages 176–178.)	Consideration is lacking in the following situations: 1. *Preexisting duty*—Consideration is not legally sufficient if one is either by law or by contract under a *preexisting duty* to perform the action being offered as consideration for a new contract. 2. *Past consideration*—Actions or events that have already taken place do not constitute legally sufficient consideration. 3. *Illusory promises*—When the nature or extent of performance is too uncertain, the promise is rendered illusory (without consideration and unenforceable).
Settlement of Claims (See page 178.)	1. *Accord and satisfaction*—An *accord* is an agreement in which a debtor offers to pay a lesser amount than the creditor claims is owed. *Satisfaction* may take place when the accord is executed. 2. *Release*—An agreement in which, for consideration, a party forfeits the right to seek further recovery beyond the terms specified in the release. 3. *Covenant not to sue*—An agreement not to sue on a present, valid claim.
Promissory Estoppel (See page 179.)	The equitable doctrine of promissory estoppel applies when a promisor reasonably expects a promise to induce definite and substantial action or forbearance by the promisee, and the promisee does act in reliance on the promise. Such a promise is binding if injustice can be avoided only by enforcement of the promise. Also known as the doctrine of *detrimental reliance*.

FOR REVIEW

Answers for the even-numbered questions in this **For Review** *section can be found on this text's accompanying Web site at* **www.cengage.com/blaw/fbl.** *Select "Chapter 8" and click on "For Review."*

1 What elements are necessary for an effective offer? What are some examples of nonoffers?

2 In what circumstances will an offer be irrevocable?

3 What are the elements that are necessary for an effective acceptance?

4 What is consideration? What is required for consideration to be legally sufficient?

5 In what circumstances might a promise be enforced despite a lack of consideration?

QUESTIONS AND CASE PROBLEMS

 HYPOTHETICAL SCENARIOS AND CASE PROBLEMS

8.1 Agreement. Ball writes to Sullivan and inquires how much Sullivan is asking for a specific forty-acre tract of land Sullivan owns. In a letter received by Ball, Sullivan states, "I will not take less than $60,000 for the forty-acre tract as specified." Ball immediately sends Sullivan a telegram stating, "I accept your offer for $60,000 for the forty-acre tract as specified." Discuss whether Ball can hold Sullivan to a contract for sale of the land.

8.2 Hypothetical Question with Sample Answer. Chernek, the sole owner of a small business, has a large piece of used farm equipment for sale. He offers to sell the equipment to Bollow for $10,000. Discuss the legal effects of the following events on the offer:

1 Chernek dies prior to Bollow's acceptance, and at the time she accepts, Bollow is unaware of Chernek's death.

2 The night before Bollow accepts, a fire destroys the equipment.

3 Bollow pays $100 for a thirty-day option to purchase the equipment. During this period, Chernek dies, and Bollow accepts the offer, knowing of Chernek's death.

4 Bollow pays $100 for a thirty-day option to purchase the equipment. During this period, Bollow dies, and Bollow's estate accepts Chernek's offer within the stipulated time period.

For a sample answer to Question 8.2, go to Appendix E at the end of this text.

8.3 Consideration. Daniel, a recent college graduate, is on his way home for the Christmas holidays from his new job. He gets caught in a snowstorm and is taken in by an elderly couple, who provide him with food and shelter. After the snowplows have cleared the road, Daniel proceeds home. Daniel's father, Fred, is most appreciative of the elderly couple's action and in a letter promises to pay them $500. The elderly couple, in need of funds, accept Fred's offer. Then, because of a dispute with Daniel, Fred refuses to pay the elderly couple the $500. Discuss whether the couple can hold Fred liable in contract for the services rendered to Daniel.

8.4 Intention. Music that is distributed on compact discs and similar media generates income in the form of "mechanical" royalties. Music that is publicly performed, such as when a song is played on the radio, included in a movie or commercial, or sampled in another song, produces "performance" royalties. Both types of royalties are divided between the songwriter and the song's publisher. Vincent Cusano is a musician and songwriter who performed under the name "Vinnie Vincent" as a guitarist with the group KISS in the early 1980s. Cusano co-wrote three songs entitled "Killer," "I Love It Loud," and "I Still Love You," which KISS recorded and released in 1982 on an album titled *Creatures of the Night*. Cusano left KISS in 1984. Eight years later, Cusano sold to Horipro Entertainment Group "one hundred (100%) percent undivided interest" of his rights in the songs "other than Songwriter's share of performance income." Later, Cusano filed a suit in a federal district court against Horipro, claiming in part that he never intended to sell the writer's share of the mechanical royalties. Horipro filed a motion for summary judgment. Should the court grant the motion? Explain. [*Cusano v. Horipro Entertainment Group,* 301 F.Supp.2d 272 (S.D.N.Y. 2004)]

8.5 Consideration. As a child, Martha Carr once visited her mother's 108-acre tract of unimproved land in Richland County, South Carolina. In 1968, Betty and Raymond Campbell leased the land. Carr, a resident of New York, was diagnosed as having schizophrenia and depression in 1986, was hospitalized five or six times, and takes prescription drugs for the illnesses. In 1996, Carr inherited the Richland property and, two years later, contacted the Campbells about selling the land. Carr asked Betty about the value of the land, and Betty said that the county tax assessor had determined that the land's *agricultural value* was $54,000. The Campbells knew at the time that the county had assessed the total property value at $103,700 for tax purposes. On August 6, Carr signed a contract to sell the land to the Campbells for

$54,000. Believing the price to be unfair, however, Carr did not deliver the deed. The Campbells filed a suit in a South Carolina state court against Carr, seeking specific performance of the contract. At trial, an expert real estate appraiser testified that the *real market value* of the property was $162,000 at the time of the contract. Under what circumstances will a court examine the adequacy of consideration? Are those circumstances present in this case? Should the court enforce the contract between Carr and the Campbells? Explain. [*Campbell v. Carr,* 361 S.C. 258, 603 S.E.2d 625 (2004)]

8.6 Case Problem with Sample Answer. In 2000, David and Sandra Harless leased 2.3 acres of real property at 2801 River Road S.E. in Winnabow, North Carolina, to their son-in-law and daughter, Tony and Jeanie Connor. The Connors planned to operate a "general store/variety store" on the premises. They agreed to lease the property for sixty months with an option to renew for an additional sixty months. The lease included an option to buy the property for "fair market value at the time of such purchase (based on at least two appraisals)." In March 2003, Tony told David that the Connors wanted to buy the property. In May, Tony gave David an appraisal that estimated the property's value at $140,000. In July, the Connors presented a second appraisal that put the value at $160,000. The Connors offered $150,000. The Harlesses replied that "under no circumstances would they ever agree to sell their old store building and approximately 2.5 acres to their daughter . . . and their son-in-law." The Connors filed a suit in a North Carolina state court against the Harlesses, alleging breach of contract. Did these parties have a contract to sell the property? If so, what were its terms? If not, why not? [*Connor v. Harless,* 176 N.C.App. 402, 626 S.E.2d 755 (2006)]

After you have answered Problem 8.6, compare your answer with the sample answer given on the Web site that accompanies this text. Go to www.cengage.com/blaw/fbl, select "Chapter 8," and click on "Case Problem with Sample Answer."

8.7 Offer. In August 2000, in California, Terry Reigelsperger sought treatment for pain in his lower back from chiropractor James Siller. Reigelsperger felt better after the treatment and did not intend to return for more, although he did not mention this to Siller. Before leaving the office, Reigelsperger signed an "informed consent" form that read, in part, "I intend this consent form to cover the entire course of treatment for my present condition and for any future condition(s) for which I seek treatment." He also signed an agreement that required the parties to submit to arbitration "any dispute as to medical malpractice. . . .This agreement is intended to bind the patient and the health care provider . . . who now or in the future treat[s] the patient." Two years later, Reigelsperger sought treatment from Siller for a different condition relating to his cervical spine and shoulder. Claiming malpractice with respect to the second treatment, Reigelsperger filed a suit in a California state court against

Siller. Siller asked the court to order the submission of the dispute to arbitration. Does Reigelsperger's lack of intent to return to Siller after his first treatment affect the enforceability of the arbitration agreement and consent form? Why or why not? [*Reigelsperger v. Siller*, 40 Cal.4th 574, 53 Cal.Rptr.3d 887, 150 P.3d 764 (2007)]

8.8 **A Question of Ethics.** *John Sasson and Emily Springer met in January 2002. John worked for the U.S. Army as an engineer. Emily was an attorney with a law firm. When, six months later, John bought a townhouse in Randolph, New Jersey, he asked Emily to live with him. She agreed, but retained the ownership of her home in Monmouth Beach. John paid the mortgage and the other expenses on the townhouse. He urged Emily to quit her job and work from "our house." In May 2003, Emily took John's advice and started her own law practice. In December, John made her the beneficiary of his $150,000 individual retirement account (IRA) and said that he would give her his 2002 BMW M3 car before the end of the next year. He proposed to her in September 2004, giving her a diamond engagement ring and promising to "take care*

of her" for the rest of her life. Less than a month later, John was critically injured by an accidental blow to his head during a basketball game and died. On behalf of John's estate, which was valued at $1.1 million, his brother Steven filed a complaint in a New Jersey state court to have Emily evicted from the townhouse. Given these facts, consider the following questions. [In re Estate of Sasson, 387 N.J.Super. 459, 904 A.2d 769 (App.Div. 2006)]

1 Based on John's promise to "take care of her" for the rest of her life, Emily claimed that she was entitled to the townhouse, the BMW, and an additional portion of John's estate. Under what circumstances would such a promise constitute a valid, enforceable contract? Does John's promise meet these requirements? Why or why not?

2 Whether or not John's promise is legally binding, is there an ethical basis on which it should be enforced? Is there an ethical basis for *not* enforcing it? Are there any circumstances under which a promise of support should be—or should *not* be—enforced? Discuss.

CRITICAL THINKING AND WRITING ASSIGNMENTS

8.9 Critical Legal Thinking. Under what circumstances should courts examine the adequacy of consideration?

8.10 **Video Question.** Go to this text's Web site at **www.cengage.com/blaw/fbl** and select "Chapter 8." Click on "Video Questions" and view the video titled *Offer and Acceptance.* Then answer the following questions.

1 On the video, Vinny indicates that he can't sell his car to Oscar for four thousand dollars; then he says, "maybe

five . . . ." Discuss whether Vinny has made an offer or a counteroffer.

2 Oscar then says to Vinny, "Okay, I'll take it. But you gotta let me pay you four thousand now and the other thousand in two weeks." According to the chapter, do Oscar and Vinny have an agreement? Why or why not?

3 When Maria later says to Vinny, "I'll take it," has she accepted an offer? Why or why not?

ACCESSING THE INTERNET

For updated links to resources available on the Web, as well as a variety of other materials, visit this text's Web site at

www.cengage.com/blaw/fbl

You can read an overview of contract law and access contracts cases decided by the United States Supreme Court and federal appellate courts (as well as federal statutory law on contracts) at Cornell University's School of Law site:

topics.law.cornell.edu/wex/Contracts

To view the terms of a sample contract, go to the "forms" pages of the 'Lectric Law Library at

www.lectlaw.com/formb.htm

and select one of the types of contracts listed there to review.

FindLaw offers a collection of sample contracts from U.S. companies that you can explore at

contracts.corporate.findlaw.com/index.html

The *New Hampshire Consumer's Sourcebook* provides information on contract law from a consumer's perspective. You can access this book online at

doj.nh.gov/consumer/index.html

PRACTICAL INTERNET EXERCISES

Go to this text's Web site at **www.cengage.com/blaw/fbl**, select "Chapter 8," and click on "Practical Internet Exercises." There you will find the following Internet research exercises that you can perform to learn more about the topics covered in this chapter.

PRACTICAL INTERNET EXERCISE 8–1   LEGAL PERSPECTIVE—Contract Terms

PRACTICAL INTERNET EXERCISE 8–2   ETHICAL PERSPECTIVE—Offers and Advertisements

PRACTICAL INTERNET EXERCISE 8–3   MANAGEMENT PERSPECTIVE—Promissory Estoppel

BEFORE THE TEST

Go to this text's Web site at **www.cengage.com/blaw/fbl**, select "Chapter 8," and click on "Interactive Quizzes." You will find a number of interactive questions relating to this chapter.

4

Capacity and Legality

AFTER READING THIS CHAPTER, YOU SHOULD BE ABLE TO ANSWER THE FOLLOWING QUESTIONS:

1 What are some exceptions to the rule that a minor can disaffirm (avoid) any contract?

2 Does an intoxicated person have the capacity to enter into an enforceable contract?

3 Does the mental incompetence of one party necessarily make a contract void?

4 Under what circumstances will a covenant not to compete be enforceable? When will such covenants not be enforced?

5 What is an exculpatory clause? In what circumstances might exculpatory clauses be enforced? When will they not be enforced?

C ourts generally want contracts to be enforceable, and much of the law is devoted to aiding the enforceability of contracts. Nonetheless, not all people can make legally binding contracts at all times. Contracts entered into by persons lacking the capacity to do so may be voidable. Similarly, contracts calling for the performance of an illegal act are illegal and thus void—they are not contracts at all. In this chapter, we examine contractual capacity and some aspects of illegal bargains.

CONTRACTUAL CAPACITY

Contractual capacity is the legal ability to enter into a contractual relationship. Courts generally presume the existence of contractual capacity, but in some situations, capacity is lacking or may be questionable. A person who has been determined by a court to be mentally incompetent, for example, cannot form a legally binding contract with another party. In other situations, a party may have the capacity to enter into a valid contract but may also have the right to avoid liability under it. For example, minors—or *infants*, as they are commonly referred to in the law—usually are not legally bound by contracts. In this section, we look at the effect of youth, intoxication, and mental incompetence on contractual capacity.

Minors

Today, in virtually all states, the *age of majority* (when a person is no longer a minor) for contractual purposes is eighteen years—the so-called coming of age. (The age of majority may still be twenty-one for other purposes, however, such as the purchase and consumption of alcohol.) In addition, some states provide for the termination of minority on marriage. Minority status may also be terminated by a minor's **emancipation,** which occurs when a child's parent or legal guardian relinquishes the legal right to exercise control over the child. Normally, minors who leave home to support themselves are considered emancipated. Several jurisdictions permit minors to petition a court for emancipation themselves. For business purposes, a minor may petition a court to be treated as an adult.

The general rule is that a minor can enter into any contract an adult can, provided that the contract is not one prohibited by law for minors (for example, the sale of alcoholic beverages or tobacco). A contract entered into by a minor, however, is voidable at the option of that minor, subject to certain exceptions (to be discussed shortly). To exercise the option to avoid a contract, a minor need only manifest an intention not to be bound by it. The minor "avoids" the contract by disaffirming it.

Disaffirmance The legal avoidance, or setting aside, of a contractual obligation is referred to as **disaffirmance**. To disaffirm, a minor must express, through words or conduct, his or her intent not to be bound to the contract. The minor must disaffirm the entire contract, not merely a portion of it. For instance, a minor cannot decide to keep part of the goods purchased under a contract and return the remaining goods. When a minor disaffirms a contract, the minor can recover any property that she or he transferred to the adult as consideration for the contract, even if it is then in the possession of a third party.[1]

A contract can ordinarily be disaffirmed at any time during minority[2] or for a reasonable time after the minor comes of age. What constitutes a "reasonable" time may vary. Two months would probably be considered reasonable, but except in unusual circumstances, a court may not find it reasonable to wait a year or more after coming of age to disaffirm. If an individual fails to disaffirm an executed contract within a reasonable time after reaching the age of majority, a court will likely hold that the contract has been ratified (*ratification* will be discussed shortly).

Note that an adult who enters into a contract with a minor cannot avoid his or her contractual duties on the ground that the minor can do so. Unless the minor exercises the option to disaffirm the contract, the adult party normally is bound by it.

A Minor's Obligations on Disaffirmance Although all states' laws permit minors to disaffirm contracts (with certain exceptions), including executed contracts, state laws differ on the extent of a minor's obligations on disaffirmance.

Majority Rule. Courts in a majority of states hold that the minor need only return the goods (or other consideration) subject to the contract, provided the goods are in the minor's possession or control. **■EXAMPLE 9.1** Jim Garrison, a seventeen-year-old, purchases a computer from Radio Shack. While transporting the computer to his home, Garrison, through no fault of his own, is involved in a car accident. As a result of the accident, the plastic casing of the computer is broken. The next day, he returns the computer to Radio Shack and disaffirms the contract. Under the majority view,

this return fulfills Garrison's duty even though the computer is now damaged. Garrison is entitled to receive a refund of the purchase price (if paid in cash) or to be relieved of any further obligations under an agreement to purchase the computer on credit. **■**

Minority Rule. A growing number of states, either by statute or by court decision, place an additional duty on the minor — the duty to restore the adult party to the position she or he held before the contract was made. **■EXAMPLE 9.2** Sixteen-year-old Joseph Dodson bought a pickup truck for $4,900 from a used-car dealer. Although the truck developed mechanical problems nine months later, Dodson continued to drive it until the engine blew up and it stopped running. Then Dodson disaffirmed the contract and attempted to return the truck to the dealer for a refund of the full purchase price. The dealer refused to accept the pickup or refund the money. Dodson filed suit. Ultimately, the Tennessee Supreme Court allowed Dodson to disaffirm the contract but required him to compensate the seller for the depreciated value — not the purchase price — of the pickup.[3] **■** This example illustrates the trend among today's courts to hold a minor responsible for damage, ordinary wear and tear, and depreciation of goods that the minor used prior to disaffirmance.

Exceptions to the Minor's Right to Disaffirm State courts and legislatures have carved out several exceptions to the minor's right to disaffirm. Some contracts cannot be avoided simply as a matter of law, on the ground of public policy. For example, marriage contracts and contracts to enlist in the armed services fall into this category. Other contracts may not be disaffirmed for different reasons, including those discussed here.

Misrepresentation of Age. Suppose that a minor tells a seller she is twenty-one years old when she is really seventeen. Ordinarily, the minor can disaffirm the contract even though she has misrepresented her age. Moreover, in some jurisdictions the minor is not liable for the tort of fraudulent misrepresentation, the rationale being that such a tort judgment might indirectly force the minor to perform the contract.

In many jurisdictions, however, a minor who has misrepresented his or her age can be bound by a contract under certain circumstances. First, several states have enacted statutes for precisely this purpose. In these states, misrepresentation of age is enough to prohibit disaffirmance. Other statutes prohibit disaffirmance by a minor who has engaged in business

---

1. The Uniform Commercial Code (UCC), in Section 2–403(1), allows an exception if the third party is a "good faith purchaser for value." See Chapter 15.

2. In some states, however, a minor who enters into a contract for the sale of land cannot disaffirm the contract until she or he reaches the age of majority.

3. *Dodson v. Shrader,* 824 S.W.2d 545 (Tenn. 1992). See also *Restatement (Third) of Restitution,* Sections 16 and 33 (2004).

as an adult. Second, some courts refuse to allow minors to disaffirm executed (fully performed) contracts unless they can return the consideration received. The combination of the minors' misrepresentations and their unjust enrichment has persuaded these courts to *estop* (prevent) the minors from asserting contractual incapacity.

Contracts for Necessaries. A minor who enters into a contract for necessaries may disaffirm the contract but remains liable for the reasonable value of the goods used. **Necessaries** are basic needs, such as food, clothing, shelter, and medical services, at a level of value required to maintain the minor's standard of living or financial and social status. Thus, what will be considered a necessary for one person may be a luxury for another. Additionally, what is considered a necessary depends on whether the minor is under the care or control of his or her parents, who are required by law to provide necessaries for the minor. If a minor's parents provide the minor with shelter, for example, then a contract to lease shelter (such as an apartment) normally will not be regarded as a contract for necessaries.

Generally, then, to qualify as a contract for necessaries, (1) the item contracted for must be necessary to the minor's existence, (2) the value of the necessary item may be up to a level required to maintain the minor's standard of living or financial and social status, and (3) the minor must not be under the care of a parent or guardian who is required to supply this item. Unless these three criteria are met, the minor can normally disaffirm the contract *without* being liable for the reasonable value of the goods used.

Insurance and Loans. Traditionally, insurance has not been viewed as a necessary, so minors can ordinarily disaffirm their insurance contracts and recover all premiums paid. Nevertheless, some jurisdictions prohibit disaffirming insurance contracts—for example, when minors contract for life insurance on their own lives. Financial loans are seldom considered to be necessaries, even if the minor spends the borrowed funds on necessaries. If, however, a lender makes a loan to a minor for the express purpose of enabling the minor to purchase necessaries, and the lender personally makes sure the funds are so spent, the minor normally is obligated to repay the loan.

Ratification In contract law, **ratification** is the act of accepting and giving legal force to an obligation that previously was not enforceable. A minor who has reached the age of majority can ratify a contract expressly or impliedly. *Express* ratification occurs when the individual, on reaching the age of majority, states orally or in writing that she or he intends to be bound by the contract. *Implied* ratification

takes place when the minor, on reaching the age of majority, indicates an intent to abide by the contract.

■EXAMPLE 9.3 Lin enters a contract to sell her laptop to Arturo, a minor. If Arturo does not disaffirm the contract and, on reaching the age of majority, writes a letter to Lin stating that he still agrees to buy the laptop, he has expressly ratified the contract. If, instead, Arturo takes possession of the laptop as a minor and continues to use it well after reaching the age of majority, he has impliedly ratified the contract. ■

If a minor fails to disaffirm a contract within a reasonable time after reaching the age of majority, then a court must determine whether the conduct constitutes implied ratification or disaffirmance. Generally, courts presume that a contract that is *executed* (fully performed by both sides) was ratified. A contract that is still *executory* (not yet performed by both parties) is normally considered to be disaffirmed.

Parents' Liability As a general rule, parents are not liable for the contracts made by minor children acting on their own, except contracts for necessaries, which the parents are legally required to provide. This is why businesses ordinarily require parents to cosign any contract made with a minor. The parents then become personally obligated to perform the conditions of the contract, even if their child avoids liability.

Normally, minors are personally liable for their own torts. The parents of the minor can *also* be held liable in certain situations. In some states, parents may be liable if they failed to exercise proper parental control when they knew or should have known that this lack of control posed an unreasonable risk of harm to others. **■EXAMPLE 9.4** An eleven-year-old's parents allow him to drive a car on public roads. If the child drives negligently and causes someone else to be injured, the parents may be held liable for the minor's tort (negligence). ■ Other states have enacted statutes that impose liability on parents for certain kinds of tortious acts committed by their children, such as those that are willful and malicious.

Intoxicated Persons

Contractual capacity also becomes an issue when a party to a contract was intoxicated at the time the contract was made. Intoxication is a condition in which a person's normal capacity to act or think is inhibited by alcohol or some other drug. If the person was sufficiently intoxicated to lack mental capacity, the contract may be voidable even if the intoxication was purely voluntary. For the contract to be voidable, however, the person must prove that the intoxication impaired her or his reason and judgment so severely that she or he did not comprehend the legal consequences of entering into the contract. In addition, to avoid the contract in the majority of states, the person claiming intoxication must be able to return all consideration received.

If, despite intoxication, the person understood the legal consequences of the agreement, the contract is enforceable. The fact that the terms of the contract are foolish or obviously favor the other party does not make the contract voidable (unless the other party fraudulently induced the person to become intoxicated). As a practical matter, courts rarely permit contracts to be avoided on the ground of intoxication, because it is difficult to determine whether a party was sufficiently intoxicated to avoid legal duties. Rather than inquire into the intoxicated person's mental state, many courts instead focus on objective indications of capacity to determine whether the contract is voidable owing to intoxication.[4]

Mentally Incompetent Persons

Contracts made by mentally incompetent persons can be void, voidable, or valid. We look here at the circumstances that determine when these classifications apply.

When the Contract Will Be Void   If a court has previously determined that a person is mentally incompetent and has appointed a guardian to represent the person, any contract made by that mentally incompetent person is *void*—no contract exists. Only the guardian can enter into a binding contract on behalf of the mentally incompetent person.

When the Contract Will Be Voidable   If a court has not previously judged a person to be mentally incompetent but in fact the person was incompetent at the time, the contract may be *voidable*. A contract is voidable if the person did not know he or she was entering into the contract or lacked the mental capacity to comprehend its nature, purpose, and consequences. In such situations, the contract is voidable at the option of the mentally incompetent person but not the other party. The contract may then be disaffirmed or ratified (if the person regains mental competence). Like intoxicated persons, mentally incompetent persons must return any consideration and pay for the reasonable value of any necessaries they receive.

■**EXAMPLE 9.5** Milo, a mentally incompetent man who had not been previously declared incompetent by a judge, agrees to sell twenty lots in a prime residential neighborhood to Anastof. At the time of entering the contract, Milo is confused over which lots he is selling and how much they are worth. As a result, he contracts to sell the properties for substantially less than their market value. If the court finds that Milo was unable

to understand the nature and consequences of the contract, the contract is voidable. Milo can avoid the sale, provided that he returns any consideration he received. ■

When the Contract Will Be Valid   A contract entered into by a mentally incompetent person (whom a court has not previously declared incompetent) may also be *valid* if the person had capacity *at the time the contract was formed*. For instance, a person may be able to understand the nature and effect of entering into a certain contract yet simultaneously lack capacity to engage in other activities. In such cases, the contract ordinarily will be valid because the person is not legally mentally incompetent for contractual purposes.[5] Similarly, an otherwise mentally incompetent person may have a *lucid interval*—a temporary restoration of sufficient intelligence, judgment, and will to enter into contracts—during which she or he will be considered to have full legal capacity.

LEGALITY

To this point, we have discussed three of the requirements for a valid contract to exist—agreement, consideration, and contractual capacity. Now we examine the fourth—legality. For a contract to be valid and enforceable, it must be formed for a legal purpose. A contract to do something that is prohibited by federal or state statutory law is illegal and, as such, void from the outset and thus unenforceable. Additionally, a contract to commit a tortious act or to commit an action that is contrary to public policy is illegal and unenforceable.

Contracts Contrary to Statute

Statutes often set forth rules specifying which terms and clauses may be included in contracts and which are prohibited. We examine here several ways in which contracts may be contrary to a statute and thus illegal.

Contracts to Commit a Crime   Any contract to commit a crime is a contract in violation of a statute. Thus, a contract to sell an illegal drug (the sale of which is prohibited by statute) is not enforceable. If the object or performance of the contract is rendered illegal by statute *after* the contract has been entered into, the contract is considered to be discharged by law. (See the discussion of *impossibility of performance* in Chapter 11.)

---

4. See, for example, the court's decision in *Lucy v. Zehmer*, presented as Case 8.1 in Chapter 8 on pages 168 and 169.

5. Modern courts no longer require a person to be completely irrational to disaffirm contracts on the basis of mental incompetence. A contract may be voidable if, by reason of a mental illness or defect, an individual was unable to act reasonably with respect to the transaction and the other party had reason to know of the condition.

Usury Virtually every state has a statute that sets the maximum rate of interest that can be charged for different types of transactions, including ordinary loans. A lender who makes a loan at an interest rate above the lawful maximum commits **usury.** The maximum rate of interest varies from state to state, as do the consequences for lenders who make usurious loans. Some states allow the lender to recover only the principal of a loan along with interest up to the legal maximum. In effect, the lender is denied recovery of the excess interest. In other states, the lender can recover the principal amount of the loan but no interest.

Although usury statutes place a ceiling on allowable rates of interest, exceptions are made to facilitate business transactions. For example, many states exempt corporate loans from the usury laws. In addition, almost all states have special statutes allowing much higher interest rates on small loans to help those borrowers who need funds and could not otherwise obtain loans.

Gambling All states have statutes that regulate gambling—defined as any scheme that involves the distribution of property by chance among persons who have paid valuable consideration for the opportunity (chance) to receive the property. Gambling is the creation of risk for the purpose of assuming it. Traditionally, the states have deemed gambling contracts illegal and thus void.

In several states, however, including Louisiana, Michigan, Nevada, and New Jersey, casino gambling is legal. In other states, certain forms of gambling are legal. California, for example, has not defined draw poker as a crime, although criminal statutes prohibit numerous other types of gambling games. A number of states allow gambling on horse races, and the majority of states have legalized state-operated lotteries, as well as lotteries (such as bingo) conducted for charitable purposes. Many states also allow gambling on Indian reservations.

Sometimes, it is difficult to distinguish a gambling contract from the risk sharing inherent in almost all contracts. **■EXAMPLE 9.6** In one case, five co-workers each received some free lottery tickets from a customer and agreed to split the winnings if one of the tickets turned out to be the winner. At first glance, this may seem entirely legal. The court, however, noted that the oral contract in this case "was an exchange of promises to share winnings from the parties' individually owned lottery tickets upon the happening of the uncertain event" that one of the tickets would win. Consequently, concluded the court, the agreement at issue was "founded on a gambling consideration" and therefore was void.[6] **■**

Online Gambling A significant issue today is how gambling laws can be applied in the Internet context. Because state laws pertaining to gambling differ, online gambling raises a number of unique issues. For example, in those states that do not allow casino gambling or offtrack betting, what can a state government do if residents of the state place bets online? Also, where does the actual act of gambling occur? Suppose that a resident of New York places bets via the Internet at a gambling site located in Antigua. Is the actual act of "gambling" taking place in New York or in Antigua? According to a New York court in one case, "if the person engaged in gambling is located in New York, then New York is the location where the gambling occurred."[7] Courts of other states may take a different view, however.

Another issue that is being debated is whether entering contracts that involve gambling on sports teams that do not really exist—fantasy sports—is a form of gambling. For a discussion of this issue, see this chapter's *Adapting the Law to the Online Environment* feature on the following page.

Sabbath (Sunday) Laws Statutes referred to as Sabbath (Sunday) laws prohibit the formation or performance of certain contracts on a Sunday. These laws, which date back to colonial times, are often called **blue laws.** Blue laws get their name from the blue paper on which New Haven, Connecticut, printed its town ordinance in 1781 that prohibited work and required businesses to close on Sunday. According to a few state and local laws, all contracts entered into on a Sunday are illegal. Laws in other states or municipalities prohibit only the sale of certain types of merchandise, such as alcoholic beverages, on a Sunday.

In most states with such statutes, contracts that were entered into on a Sunday can be ratified during a weekday. Also, if a contract that was entered into on a Sunday has been fully performed (executed), normally it cannot be rescinded (canceled). Exceptions to Sunday laws permit contracts for necessities (such as food) and works of charity. Many states do not enforce Sunday laws, and some state courts have held these laws to be unconstitutional because they interfere with the freedom of religion. *Not inforced*

Mew Jersey does enforced

Licensing Statutes All states require that members of certain professions obtain licenses allowing them to practice. Physicians, lawyers, real estate brokers, architects, electricians, and stockbrokers are but a few of the people who must be licensed. Some licenses are obtained only after extensive schooling and examinations, which indicate to the public that a special skill has been acquired. Others require only that the particular person be of good moral character and pay a fee.

---

6. *Dickerson v. Deno*, 770 So.2d 63 (Ala. 2000).

7. *United States v. Cohen*, 260 F.3d 68 (2d Cir. 2001).

Take a loan for gambling in nevada you must pay back loan. Same thing in Iowa gambling is illegal do not have to pay.

ADAPTING THE LAW TO THE ONLINE ENVIRONMENT   Are Online Fantasy Sports Just Another Form of Real-Life Gambling?

As many as 20 million adults in the United States play some form of fantasy sports via the Internet. A fantasy sport is a game in which participants, often called owners, build teams composed of real-life players from different real-life teams. Each fantasy team competes against the fantasy teams belonging to other owners. At the end of each week, the statistical performances of all the real-life players are translated into points, and the points of all the players on an owner's fantasy team are totaled. Although a wide variety of fantasy games are available, most participants play fantasy football. On many fantasy sports sites, participants pay a fee in order to play and use the site's facilities, such as statistical tracking and message boards. At the end of the season, prizes ranging from T-shirts to flat-screen televisions are awarded to the winners.

In other instances, the participants in fantasy sports gamble directly on the outcome. In a fantasy football league, for example, each participant-owner adds a given amount to the pot and then "drafts" his or her fantasy team from actual National Football League players. At the end of the football season, each owner's points are totaled, and the owner with the most points wins the pot.

Congress Weighs In

As online gambling has expanded, Congress has attempted to regulate it. In late 2006, a federal law went into effect that makes it illegal for credit-card companies and banks to engage in transactions with Internet gambling companies.[a] Although the law does not prohibit individuals from placing online bets, in effect it makes it almost impossible for them to do so by preventing them from obtaining financing for online gambling. At first glance, the legislation appears comprehensive, but it specifically exempts Internet wagers on horse racing, state lotteries, and fantasy sports. Hence, one could argue that Congress has determined that fantasy sports do not constitute a prohibited Internet gambling activity.

Testing the Gambling Aspect in Court

Thus far, the courts have had the opportunity to rule only on whether the pay-to-play fantasy sports sites that charge an entrance fee and offer prizes to the winners are running gambling operations. Charles Humphrey brought a lawsuit against Viacom, ESPN, *The Sporting News*, and other hosts of such fantasy sports sites under a New Jersey statute that allows the recovery of gambling losses. Humphrey claimed that the fantasy sports leagues were games of chance, not games of skill, because events beyond the participants' control could determine the outcome—for example, a star quarterback might be injured. He also pointed out that in the offline world, federal law prohibits any games of chance, such as sweepstakes or drawings, that require entrants to submit consideration in order to play. *Consideration* has been defined as the purchase of a product or the payment of money. For these reasons, he argued, the entrance fees constituted gambling losses that could be recovered.

The federal district court that heard the case ruled against Humphrey, mostly on procedural grounds, but the court did conclude that as a matter of law the entrance fees did not constitute "bets" or "wagers" because the fees are paid unconditionally, the prizes offered are for a fixed amount and certain to be awarded, and the defendants do not compete for the prizes.[b] The court also observed that if a combination of entrance fees and prizes constituted gambling, a host of contests ranging from golf tournaments to track meets to spelling bees and beauty contests would be gambling operations—a conclusion that the court deemed "patently absurd."[c] Note, however, that the case involved only pay-to-play sites. The court did not have to address the question of whether fantasy sports sites that enable participants to contribute to a pot in the hopes of winning it at the end of the season constitute gambling sites.

FOR CRITICAL ANALYSIS *What arguments can be used to support the idea that playing fantasy sports requires skill?*

---

a. Security and Accountability for Every Port Act, Public L. No. 109-347, Sections 5361–5367, 120 Stat. 1884 (2006). (A version of the Unlawful Internet Gambling Enforcement Act of 2006 was incorporated into this statute as Title VIII.)

b. *Humphrey v. Viacom, Inc.,* 2007 WL1797648 (D.N.J. 2007).
c. In reaching this conclusion, the federal district court cited portions of an Arizona Supreme Court ruling, *State v. American Holiday Association, Inc.,* 151 Ariz. 312, 727 P.2d 807 (1986).

Unlicensed can sue can sue for no performance or payment.

1) Protect the Public
Kaise Money Rg
2) Kaise Money Rg

The Purpose of Licensing Statutes. Generally, business licenses provide a means of regulating and taxing certain businesses and protecting the public against actions that could threaten the general welfare. For example, in nearly all states, a stockbroker must be licensed and must file a bond with the state to protect the public from fraudulent transactions in stocks. Similarly, a plumber must be licensed and bonded to protect the public against incompetent plumbers and to protect the public health. Only persons or businesses possessing the qualifications and complying with the conditions required by statute are entitled to licenses. For instance, the owner of a bar can be required to sell food as a condition of obtaining a license to serve liquor.

Contracts with Unlicensed Practitioners. A contract with an unlicensed practitioner may still be enforceable, depending on the nature of the licensing statute. Some states expressly provide that the lack of a license in certain occupations bars the enforcement of work-related contracts. If the statute does not expressly state this, one must look to the underlying purpose of the licensing requirements for a particular occupation. If the purpose is to protect the public from unauthorized practitioners, a contract involving an unlicensed individual is illegal and unenforceable. If, however, the underlying purpose of the statute is to raise government revenues, a contract with an unlicensed practitioner is enforceable—although the unlicensed person is usually fined.

Contracts Contrary to Public Policy

Although contracts involve private parties, some are not enforceable because of the negative impact they would have on society. These contracts are said to be *contrary to public policy.* Examples include a contract to commit an immoral act, such as selling a child, and a contract that prohibits marriage. **■EXAMPLE 9.7** Everett offers a young man $10,000 if he refrains from marrying Everett's daughter. If the young man accepts, no contract is formed (the contract is void) because it is contrary to public policy. Thus, if the man marries Everett's daughter, Everett cannot sue him for breach of contract. ■ Business contracts that may be contrary to public policy include contracts in restraint of trade and unconscionable contracts or clauses.

Contracts in Restraint of Trade Contracts in restraint of trade (anticompetitive agreements) usually adversely affect the public policy that favors competition in the economy. Typically, such contracts also violate one or more federal or state statutes.[8] An exception is recognized when the restraint

is reasonable and is part of, or supplemental to, a contract for the sale of a business or an **employment contract** (a contract stating the terms and conditions of employment). Many such exceptions involve a type of restraint called a **covenant not to compete,** or a restrictive covenant.

Covenants Not to Compete and the Sale of an Ongoing Business. Covenants (promises) not to compete are often contained as ancillary (secondary, or subordinate) clauses in contracts concerning the sale of an ongoing business. A covenant not to compete is created when a seller agrees not to open a new store in a certain geographic area surrounding the old store. Such agreements enable the seller to sell, and the purchaser to buy, the goodwill and reputation of an ongoing business. If, for example, a well-known merchant sells his or her store and opens a competing business a block away, many of the merchant's customers will likely do business at the new store. This renders less valuable the good name and reputation sold to the other merchant for a price. If a covenant not to compete is not ancillary to a sales agreement, however, it will be void because it unreasonably restrains trade and is contrary to public policy.

Covenants Not to Compete in Employment Contracts. Agreements not to compete, or *noncompete agreements,* can also be contained in employment contracts. People in middle- or upper-level management positions commonly agree not to work for competitors or not to start competing businesses for a specified period of time after termination of employment. Such agreements are legal in most states so long as the specified period of time (of restraint) is not excessive in duration and the geographic restriction is reasonable. What constitutes a reasonable time period may be shorter in the online environment than in conventional employment contracts because the restrictions apply worldwide. (For a further discussion of this issue, see this chapter's *Management Perspective* feature on page 193.)

To be reasonable, a restriction on competition must protect a legitimate business interest and must not be any greater than necessary to protect that interest.[9] In the following case, the court had to decide whether it was reasonable for an employer's noncompete agreement to restrict a former employee from competing "in any area of business" in which the employer was engaged.

Time and distance must be reasonable.

---

8. Federal statutes prohibiting anticompetitive agreements include the Sherman Antitrust Act, the Clayton Act, and the Federal Trade Commission Act.

9. See, for example, *Gould & Lamb, LLC v. D'Alusio,* 949 So.2d 1212 (Fla.App. 2007). See also *Moore v. Midwest Distribution, Inc.,* 76 Ark.App. 397, 65 S.W.3d 490 (2002).

CASE 9.1   Stultz v. Safety and Compliance Management, Inc.

Court of Appeals of Georgia, 285 Ga.App. 799, 648 S.E.2d 129 (2007).

FACTS Safety and Compliance Management, Inc. (S&C), in Rossville, Georgia, provides alcohol- and drug-testing services in multiple states. In February 2002, S&C hired Angela Burgess. Her job duties included providing customer service, ensuring that specimens were properly retrieved from clients and transported to the testing lab, contacting clients, and managing the office. Burgess signed a covenant not to compete "in any area of business conducted by Safety and Compliance Management . . . for a two-year period . . . beginning at the termination of employment." In May 2004, Burgess quit her job to work at Rossville Medical Center (RMC) as a medical assistant. RMC provides medical services, including occupational medicine, medical physicals, and workers' compensation injury treatment. RMC also offers alcohol- and drug-testing services. Burgess's duties included setting patient appointments, taking patient medical histories, checking vital signs, performing urinalysis testing, administering injections, conducting alcohol-breath tests, and collecting specimens for drug testing. S&C filed a suit in a Georgia state court against Burgess and others (including a defendant named Stultz), alleging, among other things, that she had violated the noncompete agreement. The court issued a summary judgment in S&C's favor. Burgess appealed to a state intermediate appellate court.

ISSUE Was a two-year noncompete clause that prevented a former employee from working in "any area of business" conducted by the employer a reasonable restraint?

DECISION No. The appellate court reversed the judgment of the lower court, finding that the noncompete clause was unreasonable as to the scope of the activity prohibited and was therefore unenforceable.

REASON The court pointed out that noncompete clauses in employment contracts cannot impose an unreasonable restraint of trade. "A three-element test of duration, territorial coverage, and scope of activity has evolved as a helpful tool in examining the reasonableness of the particular factual setting to which it is applied." The noncompete clause in Angela Burgess's employment contract stated that she would "not compete in any area of business conducted by [her employer]." This agreement, the court reasoned, was intended to prevent any type of competing activity whatsoever. Therefore, the covenant not to compete was "overly broad and indefinite."

 FOR CRITICAL ANALYSIS—Global Consideration *Should an employer be permitted to restrict a former employee from engaging in a competing business on a global level? Why or why not?*

▪

Enforcement Problems. The laws governing the enforceability of covenants not to compete vary significantly from state to state. In some states, such as Texas, such a covenant will not be enforced unless the employee has received some benefit in return for signing the noncompete agreement. This is true even if the covenant is reasonable as to time and area. If the employee receives no benefit, the covenant will be deemed void. California prohibits the enforcement of covenants not to compete altogether.

Occasionally, depending on the jurisdiction, courts will *reform* covenants not to compete. If a covenant is found to be unreasonable in time or geographic area, the court may convert the terms into reasonable ones and then enforce the reformed covenant. This presents a problem, however, in that the judge has implicitly become a party to the contract. Consequently, courts usually resort to contract **reformation** only when necessary to prevent undue burdens or hardships.

Unconscionable Contracts or Clauses Ordinarily, a court does not look at the fairness or equity of a contract; for example, a court normally will not inquire into the adequacy of consideration. Persons are assumed to be reasonably intelligent, and the court does not come to their aid just because they have made unwise or foolish bargains. In certain circumstances, however, bargains are so oppressive that the courts relieve innocent parties of part or all of their duties. Such a bargain is called an **unconscionable contract** (or **unconscionable clause**). Both the Uniform Commercial Code (UCC) and the Uniform Consumer Credit Code (UCCC) embody the unconscionability concept—the former with regard to the sale of goods and the latter with regard to consumer loans and the waiver of rights.[10] A contract can be unconscionable on either procedural or substantive grounds, as discussed in the follow-

---

10. See, for example, UCC 2–302 and 2–719, and UCCC 5–108 and 1–107.

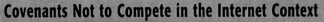

Covenants Not to Compete in the Internet Context

Management Faces a Legal Issue

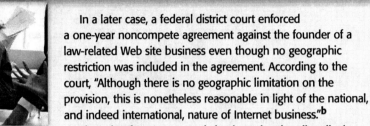

For some companies, particularly those in high-tech industries, trade secrets are their most valuable assets. Often, to prevent departing employees from disclosing trade secrets to competing employers, a company asks its key employees to sign *covenants not to compete,* in which they agree not to set up a competing business or work for a competitor in a specified geographic area for a certain period of time. Generally, the time and geographic restrictions must be reasonable. A serious issue facing management today is whether time and space restrictions that have been deemed reasonable in the past will be considered reasonable in today's changing legal landscape, which includes the Internet environment.

What the Courts Say

There is little case law to guide management on this issue. One case involved Mark Schlack, who worked as a Web site manager for EarthWeb, Inc., in New York. Schlack signed a covenant stating that, on termination of his employment, he would not work for any competing company for one year. When he resigned and accepted an offer from a company in Massachusetts to design a Web site, EarthWeb sued to enforce the covenant not to compete. The court refused to enforce the covenant, in part, because there was no evidence that Schlack had misappropriated any of EarthWeb's trade secrets or clients. The court also stated that because the Internet lacks physical borders, a covenant prohibiting an employee from working for a competitor anywhere in the world for one year is excessive in duration.[a]

a. *EarthWeb, Inc. v. Schlack,* 71 F.Supp.2d 299 (S.D.N.Y. 1999).

In a later case, a federal district court enforced a one-year noncompete agreement against the founder of a law-related Web site business even though no geographic restriction was included in the agreement. According to the court, "Although there is no geographic limitation on the provision, this is nonetheless reasonable in light of the national, and indeed international, nature of Internet business."[b]

The sale of an Internet-only business involves literally the full worldwide scope of the Internet itself. In a recent case, a company selling vitamins over the Internet was sold for more than $2 million. The purchase agreement contained a noncompete clause that prohibited the seller from engaging in the sale of nutritional and health products via the Internet for four years. Despite the noncompete agreement, after the sale, the seller created at least two Internet sites from which he sold health products and vitamins. When the buyer sued to enforce the noncompete agreement, the court held for the buyer and enjoined (prevented) the seller from violating the agreement.[c] The court pointed out that the seller could still engage in his former business by using non-Internet markets. The seller also remained free to sell other types of products on the Internet.

Implications for Managers

Management in high-tech companies should avoid overreaching in terms of time and geographic restrictions in noncompete agreements. Additionally, when considering whether time and place restrictions are reasonable, the courts tend to balance time restrictions against other factors, such as geographic restrictions. Because for Web-based work the geographic restriction can be worldwide, the time restriction should be narrowed considerably to compensate for the extensive geographic restriction.

b. *West Publishing Corp. v. Stanley,* 2004 WL 73590 (D.N.D. 2004).
c. *MyVitaNet.com v. Kowalski,* __ F.Supp.2d __ , 2008 WL 203008 (S.D. Ohio 2008).

ing subsections and illustrated graphically in Exhibit 9–1 on the next page.

Procedural Unconscionability. Procedural unconscionability has to do with how a term becomes part of a contract and relates to factors bearing on a party's lack of knowledge or understanding of the contract terms because of inconspicuous print, unintelligible language ("legalese"), lack of opportunity to read the contract, lack of opportunity

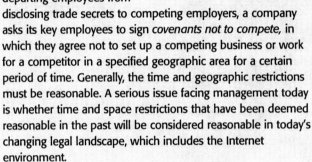
very fine print / hidden in the contract.

to ask questions about the contract's meaning, and other factors. Procedural unconscionability sometimes relates to purported lack of voluntariness because of a disparity in bargaining power between the two parties. Contracts entered into because of one party's vastly superior bargaining power may be deemed unconscionable. Such contracts are often referred to as **adhesion contracts.** An adhesion contract is written exclusively by one party (the dominant party, usually the seller or creditor) and presented to the other (the

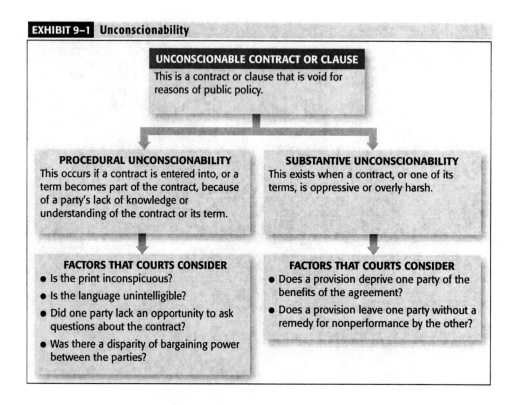

EXHIBIT 9–1 Unconscionability

UNCONSCIONABLE CONTRACT OR CLAUSE
This is a contract or clause that is void for reasons of public policy.

PROCEDURAL UNCONSCIONABILITY
This occurs if a contract is entered into, or a term becomes part of the contract, because of a party's lack of knowledge or understanding of the contract or its term.

SUBSTANTIVE UNCONSCIONABILITY
This exists when a contract, or one of its terms, is oppressive or overly harsh.

FACTORS THAT COURTS CONSIDER
- Is the print inconspicuous?
- Is the language unintelligible?
- Did one party lack an opportunity to ask questions about the contract?
- Was there a disparity of bargaining power between the parties?

FACTORS THAT COURTS CONSIDER
- Does a provision deprive one party of the benefits of the agreement?
- Does a provision leave one party without a remedy for nonperformance by the other?

adhering party, usually the buyer or borrower) on a take-it-or-leave-it basis. In other words, the adhering party has no opportunity to negotiate the terms of the contract.

Substantive Unconscionability. *Substantive* unconscionability characterizes those contracts, or portions of contracts, that are oppressive or overly harsh. Courts generally focus on provisions that deprive one party of the benefits of the agreement or leave that party without remedy for nonperformance by the other. ▪EXAMPLE 9.8 A person with little income and only a fourth-grade education agrees to purchase a refrigerator for $4,000 and signs a two-year installment contract. The same type of refrigerator usually sells for $900 on the market. Some courts have held that this type of contract is unconscionable because the contract terms are so oppressive as to "shock the conscience" of the court.[11] ▪

Substantive unconscionability can arise in a wide variety of business contexts. For example, a contract clause that gives the business entity free access to the courts but requires the other party to arbitrate any dispute with the firm may be unconscionable.[12] Similarly, an arbitration clause in a credit-

card agreement that prevents credit cardholders from obtaining relief for abusive debt-collection practices under consumer law may be unconscionable.[13] Contracts drafted by insurance companies and cell phone providers have been struck down as substantively unconscionable when they included provisions that were overly harsh or one sided.[14]

Exculpatory Clauses Closely related to the concept of unconscionability are **exculpatory clauses**—clauses that release a party from liability in the event of monetary or physical injury *no matter who is at fault.* Indeed, courts sometimes refuse to enforce such clauses on the ground that they are unconscionable. ▪EXAMPLE 9.9 An employer requires its employees to sign a contract containing a provision that shields the employer from liability for any injuries to those employees. In that situation, a court would usually hold the exculpatory clause to be contrary to public policy. ▪ Exculpatory clauses found in rental agreements for commercial property are fre-

---

11. See, for example, *Jones v. Star Credit Corp.*, 59 Misc.2d 189, 298 N.Y.S.2d 264 (1969). This case will be presented in Chapter 14 as Case 14.3.
12. See, for example, *Wisconsin Auto Loans, Inc. v. Jones*, 290 Wis.2d 514, 714 N.W.2d 155 (2006).

13. See, for example, *Coady v. Cross County Bank*, 2007 WI App 26, 299 Wis.2d 420, 729 N.W.2d 732 (2007).
14. See, for example, *Gatton v. T-Mobile USA, Inc.*, 152 Cal.App.4th 571, 61 Cal.Rptr.3d 344 (2007); *Kinkel v. Cingular Wireless, LLC*, 223 Ill.2d 1, 857 N.E.2d 250, 306 Ill.Dec. 157 (2006); and *Aul v. Golden Rule Insurance Co.*, 2007 WI App 165, 737 N.W.2d 24 (2007).

quently held to be contrary to public policy, and such clauses are almost always unenforceable in residential property leases.

Although courts view exculpatory clauses with disfavor, they do enforce such clauses when they do not contravene public policy, are not ambiguous, and do not claim to protect parties from liability for intentional misconduct. Businesses such as health clubs, racetracks, amusement parks, skiing facilities, horse-rental operations, golf-cart concessions, and skydiving organizations frequently use exculpatory clauses to limit their liability for patrons' injuries. Because these services are not essential, the firms offering them are sometimes considered to have no relative advantage in bargaining strength, and anyone contracting for their services is considered to do so voluntarily.

Sometimes, a company includes an indemnification provision in its contracts with *independent contractors* (see Chapter 22). Such a provision, or clause, removes any responsibility on the company's part for accidents that happen to the independent contractor while working for the company. When is such a provision against public policy? This was the main question in the following case.

CASE 9.2   Speedway SuperAmerica, LLC v. Erwin

Court of Appeals of Kentucky, 250 S.W.3d 339 (2008).

FACTS Speedway SuperAmerica, LLC, hired Sebert Erwin to provide "General Contracting" for five years, but reserved the right to end the contract at any time. The contract contained an *indemnification* clause. Under that clause, Erwin promised to "hold harmless" Speedway for anything that happened to him while working for the company. One day, Erwin was told to report to a Speedway gas station in another city and help remove a walk-in freezer. When he was helping load it on a truck, he fell and was injured. Erwin sued Speedway for damages resulting from the injury he had suffered. Speedway counterclaimed, seeking enforcement of the contract's indemnification clause. Erwin moved to dismiss the counterclaim on the ground that the indemnification clause was invalid because it was against public policy. The trial court held for Erwin. Speedway appealed.

ISSUE Was the indemnification (exculpatory) clause that Erwin signed agreeing not to hold Speedway liable for any injuries he might receive while working for it contrary to public policy?

DECISION Yes. The Kentucky appellate court affirmed the trial court's ruling, holding that the indemnification clause was contrary to public policy and could not be enforced.

REASON The court noted, "The predominant fact of this case is the disparity in bargaining power existing between these two parties." The contract was one sided because it was between a chain of convenience stores and a single worker. While such contracts are not always against public policy, they are when there is no bargaining between parties of similar strength. Here, the situation involved one worker with an eighth-grade education contracting with a large company; the bargaining powers were clearly unequal. Erwin was called an independent contractor despite not having control over his work. The contract stated that he agreed to defend the owner and hold it harmless in the event of any negligence. As an independent contractor (rather than an employee), Erwin had no right to workers' compensation or other benefits that normally would be due to an employee. The court reasoned that the contract was the equivalent of an exculpatory clause, releasing the employer from any liability regardless of fault.

WHAT IF THE FACTS WERE DIFFERENT? *Suppose that Erwin worked for another company as a mover and his employer had sent him to help Speedway move the freezer. Suppose further that the indemnification clause was in a contract signed between Speedway and Erwin's employer. Would that clause be valid? Explain your answer.*

THE EFFECT OF ILLEGALITY

In general, an illegal contract is void: the contract is deemed never to have existed, and the courts will not aid either party. In most illegal contracts, both parties are considered to be equally at fault—*in pari delicto*. If the contract is executory (not yet fulfilled), neither party can enforce it. If it has been executed, there can be neither contractual nor quasi-contractual recovery.

That one wrongdoer in an illegal contract is unjustly enriched at the expense of the other is of no concern to the law—except under certain circumstances (to be discussed shortly). The major justification for this hands-off attitude is that it is improper to place the machinery of justice at the disposal of a plaintiff who has broken the law by entering into an illegal bargain. Another justification is the hoped-for deterrent effect of this general rule. A plaintiff who suffers a loss because of an illegal bargain will presumably be deterred from entering into similar illegal bargains in the future.

There are exceptions to the general rule that neither party to an illegal bargain can sue for breach and neither party can recover for performance rendered. We look at these exceptions here.

Justifiable Ignorance of the Facts

When one of the parties to a contract is relatively innocent (has no reason to know that the contract is illegal), that party can often recover any benefits conferred in a partially executed contract. In this situation, the courts will not enforce the contract but will allow the parties to return to their original positions.

A court may sometimes permit an innocent party who has fully performed under a contract to enforce the contract against the guilty party. **■EXAMPLE 9.10** A trucking company contracts with Gillespie to carry crated goods to a specific destination for a normal fee of $5,000. The trucker delivers the crates and later finds out that they contained illegal goods. Although the shipment, use, and sale of the goods are illegal under the law, the trucker, being an innocent party, normally can still legally collect the $5,000 from Gillespie. ■

Members of Protected Classes

When a statute protects a certain class of people, a member of that class can enforce an illegal contract even though the other party cannot. **■EXAMPLE 9.11** Statutes prohibit certain employees (such as flight attendants) from working more than a specified number of hours per month. These employees thus constitute a class protected by statute. An employee who is required to work more than the maximum can recover for those extra hours of service. ■

Other examples of statutes designed to protect a particular class of people are **blue sky laws**—state laws that regulate the offering and sale of securities for the protection of the public (see Chapter 27)—and state statutes regulating the sale of insurance. If an insurance company violates a statute when selling insurance, the purchaser can nevertheless enforce the policy and recover from the insurer.

Withdrawal from an Illegal Agreement

If the illegal part of a bargain has not yet been performed, the party rendering performance can withdraw from the contract and recover the performance or its value. **■EXAMPLE 9.12** Marta and Amil decide to wager (illegally) on the outcome of a boxing match. Each deposits funds with a stakeholder, who agrees to pay the winner of the bet. At this point, each party has performed part of the agreement, but the illegal part of the agreement will not occur until the funds are paid to the winner. Before such payment occurs, either party is entitled to withdraw from the agreement by giving notice to the stakeholder of his or her withdrawal. ■

Severable, or Divisible, Contracts

A contract that is *severable*, or divisible, consists of distinct parts that can be performed separately, with separate consideration provided for each part. With an *indivisible* contract, in contrast, the parties intended that complete performance by each party would be essential, even if the contract contains a number of seemingly separate provisions.

If a contract is divisible into legal and illegal portions, a court may enforce the legal portion but not the illegal one, so long as the illegal portion does not affect the essence of the bargain. This approach is consistent with the basic policy of enforcing the legal intentions of the contracting parties whenever possible. **■EXAMPLE 9.13** Cole signs an employment contract that includes an overly broad and thus illegal covenant not to compete. In this situation, the court may allow the employment contract to be enforceable but reform the unreasonably broad covenant by converting its terms into reasonable ones. Alternatively, the court could declare the covenant illegal (and thus void) and enforce the remaining employment terms. ■

Contracts Illegal through Fraud, Duress, or Undue Influence

Often, one party to an illegal contract is more at fault than the other. When a party has been induced to enter into an illegal bargain through fraud, duress, or undue influence on the part of the other party to the agreement, the first party will be allowed to recover for the performance or its value.

REVIEWING Capacity and Legality

Renee Beaver started racing go-karts competitively in 2007, when she was fourteen. Many of the races required her to sign an exculpatory clause to participate, which she or her parents regularly signed. In 2010, right before her birthday, she participated in the annual Elkhart Grand Prix, a series of races in Elkhart, Indiana. During the event in which she drove, a piece of foam padding used as a course barrier was torn from its base and ended up on the track. A portion of the padding struck Beaver in the head, and another portion was thrown into oncoming traffic, causing a multikart collision during which she sustained severe injuries. Beaver filed an action against the race organizers for negligence. The organizers could not locate the exculpatory clause that Beaver was supposed to have signed. Race organizers argued that she must have signed one to enter the race, but even if she had not signed one, her actions showed her intent to be bound by its terms. Using the information presented in the chapter, answer the following questions.

1 Did Beaver have the contractual capacity to enter a contract with an exculpatory clause? Why or why not?

2 Assuming that Beaver did, in fact, sign the exculpatory clause, did she later disaffirm or ratify the contract? Explain.

3 Now assume that Beaver had stated that she was eighteen years old at the time that she signed the exculpatory clause. How might this affect Beaver's ability to disaffirm or ratify the contract?

4 If Beaver did not actually sign the exculpatory clause, could a court conclude that she impliedly accepted its terms by participating in the race? Why or why not?

TERMS AND CONCEPTS

adhesion contract 193
blue laws 189
blue sky laws 196
contractual capacity 185
covenant not to compete 191

disaffirmance 186
emancipation 185
employment contract 191
exculpatory clause 194
necessaries 187

ratification 187
reformation 192
unconscionable contract or clause 192
usury 189

CHAPTER SUMMARY Capacity and Legality

CONTRACTUAL CAPACITY

Minors (See pages 185–187.)	A minor is a person who has not yet reached the age of majority. In most states, the age of majority is eighteen for contract purposes. Contracts with minors are voidable at the option of the minor.
	1. *Disaffirmance*—The legal avoidance of a contractual obligation.
	a. Disaffirmance can take place (in most states) at any time during minority and within a reasonable time after the minor has reached the age of majority.
	b. If a minor disaffirms part of a contract, the entire contract must be disaffirmed.
	c. When disaffirming executed contracts, the minor has a duty to return received goods if they are still in the minor's control or (in some states) to pay their reasonable value.
	d. A minor who has committed an act of fraud (such as misrepresentation of age) will be denied the right to disaffirm by some courts.

(Continued)

CHAPTER SUMMARY	**Capacity and Legality—Continued**
Minors—Continued	e. A minor may disaffirm a contract for necessaries but remains liable for the reasonable value of the goods.
	2. *Ratification*—The acceptance, or affirmation, of a legal obligation; may be express or implied.
	a. Express ratification—Exists when the minor, through a writing or an oral agreement, explicitly assumes the obligations imposed by the contract.
	b. Implied ratification—Exists when the conduct of the minor is inconsistent with disaffirmance or when the minor fails to disaffirm an executed contract within a reasonable time after reaching the age of majority.
	3. *Parents' liability*—Generally, except for contracts for necessaries, parents are not liable for the contracts made by minor children acting on their own, nor are parents liable for minors' torts except in certain circumstances.
	4. *Emancipation*—Occurs when a child's parent or legal guardian relinquishes the legal right to exercise control over the child. Normally, a minor who leaves home to support himself or herself is considered emancipated. In some jurisdictions, minors themselves are permitted to petition for emancipation for limited purposes.
Intoxicated Persons (See pages 187–188.)	1. A contract entered into by an intoxicated person is voidable at the option of the intoxicated person if the person was sufficiently intoxicated to lack mental capacity, even if the intoxication was voluntary.
	2. A contract with an intoxicated person is enforceable if, despite being intoxicated, the person understood the legal consequences of entering into the contract.
Mentally Incompetent Persons (See page 188.)	1. A contract made by a person previously judged by a court to be mentally incompetent is void.
	2. A contract made by a mentally incompetent person whom a court has not previously declared to be mentally incompetent is voidable at the option of the mentally incompetent person.

LEGALITY

Contracts Contrary to Statute (See pages 188–191.)	1. *Usury*—Usury occurs when a lender makes a loan at an interest rate above the lawful maximum. The maximum rate of interest varies from state to state.
	2. *Gambling*—Gambling contracts that contravene (go against) state statutes are deemed illegal and thus void.
	3. *Sabbath (Sunday) laws*—These laws prohibit the formation or performance of certain contracts on Sunday. Such laws vary widely from state to state, and many states do not enforce them.
	4. *Licensing statutes*—Contracts entered into by persons who do not have a license, when one is required by statute, will not be enforceable *unless* the underlying purpose of the statute is to raise government revenues (and not to protect the public from unauthorized practitioners).
Contracts Contrary to Public Policy (See pages 191–195.)	1. *Contracts in restraint of trade*—Contracts to reduce or restrain free competition are illegal and prohibited by statutes. An exception is a *covenant not to compete*. It is usually enforced by the courts if the terms are secondary to a contract (such as a contract for the sale of a business or an employment contract) and are reasonable as to time and area of restraint. Courts tend to scrutinize covenants not to compete closely and, at times, may reform them if they are overbroad rather than declaring the entire covenant unenforceable.
	2. *Unconscionable contracts and clauses*—When a contract or contract clause is so unfair that it is oppressive to one party, it may be deemed unconscionable; as such, it is illegal and cannot be enforced.
	3. *Exculpatory clauses*—An exculpatory clause is a clause that releases a party from liability in the event of monetary or physical injury, no matter who is at fault. In certain situations, exculpatory clauses may be contrary to public policy and thus unenforceable.

CHAPTER SUMMARY Capacity and Legality—Continued

THE EFFECT OF ILLEGALITY

General Rule (See pages 195–196.)	In general, an illegal contract is void, and the courts will not aid either party when both parties are considered to be equally at fault (*in pari delicto*). If the contract is executory, neither party can enforce it. If the contract is executed, there can be neither contractual nor quasi-contractual recovery.
Exceptions (See page 196.)	Several exceptions exist to the general rule that neither party to an illegal bargain will be able to recover. In the following situations, the court may grant recovery: 1. *Justifiable ignorance of the facts*—When one party to the contract is relatively innocent. 2. *Members of protected classes*—When one party to the contract is a member of a group of persons protected by statute, such as certain employees. 3. *Withdrawal from an illegal agreement*—When either party seeks to recover consideration given for an illegal contract before the illegal act is performed. 4. *Severable, or divisible, contracts*—When the court can divide the contract into illegal and legal portions and the illegal portion is not essential to the bargain. 5. *Fraud, duress, or undue influence*—When one party was induced to enter into an illegal bargain through fraud, duress, or undue influence.

FOR REVIEW

*Answers for the even-numbered questions in this **For Review** section can be found on this text's accompanying Web site at* **www.cengage.com/blaw/fbl**. *Select "Chapter 9" and click on "For Review."*

1 What are some exceptions to the rule that a minor can disaffirm (avoid) any contract?

2 Does an intoxicated person have the capacity to enter into an enforceable contract?

3 Does the mental incompetence of one party necessarily make a contract void?

4 Under what circumstances will a covenant not to compete be enforceable? When will such covenants not be enforced?

5 What is an exculpatory clause? In what circumstances might exculpatory clauses be enforced? When will they not be enforced?

QUESTIONS AND CASE PROBLEMS

HYPOTHETICAL SCENARIOS AND CASE PROBLEMS

9.1 Contracts by Minors. Kalen is a seventeen-year-old minor who has just graduated from high school. He is attending a university two hundred miles from home and has contracted to rent an apartment near the university for one year at $500 per month. He is working at a convenience store to earn enough income to be self-supporting. After living in the apartment and paying monthly rent for four months, he becomes involved in a dispute with his landlord. Kalen, still a minor, moves out and returns the key to the landlord. The landlord wants to hold Kalen liable for the balance of the payments due under the lease. Discuss fully Kalen's liability in this situation.

9.2 Hypothetical Question with Sample Answer. A famous New York City hotel, Hotel Lux, is noted for its food as well as its luxury accommodations. Hotel Lux contracts with a famous chef, Chef Perlee, to become its head chef at $6,000 per month. The contract states that should Perlee leave the employment of Hotel Lux for any reason, he will not work as a chef for any hotel or restaurant in New York, New Jersey, or Pennsylvania for a period of one year. During the first six months of the contract, Hotel Lux extensively advertises Perlee as its head chef, and business at the hotel is excellent. Then a dispute arises between the hotel management and

Perlee, and Perlee terminates his employment. One month later, he is hired by a famous New Jersey restaurant just across the New York state line. Hotel Lux learns of Perlee's employment through a large advertisement in a New York City newspaper. It seeks to enjoin (prevent) Perlee from working in that restaurant as a chef for one year. Discuss how successful Hotel Lux will be in its action.

For a sample answer to Question 9.2, go to Appendix E at the end of this text.

9.3 Mental Incompetence. Joanne is a seventy-five-year-old widow who survives on her husband's small pension. Joanne has become increasingly forgetful, and her family worries that she may have Alzheimer's disease (a brain disorder that seriously affects a person's ability to carry out daily activities). No physician has diagnosed her, however, and no court has ruled on Joanne's legal competence. One day while out shopping, Joanne stops by a store that is having a sale on pianos and enters into a fifteen-year installment contract to buy a grand piano. When the piano arrives the next day, Joanne seems confused and repeatedly asks the delivery-person why a piano is being delivered. Joanne claims that she does not recall buying a piano. Explain whether this contract is void, voidable, or valid. Can Joanne avoid her contractual obligation to buy the piano? If so, how?

9.4 Covenants Not to Compete. In 1993, Mutual Service Casualty Insurance Co. and its affiliates (collectively, MSI) hired Thomas Brass as an insurance agent. Three years later, Brass entered into a career agent's contract with MSI. This contract contained provisions regarding Brass's activities after termination. These provisions stated that, for a period of not less than one year, Brass could not solicit any MSI customers to "lapse, cancel, or replace" any insurance contract in force with MSI in an effort to take that business to a competitor. If he did, MSI could at any time refuse to pay the commissions that it otherwise owed him. The contract also restricted Brass from working for American National Insurance Co. for three years after termination. In 1998, Brass quit MSI and immediately went to work for American National, soliciting MSI customers. MSI filed a suit in a Wisconsin state court against Brass, claiming that he had violated the noncompete terms of his MSI contract. Should the court enforce the covenant not to compete? Why or why not? [*Mutual Service Casualty Insurance Co. v. Brass*, 242 Wis.2d 733, 625 N.W.2d 648 (App. 2001)]

9.5 Misrepresentation of Age. Millennium Club, Inc., operates a tavern in South Bend, Indiana. In January 2003, Pamela Avila and other minors gained admission by misrepresenting that they were at least twenty-one years old. According to Millennium's representatives, the minors used false driver's licenses, "fraudulent transfer of a stamp used to gain admission by another patron or other means of false identification." To gain access, the minors also signed affidavits falsely attesting that they were twenty-one or older. When the state filed criminal charges against the Millennium Club, Millennium

filed a suit in an Indiana state court against Avila and more than two hundred others, seeking damages of $3,000 each for misrepresenting their ages. The minors filed a motion to dismiss the complaint. Should the court grant the motion? What are the competing policy interests in this case? If the Millennium Club was not careful in checking the minors' identification, should it be allowed to recover? If Millennium Club reasonably relied on the minors' representations, should the minors be allowed to avoid liability? Discuss. [*Millennium Club, Inc. v. Avila*, 809 N.E.2d 906 (Ind.App. 2004)]

9.6 Case Problem with Sample Answer. Gary Forsee was an executive officer with responsibility for the U.S. operations of BellSouth Corp., a company providing global telecommunications services. Under a covenant not to compete, Forsee agreed that for a period of eighteen months after termination from employment, he would not provide services in competition with BellSouth "to any person or entity which provides products or services identical or similar to products and services provided by [BellSouth]" within the territory. *Territory* was defined to include the geographic area in which Forsee provided services to BellSouth. The *services* included "management, strategic planning, business planning, administration, or other participation in or providing advice with respect to the communications services business." Forsee announced his intent to resign and accept a position as chief executive officer of Sprint Corp., a competitor of BellSouth. BellSouth filed a suit in a Georgia state court against Forsee, claiming, in part, that his acceptance of employment with Sprint would violate the covenant not to compete. Is the covenant legal? Should it be enforced? Why or why not? [*BellSouth Corp. v. Forsee*, 265 Ga.App. 589, 595 S.E.2d 99 (2004)]

After you have answered Problem 9.6, compare your answer with the sample answer given on the Web site that accompanies this text. Go to www.cengage.com/blaw/fbl, select "Chapter 9," and click on "Case Problem with Sample Answer."

9.7 Licensing Statutes. Under California law, a contract to manage a professional boxer must be in writing and the manager must be licensed by the state athletic commission. Marco Antonio Barrera is a professional boxer and two-time world champion. In May 2003, Jose Castillo, who was not licensed by the state, orally agreed to assume Barrera's management. He "understood" that he would be paid in accord with the "practice in the professional boxing industry, but in no case less than ten percent (10%) of the gross revenue" that Barrera generated as a boxer and through endorsements. Among other accomplishments, Castillo negotiated an exclusive promotion contract for Barrera with Golden Boy Promotions, Inc., which is owned and operated by Oscar De La Hoya. Castillo also helped Barrera settle three lawsuits and resolve unrelated tax problems so that Barrera could continue boxing. Castillo did not train Barrera, pick his opponents, or arrange his fights, however. When Barrera abruptly stopped communicating with Castillo, the latter filed a suit in a California state court against Barrera and others, alleging breach of contract. Under what circumstances is a contract with an unlicensed practitioner enforceable? Is the alleged contract in this case enforceable? Why or why not? [*Castillo v. Barrera*, 146 Cal.App.4th 1317, 53 Cal.Rptr.3d 494 (2 Dist. 2007)]

9.8 **A Question of Ethics.** *Dow AgroSciences, LLC (DAS), makes and sells agricultural seed products. In 2000, Timothy Glenn, a DAS sales manager, signed a covenant not to compete. He agreed that for two years from the date of his termination, he would not "engage in or contribute my knowledge to any work or activity involving an area of technology or business that is then competitive with a technology or business with respect to which I had access to Confidential Information during the five years immediately prior to such termination." Working with DAS business, operations, and research and development personnel, and being a member of high-level*

teams, Glenn had access to confidential DAS information, including agreements with DAS's business partners, marketing plans, litigation details, product secrets, new product development, future plans, and pricing strategies. In 2006, Glenn resigned to work for Pioneer Hi-Bred International, Inc., a DAS competitor. DAS filed a suit in an Indiana state court against Glenn, asking that he be enjoined from accepting any "position that would call on him to use confidential DAS information." [*Glenn v. Dow AgroSciences, LLC*, 861 N.E.2d 1 (Ind.App. 2007)]

1 Generally, what interests are served by enforcing covenants not to compete? What interests are served by refusing to enforce them?

2 What argument could be made in support of reforming (and then enforcing) illegal covenants not to compete? What argument could be made against this practice?

3 How should the court rule in this case? Why?

CRITICAL THINKING AND WRITING ASSIGNMENTS

9.9 **Critical Legal Thinking.** Are legalized forms of gambling, such as state-operated lotteries, consistent with a continuing public policy against the enforcement of gambling contracts? Why or why not?

9.10 **Video Question.** Go to this text's Web site at **www.cengage.com/blaw/fbl** and select "Chapter 9." Click on "Video Questions" and view the video titled *The Money Pit*. Then answer the following questions.

1 Assume that a valid contract exists between Walter (Tom Hanks) and the plumber. Recall from the video that the plumber had at least two drinks before agreeing to take on the plumbing job. If the plumber was intoxicated, is the contract voidable? Why or why not?

2 Suppose that state law requires plumbers in Walter's state to have a plumber's license and that this plumber does not have a license. Would the contract be enforceable? Why or why not?

3 In the video, the plumber suggests that Walter has been "turned down by every other plumber in the valley." Although the plumber does not even look at the house's plumbing, he agrees to do the repairs if Walter gives him a check for $5,000 right then "before he changes his mind." If Walter later seeks to void the contract because it is contrary to public policy, what should he argue?

ACCESSING THE INTERNET

For updated links to resources available on the Web, as well as a variety of other materials, visit this text's Web site at

www.cengage.com/blaw/fbl

To find your state's statutes governing the emancipation of minors, visit the Legal Information Institute's Web site at

www.law.cornell.edu/topics/Table_Emancipation.htm

For a brief covering contractual capacity and mentally incompetent persons, go to

www.zlawyer2b.com/Contract-4-brief.html

For more information on restrictive covenants in employment contracts, you can access an article written by attorneys at Loose Brown & Associates, P.C., at

www.loosebrown.com/articles/art009.pdf

PRACTICAL INTERNET EXERCISES

Go to this text's Web site at **www.cengage.com/blaw/fbl**, select "Chapter 9," and click on "Practical Internet Exercises." There you will find the following Internet research exercises that you can perform to learn more about the topics covered in this chapter.

PRACTICAL INTERNET EXERCISE 9–1   MANAGEMENT PERSPECTIVE—Minors and the Law

PRACTICAL INTERNET EXERCISE 9–2   SOCIAL PERSPECTIVE—Online Gambling

PRACTICAL INTERNET EXERCISE 9–3   LEGAL PERSPECTIVE—Covenants Not to Compete

BEFORE THE TEST

Go to this text's Web site at **www.cengage.com/blaw/fbl**, select "Chapter 9," and click on "Interactive Quizzes." You will find a number of interactive questions relating to this chapter.

5

Defenses to Contract Enforceability

LEARNING OBJECTIVES

AFTER READING THIS CHAPTER, YOU SHOULD BE ABLE TO ANSWER THE FOLLOWING QUESTIONS:

1 In what types of situations might genuineness of assent to a contract's terms be lacking?

2 What is the difference between a mistake of value or quality and a mistake of fact?

3 What elements must exist for fraudulent misrepresentation to occur?

4 What contracts must be in writing to be enforceable?

5 What is parol evidence? When is it admissible to clarify the terms of a written contract?

An otherwise valid contract may still be unenforceable if the parties have not genuinely assented to its terms. As mentioned in Chapter 7, lack of genuine assent is a *defense* to the enforcement of a contract. If the law were to enforce contracts not genuinely assented to by the contracting parties, injustice would result. The first part of this chapter focuses on the kinds of factors that indicate that genuineness of assent to a contract may be lacking.

A contract that is otherwise valid may also be unenforceable if it is not in the proper form. For example, if a contract is required by law to be in writing and there is no written evidence of the contract, it may not be enforceable. In the second part of this chapter, we examine the kinds of contracts that require a writing under what is called the *Statute of Frauds*. The chapter concludes with a discussion of the parol evidence rule, under which courts determine the admissibility at trial of evidence extraneous (external) to written contracts.

GENUINENESS OF ASSENT

Genuineness of assent may be lacking because of mistake, fraudulent misrepresentation, undue influence, or duress. Generally, a party who demonstrates that he or she did not

genuinely assent (agree) to the terms of a contract can choose either to carry out the contract or to rescind (cancel) it and thus avoid the entire transaction.

Mistakes

We all make mistakes, so it is not surprising that mistakes are made when contracts are created. In certain circumstances, contract law allows a contract to be avoided on the basis of mistake. It is important to distinguish between *mistakes of fact* and *mistakes of value or quality*. Only a mistake of fact makes a contract voidable.

EXAMPLE 10.1 Paco buys a violin from Beverly for $250. Although the violin is very old, neither party believes that it is extremely valuable. Later, however, an antiques dealer informs the parties that the violin is rare and worth thousands of dollars. Here, both parties were mistaken, but the mistake is a mistake of *value* rather than a mistake of *fact* that warrants contract rescission. Therefore, Beverly cannot rescind the contract. ■

Mistakes of fact occur in two forms—*unilateral* and *bilateral (mutual)*. A unilateral mistake is made by only one of the contracting parties; a mutual mistake is made by both. We look next at these two types of mistakes and illustrate them graphically in Exhibit 10–1 on the following page.

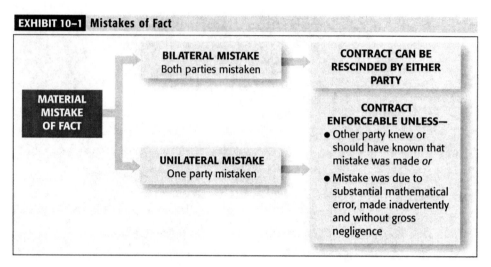

EXHIBIT 10–1 Mistakes of Fact

Unilateral Mistakes A **unilateral mistake** occurs when only one party is mistaken as to a *material fact*—that is, a fact important to the subject matter of the contract. Generally, a unilateral mistake does not give the mistaken party any right to relief from the contract. In other words, the contract normally is enforceable against the mistaken party. **■EXAMPLE 10.2** Elena intends to sell her motor home for $32,500. When she learns that Chin is interested in buying a used motor home, she sends a fax offering to sell the vehicle to him. When typing the fax, however, she mistakenly keys in the price of $23,500. Chin immediately sends Elena a fax accepting her offer. Even though Elena intended to sell her motor home for $32,500, she has made a unilateral mistake and is bound by contract to sell the vehicle to Chin for $23,500. **■**

There are at least two exceptions to this rule.[1] First, if the *other* party to the contract knows or should have known that a mistake of fact was made, the contract may not be enforceable. **■EXAMPLE 10.3** In the above example, if Chin knew that Elena intended to sell her motor home for $32,500, then Elena's unilateral mistake (stating $23,500 in her offer) may render the resulting contract unenforceable. **■** The second exception arises when a unilateral mistake of fact was due to a mathematical mistake in addition, subtraction, division, or multiplication and was made inadvertently and without gross (extreme) negligence. If a contractor's bid was significantly low because he or she made a mistake in addition when totaling the estimated costs, any contract resulting from the bid normally may be rescinded. Of course, in both situations, the mistake must still involve some *material fact*.

Bilateral (Mutual) Mistakes When both parties are mistaken about the same material fact, it is a **bilateral mistake.**

When a bilateral mistake occurs, the contract can be rescinded by either party.[2] Note that, as with unilateral mistakes, the mistake must be about a *material fact* (one that is important and central to the contract). **■EXAMPLE 10.4** Keeley buys a landscape painting from Umberto's art gallery. Both Umberto and Keeley believe that the painting is by the artist Vincent van Gogh. Later, Keeley discovers that the painting is a very clever fake. Because neither Umberto nor Keeley was aware of this fact when they made their deal, Keeley can rescind the contract and recover the purchase price of the painting. **■**

A word or term in a contract may be subject to more than one reasonable interpretation. In that situation, if the parties to the contract attach materially different meanings to the term, their mutual misunderstanding may allow the contract to be rescinded. **■EXAMPLE 10.5** In a classic case, *Raffles v. Wichelhaus*,[3] Wichelhaus purchased a shipment of cotton from Raffles to arrive on a ship called the *Peerless* from Bombay, India. Wichelhaus meant a ship called *Peerless* sailing from Bombay in October; Raffles meant a different ship called *Peerless* sailing from Bombay in December. When the goods arrived on the December *Peerless* and Raffles tried to deliver them, Wichelhaus refused to accept them. The British court held for Wichelhaus, concluding that no mutual assent existed because the parties had attached materially different meanings to an essential term of the contract (which ship *Peerless* was to transport the goods). **■**

In the following case, the court had to grapple with the question of whether a mutual mistake of fact had occurred.

---

1. The *Restatement (Second) of Contracts*, Section 153, liberalizes the general rule to take into account the modern trend of allowing avoidance in some circumstances even though only one party has been mistaken.

2. *Restatement (Second) of Contracts*, Section 152.
3. 159 Eng.Rep. 375 (1864).

CASE 10.1   Inkel v. Pride Chevrolet-Pontiac, Inc.

Supreme Court of Vermont, 945 A.2d 855 (2008).

FACTS The Inkels, who live in Vermont, called Pride Chevrolet-Pontiac, Inc., in Boston about buying a new Chevy Tahoe. They said that they would trade in a high-mileage vehicle they leased. The sales representative told them that the high-mileage penalty would probably not apply as the lease was from a bank, not a dealership. When the Inkels took delivery of the new Tahoe and left their old vehicle at Pride, the price on the contract was $41,200. In small print on the back of the agreement was a provision that the buyer was responsible for any problems with the trade-in vehicle. A month after the sale, Pride told the Inkels they owed another $16,435 because there was a misunderstanding with the leasing company about the high-mileage charge. The Inkels refused to pay. Pride demanded that they return the Tahoe and wanted to cancel the deal; the Inkels refused. The Inkels then sued Pride for breach of contract and other claims. A Vermont superior court held that a mutual mistake had been made in the contract and that the Inkels should have agreed to undo the deal. The court granted summary judgment for Pride and ordered the Inkels to pay damages. They appealed.

ISSUE Was the parties' misunderstanding about whether a high-mileage penalty would be assessed on the trade-in vehicle a mutual mistake of fact?

DECISION The Supreme Court of Vermont reversed the lower court's summary judgment in favor of Pride and remanded the case back to the trial court for further proceedings. It was unclear whether there had been a mutual mistake, and the court was concerned that Pride may have engaged in consumer fraud.

REASON For a court to find that a mutual mistake occurred, evidence would have to be produced at trial to show that both parties had been mistaken about the same material fact. Pride knew about the terms of its contract, and the Inkels knew their vehicle was high mileage. It appears that either Pride was hiding the truth about what would happen due to the high mileage on the trade-in car, or the Inkels were trying to take advantage of Pride's ignorance about the extra payoff needed to their bank for their high-mileage vehicle. Even if there was a mutual mistake, which should be determined at trial, it was not clear that Pride offered to rescind the contract when it said the Inkels could return the vehicle. The terms of a return were never clarified.

FOR CRITICAL ANALYSIS—Ethical Consideration *If a Pride sales representative led the Inkels to believe that the dealership did not care about the excessive miles on the trade-in vehicle, should Pride be willing to incur the loss? Why or why not?*

Fraudulent Misrepresentation

Although fraud is a tort, the presence of fraud also affects the genuineness of the innocent party's consent to a contract. When an innocent party consents to a contract with fraudulent terms, the contract usually can be avoided because she or he has not *voluntarily* consented to the terms.[4] Normally, the innocent party can either rescind (cancel) the contract and be restored to her or his original position or enforce the contract and seek damages for injuries resulting from the fraud.

Typically, fraud involves three elements:

1 A misrepresentation of a material fact must occur.
2 There must be an intent to deceive.
3 The innocent party must justifiably rely on the misrepresentation.

Additionally, to collect damages, a party must have been injured as a result of the misrepresentation.

Fraudulent misrepresentation can also occur in the online environment. For a case involving allegations that Yahoo fraudulently posted online personal ads, see this chapter's *Adapting the Law to the Online Environment* feature on the following page.

Misrepresentation Must Occur The first element of proving fraud is to show that misrepresentation of a material fact has occurred. This misrepresentation can take the form of words or actions. For example, an art gallery owner's statement, "This painting is a Picasso" is a misrepresentation of fact if the painting was done by another artist.

A statement of opinion is generally not subject to a claim of fraud. For example, claims such as "This computer will never break down" and "This car will last for years and years" are statements of opinion, not fact, and contracting parties should recognize them as such and not rely on them. A fact is

---

4. *Restatement (Second) of Contracts*, Sections 163 and 164.

ADAPTING THE LAW TO THE ONLINE ENVIRONMENT   Online Personals—Fraud and Misrepresentation Issues

Keying the words *online personals* into the Google search engine will return more than 35 million hits, including Match.com, Chanceforlove.com, Widowsorwidowers.com, Makefriendsonline.com, and Yahoo! Personals. Yahoo! Personals, which calls itself the "top online dating site," offers two options. One is for people looking for casual dates. It allows users to create their own profiles, browse member profiles, and exchange e-mail or instant messages. The second option, called Yahoo! Personals Primer, is for people who want serious relationships. Users must take a relationship test. Then they can use Yahoo's computerized matching system to "zero in on marriage material." With this service, users can chat on the phone, as well as exchange e-mail.

The Thorny Problem of Misrepresentation

When singles (and others) create their profiles for online dating services, they tend to exaggerate their more appealing features and downplay or omit their less attractive attributes. All users of such services are aware that the profiles may not correspond exactly with reality, but they do assume that the profiles are not complete misrepresentations. In 2006, however, Robert Anthony, individually and on behalf of others, brought a suit against Yahoo in federal district court, alleging fraud and negligent misrepresentation, among other things.

In his complaint, Anthony claimed that Yahoo was not just posting fictitious or exaggerated profiles submitted by users but was deliberately and intentionally originating, creating, and perpetuating false and/or nonexistent profiles. According to Anthony, many profiles used the exact same phrases "with such unique dictation and vernacular [language] that such a random occurrence would not be possible." Anthony also argued that some photo images had multiple identities—that is, the same photo appeared in several different profiles. He also alleged that Yahoo continued to circulate profiles of "actual, legitimate former subscribers whose subscriptions had

expired." Finally, Anthony claimed that when a subscription neared its end date, Yahoo would send the subscriber a fake profile, heralding it as a "potential 'new match.'"

Did Yahoo Have Immunity?

Yahoo asked the court to dismiss the complaint on the grounds that the lawsuit was barred by the Communications Decency Act (CDA) of 1996.[a] As discussed in Chapter 4, the CDA shields Internet service providers (ISPs) from liability for any information submitted by another information content provider. In other words, an interactive computer service cannot be held liable under state law as a publisher of information that originates from a third party information content provider. The CDA defines an information content provider as "any person or entity that is responsible, in whole or in part, for the creation or development of information provided through the Internet or any other interactive computer service."[b]

The court rejected Yahoo's claim that it had immunity under the CDA and held that Yahoo had become an information content provider itself when it created bogus user profiles. The court observed that "no case of which this court is aware has immunized a defendant from allegations that *it* created tortious content."[c] Thus, the court denied Yahoo's motion to dismiss and allowed Anthony's claims of fraud and negligent misrepresentation to proceed to trial.[d]

FOR CRITICAL ANALYSIS *Assume that Anthony had contacted various users of Yahoo's online dating service only to discover that each user's profile exaggerated the person's physical appearance, intelligence, and occupation. Would Anthony prevail if he brought a lawsuit for fraudulent misrepresentation against Yahoo in that situation? Why or why not?*

a. 47 U.S.C. Section 230.

b. 47 U.S.C. Section 230(f)(3).

c. For an example of the type of cases that have been brought against Internet dating services, see *Carafano v. Metrosplash.com, Inc.,* 339 F.3d 1119 (9th Cir. 2003).

d. *Anthony v. Yahoo!, Inc.,* 421 F.Supp.2d 1257 (N.D.Cal. 2006). See also *Doe v. SexSearch.com,* 502 F.Supp.2d 719 (N.D. Ohio 2007).

---

objective and verifiable; an opinion is usually subject to debate. Therefore, a seller is allowed to "huff and puff his [or her] wares" without being liable for fraud. In certain cases, however, particularly when a naïve purchaser relies on an expert's opinion, the innocent party may be entitled to *rescission* (cancellation) or *reformation* (an equitable remedy

granted by a court in which the terms of a contract are altered to reflect the true intentions of the parties).

Misrepresentation by Conduct. Misrepresentation can occur by conduct, as well as through express oral or written statements. For example, if a seller, by her or his actions, prevents a buyer from learning of some fact that is material to the contract, such behavior constitutes misrepresentation by conduct.[5] **■EXAMPLE 10.6** Cummings contracts to purchase a racehorse from Garner. The horse is blind in one eye, but when Garner shows the horse, he skillfully conceals this fact by keeping the horse's head turned so that Cummings does not see the defect. The concealment constitutes fraud. ■ Another example of misrepresentation by conduct is the untruthful denial of knowledge or information concerning facts that are material to the contract when such knowledge or information is requested.

Misrepresentation of Law. Misrepresentation of law *ordinarily* does not entitle a party to be relieved of a contract. **■EXAMPLE 10.7** Debbie has a parcel of property that she is trying to sell to Barry. Debbie knows that a local ordinance prohibits building anything higher than three stories on the property. Nonetheless, she tells Barry, "You can build a condominium one hundred stories high if you want to." Barry buys the land and later discovers that Debbie's statement is false. Normally, Barry cannot avoid the contract because under the common law, people are assumed to know state and local laws. ■ Exceptions to this rule occur, however, when the misrepresenting party is in a profession known to require greater knowledge of the law than the average citizen possesses.

Misrepresentation by Silence. Ordinarily, neither party to a contract has a duty to come forward and disclose facts, and a contract normally will not be set aside because certain pertinent information has not been volunteered. **■EXAMPLE 10.8** You are selling a car that has been in an accident and has been repaired. You do not need to volunteer this information to a potential buyer. If, however, the purchaser asks you if the car has had extensive bodywork and you lie, you have committed a fraudulent misrepresentation. ■

Generally, if the seller knows of a serious defect or a serious potential problem about which the buyer cannot reasonably be expected to know, the seller may have a duty to speak. Normally, the seller must disclose only "latent" defects—that is, defects that could not readily be discovered. Thus, termites in a house may not be a latent defect because a buyer could normally discover their presence through a termite inspection. Also, when the parties are in a *fiduciary relationship* (one of trust, such as partners, physician and patient, or attorney and client), there is a duty to disclose material facts; failure to do so may constitute fraud.

Intent to Deceive The second element of fraud is knowledge on the part of the misrepresenting party that facts have been misrepresented. This element, usually called *scienter*,[6] or "guilty knowledge," generally signifies that there was an intent to deceive. *Scienter* clearly exists if a party knows that a fact is not as stated. *Scienter* also exists if a party makes a statement that he or she believes not to be true or makes a statement recklessly, without regard to whether it is true or false. Finally, this element is met if a party says or implies that a statement is made on some basis, such as personal knowledge or personal investigation, when it is not.

■EXAMPLE 10.9 A convicted felon, Robert Sarvis, applied for a position as an adjunct professor two weeks after his release from prison. On his résumé, he lied about his past work history by representing that he had been the president of a corporation for fourteen years and had taught business law at another college. At his interview, Sarvis stated that he was "well equipped to teach" business law and ethics and that he had "a great interest and knowledge of business law." After he was hired and began working, Sarvis's probation officer alerted the school to his criminal history. The school immediately fired Sarvis, and he brought a lawsuit against the school for breaching his employment contract. The school claimed that it was not liable for the breach because of Sarvis's fraudulent misrepresentations during the hiring process. The court agreed. Sarvis had not fully disclosed his personal history, he clearly had an intent to deceive, and the school had justifiably relied on his misrepresentations. Therefore, the school could rescind Sarvis's employment contract.[7] ■

Reliance on the Misrepresentation The third element of fraud is *justifiable reliance* on the misrepresentation of fact. The deceived party must have a justifiable reason for relying on the misrepresentation, and the misrepresentation must be an important factor (but not necessarily the sole factor) in inducing the party to enter into the contract.

Reliance is not justified if the innocent party knows the true facts or, alternatively, relies on obviously extravagant statements. **■EXAMPLE 10.10** If a used-car dealer tells you, "This old Cadillac will get over sixty miles to the gallon," you normally would not be justified in relying on this statement. Suppose, however, that Merkel, a bank director, induces O'Connell, a co-director, to sign a statement that the bank has sufficient assets to meet its liabilities by telling O'Connell, "We have plenty of assets to satisfy our creditors." This statement is false. If O'Connell knows the true facts or, as a bank director, should know the true facts, he is not justified in relying on Merkel's statement. If O'Connell does not know the true facts, however, *and has no way of finding them out*, he may be justified in relying on the statement. ■

---

5. *Restatement (Second) of Contracts*, Section 160.

6. Pronounced sy-*en*-ter.

7. *Sarvis v. Vermont State Colleges*, 172 Vt. 76, 772 A.2d 494 (2001).

Employers sometimes run into problems by exaggerating their companies' future prospects or financial health when they are interviewing prospective employees. Obviously, an employer wants to paint the future as bright, but should be careful to avoid making representations that an interviewee may rely on to her or his detriment. **EXAMPLE 10.11** In one case, an employee accepted a job with a brokerage firm, relying on assurances that the firm was not about to be sold. In fact, as the employee was able to prove in his later lawsuit against the firm for fraud, negotiations to sell the firm were under way at the time he was hired. The trial court awarded the employee more than $6 million in damages, a decision that was affirmed on appeal.[8] ■ Generally, employers must be truthful during their hiring procedures to avoid possible lawsuits for fraudulent misrepresentation.

Injury to the Innocent Party   Most courts do not require a showing of injury when the action is to rescind (cancel) the contract—these courts hold that because rescission returns the parties to the positions they held before the contract was made, a showing of injury to the innocent party is unnecessary.

To recover damages caused by fraud, however, proof of an injury is universally required. The measure of damages is ordinarily equal to the property's value had it been delivered as represented, less the actual price paid for the property. In actions based on fraud, courts often award *punitive*, or *exemplary, damages*, which are granted to a plaintiff over and above the compensation for the actual loss. As pointed out in Chapter 4, punitive damages are based on the public-policy consideration of punishing the defendant or setting an example to deter similar wrongdoing by others.

PREVENTING LEGAL DISPUTES   To avoid making comments that might later be construed as a misrepresentation of material fact, be careful what you say to clients and customers. Those in the business of selling products or services should assume that all customers are naïve and are relying on the seller's representations. Instruct employees to phrase their comments so that customers understand that any statements that are not factual are the employee's opinion. If someone asks a question that is beyond the employee's knowledge, it is better to say that he or she does not know than to guess and have the customer rely on a representation that turns out to be false. This can be particularly important when the questions concern topics such as compatibility or speed of electronic and digital goods, software, or related services.

Also be prudent about what you say when interviewing potential employees. Do not speculate on the financial health of the firm or exaggerate the company's future prospects. Exercising caution in your statements to others in a business context is the best way to avoid potential legal actions for fraudulent misrepresentation.

■

Undue Influence

Undue influence arises from special kinds of relationships in which one party can greatly influence another party, thus overcoming that party's free will. A contract entered into under excessive or undue influence lacks voluntary assent and is therefore voidable.

There are various types of relationships in which one party may dominate another party, thus unfairly influencing him or her. Minors and elderly people, for example, are often under the influence of guardians (persons who are legally responsible for others). If a guardian induces a young or elderly ward (the person whom the guardian looks after) to enter into a contract that benefits the guardian, undue influence may have been exerted. Undue influence can arise from a number of confidential or fiduciary relationships: attorney-client, physician-patient, guardian-ward, parent-child, husband-wife, or trustee-beneficiary.

The essential feature of undue influence is that the party being taken advantage of does not, in reality, exercise free will in entering into a contract. It is not enough that a person is elderly or suffers from some mental or physical impairment. There must be clear and convincing evidence that the person did not act out of her or his free will.

Duress

Assent to the terms of a contract is not genuine if one of the parties is forced into the agreement. Forcing a party to enter into a contract because of the fear created by threats is referred to as **duress**.[9] Inducing consent to a contract through blackmail or extortion also constitutes duress. Duress is both a defense to the enforcement of a contract and a ground for rescission of a contract. Therefore, a party who signs a contract under duress can choose to carry out the contract or to avoid the entire transaction. (The wronged party usually has this choice in cases in which assent is not real or genuine.)

Economic need is generally not sufficient to constitute duress, even when one party exacts a very high price for an

---

8. *McConkey v. AON Corp.*, 354 N.J.Super. 25, 804 A.2d 572 (A.D. 2002).

9. *Restatement (Second) of Contracts*, Sections 174 and 175.

item the other party needs. If the party exacting the price also creates the need, however, economic duress may be found. **EXAMPLE 10.12** The Internal Revenue Service (IRS) assessed a large tax and penalty against Weller. Weller retained Eyman to contest the assessment. Two days before the deadline for filing a reply with the IRS, Eyman declined to represent Weller unless he agreed to pay a very high fee for Eyman's services. The agreement was held to be unenforceable.[10] Although Eyman had threatened only to withdraw his services, something that he was legally entitled to do, he was responsible for delaying his withdrawal until just before the deadline. Because Weller was forced into either signing the contract or losing his right to challenge the IRS assessment, the agreement was secured under duress. ■

THE STATUTE OF FRAUDS— REQUIREMENT OF A WRITING

Today, every state has a statute that stipulates what types of contracts must be in writing or be evidenced by a record. In this text, we refer to such a statute as the **Statute of Frauds.** The primary purpose of the statute is to ensure that, for certain types of contracts, there is reliable evidence of the contracts and their terms. These types of contracts are those historically deemed to be important or complex. Although the statutes vary slightly from state to state, the following types of contracts are normally required to be in writing or evidenced by a written memorandum:

1 Contracts involving interests in land.

2 Contracts that cannot by their terms be performed within one year from the date of formation.

3 Collateral contracts, such as promises to answer for the debt or duty of another.

4 Promises made in consideration of marriage.

5 Contracts for the sale of goods priced at $500 or more (under the Uniform Commercial Code, or UCC—see Chapter 14).

Agreements or promises that fit into one or more of these categories are said to "fall under" or "fall within" the Statute of Frauds. (Certain exceptions are made to the Statute of Frauds, however, as you will read later in this section.)

The actual name of the Statute of Frauds is misleading because it does not apply to fraud. Rather, the statute denies enforceability to certain contracts that do not comply with its requirements.

10. *Thompson Crane & Trucking Co. v. Eyman,* 123 Cal.App.2d 904, 267 P.2d 1043 (1954).

Contracts Involving Interests in Land

Land is a form of *real property*, or real estate, which includes not only land but all physical objects that are permanently attached to the soil, such as buildings, plants, trees, and the soil itself. Under the Statute of Frauds, a contract involving an interest in land must be evidenced by a writing to be enforceable.[11] **EXAMPLE 10.13** If Carol contracts orally to sell Seaside Shelter to Axel but later decides not to sell, Axel cannot enforce the contract. Similarly, if Axel refuses to close the deal, Carol cannot force Axel to pay for the land by bringing a lawsuit. The Statute of Frauds is a *defense* to the enforcement of this type of oral contract. ■

A contract for the sale of land ordinarily involves the entire interest in the real property, including buildings, growing crops, vegetation, minerals, timber, and anything else affixed to the land. Therefore, a *fixture* (personal property so affixed or so used as to become a part of the realty—see Chapter 29) is treated as real property.

The Statute of Frauds requires written contracts not just for the sale of land but also for the transfer of other interests in land, such as mortgages and leases. We will describe these other interests in Chapter 29.

The One-Year Rule

Contracts that cannot, *by their own terms*, be performed within one year *from the day after* the contract is formed must be in writing to be enforceable. Because disputes over such contracts are unlikely to occur until some time after the contracts are made, resolution of these disputes is difficult unless the contract terms have been put in writing. The one-year period begins to run *the day after the contract is made.* **EXAMPLE 10.14** Superior University forms a contract with Kimi San stating that San will teach three courses in history during the coming academic year (September 15 through June 15). If the contract is formed in March, it must be in writing to be enforceable—because it cannot be performed within one year. If the contract is not formed until July, however, it will not have to be in writing to be enforceable—because it can be performed within one year. ■ Exhibit 10–2 on the next page graphically illustrates the one-year rule.

Normally, the test for determining whether an oral contract is enforceable under the one-year rule of the Statute of Frauds is whether performance is *possible* within one year from the day after the date of contract formation—not whether the agreement is *likely* to be performed within one year. When

11. In some states, the contract will be enforced if each party admits to the existence of the oral contract in court or admits to its existence during discovery before trial (see Chapter 2).

EXHIBIT 10–2 The One-Year Rule

Under the Statute of Frauds, contracts that by their terms are impossible to perform within one year from the day after the date of contract formation must be in writing to be enforceable. Put another way, if it is at all possible to perform an oral contract within one year from the day after the contract is made, the contract will fall outside the Statute of Frauds and be enforceable.

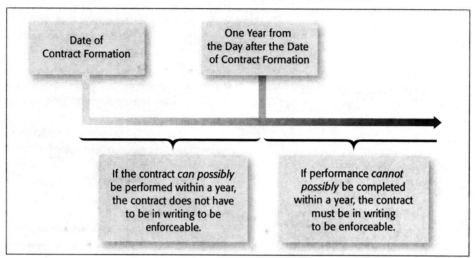

performance of a contract is objectively impossible during the one-year period, the oral contract will be unenforceable.

Collateral Promises

A **collateral promise,** or secondary promise, is one that is ancillary (subsidiary) to a principal transaction or primary contractual relationship. In other words, a collateral promise is one made by a third party to assume the debts or obligations of a primary party to a contract if that party does not perform. Any collateral promise of this nature falls under the Statute of Frauds and therefore must be in writing to be enforceable. To understand this concept, it is important to distinguish between primary and secondary promises and obligations.

Primary versus Secondary Obligations A contract in which a party assumes a primary obligation normally does not need to be in writing to be enforceable. **■EXAMPLE 10.15** Kenneth orally contracts with Joanne's Floral Boutique to send his mother a dozen roses for Mother's Day. Kenneth promises to pay the boutique when he receives the bill for the flowers. Kenneth is a direct party to this contract and has incurred a *primary* obligation under the contract. Because he is a party to the contract and has a primary obligation to Joanne's Floral Boutique, this contract does not fall under the Statute of Frauds and does not have to be in writing to be enforceable. If Kenneth fails to pay the florist and the florist sues him for payment, Kenneth cannot raise the Statute of Frauds as a defense. He cannot claim that the contract is unenforceable because it was not in writing. ■

In contrast, a contract in which a party assumes a secondary obligation does have to be in writing to be enforceable. **■EXAMPLE 10.16** Kenneth's mother borrows $10,000 from the Medford Trust Company on a promissory note payable six months later. Kenneth promises the bank officer handling the loan that he will pay the $10,000 *if his mother does not pay the loan on time.* Kenneth, in this situation, becomes what is known as a *guarantor* on the loan. He is guaranteeing to the bank (the creditor) that he will pay the loan if his mother fails to do so. This kind of collateral promise, in which the guarantor states that he or she will become responsible only if the primary party does not perform, must be in writing to be enforceable. ■ We return to the concept of guaranty and the distinction between primary and secondary obligations in Chapter 21, in the context of creditors' rights.

An Exception—The "Main Purpose" Rule An oral promise to answer for the debt of another is covered by the Statute of Frauds *unless* the guarantor's purpose in accepting secondary liability is to secure a personal benefit. Under the "main purpose" rule, this type of contract need not be in writing.[12] The assumption is that a court can infer from the circum-

---

12. *Restatement (Second) of Contracts,* Section 116.

stances of a case whether a "leading objective" of the promisor was to secure a personal benefit.

EXAMPLE 10.17 Carrie Oswald contracts with Machine Manufacturing Company to have some machines custom made for her factory. To ensure that Machine Manufacturing will have the supplies it needs to make the machines, Oswald promises Allrite Materials Supply Company, Machine Manufacturing's supplier, that if Allrite continues to deliver materials to Machine Manufacturing, she will guarantee payment. This promise need not be in writing, even though the effect may be to pay the debt of another, because Oswald's main purpose is to secure a benefit for herself. ■

Another typical application of the so-called main purpose doctrine occurs when one creditor guarantees the debtor's debt to another creditor to forestall litigation. This allows the debtor to remain in business long enough to generate profits sufficient to pay *both* creditors. In this situation, the guaranty does not need to be in writing to be enforceable.

Promises Made in Consideration of Marriage

A unilateral promise to make a monetary payment or to give property in consideration of marriage must be in writing. If Mr. Baumann promises to pay Joe Villard $10,000 if Villard marries Baumann's daughter, the promise must be in writing to be enforceable. The same rule applies to **prenuptial agreements**—agreements made before marriage (also called *antenuptial agreements*) that define each partner's ownership rights in the other partner's property. A prospective wife or husband may wish to limit the amount the prospective spouse can obtain if the marriage ends in divorce. Prenuptial agreements made in consideration of marriage must be in writing to be enforceable.

Generally, courts tend to give more credence to prenuptial agreements that are accompanied by consideration. **EXAMPLE 10.18** Maureen, who is not wealthy, marries Kaiser, who has a net worth of $300 million. Kaiser has several children, and he wants them to receive most of his wealth on his death. Prior to their marriage, Maureen and Kaiser draft and sign a prenuptial agreement in which Kaiser promises to give Maureen $100,000 per year for the rest of her life if they divorce. As consideration for consenting to this amount, Kaiser offers Maureen $1 million. If Maureen consents to the agreement and accepts the $1 million, very likely a court would hold that this prenuptial agreement is valid, should it ever be contested. ■

Contracts for the Sale of Goods

The Uniform Commercial Code (UCC) includes Statute of Frauds provisions that require written evidence of a contract. Section 2–201 contains the major provision, which generally requires a writing or memorandum for the sale of goods priced at $500 or more under the UCC (see Chapter 14). A writing that will satisfy the UCC requirement need only state the quantity term; other terms agreed on need not be stated "accurately" in the writing, as long as they adequately reflect both parties' intentions. The contract will not be enforceable, however, for any quantity greater than that set forth in the writing. In addition, the writing must be signed by the person against whom enforcement is sought. Beyond these two requirements, the writing need not designate the buyer or the seller, the terms of payment, or the price.

Exceptions to the Statute of Frauds

Exceptions to the applicability of the Statute of Frauds are made in certain situations. We describe those situations here.

Partial Performance   In cases involving oral contracts for the transfer of interests in land, if the purchaser has paid part of the price, taken possession, and made valuable improvements to the property, and if the parties cannot be returned to their positions prior to the contract, a court may grant *specific performance* (performance of the contract according to its precise terms). Whether a court will enforce an oral contract for an interest in land when partial performance has taken place is usually determined by the degree of injury that would be suffered if the court chose *not* to enforce the oral contract. In some states, mere reliance on certain types of oral contracts is enough to remove them from the Statute of Frauds.

Under the UCC, an oral contract for goods priced at $500 or more is enforceable to the extent that a seller accepts payment or a buyer accepts delivery of the goods.[13] **EXAMPLE 10.19** If the president of Ajax Corporation orders by telephone thirty crates of bleach from Cloney, Inc., and repudiates the contract after ten crates have been delivered and accepted, Cloney can enforce the contract to the extent of the ten crates accepted by Ajax. ■

The existence and extent of a contract to supply computer kiosks for use in school cafeterias was in dispute in the following case.

---

13. UCC 2–201(3)(c). See Chapter 14.

CASE 10.2   School-Link Technologies, Inc. v. Applied Resources, Inc.

United States District Court, District of Kansas, 471 F.Supp.2d 1101 (2007).

FACTS Applied Resources, Inc. (ARI), makes computer hardware for point-of-sale systems: kiosks that consist of computers encased in chassis on which card readers or other payment devices are mounted. School-Link Technologies, Inc. (SLT), sells food-service technology to schools. In August 2003, the New York City Department of Education (NYCDOE) asked SLT to propose a cafeteria payment system that included kiosks. SLT asked ARI to participate in a pilot project, orally promising ARI that it would be the exclusive supplier of as many as 1,500 kiosks if the NYCDOE awarded the contract to SLT. ARI agreed. SLT intended to cut ARI out of the deal, however, and told the NYCDOE that SLT would be making its own kiosks. Meanwhile, SLT paid ARI in advance for a certain number of goods, but insisted on onerous terms for a written contract to which ARI would not agree. ARI suspended production of the prepaid items and refused to refund over $55,000 of SLT's funds. SLT filed a suit in a federal district court against ARI. ARI responded in part with a counterclaim for breach of contract, asserting that SLT failed to use ARI as an exclusive supplier as promised. ARI sought the expenses it incurred for the pilot project and the amount of profit that it would have realized on the entire deal. SLT filed a motion for summary judgment on this claim.

ISSUE Was the oral agreement for the kiosks enforceable to the extent to which it had been performed?

DECISION Yes. The court denied SLT's motion for summary judgment on ARI's counterclaim for breach of contract "with respect to goods which SLT already received and accepted, i.e., the goods for the pilot program with the NYCDOE."

REASON The court acknowledged that, according to the Uniform Commercial Code, a contract for a sale of goods for a price of $500 or more generally must be in writing and must be signed by the party against whom enforcement is sought. The court reasoned that "because the NYCDOE contract undisputedly involved the sale of goods in excess of $500, the parties' oral contract that ARI would be the exclusive supplier of kiosks for the project is not enforceable in the absence of an applicable exception to this general rule." Under the partial performance exception to the rule, an oral contract for a sale of goods over $500 that would otherwise be unenforceable for the lack of a writing is enforceable to the extent that the seller delivers the goods and the buyer accepts them. In that situation, the performance serves as a substitute for the required writing. Thus, in this case, the court concluded that the alleged oral contract between SLT and ARI, to the effect that ARI would be the exclusive supplier of kiosks for SLT's contract with the NYCDOE, was enforceable to the extent that ARI had delivered the kiosks for the pilot project and SLT had accepted them. The court added, however, that "the remaining aspect of that claim is barred by the Statute of Frauds."

FOR CRITICAL ANALYSIS–Social Consideration *Could ARI successfully assert a claim against SLT based on fraudulent misrepresentation? Explain.*

Admissions In some states, if a party against whom enforcement of an oral contract is sought admits in pleadings, testimony, or otherwise in court proceedings that a contract for sale was made, the contract will be enforceable.[14] A contract subject to the UCC will be enforceable, but only to the extent of the quantity admitted.[15] **EXAMPLE 10.20** Suppose that the president of Ajax Corporation in the previous example admits under oath that an oral agreement was made with Cloney, Inc., for twenty crates of bleach. In this situation, even if Cloney, Inc., claims that Ajax had contracted for thirty crates, the agreement will be enforceable only to the extent admitted (for twenty rather than thirty crates of bleach). ■

Promissory Estoppel In some states, an oral contract that would otherwise be unenforceable under the Statute of Frauds may be enforced under the doctrine of promissory estoppel, or detrimental reliance. Recall from Chapter 8 that if a promisor makes a promise on which the promisee justifiably relies to her or his detriment, a court may *estop* (prevent) the promisor from denying that a contract exists. Section 139 of the *Restatement (Second) of Contracts* provides that in these circumstances, an oral promise can be enforceable, notwithstanding the Statute of Frauds, if the reliance was foreseeable to the person making the promise and if injustice can be avoided only by enforcing the promise.

Special Exceptions under the UCC Special exceptions to the applicability of the Statute of Frauds exist for sales con-

---

14. *Restatement (Second) of Contracts*, Section 133.
15. UCC 2–201(3)(b). See Chapter 14.

tracts. Oral contracts for customized goods may be enforced in certain circumstances. Another exception has to do with oral contracts between merchants that have been confirmed in writing. We will examine these exceptions in Chapter 14. Exhibit 10–3 graphically summarizes the types of contracts that fall under the Statute of Frauds and the various exceptions that apply.

THE STATUTE OF FRAUDS— SUFFICIENCY OF THE WRITING

A written contract will satisfy the writing requirement of the Statute of Frauds. A *written memorandum* (written evidence of the oral contract) signed by the party against whom enforcement is sought will also satisfy the writing requirement.[16] The signature need not be placed at the end of the document but can be anywhere in the writing; it can even be initials rather than the full name.

A significant issue in today's business world has to do with how "signatures" can be created and verified on electronic contracts and other documents. We will examine electronic signatures in Chapter 13.

What Constitutes a Writing?

A writing can consist of any confirmation, invoice, sales slip, check, fax, or e-mail—or such items in combination. The written contract need not consist of a single document to constitute an enforceable contract. One document may incorpo-

---

16. As mentioned earlier, under the UCC's Statute of Frauds, a writing is required only for contracts for the sale of goods priced at $500 or more (see Chapter 14).

rate another document by expressly referring to it. Several documents may form a single contract if they are physically attached, such as by staple, paper clip, or glue. Several documents may form a single contract even if they are only placed in the same envelope.

■ **EXAMPLE 10.21** Sam orally agrees to sell some land next to a shopping mall to Terry. Sam gives Terry an unsigned memo that contains a legal description of the property, and Terry gives Sam an unsigned first draft of their contract. Sam sends Terry a signed letter that refers to the memo and to the first and final drafts of the contract. Terry sends Sam an unsigned copy of the final draft of the contract with a signed check stapled to it. Together, the documents can constitute a writing sufficient to satisfy the Statute of Frauds and bind both parties to the terms of the contract as evidenced by the writings. ■

What Must Be Contained in the Writing?

A memorandum evidencing the oral contract need only contain the essential terms of the contract. Under most provisions of the Statute of Frauds, the writing must name the parties and identify the subject matter, consideration, and quantity. With respect to contracts for the sale of land, some states require that the memorandum also set forth the essential terms of the contract, such as location and price, with sufficient clarity to allow the terms to be determined from the memo itself, without reference to any outside sources. Under the UCC, in regard to the sale of goods, the writing need only state the quantity and be signed by the party against whom enforcement is sought.

Because only the party against whom enforcement is sought must have signed the writing, a contract may be

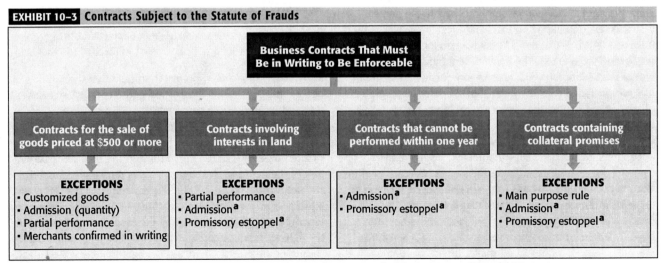

EXHIBIT 10–3 Contracts Subject to the Statute of Frauds

Business Contracts That Must Be in Writing to Be Enforceable

Contracts for the sale of goods priced at $500 or more	Contracts involving interests in land	Contracts that cannot be performed within one year	Contracts containing collateral promises
EXCEPTIONS • Customized goods • Admission (quantity) • Partial performance • Merchants confirmed in writing	**EXCEPTIONS** • Partial performance • Admission[a] • Promissory estoppel[a]	**EXCEPTIONS** • Admission[a] • Promissory estoppel[a]	**EXCEPTIONS** • Main purpose rule • Admission[a] • Promissory estoppel[a]

a. Some states follow Section 133 (on admissions) and Section 139 (on promissory estoppel) of the *Restatement (Second) of Contracts*.

enforceable by one of its parties but not by the other. **EXAMPLE 10.22** Rock orally agrees to buy Betty Devlin's lake house and lot for $350,000. Devlin writes Rock a letter confirming the sale by identifying the parties and the essential terms of the sales contract—price, method of payment, and legal address—and signs the letter. Devlin has made a written memorandum of the oral land contract. Because she signed the letter, she normally can be held to the oral contract by Rock. Rock, however, because he has not signed or entered into a written contract or memorandum, can plead the Statute of Frauds as a defense, and Devlin cannot enforce the contract against him. ■

THE PAROL EVIDENCE RULE

Sometimes, a written contract does not include—or contradicts—an oral understanding reached by the parties before or at the time of contracting. For example, suppose a person signs a lease agreement that says no pets are allowed because the landlord orally represented at the time of the lease contract that tenants were allowed to have cats. Can the tenant have a cat despite what the lease agreement says? In determining the outcome of such disputes, the courts look to a common law rule governing the admissibility in court of oral evidence, or *parol evidence.*

Under the **parol evidence rule,** if a court finds that a written contract represents the complete and final statement of the parties' agreement, then it will not allow either party to present parol evidence (testimony or other evidence of communications between the parties that are not contained in the contract itself). In other words, a party cannot introduce in court evidence of the parties' prior negotiations, prior agreements, or contemporaneous oral agreements if that evidence contradicts or varies the terms of the parties' written contract.[17]

Does a football team's agreement with its fans to sell "stadium builder licenses" (SBLs) for seats represent the parties' entire contract, or can an SBL brochure explain or vary the agreement? That was the question in the following case.

---

17. *Restatement (Second) of Contracts,* Section 213.

CASE 10.3   **Yocca v. Pittsburgh Steelers Sports, Inc.**

Supreme Court of Pennsylvania, 578 Pa. 479, 854 A.2d 425 (2004).

FACTS In October 1998, Pittsburgh Steelers Sports, Inc., and others (collectively, the Steelers) sent Ronald Yocca a brochure that advertised a new stadium to be built for the Pittsburgh Steelers football team. The brochure publicized the opportunity to buy stadium builder licenses (SBLs), which grant the right to buy annual season tickets to the games. Prices varied, depending on the seats' locations, which were indicated by small diagrams. Yocca applied for an SBL, listing his seating preferences. The Steelers sent him a letter notifying him of the section in which his seat was located. A diagram that was included with the letter showed different parameters of the seating section than were shown in the brochure's diagrams. The Steelers also sent Yocca documents setting out the terms of the SBL and requiring his signature. These documents included a clause that read, "This Agreement contains the entire agreement of the parties." Yocca signed the documents, and the Steelers told him the specific location of his seat. When he arrived at the stadium, however, the seat was not where he expected it to be. Yocca and other SBL buyers filed a suit in a Pennsylvania state court against the Steelers, alleging, among other things, breach of contract. The court ordered the dismissal of the complaint. The plaintiffs appealed to a state intermediate appellate court, which reversed this order. The defendants appealed to the state supreme court.

ISSUE Did the documents that the Steelers sent to Yocca setting forth the terms of the SBL constitute the parties' entire agreement and preclude the introduction of parol evidence?

DECISION Yes. The Pennsylvania Supreme Court reversed the lower court's judgment and ruled in favor of the Steelers.

REASON The state supreme court held that the SBL documents constituted the parties' entire contract and under the parol evidence rule could not be supplemented by previous negotiations or agreements. Because the plaintiffs' complaint was based on the claim that the defendants violated the terms of the brochure, and the brochure was not part of the contract, the complaint was properly dismissed. The court explained that "the SBL Brochure did not represent a promise by the Steelers to sell SBLs to Appellees. Rather, the Brochure was merely an offer by the Steelers to sell Appellees the right to be assigned an unspecified seat in an unspecified section of the new stadium and the right to receive a contract to buy an SBL for that later-assigned seat. *   *   * The SBL

CASE 10.3—Continued

Agreement clearly represented the parties' contract concerning the sale of SBLs. Unlike the SBL Brochure, the SBL Agreement reflected a promise by the Steelers to actually sell Appellees a specific number of SBL seats in a specified section. Furthermore, the SBL Agreement * * * explicitly stated that it represented the parties' entire contract regarding the sale of SBLs."

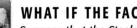 **WHAT IF THE FACTS WERE DIFFERENT?**
Suppose that the Steelers had not sent Yocca a diagram with the letter notifying him of his seat's section and that the SBL documents had not included a clause stating that the documents contained the entire agreement of the parties. Would the result have been different? Why or why not?

Exceptions to the Parol Evidence Rule

Because of the rigidity of the parol evidence rule, courts make several exceptions. These exceptions include the following:

1 Evidence of a *subsequent modification* of a written contract can be introduced in court. Keep in mind that the oral modifications may not be enforceable if they come under the Statute of Frauds—for example, if they increase the price of the goods for sale to $500 or more or increase the term for performance to more than one year. Also, oral modifications will not be enforceable if the original contract provides that any modification must be in writing.[18]

2 Oral evidence can be introduced in all cases to show that the contract was voidable or void (for example, induced by mistake, fraud, or misrepresentation). In this situation, if deception led one of the parties to agree to the terms of a written contract, oral evidence indicating fraud should not be excluded. Courts frown on bad faith and are quick to allow the introduction at trial of parol evidence when it establishes fraud.

3 When the terms of a written contract are ambiguous, evidence is admissible to show the meaning of the terms.

4 Evidence is admissible when the written contract is incomplete in that it lacks one or more of the essential terms. The courts allow evidence to "fill in the gaps" in the contract.

5 Under the UCC, evidence can be introduced to explain or supplement a written contract by showing a prior dealing, course of performance, or usage of trade.[19] We will discuss these terms in further detail in Chapter 14, in the context of sales contracts. Here, it is sufficient to say that when buyers and sellers deal with each other over extended periods of time, certain customary practices develop. These practices are often overlooked in the writing of the contract, so courts allow the introduction of evi-

dence to show how the parties have acted in the past. Usage of trade—practices and customs generally followed in a particular industry—can also shed light on the meaning of certain contract provisions, and thus evidence of trade usage may be admissible.

6 The parol evidence rule does not apply if the existence of the entire written contract is subject to an orally agreed-on condition. Proof of the condition does not alter or modify the written terms but affects the *enforceability* of the written contract. **■EXAMPLE 10.23** Jelek orally agrees to purchase Armand's car for $8,000, but only if Jelek's mechanic, Frank, inspects the car and approves of the purchase. Frank cannot do an inspection for another week, and Armand is leaving town for the weekend. Jelek wants to use the car right away, so he drafts a contract of sale that does not include the agreed-on condition of a mechanical inspection. Both parties sign the contract. The following week Frank, the mechanic, inspects the car but does not recommend its purchase. When Jelek does not buy the car, Armand sues him for breach of contract. In this case, Jelek's oral agreement did not alter or modify the terms of the written agreement but concerned whether the contract existed at all. Therefore, the parol evidence rule does not apply. ■

7 When an *obvious* or *gross* clerical (or typographic) error exists that clearly would not represent the agreement of the parties, parol evidence is admissible to correct the error. **■EXAMPLE 10.24** Sempter agrees to lease 1,000 square feet of office space from Stone Enterprises at the current monthly rate of $3 per square foot. The signed written lease provides for a monthly lease payment of $300 rather than the $3,000 agreed to by the parties. Because the error is obvious, Stone Enterprises would be allowed to admit parol evidence to correct the mistake. ■

Integrated Contracts

The determination of whether evidence will be allowed basically depends on whether the written contract is intended to be a complete and final statement of the terms of the

---

18. UCC 2–209(2), (3). See Chapter 14.
19. UCC 1–205, 2–202. See Chapter 14.

agreement. If it is so intended, it is referred to as an **integrated contract**, and extraneous evidence (evidence from outside the contract) is excluded.

An integrated contract can be either completely or partially integrated. If it contains all of the terms of the parties' agreement, then it is completely integrated. If it contains only some of the terms that the parties agreed on and not others, it is partially integrated. If the contract is only partially integrated, evidence of consistent additional terms is admissi-

ble to supplement the written agreement.[20] Note that for both completely and partially integrated contracts, courts exclude any evidence that *contradicts* the writing and allow parol evidence only to add to the terms of a partially integrated contract. Exhibit 10–4 illustrates the relationship between integrated contracts and the parol evidence rule.

20. *Restatement (Second) of Contracts*, Section 216.

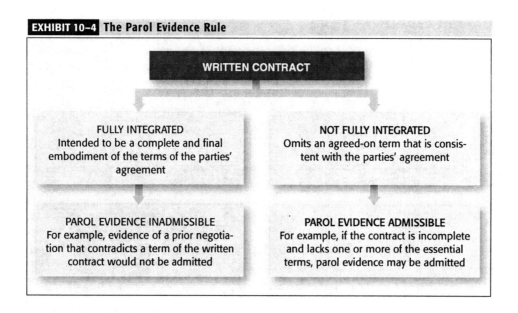

EXHIBIT 10–4 The Parol Evidence Rule

WRITTEN CONTRACT

FULLY INTEGRATED
Intended to be a complete and final embodiment of the terms of the parties' agreement

NOT FULLY INTEGRATED
Omits an agreed-on term that is consistent with the parties' agreement

PAROL EVIDENCE INADMISSIBLE
For example, evidence of a prior negotiation that contradicts a term of the written contract would not be admitted

PAROL EVIDENCE ADMISSIBLE
For example, if the contract is incomplete and lacks one or more of the essential terms, parol evidence may be admitted

REVIEWING Defenses to Contract Enforceability

Charter Golf, Inc., manufactures and sells golf apparel and supplies. Ken Odin had worked as a Charter sales representative for six months when he was offered a position with a competing firm. Charter's president, Jerry Montieth, offered Odin a 10 percent commission "for the rest of his life" if Ken would turn down the offer and stay on with Charter. He also promised that Odin would not be fired unless he was dishonest. Odin turned down the competitor's offer and stayed with Charter. Three years later, Charter fired Odin for no reason. Odin sued, alleging breach of contract. Using the information presented in the chapter, answer the following questions.

1 Would a court likely decide that Odin's employment contract falls within the Statute of Frauds? Why or why not?

2 Assume that the court does find that the contract falls within the Statute of Frauds and that the state in which the court sits recognizes every exception to the Statute of Frauds discussed in the chapter. What exception provides Odin with the best chance of enforcing the oral contract in this situation?

3 Now suppose that Montieth had taken out a pencil, written "10 percent for life" on the back of a register receipt, and handed it to Odin. Would this satisfy the Statute of Frauds? Why or why not?

4 Assume that Odin had signed a written employment contract at the time he was hired to work for Charter, but it was not completely integrated. Would a court allow Odin to present parol evidence of Montieth's subsequent promises?

TERMS AND CONCEPTS

bilateral mistake 204	integrated contract 216	*scienter* 207
collateral promise 210	parol evidence rule 214	Statute of Frauds 209
duress 208	prenuptial agreement 211	unilateral mistake 204

CHAPTER SUMMARY — Defenses to Contract Enforceability

GENUINENESS OF ASSENT

Mistakes
(See pages 203–205.)

1. *Unilateral*—Generally, the mistaken party is bound by the contract *unless* (a) the other party knows or should have known of the mistake or (b) the mistake is an inadvertent mathematical error—such as an error in addition or subtraction—committed without gross negligence.

2. *Bilateral (mutual)*—When both parties are mistaken about the same material fact, such as identity, either party can avoid the contract.

Fraudulent Misrepresentation
(See pages 205–208.)

When fraud occurs, usually the innocent party can enforce or avoid the contract. The elements necessary to establish fraud are as follows:

1. A misrepresentation of a material fact must occur.

2. There must be an intent to deceive.

3. The innocent party must justifiably rely on the misrepresentation.

Undue Influence
(See page 208.)

Undue influence arises from special relationships, such as fiduciary or confidential relationships, in which one party's free will has been overcome by the undue influence exerted by the other party. Usually, the contract is voidable.

Duress
(See pages 208–209.)

Duress is the tactic of forcing a party to enter a contract under the fear of a threat—for example, the threat of violence or serious economic loss. The party forced to enter the contract can rescind the contract.

FORM

The Statute of Frauds—Requirement of a Writing
(See pages 209–213.)

1. *Applicability*—The following types of contracts fall under the Statute of Frauds and must be in writing to be enforceable:

   a. Contracts involving interests in land—The statute applies to any contract for an interest in realty, such as a sale, a lease, or a mortgage.

   b. Contracts that cannot by their terms be performed within one year—The statute applies only to contracts that are objectively impossible to perform fully within one year from (the day after) the contract's formation.

   c. Collateral promises—The statute applies only to express contracts made between the guarantor and the creditor that make the guarantor secondarily liable. Exception: the main purpose rule.

   d. Promises made in consideration of marriage—The statute applies to promises to make a monetary payment or give property in consideration of a promise to marry and to prenuptial agreements made in consideration of marriage.

   e. Contracts for the sale of goods priced at $500 or more—See the Statute of Frauds provision in Section 2–201 of the Uniform Commercial Code (UCC).

2. *Exceptions*—Partial performance, admissions, and promissory estoppel.

(Continued)

CHAPTER SUMMARY	Defenses to Contract Enforceability—Continued
The Statute of Frauds—Sufficiency of the Writing (See pages 213–214.)	To constitute an enforceable contract under the Statute of Frauds, a writing must be signed by the party against whom enforcement is sought, name the parties, identify the subject matter, and state with reasonable certainty the essential terms of the contract. In a sale of land, the price and a description of the property may need to be stated with sufficient clarity to allow them to be determined without reference to outside sources. Under the UCC, a contract for a sale of goods is not enforceable beyond the quantity of goods shown in the contract.
The Parol Evidence Rule (See pages 214–216.)	The parol evidence rule prohibits the introduction at trial of evidence of the parties' prior negotiations, prior agreements, or contemporaneous oral agreements that contradicts or varies the terms of the parties' written contract. The written contract is assumed to be the complete embodiment of the parties' agreement. Exceptions are made in the following circumstances: 1. To show that the contract was subsequently modified. 2. To show that the contract was voidable or void. 3. To clarify the meaning of ambiguous terms. 4. To clarify the terms of the contract when the written contract lacks one or more of its essential terms. 5. Under the UCC, to explain the meaning of contract terms in light of a prior dealing, course of performance, or usage of trade. 6. To show that the entire contract is subject to an orally agreed-on condition. 7. When an obvious clerical or typographic error was made.

FOR REVIEW

Answers for the even-numbered questions in this **For Review** *section can be found on this text's accompanying Web site at* **www.cengage.com/blaw/fbl.** *Select "Chapter 10" and click on "For Review."*

1 In what types of situations might genuineness of assent to a contract's terms be lacking?

2 What is the difference between a mistake of value or quality and a mistake of fact?

3 What elements must exist for fraudulent misrepresentation to occur?

4 What contracts must be in writing to be enforceable?

5 What is parol evidence? When is it admissible to clarify the terms of a written contract?

QUESTIONS AND CASE PROBLEMS

 ## HYPOTHETICAL SCENARIOS AND CASE PROBLEMS

10.1 Genuineness of Assent. Jerome is an elderly man who lives with his nephew, Philip. Jerome is totally dependent on Philip's support. Philip tells Jerome that unless Jerome transfers a tract of land he owns to Philip for a price 30 percent below market value, Philip will no longer support and take care of him. Jerome enters into the contract. Discuss fully whether Jerome can set aside this contract.

10.2 Hypothetical Question with Sample Answer. Gemma promises a local hardware store that she will pay for a lawn mower that her brother is purchasing on credit if the brother fails to pay

the debt. Must this promise be in writing to be enforceable? Why or why not?

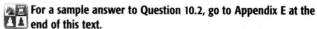 **For a sample answer to Question 10.2, go to Appendix E at the end of this text.**

10.3 Fraudulent Misrepresentation. Larry offered to sell Stanley his car and told Stanley that the car had been driven only 25,000 miles and had never been in an accident. Stanley hired Cohen, a mechanic, to appraise the condition of the car, and Cohen said that the car probably had at least 50,000 miles on it and probably had been in an accident. In spite of this information, Stanley still thought the car would be a good buy for the price, so he purchased it. Later, when the car developed numerous mechanical problems, Stanley sought to rescind the contract on the basis of Larry's fraudulent misrepresentation of the auto's condition. Will Stanley be able to rescind his contract? Discuss.

10.4 Statute of Frauds. Sierra Bravo, Inc., and Shelby's, Inc., entered into a written "Waste Disposal Agreement" under which Shelby's allowed Sierra to deposit on Shelby's land waste products, deleterious (harmful) materials, and debris removed by Sierra in the construction of a highway. Later, Shelby's asked Sierra why it had not constructed a waterway and a building pad suitable for a commercial building on the property, as they had orally agreed. Sierra denied any such agreement. Shelby's filed a suit in a Missouri state court against Sierra, alleging breach of contract. Sierra contended that any oral agreement was unenforceable under the Statute of Frauds. Sierra argued that because the right to remove minerals from land is considered a contract for the sale of an interest in land to which the Statute of Frauds applies, the Statute of Frauds should apply to the right to deposit soil on another person's property. How should the court rule, and why? [*Shelby's, Inc. v. Sierra Bravo, Inc.*, 68 S.W.3d 604 (Mo.App. S.D. 2002)]

10.5 The Parol Evidence Rule. Novell, Inc., owned the source code for DR DOS, a computer operating system that Microsoft Corp. targeted with anticompetitive practices in the early 1990s. Novell worried that if it filed a suit, Microsoft would retaliate with further unfair practices. Consequently, Novell sold DR DOS to Caldera, Inc., the predecessor in interest to Canopy Group. The purposes of the sale were to obligate Canopy to bring an action against Microsoft and to allow Novell to share in the recovery without revealing its role. Novell and Canopy signed two documents: a contract of sale, obligating Canopy to pay $400,000 for rights to the source code, and a temporary license, obligating Canopy to pay at least $600,000 in royalties, which included a percentage of any recovery from the suit. Canopy settled the dispute with Microsoft, deducted its expenses, and paid Novell its percentage. Novell filed a suit in a Utah state court against Canopy, alleging breach of contract for Canopy's deduction of expenses. Canopy responded that it could show that the parties had an oral agreement on this point. On what basis might the court refuse to consider this evidence? Is that the appropriate course in this case? Explain. [*Novell, Inc. v. Canopy Group, Inc.*, 2004 UT App. 162, 92 P.3d 768 (2004)]

10.6 The Parol Evidence Rule. Carlin Krieg owned a dairy farm in St. Joe, Indiana, that was appraised at $154,000 in December 1997. In August 1999, Krieg told Donald Hieber that he intended to sell the farm for $106,000. Hieber offered to buy it. Krieg also told Hieber that he wanted to retain a "right of residency" for life in the farm. In October, Krieg and Hieber executed a "Purchase Agreement" that provided that Krieg "shall transfer full and complete possession" of the farm "subject to [his] right of residency." The agreement also con-

tained an integration clause that stated "there are no conditions, representations, warranties, or agreements not stated in this instrument." In November 2000, the house was burned in a fire, rendering it unlivable. Hieber filed an insurance claim for the damage and received the proceeds, but he did not fix the house. Krieg filed a suit in an Indiana state court against Hieber, alleging breach of contract. Is there any basis on which the court can consider evidence regarding the parties' negotiations prior to their agreement for the sale of the farm? Explain. [*Krieg v. Hieber*, 802 N.E.2d 938 (Ind.App. 2004)]

10.7 Case Problem with Sample Answer. According to the student handbook at Cleveland Chiropractic College (CCC) in Missouri, *academic misconduct* includes "selling . . . any copy of any material intended to be used as an instrument of academic evaluation in advance of its initial administration." Leonard Verni was enrolled at CCC in Dr. Aleksandr Makarov's dermatology class. Before the first examination, Verni was reported to be selling copies of the test. CCC investigated and concluded that Verni had committed academic misconduct. Verni was dismissed from CCC, which informed him of his right to an appeal. According to the handbook, at the hearing on appeal a student could have an attorney or other adviser, present witnesses' testimony and other evidence, and "question any testimony . . . against him/her." At his hearing, however, Verni did not bring his attorney, present evidence on his behalf, or question any adverse witnesses. When the dismissal was upheld, Verni filed a suit in a Missouri state court against CCC and others, claiming, in part, fraudulent misrepresentation. Verni argued that because he "relied" on the handbook's "representation" that CCC would follow its appeal procedure, he was unable to properly refute the charges against him. Can Verni succeed with this argument? Explain. [*Verni v. Cleveland Chiropractic College*, 212 S.W.3d 150 (Mo. 2007)]

After you have answered Problem 10.7, compare your answer with the sample answer given on the Web site that accompanies this text. Go to www.cengage.com/blaw/fbl, select "Chapter 10," and click on "Case Problem with Sample Answer."

10.8 Contract for a Sale of Goods. Milton Blankenship agreed in writing to buy 15 acres of Ella Mae Henry's junkyard property for $15,000 per acre with a ten-year option to buy the remaining 28.32 acres. Blankenship orally agreed to (1) begin operating a car skeleton processing plant within six to fifteen months; (2) buy as many car skeletons generated by the yard as Clifford Henry wanted to sell him, at a certain premium over the market price; and (3) allow all junk vehicles on the property to remain until they were processed at the new plant. Blankenship never operated such a plant, never bought any vehicles from the yard, and demanded that all vehicles be removed from the property. To obtain the remaining 28.32 acres, Blankenship filed a suit in a Georgia state court against Henry, who responded with a counterclaim for breach of contract. Under oath during discovery,

Henry testified that their oral agreement allowed him to sell "as many of the car skeletons generated by the Henry junkyard" as he wished, and Blankenship testified that he had agreed to buy as many skeletons as Henry was willing to sell. Does the Statute of Frauds undercut or support Henry's counterclaim? Explain. [*Henry v. Blankenship*, 284 Ga.App. 578, 644 S.E.2d 419 (2007)]

10.9 **A Question of Ethics.** *On behalf of BRJM, LLC, Nicolas Kepple offered Howard Engelsen $210,000 for a parcel of land known as lot five on the north side of Barnes Road in Stonington, Connecticut. Engelsen's company, Output Systems, Inc., owned the land. Engelsen had the lot surveyed and obtained an appraisal. The appraiser valued the property at $277,000, after determining that it was 3.0 acres and thus could not be subdivided because it did not meet the town's minimum legal requirement of 3.7 acres for subdivision. Engelsen responded to Kepple's offer with a counteroffer of $230,000, which Kepple accepted. On May 3, 2002, the parties signed a contract. When Engelsen*

refused to go through with the deal, BRJM filed a suit in a Connecticut state court against Output, seeking specific performance and other relief. The defendant asserted the defense of mutual mistake on at least two grounds. [BRJM, LLC v. Output Systems, Inc., 100 Conn.App. 143, 917 A.2d 605 (2007)]

1 In the counteroffer, Engelsen asked Kepple to remove from their contract a clause requiring written confirmation of the availability of a "free split," which meant that the property could be subdivided without the town's prior approval. Kepple agreed. After signing the contract, Kepple learned that the property was not entitled to a free split. Would this circumstance qualify as a mistake on which the defendant could avoid the contract? Why or why not?

2 After signing the contract, Engelsen obtained a second appraisal that established the size of lot five as 3.71 acres, which meant that it could be subdivided, and valued the property at $490,000. Can the defendant avoid the contract on the basis of a mistake in the first appraisal? Explain.

CRITICAL THINKING AND WRITING ASSIGNMENTS

10.10 Critical Legal Thinking. Describe the types of individuals who might be capable of exerting undue influence on others.

10.11 **Video Question.** Go to this text's Web site at **www.cengage.com/blaw/fbl** and select "Chapter 10." Click on "Video Questions" and view the video titled *Mistake*. Then answer the following questions.

1 What kind of mistake is involved in the dispute shown in the video (bilateral or unilateral, mistake of fact or mistake of value)?

2 According to the chapter, in what two situations would the supermarket be able to rescind a contract to sell peppers to Melnick at the incorrectly advertised price?

3 Does it matter if the price that was advertised was a reasonable price for the peppers? Why or why not?

ACCESSING THE INTERNET

For updated links to resources available on the Web, as well as a variety of other materials, visit this text's Web site at

www.cengage.com/blaw/fbl

For information on the *Restatements of the Law*, including the *Restatement (Second) of Contracts*, go to the American Law Institute's Web site at

www.ali.org

The online version of UCC Section 2–201 on the Statute of Frauds includes links to definitions of certain terms used in the section. To access this site, go to

www.law.cornell.edu/ucc/2/2-201.html

For an interesting discussion of the history and current applicability of the Statute of Frauds, both internationally and in the United States, go to

en.wikipedia.org/wiki/Statute_of_frauds

To read more about contesting contracts on the grounds of fraud and duress, go to

www.lawyers.com/index.php

PRACTICAL INTERNET EXERCISES

Go to this text's Web site at **www.cengage.com/blaw/fbl**, select "Chapter 10," and click on "Practical Internet Exercises." There you will find the following Internet research exercises that you can perform to learn more about the topics covered in this chapter.

PRACTICAL INTERNET EXERCISE 10-1 LEGAL PERSPECTIVE—Promissory Estoppel and the Statute of Frauds

PRACTICAL INTERNET EXERCISE 10-2 MANAGEMENT PERSPECTIVE—Fraudulent Misrepresentation

PRACTICAL INTERNET EXERCISE 10-3 ECONOMIC PERSPECTIVE—Economic Duress

BEFORE THE TEST

Go to this text's Web site at **www.cengage.com/blaw/fbl**, select "Chapter 10," and click on "Interactive Quizzes." You will find a number of interactive questions relating to this chapter.

6

Third Party Rights and Discharge

AFTER READING THIS CHAPTER, YOU SHOULD BE ABLE TO ANSWER THE FOLLOWING QUESTIONS:

1 What is the difference between an assignment and a delegation?

2 What rights can be assigned despite a contract clause expressly prohibiting assignment?

3 What factors indicate that a third party beneficiary is an intended beneficiary?

4 How are most contracts discharged?

5 What is a contractual condition, and how might a condition affect contractual obligations?

Because a contract is a private agreement between the parties who have entered into it, it is fitting that these parties alone should have rights and liabilities under the contract. This concept is referred to as **privity of contract,** and it establishes the basic principle that third parties have no rights in contracts to which they are not parties.

You may be convinced by now that for every rule of contract law, there is an exception. When justice cannot be served by adherence to a rule of law, exceptions to the rule must be made. In this chapter, we look at some exceptions to the rule of privity of contract. These exceptions include *assignments* and *delegations*, as well as *third party beneficiary contracts*. We also examine how contractual obligations can be *discharged*. Normally, contract discharge is accomplished by both parties performing the acts promised in the contract. In the latter part of this chapter, we look at the degree of performance required to discharge a contractual obligation, as well as at some other ways in which contract discharge can occur.

ASSIGNMENTS

In a bilateral contract, the two parties have corresponding rights and duties. One party has a *right* to require the other to perform some task, and the other has a *duty* to perform it. Sometimes, though, a party will transfer her or his rights under the contract to someone else. The transfer of contract *rights* to

a third person is known as an **assignment.** (The transfer of contract duties is a *delegation*, as discussed later in this chapter.)

Assignments are important because they are utilized in much business financing. Lending institutions, such as banks, frequently assign the rights to receive payments under their loan contracts to other firms, which pay for those rights. If you obtain a loan from your local bank to purchase a car, you may later receive in the mail a notice stating that your bank has transferred (assigned) its rights to receive payments on the loan to another firm and that, when the time comes to repay your loan, you must make the payments to that other firm.

Lenders that make *mortgage loans* (loans to allow prospective home buyers to purchase land or a home) often assign their rights to collect the mortgage payments to a third party, such as GMAC Mortgage Corporation. Following an assignment, the home buyer is notified that future payments must be made to the third party, rather than to the original lender. Billions of dollars change hands daily in the business world in the form of assignments of rights in contracts.

Effect of an Assignment

In an assignment, the party assigning the rights to a third party is known as the **assignor,**[1] and the party receiving the rights is the **assignee.** Other traditional terminology used to describe

---

1. Pronounced uh-*sye*-nore.

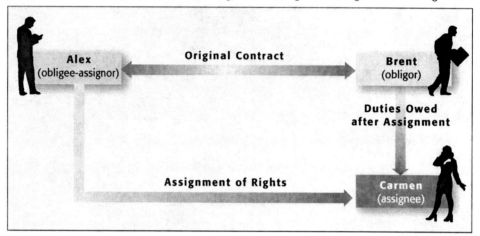

EXHIBIT 11–1 Assignment Relationships

In the assignment relationship illustrated here, Alex assigns his *rights* under a contract that he made with Brent to a third party, Carmen. Alex thus becomes the *assignor* and Carmen the *assignee* of the contractual rights. Brent, the *obligor* (the party owing performance under the contract), now owes performance to Carmen instead of Alex. Alex's original contract rights are extinguished after assignment.

Alex (obligee-assignor) — Original Contract — Brent (obligor)

Duties Owed after Assignment

Assignment of Rights — Carmen (assignee)

the parties in assignment relationships are the **obligee**[2] (the person to whom a duty, or obligation, is owed) and the **obligor** (the person who is obligated to perform the duty).

When rights under a contract are assigned unconditionally, the rights of the *assignor* (the party making the assignment) are extinguished. The third party (the *assignee*, or the party receiving the assignment) has a right to demand performance from the other original party to the contract (the *obligor*, the person who is obligated to perform). ■**EXAMPLE 11.1** Brent (the obligor) owes Alex $1,000, and Alex, the obligee, assigns to Carmen the right to receive the $1,000 (thus, Alex is now the assignor). Here, a valid assignment of a debt exists. Carmen, the assignee, can enforce the contract against Brent, the obligor, if Brent fails to perform (pay the $1,000). ■ Exhibit 11–1 illustrates assignment relationships.

The assignee obtains only those rights that the assignor originally had. Also, the assignee's rights are subject to the defenses

that the obligor has against the assignor. ■**EXAMPLE 11.2** Brent owes Alex $1,000 under a contract in which Brent agreed to buy Alex's MacBook Pro laptop. Alex assigns his right to receive the $1,000 to Carmen. Brent, in deciding to purchase the laptop, relied on Alex's fraudulent misrepresentation that the computer had 2 gigabytes of memory. When Brent discovers that the computer has only 1 gigabyte of memory, he tells Alex that he is going to return the laptop and cancel the contract. Even though Alex has assigned his "right" to receive the $1,000 to Carmen, Brent need not pay Carmen the $1,000—Brent can raise the defense of Alex's fraudulent misrepresentation to avoid payment. ■

In general, an assignment can take any form, oral or written (except when another law requires it to be in writing, such as assignments of real property interests). Problems can arise with proving oral assignments, however, especially when two parties claim to be the assignee, as the next case illustrates. In addition, like other contracts, assignments must be supported by consideration.

---
2. Pronounced ä-ble-*gee*.

CASE 11.1 Martha Graham School and Dance Foundation, Inc. v. Martha Graham Center of Contemporary Dance, Inc.

United States Court of Appeals, Second Circuit, 380 F.3d 624 (2004).

FACTS Martha Graham's career as a dancer, dance instructor, and choreographer began in the first third of the twentieth century. In the 1920s, she started a dance company and a dance school and choreographed works on commission.

In the 1940s, she funded the Martha Graham Center of Contemporary Dance, Inc. (the Center). She sold her school to the Martha Graham School of Contemporary Dance, Inc. (the

CASE 11.1—Continues next page

CASE 11.1—Continued

School), in 1956. By 1980, the Center encompassed the School. In 1989, two years before her death, Graham executed a will in which she gave Ronald Protas, the Center's general director, "any rights or interests" in "dance works, musical scores [and] scenery sets." After her death, Protas asserted ownership of all of Graham's dances and related property. In 1999, the Center's board removed Protas and, due to financial problems, suspended operations. Meanwhile, Protas founded the Martha Graham School and Dance Foundation, Inc., and began licensing Graham's dances. When the School reopened in 2001, Protas and his foundation filed a suit in a federal district court against the Center and others to enjoin their use of, among other things, seventy of the dances. The Center responded, in part, that Graham had assigned the dances to it. The court ruled that twenty-one of the dances had been assigned to the Center. The plaintiffs appealed to the U.S. Court of Appeals for the Second Circuit.

ISSUE Did Martha Graham orally assign her interest in the dances to the Center before she executed a will leaving the Center's director, Protas, any rights or interests in her dance works?

DECISION Yes. The U.S. Court of Appeals for the Second Circuit affirmed the lower court's judgment on this issue. The oral assignment of certain dances to the Center was valid.

REASON The appellate court found that although the assignment had been oral, it had been reliably proven by written testimony and supported by consideration—that is, Graham had benefited by being relieved of various administrative duties at the time of the assignment. Evidence that Graham had assigned all of her pre-1956 dances to the Center were two letters from Lee Leatherman, the Center's executive administrator at the time. The letters, written in 1968 and 1971, indicated that "recently Miss Graham assigned performing rights to all of her works to the Martha Graham Center of Contemporary Dance, Inc.," and that "Martha has assigned all rights to all of her works to the Martha Graham Center, Inc." In addition, Jeannette Roosevelt, former president of the Center's board of directors, testified that Graham had given the dances to the Center prior to 1965 or 1966, when she joined the board. There was additional evidence that the Center had acted as the owner of the dances by entering into contracts with other parties, and that Graham was aware of this and did not object. Other evidence showed that the Center received royalties for the dances and treated them as its assets.

 WHAT IF THE FACTS WERE DIFFERENT? *Suppose that Graham had not benefited from the Center's assumption of the duties associated with her choreography. Would the alleged assignment have been valid? Why or why not?*

Rights That Cannot Be Assigned

As a general rule, all rights can be assigned. Exceptions are made, however, in the following special circumstances.

When a Statute Expressly Prohibits Assignment If a statute expressly prohibits assignment, the particular right in question cannot be assigned. **■EXAMPLE 11.3** Marn is a new employee of CompuFuture, Inc. CompuFuture is an employer under workers' compensation statutes (see Chapter 23) in this state, so Marn is a covered employee. Marn has a relatively high-risk job. In need of a loan, she borrows from Stark, assigning to Stark all workers' compensation benefits due her should she be injured on the job. A state statute prohibits the assignment of *future* workers' compensation benefits, and thus such rights cannot be assigned. ■

When a Contract Is Personal in Nature When a contract is for personal services, the rights under the contract normally cannot be assigned unless all that remains is a monetary payment. **■EXAMPLE 11.4** Brent signs a contract to be a tutor for Alex's children. Alex then attempts to assign to Carmen his right to Brent's services. Carmen cannot enforce the contract against Brent. Brent may not like Carmen's children or for some other reason may not want to tutor them. Because personal services are unique to the person rendering them, rights to receive personal services cannot be assigned. ■

When an Assignment Will Significantly Change the Risk or Duties of the Obligor A right cannot be assigned if assignment will significantly increase or alter the risks or the duties of the obligor (the party owing performance under the contract).[3] **■EXAMPLE 11.5** Alex has a hotel, and to insure it, he takes out a policy with Northwest Insurance Company. The policy insures against fire, theft, floods, and vandalism. Alex attempts to assign the insurance policy to Carmen, who also owns a hotel. The assignment is ineffective because it may substantially alter the insurance company's duty of performance and the risk that the company undertakes. An insurance company evaluates the particular risk of a certain party

---

3. See Section 2–210(2) of the Uniform Commercial Code (UCC).

and tailors its policy to fit that risk. If the policy is assigned to a third party, the insurance risk is materially altered. ■

When the Contract Prohibits Assignment   If a contract stipulates that the right cannot be assigned, then *ordinarily* it cannot be assigned.   ■**EXAMPLE 11.6**   Brent agrees to build a house for Alex. The contract between Brent and Alex states, "This contract cannot be assigned by Alex without Brent's consent. Any assignment without such consent renders this contract void, and all rights hereunder will thereupon terminate." Alex then assigns his rights to Carmen, without first obtaining Brent's consent. Carmen cannot enforce the contract against Brent. ■   This rule has several exceptions:

1   A contract cannot prevent an assignment of the right to receive funds. This exception exists to encourage the free flow of funds and credit in modern business settings.

2   The assignment of ownership rights in real estate often cannot be prohibited because such a prohibition is contrary to public policy in most states. Prohibitions of this kind are called restraints against **alienation** (the voluntary transfer of land ownership).

3   The assignment of negotiable instruments (see Chapter 18) cannot be prohibited.

4   In a contract for the sale of goods, the right to receive damages for breach of contract or for payment of an account owed may be assigned even though the sales contract prohibits such an assignment.[4]

Notice of Assignment

Once a valid assignment of rights has been made to a third party, the third party should notify the obligor of the assignment (for example, in Exhibit 11–1 on page 223, Carmen should notify Brent). Giving notice is not legally necessary to establish the validity of the assignment because an assignment is effective immediately, whether or not notice is given. Two major problems arise, however, when notice of the assignment is *not* given to the obligor:

1   If the assignor assigns the same right to two different persons, the question arises as to which one has priority—that is, which one has the right to the performance by the obligor. Although the rule most often observed in the United States is that the first assignment in time is the first in right, some states follow the English rule, which basically gives priority to the first assignee who gives notice.   ■**EXAMPLE 11.7**   Brent owes Alex $5,000 on a contractual obligation. On May 1, Alex assigns this

monetary claim to Carmen, but she does not give notice of the assignment to Brent. On June 1, for services Dorman has rendered to Alex, Alex assigns the same monetary claim (to collect $5,000 from Brent) to Dorman. Dorman immediately notifies Brent of the assignment. In the majority of states, Carmen would have priority because the assignment to her was first in time. In some states, however, Dorman would have priority because he gave first notice. ■

2   Until the obligor has notice of an assignment, the obligor can discharge his or her obligation by performance to the assignor, and this performance constitutes a discharge to the assignee. Once the obligor receives proper notice, only performance to the assignee can discharge the obligor's obligations.   ■**EXAMPLE 11.8**   Suppose that Alex, in the above example, assigns to Carmen his right to collect $5,000 from Brent, and Carmen does not give notice to Brent. Brent subsequently pays Alex the $5,000. Although the assignment was valid, Brent's payment to Alex is a discharge of the debt, and Carmen's failure to notify Brent of the assignment causes her to lose the right to collect the $5,000 from Brent. (Note that Carmen still has a claim against Alex for the $5,000.) If Carmen had given Brent notice of the assignment, however, Brent's payment to Alex would not have discharged the debt. ■

PREVENTING LEGAL DISPUTES   **Providing notice of assignment, though not legally required, is one of the best ways to avoid potential legal disputes over assignments. Whether you are the assignee or the assignor, you should inform the obligor of the assignment. An assignee who does not give notice may lose the right to performance, but failure to notify the obligor may have repercussions for the assignor as well. If no notice is given and the obligor performs the duty for the assignor, the assignee, to whom the right to receive performance was assigned, can sue the assignor for breach of contract. Litigation may also ensue if the assignor has assigned a right to two different parties, which can happen when assigning rights that overlap somewhat (such as rights to receive profits from a specific enterprise).**

■

DELEGATIONS

Just as an individual party can transfer rights to a third party through an assignment, that party can also transfer duties. Duties are not assigned, however; they are *delegated*.

---

4. UCC 2–210(2).

Normally, a **delegation of duties** does not relieve the party making the delegation (the **delegator**) of the obligation to perform in the event that the party to whom the duty has been delegated (the **delegatee**) fails to perform. No special form is required to create a valid delegation of duties. As long as the delegator expresses an intention to make the delegation, it is effective; the delegator need not even use the word *delegate*. Exhibit 11–2 graphically illustrates delegation relationships.

Duties That Cannot Be Delegated

As a general rule, any duty can be delegated. This rule has some exceptions, however. Delegation is prohibited in the following circumstances:

1 When performance depends on the personal skill or talents of the obligor.

2 When special trust has been placed in the obligor.

3 When performance by a third party will vary materially from that expected by the obligee (the one to whom performance is owed) under the contract.

4 When the contract expressly prohibits delegation.

The following examples will help to clarify the kinds of duties that can and cannot be delegated:

1 Brent contracts with Alex to tutor Alex in various aspects of financial underwriting and investment banking. (Brent, an experienced businessperson known for his expertise in finance, delegates his duties to a third party, Carmen. This delegation is ineffective because Brent contracted to render a service that is founded on Brent's *expertise* and Alex placed *special trust* in Brent's teaching ability.) The delegation changes Alex's expectancy under the contract.

2 Brent, a famous musician, contracts with Alex to (*personally* perform at a concert. Then Brent receives a better offer elsewhere and delegates his duty to perform to another musician, Miles. Regardless of Miles's exceptional musical talents, the delegation is not effective without Alex's consent because the contract was for *personal* performance.)

3 Brent, an accountant, contracts to perform annual audits of Alex's business records for the next five years. The contract states that Brent must provide the services himself and cannot delegate these duties to another. Two years later, Brent is busy on other projects and delegates his obligations to perform Alex's audit to Arianna, who is a certified public accountant at the same firm. This delegation is not effective because the contract *expressly prohibited* delegation.

4 Alex is a wealthy philanthropist who just created a charitable foundation. Alex has known Brent for twenty years and knows that Brent shares his beliefs on many humanitarian issues. He contracts with Brent to be in charge of allocating funds among various charitable causes. Six months later, Brent is experiencing health problems and delegates his duties to Drew. Alex does not approve of Drew as a replacement. In this situation, Alex can claim the delegation was not effective because it *materially altered his*

EXHIBIT 11–2 **Delegation Relationships**

In the delegation relationship illustrated here, Brent delegates his *duties* under a contract that he made with Alex to a third party, Carmen. Brent thus becomes the *delegator* and Carmen the *delegatee* of the contractual duties. Carmen now owes performance of the contractual duties to Alex. Note that a delegation of duties normally does not relieve the delegator (Brent) of liability if the delegatee (Carmen) fails to perform the contractual duties.

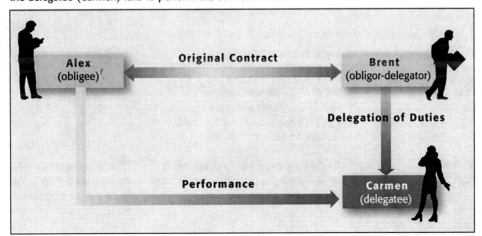

Alex (obligee)   — Original Contract —   Brent (obligor-delegator)

Delegation of Duties

Performance

Carmen (delegatee)

expectations under the contract. Alex had reasonable expectations about the types of charities to which Brent would give the foundation's funds, and substituting Drew's performance materially changes those expectations.

5 Brent contracts with Alex to pick up and deliver heavy construction machinery to Alex's property. Brent delegates this duty to Carmen, who is in the business of delivering heavy machinery. This delegation is effective. The performance required is of a routine and nonpersonal nature, and the delegation does not change Alex's expectations under the contract.

Effect of a Delegation

If a delegation of duties is enforceable, the *obligee* (the one to whom performance is owed) must accept performance from the delegatee (the one to whom the duties are delegated). **■EXAMPLE 11.9** In the fifth example in the above list, Brent delegates his duty (to pick up and deliver heavy construction machinery to Alex's property) to Carmen. In that situation, Alex (the obligee) must accept performance from Carmen (the delegatee) because the delegation was effective. The obligee can legally refuse performance from the delegatee only if the duty is one that cannot be delegated. **■**

A valid delegation of duties does not relieve the delegator of obligations under the contract. In the above example, if Carmen (the delegatee) fails to perform, Brent (the delegator) is still liable to Alex (the obligee). The obligee can also hold the delegatee liable if the delegatee made a promise of performance that will directly benefit the obligee. In this situation, there is an "assumption of duty" on the part of the delegatee, and breach of this duty makes the delegatee liable to the obligee. For example, if Carmen (the delegatee) promises Brent (the delegator), in a contract, to pick up and deliver the construction equipment to Alex's property but fails to do so, Alex (the obligee) can sue Brent, Carmen, or both. Although there are many exceptions, the general rule today is that the obligee can sue both the delegatee and the delegator.

Exhibit 11–3 summarizes the basic principles of the laws governing assignments and delegations.

"Assignment of All Rights"

Sometimes, a contract provides for an "assignment of all rights." The traditional view was that under this type of assignment, the assignee did not assume any duties. This view was based on the theory that the assignee's agreement to accept the benefits of the contract was not sufficient to imply a promise to assume the duties of the contract.

EXHIBIT 11–3 Assignments and Delegations		
Which rights can be assigned, and which duties can be delegated?	**All rights can be assigned *unless*:** 1. A statute expressly prohibits assignment. 2. The assignment will materially alter the obligor's risk or duties. 3. The contract is for personal services. 4. The contract prohibits assignment.	**All duties can be delegated *unless*:** 1. Performance depends on the obligor's personal skills or talents. 2. Special trust has been placed in the obligor. 3. Performance by a third party will materially vary from that expected by the obligee. 4. The contract prohibits delegation.
What if the contract prohibits assignment or delegation?	**No rights can be assigned *except*:** 1. Rights to receive money. 2. Ownership rights in real estate. 3. Rights to negotiable instruments. 4. Rights to payments under a sales contract or damages for breach of a sales contract.	**No duties can be delegated.**
What is the effect on the original party's rights?	On a valid assignment, effective immediately, the original party (assignor) no longer has any rights under the contract.	On a valid delegation, if the delegatee fails to perform, the original party (delegator) is liable to the obligee (who may also hold the delegatee liable).

Modern authorities, however, take the view that the probable intent in using such general words is to create both an assignment of rights and an assumption of duties.[5] Therefore, when general words are used (for example, "I assign the contract" or "all my rights under the contract"), the contract is construed as implying both an assignment of rights and an assumption of duties.

THIRD PARTY BENEFICIARIES

As mentioned earlier in this chapter, to have contractual rights, a person normally must be a party to the contract. In other words, privity of contract must exist. An exception to the doctrine of privity exists when the original parties to the contract intend, at the time of contracting, that the contract performance directly benefit a third person. In this situation, the third person becomes a **third party beneficiary** of the contract. As an **intended beneficiary** of the contract, the third party has legal rights and can sue the promisor directly for breach of the contract.

Who, though, is the promisor? In bilateral contracts, both parties to the contract are promisors because they both make promises that can be enforced. In third party beneficiary contracts, courts determine the identity of the promisor by asking which party made the promise that benefits the third party—that person is the promisor. Allowing the third party to sue the promisor directly in effect circumvents the "middle person" (the promisee) and thus reduces the burden on the courts. Otherwise, the third party would sue the promisee, who would then sue the promisor.

A classic case in the area of third party beneficiary contracts is *Lawrence v. Fox*[6]—a case decided in 1859. In that case, the court set aside the traditional requirement of privity and allowed a third party to bring a suit directly against the promisor.

Types of Intended Beneficiaries

The law distinguishes between *intended* beneficiaries and *incidental* beneficiaries. Only intended beneficiaries acquire legal rights in a contract. One type of intended beneficiary is a *creditor beneficiary*. Like the plaintiff in *Lawerence v. Fox*, a creditor beneficiary benefits from a contract in which one party (the promisor) promises another party (the promisee) to pay a debt that the promisee owes to a third party (the creditor beneficiary). As an intended beneficiary, the creditor beneficiary can sue the promisor directly to enforce the contract.

Another type of intended beneficiary is a *donee* beneficiary. When a contract is made for the express purpose of giving a *gift* to a third party, the third party (the donee beneficiary) can sue the promisor directly to enforce the promise.[7] The most common donee beneficiary contract is a life insurance contract. ▣ **EXAMPLE 11.10** Akins (the promisee) pays premiums to Standard Life, a life insurance company, and Standard Life (the promisor) promises to pay a certain amount on Akins's death to anyone Akins designates as a beneficiary. The designated beneficiary is a donee beneficiary under the life insurance policy and can enforce the promise made by the insurance company to pay her or him on Akins's death. ▣

As the law concerning third party beneficiaries evolved, numerous cases arose in which the third party beneficiary did not fit readily into either the creditor beneficiary or the donee beneficiary category. Thus, the modern view, and the one adopted by the *Restatement (Second) of Contracts*, does not draw such clear lines and distinguishes only between intended beneficiaries (who can sue to enforce contracts made for their benefit) and incidental beneficiaries (who cannot sue, as will be discussed shortly).

When the Rights of an Intended Beneficiary Vest

An intended third party beneficiary cannot enforce a contract against the original parties until the rights of the third party have *vested*, meaning that the rights have taken effect and cannot be taken away. Until these rights have vested, the original parties to the contract—the promisor and the promisee—can modify or rescind the contract without the consent of the third party. When do the rights of third parties vest? Generally, the rights vest when one of the following occurs:

1 When the third party demonstrates manifest assent to the contract, such as sending a letter or note acknowledging awareness of and consent to a contract formed for her or his benefit.

2 When the third party materially alters his or her position in detrimental reliance on the contract, such as when a donee beneficiary contracts to have a home built in reliance on the receipt of funds promised to him or her in a donee beneficiary contract.

3 When the conditions for vesting are satisfied. For example, the rights of a beneficiary under a life insurance policy vest when the insured person dies.

If the contract expressly reserves to the contracting parties the right to cancel, rescind, or modify the contract, the rights

---

5. See UCC 2–210(1), (4); and *Restatement (Second) of Contracts*, Section 328.
6. 20 N.Y. 268 (1859).

7. This principle was first enunciated in *Seaver v. Ransom*, 224 N.Y. 233, 120 N.E. 639 (1918).

of the third party beneficiary are subject to any changes that result. In such a situation, the vesting of the third party's rights does not terminate the power of the original contracting parties to alter their legal relationships.[8]

Incidental Beneficiaries

The benefit that an **incidental beneficiary** receives from a contract between two parties is unintentional. Therefore, an incidental beneficiary cannot enforce a contract to which he or she is not a party.

■EXAMPLE 11.11 In one case, spectators at a Mike Tyson boxing match in which Tyson was disqualified for biting his opponent's ear sued Tyson and the fight's promoters for a refund of their money on the basis of breach of contract. The spectators claimed that they had standing to sue the defen-

dants as third party beneficiaries of the contract between Tyson and the fight's promoters. The court, however, held that the spectators did not have standing to sue because they were not in contractual privity with any of the defendants. Furthermore, any benefits they received from the contract were incidental to the contract. The court noted that the spectators got what they paid for: "the right to view whatever event transpired."[9] ■

In the following case, a national beauty pageant organization and one of its state affiliates agreed that the national organization would accept the winner of the state contest as a competitor in the national pageant. When the state winner was asked to resign her title, she filed a suit to enforce the agreement to have herself declared a contestant in the national pageant. The national organization argued that she was an incidental, not an intended, beneficiary of the agreement.

---

8. Defenses raised against third party beneficiaries are given in the *Restatement (Second) of Contracts*, Section 309.

9. *Castillo v. Tyson*, 268 A.D.2d 336, 701 N.Y.S.2d 423 (Sup.Ct.App.Div. 2000).

CASE 11.2   Revels v. Miss America Organization

Court of Appeals of North Carolina, 182 N.C.App. 334, 641 S.E.2d 721 (2007).
www.aoc.state.nc.us/www/public/html/opinions.htm[a]

FACTS The Miss North Carolina Pageant Organization, Inc. (MNCPO), is a franchisee of the Miss America Organization (MAO). Under the "Miss America Organization Official Franchise Agreement," the MNCPO conducts a public contest (the State Finals) to select Miss North Carolina and to prepare Miss North Carolina for participation in the Miss America pageant (the National Finals).[b] In return, the MAO "accept[s] the winner of the State Finals . . . as a contestant in the National Finals." On June 22, 2002, the MNCPO designated Rebekah Revels "Miss North Carolina 2002." On July 19, the MAO received an anonymous e-mail (which was later determined to have been sent by Revels's ex-boyfriend), implying that she had formerly cohabited with a "male non-relative" and that nude photos of her existed. Revels confirmed the existence of the photos. On July 22, the MAO and the MNCPO asked Revels to resign as Miss North Carolina and told her that if she refused, she would be excluded from competing in the National Finals. On July 23, she resigned. She

then filed a suit in a North Carolina state court against the MAO, the MNCPO, and others, asserting, among other things, breach of contract. The court issued a summary judgment in the MAO's favor. Revels appealed this judgment to a state intermediate appellate court.

ISSUE Was Revels an intended beneficiary of the contract between the MAO and the MNCPO?

DECISION No. The state appellate court affirmed the lower court's judgment in favor of the MAO. Revels was an incidental rather than an intended beneficiary.

REASON The reviewing court held that "in order to establish a claim as a third-party beneficiary, plaintiff must show (1) that a contract exists between two persons or entities; (2) that the contract is valid and enforceable; and (3) that the contract was executed for the direct, and not intentional, benefit of the third party." The court pointed out that under that test, Revels was an incidental beneficiary of the agreement between the MAO and the MNCPO. Although the agreement provided that the MAO would accept the winner of the State Finals as a contestant in the National Finals, this did not establish that the two organizations intended to make the winner a direct beneficiary of the agreement. Thus, Revels was an incidental

---

a. In the "Court of Appeals Opinions" section, click on "2007." In the result, scroll to the "20 March 2007" section and click on the name of the case to access the opinion. The North Carolina Administrative Office of the Courts maintains this Web site.

b. A *franchise* is an arrangement by which the owner of a trademark, or other intellectual property, licenses the use of the mark to another party under specific conditions.

CASE 11.2—Continues next page

CASE 11.2—Continued

beneficiary and could not maintain an action against the MAO based on the agreement.

FOR CRITICAL ANALYSIS—Technological Consideration *How might Revels's third party*

status with respect to the agreement between the MAO and the MNCPO have been affected if the contracting parties had conducted their business online? Explain.

Intended versus Incidental Beneficiaries

In determining whether a third party beneficiary is an intended or an incidental beneficiary, the courts generally use the *reasonable person* test. Under this test, a beneficiary will be considered an intended beneficiary if a reasonable person in the position of the beneficiary would believe that the promisor *intended* to confer on the beneficiary the right to bring suit to enforce the contract.

In determining whether a party is an intended or an incidental beneficiary, the courts also look at a number of other factors. As you can see in Exhibit 11–4, which graphically illustrates the distinction between intended and incidental beneficiaries, the presence of one or more of the following factors strongly indicates that the third party is an intended (rather than an incidental) beneficiary to the contract:

1 Performance is rendered directly to the third party.

2 The third party has the right to control the details of performance.

3 The third party is expressly designated as a beneficiary in the contract.

CONTRACT DISCHARGE

The most common way to **discharge,** or terminate, one's contractual duties is by the **performance** of those duties. The duty to perform under a contract may be *conditioned* on the occurrence or nonoccurrence of a certain event, or the duty may be *absolute.* As shown in Exhibit 11–5, in addition to performance, a contract can be discharged in numerous other ways, including discharge by agreement of the parties and discharge by operation of law.

Conditions of Performance

In most contracts, promises of performance are not expressly conditioned or qualified. Instead, they are *absolute promises.* They must be performed, or the party promising the act will

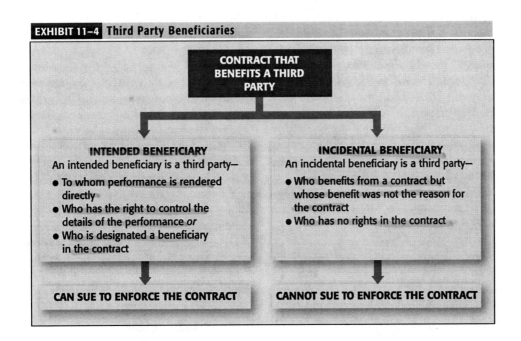

EXHIBIT 11–4 Third Party Beneficiaries

CONTRACT THAT BENEFITS A THIRD PARTY

INTENDED BENEFICIARY
An intended beneficiary is a third party—
- To whom performance is rendered directly
- Who has the right to control the details of the performance *or*
- Who is designated a beneficiary in the contract

CAN SUE TO ENFORCE THE CONTRACT

INCIDENTAL BENEFICIARY
An incidental beneficiary is a third party—
- Who benefits from a contract but whose benefit was not the reason for the contract
- Who has no rights in the contract

CANNOT SUE TO ENFORCE THE CONTRACT

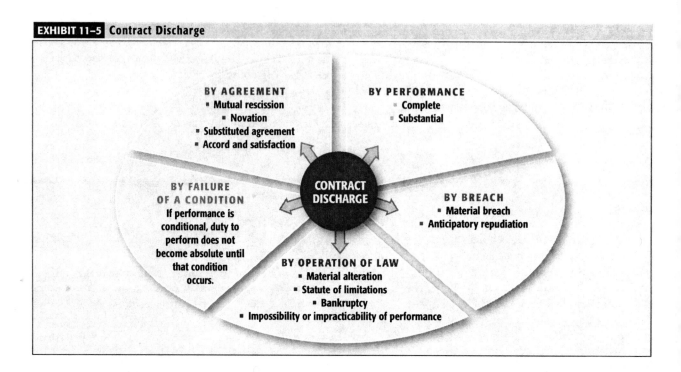

EXHIBIT 11–5 Contract Discharge

be in breach of contract. **■EXAMPLE 11.12** JoAnne contracts to sell Alfonso a painting for $10,000. The parties' promises are unconditional: JoAnne's transfer of the painting to Alfonso and Alfonso's payment of $10,000 to JoAnne. The payment does not have to be made if the painting is not transferred. ■

In some situations, however, contractual promises are conditioned. A **condition** is a possible future event, the occurrence or nonoccurrence of which will trigger the performance of a legal obligation or terminate an existing obligation under a contract. If the condition is not satisfied, the obligations of the parties are discharged. **■EXAMPLE 11.13** Suppose that Alfonso, in the above example, offers to purchase JoAnne's painting only if an independent appraisal indicates that it is worth at least $10,000. JoAnne accepts Alfonso's offer. Their obligations (promises) are conditioned on the outcome of the appraisal. Should this condition not be satisfied (for example, if the appraiser deems the value of the painting to be only $5,000), their obligations to each other are discharged and cannot be enforced. ■

We look here at three types of conditions that can be present in any given contract: *conditions precedent, conditions subsequent,* and *concurrent conditions.*

Conditions Precedent A condition that must be fulfilled before a party's promise becomes absolute is called a **condition precedent.** The condition precedes the absolute duty to perform, as in the JoAnne-Alfonso example just given. Real estate contracts frequently are conditioned on the

buyer's ability to obtain financing. **■EXAMPLE 11.14** Fisher promises to buy Calvin's house if Salvation Bank approves Fisher's mortgage application. The Fisher-Calvin contract is therefore subject to a condition precedent—the bank's approval of Fisher's mortgage application. If the bank does not approve the application, the contract will fail because the condition precedent was not met. ■ Insurance contracts frequently specify that certain conditions, such as passing a physical examination, must be met before the insurance company will be obligated to perform under the contract.

Conditions Subsequent When a condition operates to terminate a party's absolute promise to perform, it is called a **condition subsequent.** The condition follows, or is subsequent to, the absolute duty to perform. If the condition occurs, the party need not perform any further. **■EXAMPLE 11.15** A law firm hires Julia Darby, a recent law school graduate and a newly licensed attorney. Their contract provides that the firm's obligation to continue employing Darby is discharged if she fails to maintain her license to practice law. This is a condition subsequent because a failure to maintain the license will discharge a duty that has already arisen. ■

Generally, conditions precedent are common, and conditions subsequent are rare. The *Restatement (Second) of Contracts* deletes the terms *condition subsequent* and *condition precedent* and refers to both simply as "conditions."[10]

---

10. *Restatement (Second) of Contracts,* Section 224.

Concurrent Conditions When each party's absolute duty to perform is conditioned on the other party's absolute duty to perform, **concurrent conditions** are present. These conditions exist only when the parties expressly or impliedly are to perform their respective duties *simultaneously.* ■EXAMPLE 11.16 If a buyer promises to pay for goods when they are delivered by the seller, each party's absolute duty to perform is conditioned on the other party's absolute duty to perform. The buyer's duty to pay for the goods does not become absolute until the seller either delivers or attempts to deliver the goods. Likewise, the seller's duty to deliver the goods does not become absolute until the buyer pays or attempts to pay for the goods. Therefore, neither can recover from the other for breach without first tendering performance. ■

Discharge by Performance

The contract comes to an end when both parties fulfill their respective duties by performing the acts they have promised. Performance can also be accomplished by tender. **Tender** is an unconditional offer to perform by a person who is ready, willing, and able to do so. Therefore, a seller who places goods at the disposal of a buyer has tendered delivery and can demand payment according to the terms of the agreement. A buyer who offers to pay for goods has tendered payment and can demand delivery of the goods.

Once performance has been tendered, the party making the tender has done everything possible to carry out the terms of the contract. If the other party then refuses to perform, the party making the tender can consider the duty discharged and sue for breach of contract.

Complete Performance When a party performs exactly as agreed, there is no question as to whether the contract has been performed. When a party's performance is perfect, it is said to be complete.

Normally, conditions expressly stated in the contract must fully occur in all aspects for complete performance (strict performance) of the contract to take place. Any deviation breaches the contract and discharges the other party's obligations to perform. For example, most construction contracts require the builder to meet certain specifications. If the specifications are conditions, complete performance is required to avoid material breach. (*Material breach* will be discussed shortly.) If the conditions are met, the other party to the contract must then fulfill her or his obligation to pay the builder. If the specifications are not conditions and if the builder, without the other party's permission, fails to meet the specifications, performance is not complete. What effect does such a failure have on the other party's obligation to pay? The answer is part of the doctrine of *substantial performance.*

Substantial Performance A party who in good faith performs substantially all of the terms of a contract can enforce the contract against the other party under the doctrine of substantial performance. Note that good faith is required. Intentionally failing to comply with the terms is a breach of the contract.

To qualify as *substantial performance,* the performance must not vary greatly from the performance promised in the contract, and it must create substantially the same benefits as those promised in the contract. If the omission, variance, or defect in performance is unimportant and can easily be compensated for by awarding damages, a court is likely to hold that the contract has been substantially performed. Courts decide whether the performance was substantial on a case-by-case basis, examining all of the facts of the particular situation. If performance is substantial, the other party's duty to perform remains absolute (except that the party can sue for damages due to the minor deviations).

■EXAMPLE 11.17 A couple contracts with a construction company to build a house. The contract specifies that Brand X plasterboard be used for the walls. The builder cannot obtain Brand X plasterboard, and the buyers are on holiday in the mountains of Peru and virtually unreachable. The builder decides to install Brand Y instead, which he knows is identical in quality and durability to Brand X plasterboard. All other aspects of construction conform to the contract. In this situation, a court will likely hold that the builder had substantially performed his end of the bargain, and therefore the couple will be obligated to pay the builder. The court might, however, award the couple damages for the use of a different brand of plasterboard, but the couple would still have to pay the contractor the contract price, less the amount of damages. ■

Performance to the Satisfaction of Another Contracts often state that completed work must personally satisfy one of the parties or a third person. The question is whether this satisfaction becomes a condition precedent, requiring actual personal satisfaction or approval for discharge, or whether the test of satisfaction is performance that would satisfy a *reasonable person* (substantial performance).

When the subject matter of the contract is *personal,* a contract to be performed to the satisfaction of one of the parties is conditioned, and performance must actually satisfy that party. For example, contracts for portraits, works of art, and tailoring are considered personal. Therefore, only the personal satisfaction of the party fulfills the condition—unless a court finds the party is expressing dissatisfaction only to avoid payment or otherwise is not acting in good faith.

Most other contracts need to be performed only to the satisfaction of a reasonable person unless they *expressly state otherwise*. When such contracts require performance to the satisfaction of a third party (for example, "to the satisfaction of Robert Ames, the supervising engineer"), the courts are divided. A majority of courts require the work to be satisfactory to a reasonable person, but some courts hold that the personal satisfaction of the third party designated in the contract (Robert Ames, in this example) must be met. Again, the personal judgment must be made honestly, or the condition will be excused.

Material Breach of Contract A **breach of contract** is the nonperformance of a contractual duty. A breach is *material* when performance is not at least substantial. If there is a material breach, the nonbreaching party is excused from the performance of contractual duties and can sue for damages caused by the breach. If the breach is *minor* (not material), the nonbreaching party's duty to perform may sometimes be suspended until the breach is remedied, but the duty is not entirely excused. Once the minor breach is cured, the nonbreaching party must resume performance of the contractual obligations that had been undertaken.

Any breach entitles the nonbreaching party to sue for damages, but only a material breach discharges the nonbreaching party from the contract. The policy underlying these rules is that contracts should go forward when only minor problems occur, but contracts should be terminated if major problems arise.

Anticipatory Repudiation of a Contract Before either party to a contract has a duty to perform, one of the parties may refuse to perform her or his contractual obligations. This is called **anticipatory repudiation.**[11] When anticipatory repudiation occurs, it is treated as a material breach of contract, and the nonbreaching party is permitted to bring an action for damages immediately, even though the scheduled time for performance under the contract may still be in the future.[12] Until the nonbreaching party treats this early repudiation as a breach, however, the breaching party can retract the anticipatory repudiation by proper notice and restore the parties to their original obligations.[13]

An anticipatory repudiation is treated as a present, material breach for two reasons. First, the nonbreaching party should not be required to remain ready and willing to perform when the other party has already repudiated the con-

tract. Second, the nonbreaching party should have the opportunity to seek a similar contract elsewhere and may have the duty to do so to minimize his or her loss.

Quite often, an anticipatory repudiation occurs when a sharp fluctuation in market prices creates a situation in which performance of the contract would be extremely unfavorable to one of the parties. **■EXAMPLE 11.18** Martin Corporation contracts to manufacture and sell ten thousand personal computers to ComAge, a retailer of computer equipment that has five hundred outlet stores. Delivery is to be made six months from the date of the contract. The contract price is based on Martin's present costs of purchasing inventory parts from others. One month later, three suppliers of computer parts raise their prices to Martin. Because of these higher prices, Martin stands to lose $500,000 if it sells the computers to ComAge at the contract price. Martin writes to ComAge, stating that it cannot deliver the ten thousand computers at the contract price. Martin's letter is an anticipatory repudiation of the contract. ComAge has the option of treating the repudiation as a material breach and proceeding immediately to pursue remedies, even though the contract delivery date is still five months away. ■

Discharge by Agreement

Any contract can be discharged by agreement of the parties. The agreement can be contained in the original contract, or the parties can form a new contract for the express purpose of discharging the original contract.

Discharge by Rescission As mentioned in previous chapters, rescission is the process in which the parties cancel the contract and are returned to the positions they occupied prior to the contract's formation. For *mutual rescission* to take place, the parties must make another agreement that also satisfies the legal requirements for a contract—there must be an *offer*, an *acceptance*, and *consideration*. Ordinarily, if the parties agree to rescind the original contract, their promises not to perform those acts promised in the original contract will be legal consideration for the second contract.

Mutual rescission can occur in this manner when the original contract is executory on both sides (that is, neither party has completed performance). Agreements to rescind most executory contracts (with the exception of real estate contracts) are enforceable even if they are made orally and even if the original agreement was in writing.[14] When one party has fully performed, however, an agreement to rescind

---

11. *Restatement (Second) of Contracts*, Section 253; and UCC 2–610 and 2–611.

12. The doctrine of anticipatory repudiation first arose in the landmark case of *Hochster v. De La Tour*, 2 Ellis and Blackburn Reports 678 (1853), when an English court recognized the delay and expense inherent in a rule requiring a nonbreaching party to wait until the time of performance before suing on an anticipatory repudiation.

13. See UCC 2–611.

14. Agreements to rescind contracts involving transfers of realty, however, must be evidenced by a writing. Another exception has to do with the sale of goods under the UCC, when the sales contract requires written rescission.

the original contract usually is not enforceable unless additional consideration or restitution is made.[15]

Discharge by Novation The process of **novation** substitutes a third party for one of the original parties. Essentially, the parties to the original contract and one or more new parties all get together and agree to the substitution. The requirements of a novation are as follows:

1 The existence of a previous, valid obligation.

2 Agreement by all of the parties to a new contract.

3 The extinguishing of the old obligation (discharge of the prior party).

4 A new, valid contract.

A novation may appear to be similar to an assignment or delegation. Nevertheless, there is an important distinction: a novation involves a new contract, and an assignment or delegation involves the old contract.

■EXAMPLE 11.19 Union Corporation contracts to sell its pharmaceutical division to British Pharmaceuticals, Ltd. Before the transfer is completed, Union, British Pharmaceuticals, and a third company, Otis Chemicals, execute a new agreement to transfer all of British Pharmaceutical's rights and duties in the transaction to Otis Chemicals. As long as the new contract is supported by consideration, the novation will discharge the original contract (between Union and British Pharmaceuticals) and replace it with the new contract (between Union and Otis Chemicals). ■

Discharge by Accord and Satisfaction As Chapter 8 explained, in an *accord and satisfaction*, the parties agree to accept performance different from the performance originally promised. An *accord* is an executory contract (one that has not yet been performed) to perform some act to satisfy an existing contractual duty that is not yet discharged. A *satisfaction* is the performance of the accord agreement. An *accord* and its *satisfaction* discharge the original contractual obligation.

Once the accord has been made, the original obligation is merely suspended until the accord agreement is fully performed. If it is not performed, the party to whom performance is owed can bring an action on the original obligation or for breach of the accord. **■EXAMPLE 11.20** Shea obtains a judgment against Marla for $8,000. Later, both parties agree that the judgment can be satisfied by Marla's transfer of her automobile to Shea. This agreement to accept the auto in lieu of $8,000 in cash is the accord. If Marla transfers her

automobile to Shea, the accord agreement is fully performed, and the $8,000 debt is discharged. If Marla refuses to transfer her car, the accord is breached. Because the original obligation is merely suspended, Shea can sue to enforce the judgment for $8,000 in cash or bring an action for breach of the accord. ■

Discharge by Operation of Law

Under some circumstances, contractual duties may be discharged by operation of law. These circumstances include material alteration of the contract, the running of the relevant statute of limitations, bankruptcy, and impossibility of performance.

Contract Alteration To discourage parties from altering written contracts, the law allows an innocent party to be discharged when one party has materially altered a written contract without the knowledge or consent of the other party. For example, if a party alters a material term of the contract—such as the quantity term or the price term—without the knowledge or consent of the other party, the party who was unaware of the alteration can treat the contract as discharged or terminated.

Statutes of Limitations As mentioned earlier in this text, statutes of limitations limit the period during which a party can sue on a particular cause of action. After the applicable limitations period has passed, a suit can no longer be brought. For example, the limitations period for bringing lawsuits for breach of oral contracts is usually two to three years; for written contracts, four to five years; and for recovery of amounts awarded in judgment, ten to twenty years, depending on state law. Lawsuits for breach of a contract for the sale of goods must be brought within four years after the cause of action has accrued. By original agreement, the parties can agree to reduce this four-year period to not less than a one-year period. They cannot, however, agree to extend it beyond the four-year limitations period.

Bankruptcy A proceeding in bankruptcy attempts to allocate the debtor's assets to the creditors in a fair and equitable fashion. Once the assets have been allocated, the debtor receives a *discharge in bankruptcy* (see Chapter 21). A discharge in bankruptcy ordinarily bars the creditors from enforcing most of the debtor's contracts.

When Performance Is Impossible After a contract has been made, performance may become impossible in an objective sense. This is known as **impossibility of performance** and may discharge the contract. Performance may also become so

---

15. Under UCC 2–209(1), however, no consideration is needed to modify a contract for a sale of goods; see also UCC 1–107. See Chapter 14 for an extended discussion of the UCC.

difficult or costly due to some unforeseen event that a court will consider it commercially unfeasible, or impracticable, as will be discussed later in the chapter.

Objective Impossibility. *Objective impossibility* ("It can't be done") must be distinguished from subjective impossibility ("I'm sorry, I simply can't do it"). An example of subjective impossibility is the inability to pay funds on time because the bank is closed.[16] In effect, the nonperforming party is saying, "It is impossible for *me* to perform," rather than "It is impossible for *anyone* to perform." Accordingly, such excuses do not discharge a contract, and the nonperforming party is normally held in breach of contract. Three basic types of situations will generally qualify as grounds for the discharge of contractual obligations based on impossibility of performance:[17]

1 *When a party whose personal performance is essential to the completion of the contract dies or becomes incapacitated prior to performance.* **■EXAMPLE 11.21** Fred, a famous dancer, contracts with Ethereal Dancing Guild to play a leading role in its new ballet. Before the ballet can be performed, Fred becomes ill and dies. His personal performance was essential to the completion of the contract. Thus, his death discharges the contract and his estate's liability for his nonperformance. **■**

2 *When the specific subject matter of the contract is destroyed.* **■EXAMPLE 11.22** A-1 Farm Equipment agrees to sell Gudgel the green tractor on its lot and promises to have the tractor ready for Gudgel to pick up on Saturday. On Friday night, however, a truck veers off the nearby highway and smashes into the tractor, destroying it beyond repair. Because the contract was for this specific tractor, A-1's performance is rendered impossible owing to the accident. **■**

3 *When a change in the law renders performance illegal.* **■EXAMPLE 11.23** A contract to build an apartment building becomes impossible to perform when the zoning laws are changed to prohibit the construction of residential rental property at the planned location. A contract to paint a bridge using lead paint becomes impossible when the government passes new regulations forbidding the use of lead paint on bridges.[18] **■**

Temporary Impossibility. An occurrence or event that makes performance temporarily impossible operates to suspend performance until the impossibility ceases. Then, ordinarily, the parties must perform the contract as originally

planned. **■EXAMPLE 11.24** On August 22, 2005, Keefe Hurwitz contracted to sell his home in Madisonville, Louisiana, to Wesley and Gwendolyn Payne for a price of $241,500. On August 26—just four days after the parties signed the contract—Hurricane Katrina made landfall and caused extensive property damage to the house. The cost of repairs was estimated at $60,000 and Hurwitz would have to make the repairs before the *closing date* (see Chapter 29). Hurwitz did not have the funds and refused to pay $60,000 for the repairs only to sell the property to the Paynes for the previously agreed-on price of $241,500. The Paynes filed a lawsuit to enforce the contract. Hurwitz claimed that Hurricane Katrina had made it impossible for him to perform and had discharged his duties under the contract. The court, however, ruled that Hurricane Katrina had caused only a temporary impossibility. Hurwitz was required to pay for the necessary repairs and to perform the contract as written. In other words, he could not obtain a higher purchase price to offset the cost of the repairs.[19] **■**

In contrast, if the lapse of time and the change in circumstances surrounding the contract make it substantially more burdensome for the parties to perform the promised acts, the contract is discharged. A leading case on the subject, *Autry v. Republic Productions*,[20] involved an actor who was drafted into the army in 1942. Being drafted rendered the actor's contract temporarily impossible to perform, and it was suspended until the end of the war. When the actor got out of the army, the purchasing power of the dollar had so diminished that performance of the contract would have been substantially burdensome to him. Therefore, the contract was discharged.

Commercial Impracticability Courts may excuse parties from their performance obligations when the performance becomes much more difficult or expensive than originally contemplated at the time the contract was formed. For someone to invoke the doctrine of **commercial impracticability** successfully, however, the anticipated performance must become *extremely* difficult or costly.[21]

The added burden of performing not only must be extreme but also *must not have been known by the parties when the contract was made.* For example, in one case, a court held that a contract could be discharged because a party would have to pay ten times more than the original estimate to excavate a certain amount of gravel.[22] In another case, the court allowed a party to rescind a contract for the sale of land because of a potential problem with contaminated groundwater under the

---

16. *Ingham Lumber Co. v. Ingersoll & Co.*, 93 Ark. 447, 125 S.W. 139 (1910).

17. *Restatement (Second) of Contracts*, Sections 262–266; and UCC 2–615.

18. *M. J. Paquet, Inc. v. New Jersey Department of Transportation*, 171 N.J. 378, 794 A.2d 141 (2002).

19. *Payne v. Hurwitz*, 978 So.2d 1000 (La.App. 1st Cir. 2008).

20. 30 Cal.2d 144, 180 P.2d 888 (1947).

21. *Restatement (Second) of Contracts*, Section 264.

22. *Mineral Park Land Co. v. Howard*, 172 Cal. 289, 156 P. 458 (1916).

land. The court found that "the potential for substantial and unbargained-for" liability made contract performance economically impracticable. Interestingly, the court in that case also noted that the possibility of "environmental degradation with consequences extending well beyond the parties' land sale" was just as important to its decision as the economic considerations.[23]

23. *Cape-France Enterprises v. Estate of Peed*, 305 Mont. 513, 29 P.3d 1011 (2001).

The contract dispute in the following case arose out of the cancellation of a wedding reception due to a power failure. Is a power failure sufficient to invoke the doctrine of commercial impracticability?

CASE 11.3   Facto v. Pantagis

Superior Court of New Jersey, Appellate Division, 390 N.J.Super. 227, 915 A.2d 59 (2007).
lawlibrary.rutgers.edu/search.shtml[a]

FACTS Leo and Elizabeth Facto contracted with Snuffy Pantagis Enterprise, Inc., for the use of Pantagis Renaissance, a banquet hall in Scotch Plains, New Jersey, for a wedding reception in August 2002. The Factos paid the $10,578 price in advance. The contract excused Pantagis from performance "if it is prevented from doing so by an act of God [such as a flood or a power failure], or other unforeseen events or circumstances." Soon after the reception began, there was a power failure. The lights and the air conditioning shut off. The band hired for the reception refused to play without electricity to power their instruments, and the lack of lighting prevented the photographer and videographer from taking pictures. The temperature was in the 90s, the humidity was high, and the guests quickly became uncomfortable. Three hours later, after a fight between a guest and a Pantagis employee, the emergency lights began to fade, and the police evacuated the hall. The Factos filed a suit in a New Jersey state court against Pantagis, alleging breach of contract, among other things. The Factos sought to recover their prepayment, plus amounts paid to the band, the photographer, and the videographer. The court concluded that Pantagis did not breach the contract and dismissed the complaint. The Factos appealed to a state intermediate appellate court.

ISSUE Can a power failure constitute the kind of unexpected occurrence that relieves a party of the duty to perform a contract?

DECISION Yes. The state intermediate appellate court agreed that the power failure relieved Pantagis of its

contractual obligation, but held that Pantagis's inability to perform also relieved the Factos of their obligation. The court reversed the dismissal and remanded the case for an award to the Factos of the amount of their prepayment less the value of the services they received.

REASON The appellate court did not attribute any significance to the contract's reference to a power failure as "an act of God." The court reasoned that "even if a power failure caused by circumstances other than a natural event [was] not considered to be 'an act of God,' it still would constitute an unforeseen event or circumstance that would excuse performance." Of course, a power failure is not absolutely unforeseeable during hot summer months. But "absolute unforeseeability of a condition is not a prerequisite to the defense of impracticability." It is "the destruction or * * * deterioration of a specific thing necessary for the performance of the contract [that] makes performance impracticable." In this case, the power failure was area-wide and beyond the control of Pantagis, which was prevented from performing its contract. Because Pantagis was not in breach, however, did not mean that the Factos could not recover the amount they prepaid for the reception. When "one party to a contract is excused from performance as a result of an unforeseen event that makes performance impracticable, the other party is also generally excused from performance." Therefore, the power failure that relieved Pantagis of its obligation to the Factos also relieved the Factos of their obligation to Pantagis.

FOR CRITICAL ANALYSIS—Social Consideration *If Pantagis offered to reschedule the reception, should it be absolved of the obligation to refund the Factos' prepayment? Explain.*

a. In the "Search for Cases by Party Name" section, select the "Appellate Division," type "Pantagis" in the "First Name:" box, and click on "Submit Form." In the result, click on the "click here to get this case" link to access the opinion. The Rutgers University School of Law in Camden, New Jersey, maintains this Web site.

Frustration of Purpose   Closely allied with the doctrine of commercial impracticability is the doctrine of **frustration of purpose.** In principle, a contract will be discharged if supervening circumstances make it impossible to attain the purpose both parties had in mind when making the contract. As with commercial impracticability, the supervening event must not have been foreseeable at the time of the contracting.

REVIEWING **Third Party Rights and Discharge**

Val's Foods signs a contract to buy 1,500 pounds of basil from Sun Farms, a small organic herb grower, as long as an independent organization inspects and certifies that the crop contains no pesticide or herbicide residue. Val's has a contract with several restaurant chains to supply pesto and intends to use Sun Farms' basil in the pesto to fulfill these contracts. When Sun Farms is preparing to harvest the basil, an unexpected hailstorm destroys half the crop. Sun Farms attempts to purchase additional basil from other farms, but it is late in the season and the price is twice the normal market price. Sun Farms is too small to absorb this cost and immediately notifies Val's that it will not fulfill the contract. Using the information presented in the chapter, answer the following questions.

1 Suppose that the basil does not pass the chemical-residue inspection. Which concept discussed in the chapter might allow Val's to refuse to perform the contract in this situation?

2 Under which legal theory or theories might Sun Farms claim that its obligation under the contract has been discharged by operation of law? Discuss fully.

3 Suppose that Sun Farms contacts every basil grower in the country and buys the last remaining chemical-free basil anywhere. Nevertheless, Sun Farms is able to ship only 1,475 pounds to Val's. Would this fulfill Sun Farms' obligations to Val's? Why or why not?

4 Now suppose that Sun Farms sells its operations to Happy Valley Farms. As a part of the sale, all three parties agree that Happy Valley will provide the basil as stated under the original contract. What is this type of agreement called?

TERMS AND CONCEPTS

alienation 225	condition precedent 231	intended beneficiary 228
anticipatory repudiation 233	condition subsequent 231	novation 234
assignee 222	delegatee 226	obligee 223
assignment 222	delegation of duties 226	obligor 223
assignor 222	delegator 226	performance 230
breach of contract 233	discharge 230	privity of contract 222
commercial impracticability 235	frustration of purpose 237	tender 232
concurrent conditions 232	impossibility of performance 234	third party beneficiary 228
condition 231	incidental beneficiary 229	

CHAPTER SUMMARY **Third Party Rights and Discharge**

THIRD PARTY RIGHTS

Assignments
(See pages 222–225.)

1. An assignment is the transfer of rights under a contract to a third party. The person assigning the rights is the *assignor,* and the party to whom the rights are assigned is the *assignee.* The assignee has a right to demand performance from the other original party to the contract.

2. Generally, all rights can be assigned, except in the following circumstances:

    a. When assignment is expressly prohibited by statute (for example, workers' compensation benefits).

(Continued)

CHAPTER SUMMARY	**Third Party Rights and Discharge—Continued**
Assignments— Continued	b. When a contract calls for the performance of personal services.
	c. When the assignment will materially increase or alter the risks or duties of the *obligor* (the party that is obligated to perform).
	d. When the contract itself stipulates that the rights cannot be assigned (with some exceptions).
	3. The assignee should notify the obligor of the assignment. Although not legally required, notification avoids two potential problems:
	a. If the assignor assigns the same right to two different persons, generally the first assignment in time is the first in right, but in some states the first assignee to give notice takes priority.
	b. Until the obligor is notified of the assignment, the obligor can tender performance to the assignor. If the assignor accepts the performance, the obligor's duties under the contract are discharged without benefit to the assignee.
Delegations (See pages 225–228.)	1. A delegation is the transfer of duties under a contract to a third party (the *delegatee*), who then assumes the obligation of performing the contractual duties previously held by the one making the delegation (the *delegator*).
	2. As a general rule, any duty can be delegated, except in the following circumstances:
	a. When performance depends on the personal skill or talents of the obligor.
	b. When special trust has been placed in the obligor.
	c. When performance by a third party will vary materially from that expected by the obligee (the one to whom the duty is owed) under the contract.
	d. When the contract expressly prohibits delegation.
	3. A valid delegation of duties does not relieve the delegator of obligations under the contract. If the delegatee fails to perform, the delegator is still liable to the obligee.
	4. An "assignment of all rights" or an "assignment of the contract" is often construed to mean that both the rights and the duties arising under the contract are transferred to a third party.
Third Party Beneficiaries (See pages 228–230.)	A third party beneficiary contract is one made for the purpose of benefiting a third party.
	1. *Intended beneficiary*—One for whose benefit a contract is created. When the promisor (the one making the contractual promise that benefits a third party) fails to perform as promised, the third party can sue the promisor directly. Examples of third party beneficiaries are creditor and donee beneficiaries.
	2. *Incidental beneficiary*—A third party who indirectly (incidentally) benefits from a contract but for whose benefit the contract was not specifically intended. Incidental beneficiaries have no rights to the benefits received and cannot sue to have the contract enforced.
	CONTRACT DISCHARGE
Conditions of Performance (See pages 230–232.)	Contract obligations may be subject to the following types of conditions:
	1. *Condition precedent*—A condition that must be fulfilled before a party's promise becomes absolute.
	2. *Condition subsequent*—A condition that operates to terminate a party's absolute promise to perform.
	3. *Concurrent conditions*—Conditions that must be performed simultaneously. Each party's absolute duty to perform is conditioned on the other party's absolute duty to perform.
Discharge by Performance (See pages 232–233.)	A contract may be discharged by complete (strict) performance or by substantial performance. In some instances, performance must be to the satisfaction of another. Totally inadequate performance constitutes a material breach of the contract. An anticipatory repudiation of a contract allows the other party to sue immediately for breach of contract.

CHAPTER SUMMARY Third Party Rights and Discharge—Continued

Discharge by Agreement (See pages 233–234.)	Parties may agree to discharge their contractual obligations in several ways: 1. *By rescission*—The parties mutually agree to rescind (cancel) the contract. 2. *By novation*—A new party is substituted for one of the primary parties to a contract. 3. *By accord and satisfaction*—The parties agree to render and accept performance different from that on which they originally agreed.
Discharge by Operation of Law (See pages 234–237.)	Parties' obligations under contracts may be discharged by operation of law owing to one of the following: 1. Contract alteration. 2. Statutes of limitations. 3. Bankruptcy. 4. Impossibility of performance. 5. Impracticability of performance. 6. Frustration of purpose.

FOR REVIEW

Answers for the even-numbered questions in this **For Review** *section can be found on this text's accompanying Web site at* **www.cengage.com/blaw/fbl**. *Select "Chapter 11" and click on "For Review."*

1 What is the difference between an assignment and a delegation?

2 What rights can be assigned despite a contract clause expressly prohibiting assignment?

3 What factors indicate that a third party beneficiary is an intended beneficiary?

4 How are most contracts discharged?

5 What is a contractual condition, and how might a condition affect contractual obligations?

QUESTIONS AND CASE PROBLEMS

HYPOTHETICAL SCENARIOS AND CASE PROBLEMS

11.1 Third Party Beneficiaries. Wilken owes Rivera $2,000. Howie promises Wilken that he will pay Rivera the $2,000 in return for Wilken's promise to give Howie's children guitar lessons. Is Rivera an intended beneficiary of the Howie-Wilken contract? Explain.

11.2 Anticipatory Repudiation. ABC Clothiers, Inc., has a contract with Taylor & Sons, a retailer, to deliver one thousand summer suits to Taylor's place of business on or before May 1. On April 1, Taylor senior receives a letter from ABC informing him that ABC will not be able to make the delivery as scheduled. Taylor is very upset, as he had planned a big ad campaign. He wants to file a suit against ABC immediately (April 2). Taylor's son, Tom, tells his father that filing a lawsuit is not proper until ABC actually fails to deliver the suits on May 1. Discuss fully who is correct, Taylor senior or Tom.

11.3 Hypothetical Question with Sample Answer. Aron, a college student, signs a one-year lease agreement that runs from September 1 to August 31. The lease agreement specifies that the lease cannot be assigned without the landlord's consent. In late May, Aron decides not to go to summer school and assigns the balance of the lease (three months) to a close friend, Erica. The landlord objects to the assignment and denies Erica access to the apartment. Aron claims that Erica is financially sound and should be allowed the full rights and privileges of an assignee. Discuss fully whether the landlord or Aron is correct.

 For a sample answer to Question 11.3, go to Appendix E at the end of this text.

11.4 Third Party Beneficiary. The National Collegiate Athletic Association (NCAA) regulates intercollegiate amateur athletics among more than 1,200 colleges and universities with which it contracts. Among other things, the NCAA maintains rules of eligibility for student participation in intercollegiate athletic events. Jeremy Bloom, a high school football and track star, was recruited to play football at the University of Colorado (CU). Before enrolling, he competed in Olympic and professional World Cup skiing events, becoming the World Cup champion in freestyle moguls. During the Olympics, Bloom appeared on MTV and was offered other paid entertainment opportunities, including a chance to host a show on Nickelodeon. Bloom was also paid to endorse certain ski equipment and contracted to model clothing for Tommy Hilfiger. On Bloom's behalf, CU asked the NCAA to waive its rules restricting student-athlete endorsement and media activities. The NCAA refused, and Bloom quit the activities to play football for CU. He filed a suit in a Colorado state court against the NCAA, however, asserting breach of contract on the ground that its rules permitted these activities if they were needed to support a professional athletic career. The NCAA responded that Bloom did not have standing to pursue this claim. What contract has allegedly been breached in this case? Is Bloom a party to this contract? If not, is he a third party beneficiary of it, and if so, is his status intended or incidental? Explain. [*Bloom v. National Collegiate Athletic Association*, 93 P.3d 621 (Colo.App. 2004)]

11.5 Discharge by Operation of Law. Train operators and other railroad personnel use signaling systems to ensure safe train travel. Reading Blue Mountain & Northern Railroad Co. (RBMN) and Norfolk Southern Railway Co. entered into a contract for the maintenance of a signaling system that serviced a stretch of track near Jim Thorpe, Pennsylvania. The system included a series of poles, similar to telephone poles, suspending wires above the tracks. The contract provided that "the intent of the parties is to maintain the existing . . . facilities" and split the cost equally. In December 2002, a severe storm severed the wires and destroyed most of the poles. RBMN and Norfolk discussed replacing the old system, which they agreed was antiquated, inefficient, dangerous to rebuild, and expensive, but they could not agree on an alternative. Norfolk installed an entirely new system and filed a suit in a federal district court against RBMN to recover half of the cost. RBMN filed a motion for summary judgment, asserting, in part, the doctrine of frustration of purpose. What is this doctrine? Does it apply in this case? How should the court rule on RBMN's motion? Explain. [*Norfolk Southern Railway Co. v. Reading Blue Mountain & Northern Railroad Co.*, 346 F.Supp.2d 720 (M.D.Pa. 2004)]

11.6 Case Problem with Sample Answer. National Association for Stock Car Auto Racing, Inc. (NASCAR), sanctions stock car races. NASCAR and Sprint Nextel Corp. agreed that Sprint would become the Official Series Sponsor of the NASCAR NEXTEL Cup Series. The agreement granted sponsorship exclusivity to Sprint and contained a list of "Competitors" that were barred from sponsoring Series events. Excepted were existing sponsorships: in "Driver and Car Owner Agreements" between NASCAR and the cars' owners, NASCAR promised to "preserve" those sponsorships, which could continue and be renewed despite Sprint's exclusivity. RCR Team #31 owns the #31 Car. Cingular Wireless, LLC (a Sprint competitor) had been #31 Car's primary sponsor

since 2001. In 2007, Cingular changed its name to AT&T Mobility and proposed a new paint scheme for the #31 Car that called for the Cingular logo to remain on the hood while the AT&T logo would be added. NASCAR rejected the proposal. AT&T filed a suit against NASCAR, claiming that NASCAR was in breach of its "Driver and Car Owner Agreement." Can AT&T maintain an action against NASCAR based on this agreement? Explain. [*AT&T Mobility, LLC v. National Association for Stock Car Auto Racing, Inc.*, 494 F.3d 1356 (11th Cir. 2007)]

After you have answered Problem 11.6, compare your answer with the sample answer given on the Web site that accompanies this text. Go to www.cengage.com/blaw/fbl, select "Chapter 11," and click on "Case Problem with Sample Answer."

11.7 Material Breach. Kermit Johnson formed FB & I Building Products, Inc., in Watertown, South Dakota, to sell building materials. In December 1998, FB & I contracted with Superior Truss & Components in Minneota, Minnesota, "to exclusively sell Superior's open-faced wall panels, floor panels, roof trusses and other miscellaneous products." In March 2000, FB & I agreed to exclusively sell Component Manufacturing Co.'s building products in Colorado. Two months later, Superior learned of FB & I's deal with Component and terminated its contract with FB & I. That contract provided that on cancellation, "FB & I will be entitled to retain the customers that they continue to sell and service with Superior products." Superior refused to honor this provision. Between the cancellation of FB & I's contract and 2004, Superior made $2,327,528 in sales to FB & I customers without paying a commission. FB & I filed a suit in a South Dakota state court against Superior, alleging in part, breach of contract and seeking the unpaid commissions. Superior insisted that FB & I had materially breached their contract, excusing Superior from performing. In whose favor should the court rule and why? [*FB & I Building Products, Inc. v. Superior Truss & Components, a Division of Banks Lumber, Inc.*, 727 N.W.2d 474 (S.D. 2007)]

11.8 A Question of Ethics. King County, Washington, hired Frank Coluccio Construction Co. (FCCC) to act as general contractor for a public works project involving the construction of a small utility tunnel under the Duwamish Waterway. FCCC hired Donald B. Murphy Contractors, Inc. (DBM), as a subcontractor. DBM was responsible for constructing an access shaft at the eastern end of the tunnel. Problems arose during construction, including a "blow in" of the access shaft when it filled with water, soil, and debris. FCCC and DBM incurred substantial expenses from the repairs and delays. Under the project contract, King County was supposed to buy an insurance policy to "insure against physical loss or damage by perils included under an 'All Risk' Builder's Risk policy." Any claim under this policy was to be filed through the insured. King County, which had general property damage insurance, did not obtain an all-risk builder's risk policy. For the losses attributable to the blow-in, FCCC and DBM submitted builder's risk claims, which the county *denied. FCCC filed a suit in a Washington state court against King County, alleging, among other claims, breach of contract. [Frank Coluccio Construction Co. v. King County, 136 Wash.App. 751, 150 P.3d 1147 (Div. 1 2007)]*

1 King County's property damage policy specifically excluded, at the county's request, coverage of tunnels. The county drafted its contract with FCCC to require the all-risk builder's risk policy and authorize itself to "sponsor" claims. When FCCC and DBM filed their claims, the county secretly colluded with its property damage insurer to deny payment. What do these facts indicate about the county's ethics and legal liability in this situation?

2 Could DBM, as a third party to the contract between King County and FCCC, maintain an action on the contract against King County? Discuss.

3 All-risk insurance is a promise to pay on the "fortuitous" happening of a loss or damage from any cause except those that are specifically excluded. Payment is not usually made on a loss that, at the time the insurance was obtained, the claimant subjectively knew would occur. If a loss results from faulty workmanship on the part of a contractor, should the obligation to pay under an all-risk policy be discharged? Explain.

CRITICAL THINKING AND WRITING ASSIGNMENTS

11.9 Critical Legal Thinking. The concept of substantial performance permits a party to be discharged from a contract even though the party has not fully performed her or his obligations according to the contract's terms. Is this fair? What policy interests are at issue here?

11.10 Video Question. Go to this text's Web site at **www.cengage.com/blaw/fbl** and select "Chapter 11." Click on "Video Questions" and view the video titled *Third Party Beneficiaries.* Then answer the following questions.

1 Discuss whether a valid contract was formed when Oscar and Vinny bet on the outcome of a football game. Would Vinny be able to enforce the contract in court?

2 Is the Fresh Air Fund an incidental or an intended beneficiary? Why?

3 Can Maria sue to enforce Vinny's promise to donate Oscar's winnings to the Fresh Air Fund?

ACCESSING THE INTERNET

For updated links to resources available on the Web, as well as a variety of other materials, visit this text's Web site at

www.cengage.com/blaw/fbl

You can find a number of forms that can be used in the assignment of different types of contracts at

www.ilrg.com/forms/#transfers

A *New York Law Journal* article discussing leading decisions from the New York Court of Appeals on third party rights in contracts is online at

www.courts.state.ny.us/history/elecbook/thereshallbe/pg51.htm

PRACTICAL INTERNET EXERCISES

Go to this text's Web site at **www.cengage.com/blaw/fbl**, select "Chapter 11," and click on "Practical Internet Exercises." There you will find the following Internet research exercises that you can perform to learn more about the topics covered in this chapter.

PRACTICAL INTERNET EXERCISE 11–1   LEGAL PERSPECTIVE—Anticipatory Repudiation

PRACTICAL INTERNET EXERCISE 11–2   MANAGEMENT PERSPECTIVE—Commercial Impracticability

BEFORE THE TEST

Go to this text's Web site at **www.cengage.com/blaw/fbl**, select "Chapter 11," and click on "Interactive Quizzes." You will find a number of interactive questions relating to this chapter.

7

Breach and Remedies

As the Athenian political leader Solon instructed centuries ago, a contract will not be broken so long as "it is to the advantage of both" parties to fulfill their contractual obligations. Normally, a person enters into a contract with another to secure an advantage. When it is no longer advantageous for a party to fulfill her or his contractual obligations, that party may breach the contract. As noted in Chapter 11, a *breach of contract* occurs when a party fails to perform part or all of the required duties under a contract.[1] Once a party fails to perform or performs inadequately, the other party—the nonbreaching party—can choose one or more of several remedies.

The most common remedies available to a nonbreaching party under contract law include damages, rescission and restitution, specific performance, and reformation. As discussed in Chapter 1, courts distinguish between *remedies at law* and *remedies in equity*. Today, the remedy at law is normally monetary damages. We discuss this remedy in the first part of this chapter. Equitable remedies include rescission and restitution, specific performance, and reformation, all of which we will examine later in the chapter. Usually, a court will not award an equitable remedy unless the remedy at law is inadequate. In the final pages of this chapter, we will look at some special legal doctrines and concepts relating to remedies.

DAMAGES

A breach of contract entitles the nonbreaching party to sue for monetary damages. As you read in Chapter 4, damages are designed to compensate a party for harm suffered as a result of another's wrongful act. In the context of contract law, damages are designed to compensate the nonbreaching party for the loss of the bargain. Often, courts say that innocent parties are to be placed in the position they would have occupied had the contract been fully performed.[2]

Types of Damages

There are basically four broad categories of damages:

1 Compensatory (to cover direct losses and costs).

2 Consequential (to cover indirect and foreseeable losses).

3 Punitive (to punish and deter wrongdoing).

---

1. *Restatement (Second) of Contracts*, Section 235(2).

2. *Restatement (Second) of Contracts*, Section 347; and Section 1–106(1) of the Uniform Commercial Code (UCC).

4 Nominal (to recognize wrongdoing when no monetary loss is shown).

Compensatory and punitive damages were discussed in Chapter 4 in the context of tort law. Here, we look at these types of damages, as well as consequential and nominal damages, in the context of contract law.

Compensatory Damages   Damages compensating the non-breaching party for the *loss of the bargain* are known as *compensatory damages*. These damages compensate the injured party only for damages actually sustained and proved to have arisen directly from the loss of the bargain caused by the breach of contract. They simply replace what was lost because of the wrong or damage.

The standard measure of compensatory damages is the difference between the value of the breaching party's promised performance under the contract and the value of her or his actual performance. This amount is reduced by any loss that the injured party has avoided.

■**EXAMPLE 12.1** You contract with Marinot Industries to perform certain personal services exclusively for Marinot during August for a payment of $4,000. Marinot cancels the contract and is in breach. You are able to find another job during August but can earn only $3,000. You normally can sue Marinot for breach and recover $1,000 as compensatory damages. You may also recover from Marinot the amount that you spent to find the other job. ■ Expenses that are directly incurred because of a breach of contract—such as those incurred to obtain performance from another source—are called **incidental damages.**

The measurement of compensatory damages varies by type of contract. Certain types of contracts deserve special mention—contracts for the sale of goods, contracts for the sale of land, and construction contracts.

Sale of Goods.   In a contract for the sale of goods, the usual measure of compensatory damages is the difference between the contract price and the market price.[3] ■**EXAMPLE 12.2** MediQuick Laboratories contracts with Cal Computer Industries to purchase ten model UTS network servers for $8,000 each. If Cal Computer fails to deliver the ten servers, and the current market price of the servers is $8,950, MediQuick's measure of damages is $9,500 (10 × $950), plus any incidental damages (expenses) caused by the breach. ■ If the buyer breaches and the seller has not yet produced the goods, compensatory damages normally equal the seller's lost profits on the sale, rather than the difference between the contract price and the market price.

---

3. This is the difference between the contract price and the market price at the time and place at which the goods were to be delivered or tendered. [See UCC 2–708, 2–713, and 2–715(1), discussed in Chapter 15.]

Sale of Land.   Ordinarily, because each parcel of land is unique, the remedy for a seller's breach of a contract for a sale of real estate is specific performance—that is, the buyer is awarded the parcel of property for which he or she bargained (*specific performance* will be discussed more fully later in this chapter). When this remedy is unavailable (because the property has been sold, for example) or when the buyer is the party in breach, the measure of damages is typically the difference between the contract price and the market price of the land. The majority of states follow this rule.

Construction Contracts.   The measure of damages in a building or construction contract varies depending on which party breaches and when the breach occurs. The owner can breach at three different stages of the construction:

1 Before performance has begun.

2 During performance.

3 After performance has been completed.

If the owner breaches *before performance has begun*, the contractor can recover only the profits that would have been made on the contract (that is, the total contract price less the cost of materials and labor). If the owner breaches *during performance*, the contractor can recover the profits plus the costs incurred in partially constructing the building. If the owner breaches *after the construction has been completed*, the contractor can recover the entire contract price plus interest.

When the contractor breaches the construction contract—either by failing to begin construction or by stopping work partway through the project—the measure of damages is the cost of completion, which includes reasonable compensation for any delay in performance. If the contractor finishes late, the measure of damages is the loss of use.

must be known

Consequential Damages   Foreseeable damages that result from a party's breach of contract are referred to as **consequential damages,** or *special damages*. Consequential damages differ from compensatory damages in that they are caused by special circumstances beyond the contract itself. They flow from the consequences, or results, of a breach. When a seller fails to deliver goods, knowing that the buyer is planning to use or resell those goods immediately, consequential damages are awarded for the loss of profits from the planned resale.

■**EXAMPLE 12.3** Gilmore contracts to have a specific item shipped to her—one that she desperately needs to repair her printing press. In her contract with the shipper, Gilmore states that she must receive the item by Monday, or she will not be able to print her paper and will lose $3,000. If the shipper is late, Gilmore normally can recover the

not done – to expensive and time consuming

consequential damages caused by the delay—that is, the $3,000 in losses. ■ To recover consequential damages, the breaching party must know (or have reason to know) that special circumstances will cause the nonbreaching party to suffer an additional loss.[4]

PREVENTING LEGAL DISPUTES Sometimes, it is impossible to prevent contract disputes. You should understand that collecting damages through a court judgment requires litigation, which can be expensive and time consuming. Furthermore, court judgments are often difficult to enforce, particularly if the breaching party does not have sufficient assets to pay the damages awarded.[5] For these reasons, parties generally choose to settle their contract disputes before trial rather than litigate in hopes of being awarded—and being able to collect—damages (or other remedies). In sum, there is wisdom in the old saying, "a bird in the hand is worth two in the bush."

travel only

■

Punitive Damages Recall from Chapter 4 that punitive damages are designed to punish a wrongdoer and to set an example to deter similar conduct in the future. Punitive damages, or *exemplary damages*, generally are not awarded in an action for breach of contract. Such damages have no legitimate place in contract law because they are, in essence, penalties, and a breach of contract is not unlawful in a criminal sense. A contract is simply a civil relationship between the parties. The law may compensate one party for the loss of the bargain—no more and no less.

In a few situations, a person's actions can cause both a breach of contract and a tort. **■EXAMPLE 12.4** Two parties establish by contract a certain reasonable standard or duty of care. Failure to live up to that standard is a breach of the contract. The same act that breached the contract may also constitute negligence, or it may be an intentional tort if, for example, the breaching party committed fraud. In such a situation, it is possible for the nonbreaching party to recover punitive damages for the tort in addition to compensatory and consequential damages for the breach of contract. ■

---

4. UCC 2–715(2). See Chapter 16.
5. Courts dispose of cases, after trials, by entering judgments. A judgment may order the losing party to pay monetary damages to the winning party. Collecting a judgment, however, can pose problems. For example, the judgment debtor may be insolvent (unable to pay his or her bills when they come due) or have only a small net worth, or exemption laws may prevent a creditor from seizing the debtor's assets to satisfy a debt (see Chapter 21).

Nominal Damages When no actual damage or financial loss results from a breach of contract and only a technical injury is involved, the court may award **nominal damages** to the innocent party. Nominal damages awards are often small, such as one dollar, but they do establish that the defendant acted wrongfully. Most lawsuits for nominal damages are brought as a matter of principle under the theory that a breach has occurred and some damages must be imposed regardless of actual loss.

■EXAMPLE 12.5 Hernandez contracts to buy potatoes at fifty cents a pound from Lentz. Lentz breaches the contract and does not deliver the potatoes. Meanwhile, the price of potatoes falls. Hernandez is able to buy them in the open market at half the price he agreed to pay Lentz. Hernandez is clearly better off because of Lentz's breach. Thus, in a suit for breach of contract, Hernandez may be awarded only nominal damages for the technical injury he sustained, as no monetary loss was involved. ■

Mitigation of Damages

In most situations, when a breach of contract occurs, the injured party is held to a duty to mitigate, or reduce, the damages that he or she suffers. Under this doctrine of **mitigation of damages,** the required action depends on the nature of the situation.

■EXAMPLE 12.6 Some states require a landlord to use reasonable means to find a new tenant if a tenant abandons the premises and fails to pay rent. If an acceptable tenant is found, the landlord is required to lease the premises to this tenant to mitigate the damages recoverable from the former tenant. The former tenant is still liable for the difference between the amount of the rent under the original lease and the rent received from the new tenant. If the landlord has not taken the reasonable steps necessary to find a new tenant, a court will likely reduce any award by the amount of rent the landlord could have received had such reasonable means been used. ■

difference between rent at current rent and time breach

In the majority of states, a person whose employment has been wrongfully terminated has a duty to mitigate damages incurred because of the employer's breach of the employment contract. In other words, a wrongfully terminated employee has a duty to take a similar job if one is available. If the employee fails to do this, the damages awarded will be equivalent to the employee's salary less the income he or she would have received in a similar job obtained by reasonable means. The employer has the burden of proving that such jobs existed and that the employee could have been hired. Normally, the employee is under no duty to take a job that is not of the same type and rank.

Whether a tenant farmer acceptably attempted to mitigate his damages on his landlord's breach of their lease was at issue in the following case.

CASE 12.1   Hanson v. Boeder

Supreme Court of North Dakota, 2007 ND 20, 727 N.W.2d 280 (2007).
www.ndcourts.com/court/opinions.htm[a]

FACTS In 1998, Paul Hanson signed a five-year lease to farm 1,350 acres of Donald Boeder's land in Steele County, North Dakota, for $50 per acre beginning with the 1999 crop year. Under the lease, Hanson could use grain bins with a capacity of 93,000 bushels and two machine sheds on the property. The rent was $67,515 per year, with half due on April 1 and the balance due on November 1. In 2003, Boeder and Hanson renewed the lease for a second five-year period. During both terms, Boeder and Hanson disagreed about Hanson's farming practices, but during the second term, their disagreement escalated. In August 2005, Boeder told Hanson that their lease was over. Boeder also told Hanson not to till the land in the fall because it had been leased to a new tenant who wanted to do it himself. Hanson continued to work Boeder's land, however, while running ads in the local newspapers for other farmland to rent. Unable to find other land, Hanson filed a suit in a North Dakota state court against Boeder for breach of contract, asking the court to assess damages. The court awarded Hanson $315,194.26 to cover his lost profits, the lost use of the bins and sheds, and the value of the fall tillage. Boeder appealed to the North Dakota Supreme Court, arguing, among other things, that Hanson failed to mitigate his damages.

ISSUE Did Hanson take appropriate steps to mitigate his damages?

a. Click on the "By ND citation" link. In the result, click on "2007" and then the name of the case to access the opinion. The North Dakota Supreme Court maintains this Web site.

DECISION Yes. The Supreme Court of North Dakota affirmed the lower court's award of damages to Hanson.

REASON The state supreme court explained that normally, "for the breach of an obligation arising from contract, the measure of damages . . . is the amount which will compensate the party aggrieved for all the detriment proximately caused thereby or which in the ordinary course of things would be likely to result therefrom." The court recognized that "a person injured by the wrongful acts of another has a duty to mitigate or minimize the damages and must protect himself if he can do so with reasonable exertion or at trifling expense, and can recover from the delinquent party only such damages as he could not, with reasonable effort, have avoided." In this case, Hanson had not been aware of any farmland available for lease, and he had run ads in the local newspapers seeking other farmland to rent. That Hanson was unsuccessful affected the amount of his recovery, but it did not point to a failure to mitigate his damages.

FOR CRITICAL ANALYSIS—Social Consideration *During the trial, Boeder tried to retract his repudiation of the lease to allow Hanson to continue farming for the rest of the lease term. Should the court have considered this an acceptable way for Hanson to mitigate his damages?*

■

Liquidated Damages versus Penalties

[handwritten margin note: down payment loss]

A **liquidated damages** provision in a contract specifies that a certain dollar amount is to be paid in the event of a future default or breach of contract. (*Liquidated* means determined, settled, or fixed.) For example, a provision requiring a construction contractor to pay $300 for every day he or she is late in completing the project is a liquidated damages provision. Liquidated damages differ from penalties. A **penalty** specifies a certain amount to be paid in the event of a default or breach of contract and is designed to penalize the breaching party. Liquidated damages provisions normally are enforceable. In contrast, if a court finds that a provision calls for a

penalty, the agreement as to the amount will not be enforced, and recovery will be limited to actual damages.[6]

To determine whether a particular provision is for liquidated damages or for a penalty, the court must answer two questions:

1 At the time the contract was formed, was it apparent that damages would be difficult to estimate in the event of a breach?

2 Was the amount set as damages a reasonable estimate of those potential damages and not excessive?[7]

---

6. This is also the rule under the UCC. See UCC 2–718(1).
7. *Restatement (Second) of Contracts*, Section 356(1).

[handwritten note at bottom: no to any of these questions are a penalty not liquidated damages]

If the answers to both questions are yes, the provision normally will be enforced. If either answer is no, the provision normally will not be enforced. Liquidated damages provisions are frequently used in construction contracts because it is difficult to estimate the amount of damages that would be caused by a delay in completing the work.

EQUITABLE REMEDIES

In some situations, damages are an inadequate remedy for a breach of contract. In these cases, the nonbreaching party may ask the court for an equitable remedy. Equitable remedies include rescission and restitution, specific performance, and reformation.

Rescission and Restitution

As discussed in Chapter 11, *rescission* is essentially an action to undo, or cancel, a contract—to return nonbreaching parties to the positions that they occupied prior to the transaction. When fraud, mistake, duress, or failure of consideration is present, rescission is available. The failure of one party to perform under a contract entitles the other party to rescind the contract.[8] The rescinding party must give prompt notice to the breaching party.

Restitution   To rescind a contract, both parties generally must make **restitution** to each other by returning goods, property, or funds previously conveyed.[9] If the physical property or goods can be returned, they must be. If the property or goods have been consumed, restitution must be made in an equivalent dollar amount.

Essentially, restitution involves the recapture of a benefit conferred on the defendant that has unjustly enriched her or him. **■EXAMPLE 12.7** Andrea pays $32,000 to Myles in return for his promise to design a house for her. The next day, Myles calls Andrea and tells her that he has taken a position with a large architectural firm in another state and cannot design the house. Andrea decides to hire another architect that afternoon. Andrea can require restitution of $32,000 because Myles has received an unjust benefit of $32,000. ■

Restitution Is Not Limited to Rescission Cases Restitution may be required when a contract is rescinded, but the right to restitution is not limited to rescission cases.

Restitution may be sought in actions for breach of contract, tort actions, and other actions at law or in equity. Usually, restitution can be obtained when funds or property has been transferred by mistake or because of fraud. An award in a case may include restitution of funds or property obtained through embezzlement, conversion, theft, copyright infringement, or misconduct by a party in a confidential or other special relationship.

Specific Performance

The equitable remedy of **specific performance** calls for the performance of the act promised in the contract. This remedy is often attractive to a nonbreaching party because it provides the exact bargain promised in the contract. It also avoids some of the problems inherent in a suit for monetary damages. First, the nonbreaching party need not worry about collecting the judgment. Second, the nonbreaching party need not look around for another contract. Third, the actual performance may be more valuable than the monetary damages.

Normally, however, specific performance will not be granted unless the party's legal remedy (monetary damages) is inadequate.[10] For this reason, contracts for the sale of goods rarely qualify for specific performance. Monetary damages ordinarily are adequate in such situations because substantially identical goods can be bought or sold in the market. Only if the goods are unique will a court grant specific performance. For instance, paintings, sculptures, and rare books and coins are often unique, and monetary damages will not enable a buyer to obtain substantially identical substitutes in the market.

Sale of Land   A court will grant specific performance to a buyer in an action for a breach of contract involving the sale of land. In this situation, the legal remedy of monetary damages will not compensate the buyer adequately because every parcel of land is unique; obviously, the buyer cannot obtain the same land in the same location elsewhere. Only when specific performance is unavailable (for example, when the seller has sold the property to someone else) will damages be awarded instead.

Is specific performance warranted when one of the parties has substantially—but not *fully*—performed under the contract? That was the question in the following case.

---

8. The rescission discussed here refers to *unilateral* rescission, in which only one party wants to undo the contract. In *mutual* rescission, both parties agree to undo the contract. Mutual rescission discharges the contract; unilateral rescission is generally available as a remedy for breach of contract.

9. *Restatement (Second) of Contracts*, Section 370.

---

10. *Restatement (Second) of Contracts*, Section 359.

CASE 12.2   Stainbrook v. Low

Court of Appeals of Indiana, 842 N.E.2d 386 (2006).

FACTS In April 2004, Howard Stainbrook agreed to sell to Trent Low forty acres of land in Jennings County, Indiana, for $45,000. Thirty-two of the acres were wooded and eight were tillable. Under the agreement, Low was to pay for a survey of the property and other costs, including a tax payment due in November. Low gave Stainbrook a check for $1,000 to show his intent to fulfill the contract. They agreed to close the deal on May 11, and Low made financial arrangements to meet his obligations. On May 8, a tractor rolled over on Stainbrook, and he died. Stainbrook's son David became the executor of his father's estate. David asked Low to withdraw his offer to buy the forty acres. Low refused and filed a suit in an Indiana state court against David, seeking to enforce the contract. The court ordered specific performance. David appealed to a state intermediate appellate court, arguing, among other things, that his father's contract with Low was "ambiguous and inequitable."

ISSUE Is complete performance of a contract required for the party to be entitled to the remedy of specific performance?

DECISION No. A party who has substantially performed or offered to perform his or her obligations under a contract is entitled to pursue specific performance as a remedy. The state intermediate appellate court held that specific performance was an appropriate remedy in this case and affirmed the lower court's order.

REASON The appellate court explained that a contracting party's substantial performance is sufficient to support a court's order for specific performance. Here, "Low both offered to perform and substantially performed his contractual obligations." The appellate court found that Low had offered to make the tax payment that was due, but Stainbrook's estate refused the offer. Also, Low had obtained financing before the closing date, and there was nothing to indicate that he was not prepared to meet his financial obligations and go forward with the sale. Moreover, although the survey had not yet been arranged, there was no evidence that Low would not have paid for the survey of the land as required by the contract. Because Low had substantially performed under the terms of the contract, the court held that Low was entitled to the remedy of specific performance.

 WHY IS THIS CASE IMPORTANT? *The court reaffirmed the principle that "specific performance is a matter of course when it involves contracts to purchase real estate." The court also emphasized that "a party seeking specific performance of a real estate contract must prove that he has substantially performed his contract obligations or offered to do so." The court's reasoning underscores the importance of focusing on the elements of a principle to resolve a case fairly.*

Contracts for Personal Services   Personal-service contracts require one party to work personally for another party. Courts normally refuse to grant specific performance of contracts for personal services. This is because to order a party to perform personal services against his or her will amounts to a type of involuntary servitude, which is contrary to the public policy expressed in the Thirteenth Amendment to the U.S. Constitution. Moreover, the courts do not want to monitor contracts for personal services.

■EXAMPLE 12.8 If you contract with a brain surgeon to perform brain surgery on you and the surgeon refuses to perform, the court will not compel (and you certainly would not want) the surgeon to perform under these circumstances. There is no way the court can assure meaningful performance in such a situation.[11] ■

Reformation

Reformation is an equitable remedy used when the parties have *imperfectly* expressed their agreement in writing. Reformation allows a court to rewrite the contract to reflect the parties' true intentions. Courts order reformation most often when fraud or mutual mistake is present. ■EXAMPLE 12.9 If Keshan contracts to buy a forklift from Shelley but the written contract refers to a crane, a mutual mistake has occurred. Accordingly, a court could reform the contract so that the writing conforms to the parties' original intention as to which piece of equipment is being sold. ■

Courts frequently reform contracts in two other situations. The first occurs when two parties who have made a binding oral contract agree to put the oral contract in writing but, in doing so, make an error in stating the terms. Universally, the courts allow into evidence the correct terms of the oral contract, thereby reforming the written contract. The second situation occurs when the parties have executed a written

---

11. Similarly, courts often refuse to order specific performance of construction contracts because courts are not set up to operate as construction supervisors or engineers.

covenant not to compete (see Chapter 9). If the covenant not to compete is for a valid and legitimate purpose (such as the sale of a business) but the area or time restraints are unreasonable, some courts will reform the restraints by making them reasonable and will enforce the entire contract as reformed. Other courts, however, will throw the entire restrictive covenant out as illegal. Exhibit 12–1 graphically presents the remedies, including reformation, that are available to the nonbreaching party.

RECOVERY BASED ON QUASI CONTRACT

Recall from Chapter 7 that a quasi contract is not a true contract but rather a fictional contract that is imposed on the parties to prevent unjust enrichment. Hence, a quasi contract provides a basis for relief when no enforceable contract exists. The legal obligation arises because the law considers that the party accepting the benefits has made an implied promise to pay for them. Generally, when one party confers a benefit on another party, justice requires that the party receiving the benefit pay a reasonable value for it.

When Quasi Contracts Are Used

Quasi contract is a legal theory under which an obligation is imposed in the absence of an agreement. It allows the courts to act as if a contract exists when there is no actual contract or agreement between the parties. The courts can also use this theory when the parties have a contract, but it is unenforceable for some reason.

Quasi-contractual recovery is often granted when one party has partially performed under a contract that is unenforceable. It provides an alternative to suing for damages and allows the party to recover the reasonable value of the partial performance. **■EXAMPLE 12.10** Ericson contracts to build two oil derricks for Petro Industries. The derricks are to be built over a period of three years, but the parties do not create a written contract. Therefore, the Statute of Frauds will bar the enforcement of the contract.[12] After Ericson completes one derrick, Petro Industries informs him that it will not pay for the derrick. Ericson can sue Petro Industries under the theory of quasi contract. ■

The Requirements of Quasi Contract

To recover on a quasi contract theory, the party seeking recovery must show the following:

1 The party conferred a benefit on the other party.
2 The party conferred the benefit with the reasonable expectation of being paid.
3 The party did not act as a volunteer in conferring the benefit.
4 The party receiving the benefit would be unjustly enriched by retaining the benefit without paying for it.

■EXAMPLE 12.11 In Example 12.10, Ericson can sue in quasi contract because all of the conditions for quasi-contractual recovery have been fulfilled. Ericson built the oil derrick with the expectation of being paid. The derrick conferred an obvious benefit on Petro Industries, and Petro Industries would be unjustly enriched if it was allowed to keep the derrick without paying Ericson for the work. Therefore, Ericson should be able to recover the reasonable value of the oil derrick that was built (under the theory of *quantum meruit*[13] — "as much as he or she deserves"). The reasonable value is ordinarily equal to the fair market value. ■

---

12. Contracts that by their terms cannot be performed within one year from the day after the date of contract formation must be in writing to be enforceable (see Chapter 10).
13. Pronounced *kwahn*-tuhm *mehr*-oo-wuht.

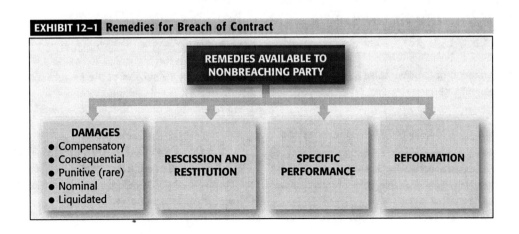

EXHIBIT 12–1 Remedies for Breach of Contract

REMEDIES AVAILABLE TO NONBREACHING PARTY

DAMAGES
• Compensatory
• Consequential
• Punitive (rare)
• Nominal
• Liquidated

RESCISSION AND RESTITUTION

SPECIFIC PERFORMANCE

REFORMATION

CONTRACT PROVISIONS LIMITING REMEDIES

A contract may include provisions stating that no damages can be recovered for certain types of breaches or that damages will be limited to a maximum amount. The contract may also provide that the only remedy for breach is replacement, repair, or refund of the purchase price. Provisions stating that no damages can be recovered are called *exculpatory clauses* (see Chapter 9). Provisions that affect the availability of certain remedies are called *limitation-of-liability clauses.*

Whether these contract provisions and clauses will be enforced depends on the type of breach that is excused by the provision. For example, a clause excluding liability for negligence may be enforced in some cases. When an exculpatory

clause for negligence is contained in a contract made between parties who have roughly equal bargaining power, the clause usually will be enforced. The Uniform Commercial Code (UCC) specifically allows limitation-of-liability clauses to be included in contracts for the sale of goods, as will be discussed in detail in Chapter 16.[14] A provision excluding liability for fraudulent or intentional injury, however, will not be enforced. Likewise, a clause excluding liability for illegal acts or violations of the law will not be enforced.

At issue in the following case was the enforceability of a limitation-of-liability clause in a home-inspection contract.

---

14. UCC 2–719.

CASE 12.3   Lucier v. Williams

Superior Court of New Jersey, Appellate Division, 366 N.J.Super. 485, 841 A.2d 907 (2004).
lawlibrary.rutgers.edu/search.shtml[a]

FACTS Eric Lucier and Karen Haley, first-time home buyers, contracted to buy a single-family home for $128,500 from James and Angela Williams in Berlin Township, New Jersey. The buyers asked Cambridge Associates, Limited (CAL), to perform a home inspection. CAL presented the buyers with a contract that limited CAL's liability to "$500, or 50% of fees actually paid to CAL by Client, whichever sum is smaller. Such causes include, but are not limited to, CAL's negligence, errors, omissions, * * * [or] breach of contract." Lucier reluctantly signed the contract. On CAL's behalf, Al Vasys performed the inspection and issued a report. The buyers paid CAL $385. Shortly after Lucier and Haley moved into the house, they noticed leaks, which required roof repairs estimated to cost $8,000 to $10,000. They filed a suit in a New Jersey state court against CAL and others, seeking damages for the loss. CAL filed a motion for summary judgment, claiming that under the limitation-of-liability clause, its liability, if any, was limited to one-half of the contract price, or $192.50. The court granted the motion. The plaintiffs appealed to a state intermediate appellate court.

ISSUE Did the limitation-of-liability clause in the CAL contract limit the plaintiffs' recovery?

DECISION No. The state intermediate appellate court held that the provision was unenforceable. The court reversed the

ruling of the lower court and remanded the case for further proceedings.

REASON The appellate court held that the limitation-of-liability clause was unenforceable for three reasons: (1) the contract was an adhesion contract prepared by the home inspector (an *adhesion contract* is a standard-form contract presented on a take-it-or-leave-it basis—see Chapter 9); (2) the parties had grossly unequal bargaining power; and (3) the provision undermined the fundamental purpose of the contract, having "the practical effect of avoiding almost all responsibility for the professional's negligence." Additionally, the court explained that limiting liability in home-inspection contracts is contrary to the state's public policy of requiring "reliable evaluation of a home's fitness for purchase and holding professionals to certain industry standards." The court added that "the foisting [forcing] of a contract of this type in this setting on an inexperienced consumer clearly demonstrates a lack of fair dealing by the professional. * * * If, upon the occasional dereliction, the home inspector's only consequence is the obligation to refund a few hundred dollars (the smaller of 50 percent of the inspection contract price or $500), there is no meaningful incentive to act diligently in the performance of home inspection contracts."

---

a. Click on the link to "Search by party name." Select "Appellate Division," and type "Lucier" in the first box and "Williams" in the second box. Click on "Submit Form" to access the opinion. Rutgers University School of Law in Camden, New Jersey, maintains this Web site.

FOR CRITICAL ANALYSIS—Social Consideration *What is the difference between the limitation-of-liability clause in this case and an exculpatory clause (discussed in Chapter 9)?*

ELECTION OF REMEDIES

In many cases, a nonbreaching party has several remedies available. Because the remedies may be inconsistent with one another, the common law of contracts requires the party to choose which remedy to pursue. This is called *election of remedies*. The purpose of the doctrine of election of remedies is to prevent double recovery. **■EXAMPLE 12.12** Jefferson agrees to sell his land to Adams. Then Jefferson changes his mind and repudiates the contract. Adams can sue for compensatory damages or for specific performance. If Adams receives damages as a result of the breach, she should not also be granted specific performance of the sales contract because that would mean she would unfairly end up with both the land and the damages. The doctrine of election of remedies requires Adams to choose the remedy she wants, and it eliminates any possibility of double recovery. ■

In contrast, remedies under the UCC are cumulative. They include all of the remedies available under the UCC for breach of a sales or lease contract.[15] We will examine the UCC provisions on limited remedies in Chapter 16, in the context of the remedies available on the breach of a contract for the sale or lease of goods.

---

15. See UCC 2–703 and 2–711.

REVIEWING Breach and Remedies

Kyle Bruno enters into a contract with X Entertainment to be a stuntman in a movie that X Entertainment is producing. Bruno is widely known as the best motorcycle stuntman in the business, and the movie, *Xtreme Riders,* has numerous scenes involving high-speed freestyle street-bike stunts. Filming is set to begin August 1 and end by December 1 so that the film can be released the following summer. Both parties to the contract have stipulated that the filming must end on time in order to capture the profits from the summer movie market. The contract states that Bruno will be paid 10 percent of the net proceeds from the movie for his stunts. The contract also includes a liquidated damages provision, which specifies that if Bruno breaches the contract, he will owe X Entertainment $1 million. In addition, the contract includes a limitation-of-liability clause stating that if Bruno is injured during filming, X Entertainment's liability is limited to nominal damages. Using the information presented in the chapter, answer the following questions.

1 One day, while Bruno is preparing for a difficult stunt, he gets into an argument with the director and refuses to perform any stunts. Can X Entertainment seek specific performance of the contract? Why or why not?

2 Suppose that while performing a high-speed wheelie on a motorcycle, Bruno is injured by an intentionally reckless act of an X Entertainment employee. Will a court be likely to enforce the limitation-of-liability clause? Why or why not?

3 What factors would a court consider to determine if the $1 million liquidated damages clause is valid or is a penalty?

4 Suppose that there was no liquidated damages clause (or the court refused to enforce it) and X Entertainment breached the contract. The breach caused the release of the film to be delayed until after summer. Could Bruno seek consequential (special) damages for lost profits from the summer movie market in that situation? Explain.

TERMS AND CONCEPTS

consequential damages 243
incidental damages 243
liquidated damages 245

mitigation of damages 244
nominal damages 244
penalty 245

restitution 246
specific performance 246

CHAPTER SUMMARY Breach and Remedies

COMMON REMEDIES AVAILABLE TO NONBREACHING PARTY

Damages (See pages 242–246.)	The legal remedy designed to compensate the nonbreaching party for the loss of the bargain. By awarding monetary damages, the court tries to place the parties in the positions that they would

CHAPTER SUMMARY   Breach and Remedies—Continued

Damages—Continued	have occupied had the contract been fully performed. The nonbreaching party frequently has a duty to *mitigate* (lessen or reduce) the damages incurred as a result of the contract's breach. Damages can be classified in the following broad categories:

1. *Compensatory damages*—Damages that compensate the nonbreaching party for injuries actually sustained and proved to have arisen directly from the loss of the bargain resulting from the breach of contract.

   a. In breached contracts for the sale of goods, the usual measure of compensatory damages is the difference between the contract price and the market price.

   b. In breached contracts for the sale of land, the measure of damages is ordinarily the same as in contracts for the sale of goods.

   c. In breached construction contracts, the measure of damages depends on which party breaches and at what stage of construction the breach occurs.

2. *Consequential damages*—Damages resulting from special circumstances beyond the contract itself; the damages flow only from the consequences of a breach. For a party to recover consequential damages, the damages must be the foreseeable result of a breach of contract, and the breaching party must have known at the time the contract was formed that special circumstances existed that would cause the nonbreaching party to incur additional loss on breach of the contract. Also called *special damages*.

3. *Punitive damages*—Damages awarded to punish the breaching party. Usually not awarded in an action for breach of contract unless a tort is involved.

4. *Nominal damages*—Damages small in amount (such as one dollar) that are awarded when a breach has occurred but no actual injury has been suffered. Awarded only to establish that the defendant acted wrongfully.

5. *Liquidated damages*—Damages that may be specified in a contract as the amount to be paid to the nonbreaching party in the event the contract is breached in the future. Clauses providing for liquidated damages are enforced if the damages were difficult to estimate at the time the contract was formed and if the amount stipulated is reasonable. If the amount is construed to be a penalty, the clause will not be enforced.

Rescission and Restitution (See page 246.)	1. *Rescission*—A remedy whereby a contract is canceled and the parties are restored to the original positions that they occupied prior to the transaction. Available when fraud, a mistake, duress, or failure of consideration is present. The rescinding party must give prompt notice of the rescission to the breaching party. 2. *Restitution*—When a contract is rescinded, both parties must make restitution to each other by returning the goods, property, or funds previously conveyed. Restitution prevents the unjust enrichment of the parties.
Specific Performance (See pages 246–247.)	An equitable remedy calling for the performance of the act promised in the contract. This remedy is available only in special situations—such as those involving contracts for the sale of unique goods or land—and when monetary damages would be an inadequate remedy. Specific performance is not available as a remedy for breached contracts for personal services.
Reformation (See pages 247–248.)	An equitable remedy allowing a contract to be "reformed," or rewritten, to reflect the parties' true intentions. Available when an agreement is imperfectly expressed in writing.
Recovery Based on Quasi Contract (See page 248.)	An equitable theory imposed by the courts to obtain justice and prevent unjust enrichment in a situation in which no enforceable contract exists. The party seeking recovery must show the following:

(Continued)

CHAPTER SUMMARY   Breach and Remedies—Continued

Recovery Based on Quasi Contract—Continued	1. A benefit was conferred on the other party. 2. The party conferring the benefit did so with the expectation of being paid. 3. The benefit was not volunteered. 4. Retaining the benefit without paying for it would result in the unjust enrichment of the party receiving the benefit.
	CONTRACT DOCTRINES RELATING TO REMEDIES
Contract Provisions Limiting Remedies (See page 249.)	A contract may provide that no damages (or only a limited amount of damages) can be recovered in the event the contract is breached. Clauses excluding liability for fraudulent or intentional injury or for illegal acts cannot be enforced. Clauses excluding liability for negligence may be enforced if both parties hold roughly equal bargaining power. Under the Uniform Commercial Code (UCC), remedies may be limited in contracts for the sale of goods.
Election of Remedies (See page 250.)	A common law doctrine under which a nonbreaching party must choose one remedy from those available. This doctrine prevents double recovery. Under the UCC, remedies are cumulative for the breach of a contract for the sale of goods.

FOR REVIEW

Answers for the even-numbered questions in this **For Review** *section can be found on this text's accompanying Web site at* **www.cengage.com/blaw/fbl**. *Select "Chapter 12" and click on "For Review."*

1 What is the difference between compensatory damages and consequential damages? What are nominal damages, and when do courts award nominal damages?

2 What is the standard measure of compensatory damages when a contract is breached? How are damages computed differently in construction contracts?

3 Under what circumstances is the remedy of rescission and restitution available?

4 When do courts grant specific performance as a remedy?

5 What is the rationale underlying the doctrine of election of remedies?

QUESTIONS AND CASE PROBLEMS

HYPOTHETICAL SCENARIOS AND CASE PROBLEMS

12.1 Liquidated Damages. Carnack contracts to sell his house and lot to Willard for $100,000. The terms of the contract call for Willard to pay 10 percent of the purchase price as a deposit toward the purchase price, or as a down payment. The terms further stipulate that should the buyer breach the contract, Carnack will retain the deposit as liquidated damages. Willard pays the deposit, but because her expected financing of the $90,000 balance falls through, she breaches the contract. Two weeks later, Carnack sells the house and lot to Balkova for $105,000. Willard demands her $10,000 back, but Carnack refuses, claiming that Willard's breach and the contract terms entitle him to keep the deposit. Discuss who is correct.

12.2 Hypothetical Question with Sample Answer. In which of the following situations might a court grant specific performance as a remedy for the breach of the contract?

1 Tarrington contracts to sell her house and lot to Rainier. Then, on finding another buyer willing to pay a higher purchase price, she refuses to deed the property to Rainier.

2 Marita contracts to sing and dance in Horace's nightclub for one month, beginning June 1. She then refuses to perform.

3 Juan contracts to purchase a rare coin from Edmund, who is breaking up his coin collection. At the last minute, Edmund decides to keep his coin collection intact and refuses to deliver the coin to Juan.

4 Astro Computer Corp. has three shareholders: Coase, who owns 48 percent of the stock; De Valle, who owns 48 percent; and Cary, who owns 4 percent. Cary contracts to sell his 4 percent to De Valle but later refuses to transfer the shares to him.

For a sample answer to Question 12.2, go to Appendix E at the end of this text.

12.3 Measure of Damages. Johnson contracted to lease a house to Fox for $700 a month, beginning October 1. Fox stipulated in the contract that before he moved in, the interior of the house had to be completely repainted. On September 9, Johnson hired Keever to do the required painting for $1,000. He told Keever that the painting had to be finished by October 1 but did not explain why. On September 28, Keever quit for no reason, having completed approximately 80 percent of the work. Johnson then paid Sam $300 to finish the painting, but Sam did not finish until October 4. When Fox found that the painting had not been completed as stipulated in his contract with Johnson, he leased another home. Johnson found another tenant who would lease the property at $700 a month, beginning October 15. Johnson then sued Keever for breach of contract, claiming damages of $650. This amount included the $300 Johnson paid Sam to finish the painting and $350 for rent for the first half of October, which Johnson had lost as a result of Keever's breach. Johnson had not yet paid Keever anything for Keever's work. Can Johnson collect the $650 from Keever? Explain.

12.4 Waiver of Breach. In May 1998, RDP Royal Palm Hotel, L.P., contracted with Clark Construction Group, Inc., to build the Royal Palms Crowne Plaza Resort in Miami Beach, Florida. The deadline for "substantial completion" was February 28, 2000, but RDP could ask for changes, and the date would be adjusted accordingly. During construction, Clark faced many setbacks, including a buried seawall, contaminated soil, the unforeseen deterioration of the existing hotel, and RDP's issue of hundreds of change orders. Clark requested extensions of the deadline, and RDP agreed, but the parties never specified a date. After the original deadline passed, RDP continued to issue change orders, Clark continued to perform, and RDP accepted the work. In March 2002, when the resort was substantially complete, RDP stopped paying Clark. Clark stopped working. RDP hired another contractor to finish the resort, which opened in May. RDP filed a suit in a federal district court against Clark, alleging, among other things, breach of contract for the two-year delay in the resort's completion. In whose favor should the court rule, and why? Discuss. [*RDP Royal Palm Hotel, L.P. v. Clark Construction Group, Inc.*, __ F.3d __ (11th Cir. 2006)]

12.5 Case Problem with Sample Answer. Tyna Ek met Russell Peterson in Seattle, Washington. Peterson persuaded Ek to buy a boat that he had once owned, the *O'Hana Kai*, which was in Juneau, Alaska. Ek paid the boat's current owner $43,000 for the boat, and in January 2000, she and Peterson entered into a contract, under which Peterson agreed to make the vessel seaworthy so that within one month it could be transported to Seattle, where he would pay its moorage costs. He would renovate the boat at his own expense in return for a portion of the profit on its resale in 2001. On the sale, Ek would recover her costs, and then Peterson would be reimbursed for his. Ek loaned Peterson her cell phone so that they could communicate while he prepared the vessel for the trip to Seattle. In March, Peterson, who was still in Alaska, borrowed $4,000 from Ek. Two months later, Ek began to receive unanticipated, unauthorized bills for vessel parts and moorage, the use of her phone, and charges on her credit card. She went to Juneau to take possession of the boat. Peterson moved it to Petersburg, Alaska, where he registered it under a false name, and then to Taku Harbor, where the police seized it. Ek filed a suit in an Alaska state court against Peterson, alleging breach of contract and seeking damages. If the court finds in Ek's favor, what should her damages include? Discuss. [*Peterson v. Ek*, 93 P.3d 458 (Alaska 2004)]

After you have answered Problem 12.5, compare your answer with the sample answer given on the Web site that accompanies this text. Go to www.cengage.com/blaw/fbl, select "Chapter 12," and click on "Case Problem with Sample Answer."

12.6 Remedies. On July 7, 2000, Frances Morelli agreed to sell to Judith Bucklin a house at 126 Lakedell Drive in Warwick, Rhode Island, for $77,000. Bucklin made a deposit on the house. The closing at which the parties would exchange the deed for the price was scheduled for September 1. The agreement did not state that "time is of the essence," but it did provide, in "Paragraph 10" that "[i]f Seller is unable to [convey good, clear, insurable, and marketable title], Buyer shall have the option to: (a) accept such title as Seller is able to convey without abatement or reduction of the Purchase Price, or (b) cancel this Agreement and receive a return of all Deposits." An examination of the public records revealed that the house did not have marketable title. Wishing to be flexible, Bucklin offered Morelli time to resolve the problem, and the closing did not occur as scheduled. Morelli decided "the deal is over" and offered to return the deposit. Bucklin refused and, in mid-October, decided to exercise her option under Paragraph 10(a). She notified Morelli, who did not respond. Bucklin filed a suit in a Rhode Island state court against Morelli. In whose favor should the court rule? Should damages be awarded? If not, what is the appropriate remedy? Why? [*Bucklin v. Morelli*, 912 A.2d 931 (R.I. 2007)]

12.7 Contract Limits on Damages. David Hanson was flying on American West Airlines. In his carry-on duffel bag, he carried a robotic head that was worth about $750,000. (This head was used in making movies.) When he transferred to another plane, he forgot about his duffel bag, which he had stored above his seat. When he got to his final destination, he reported the loss and was told that the airline had retrieved the bag and its contents and that the airlines would send it to him. But it never arrived. Hanson sued for damages for breach of contract. The airline requested a summary judgment. The ticket Hanson had purchased stated that there was a $2,800 damage limit for checked baggage, per passenger, and that there was no liability for items passengers carry on board a plane. Is this sort of damage restriction by American West Airlines reasonable? Why or why not? [*Hanson v. American West Airlines,* 544 F.Supp.2d 1038 (C.D. Cal. 2008)]

12.8 **A Question of Ethics.** *In 2004, Tamara Cohen, a real estate broker, began showing property in Manhattan to Steven Galistinos, who represented comedian Jerry Seinfeld and his wife, Jessica. According to Cohen, she told Galistinos that her commission would be 5 or 6 percent, and he agreed. According to Galistinos, there was no such agreement. Cohen spoke with Maximillan Sanchez, another broker, about a townhouse owned by Ray and Harriet Mayeri. According to Cohen, Sanchez said that the commission would be 6 percent, which they agreed to split equally. Sanchez later acknowledged that they agreed to split the fee, but claimed that they did not discuss a specific amount. On a Friday in February 2005, Cohen showed the townhouse to Jessica. According to Cohen, she told Jessica that the commission would be 6 percent, with the Seinfelds paying half, and Jessica agreed. According to Jessica, there was no such conversation. Later that day, Galistinos asked Cohen to arrange for the Seinfelds to see the premises again. Cohen told Galistinos that her religious beliefs prevented her from showing property on Friday evenings or Saturdays before sundown. She suggested the following Monday or Tuesday, but Galistinos said that Jerry would not be available and asked her to contact Carolyn Liebling, Jerry's business manager. Cohen left Liebling a message. Over the weekend, the Seinfelds toured the building on their own and agreed to buy the property for $3.95 million. Despite repeated attempts, they were unable to contact Cohen.* [*Cohen v. Seinfeld,* 15 Misc.3d 1118(A), 839 N.Y.S.2d 432 (Sup. 2007)]

1 The contract between the Seinfelds and the Mayeris stated that the sellers would pay Sanchez's fee and the "buyers will pay buyer's real estate broker's fees." The Mayeris paid Sanchez $118,500, which is 3 percent of $3.95 million. The Seinfelds refused to pay Cohen. She filed a suit in a New York state court against them, asserting, among other things, breach of contract. Should the court order the Seinfelds to pay Cohen? If so, is she entitled to a full commission even though she was not available to show the townhouse when the Seinfelds wanted to see it? Explain.

2 What obligation do parties involved in business deals owe to each other with respect to their religious beliefs? How might the situation in this case have been avoided?

CRITICAL THINKING AND WRITING ASSIGNMENTS

12.9 Critical Legal Thinking. Review the discussion of the doctrine of election of remedies in this chapter. What are some of the advantages and disadvantages of this doctrine?

12.10 **Video Question.** Go to this text's Web site at **www.cengage.com/blaw/fbl** and select "Chapter 12." Click on "Video Questions" and view the video titled *Midnight Run.* Then answer the following questions.

1 In the video, Eddie (Joe Pantoliano) and Jack (Robert De Niro) negotiate a contract for Jack to find "the Duke," a mob accountant who embezzled funds, and bring him back for trial. Assume that the contract is valid. If Jack breaches the contract by failing to bring in the Duke, what kinds of remedies, if any, can Eddie seek? Explain your answer.

2 Would the equitable remedy of specific performance be available to either Jack or Eddie in the event of a breach? Why or why not?

3 Now assume that the contract between Eddie and Jack is unenforceable. Nevertheless, Jack performs his side of the bargain by bringing in the Duke. Does Jack have any legal recourse in this situation? Explain.

ACCESSING THE INTERNET

For updated links to resources available on the Web, as well as a variety of other materials, visit this text's Web site at

www.cengage.com/blaw/fbl

The following site offers a brief summary of and several related articles on breach of contract:

www.legalmatch.com/law-library/article/breach-of-contract.html

PRACTICAL INTERNET EXERCISES

Go to this text's Web site at **www.cengage.com/blaw/fbl**, select "Chapter 12," and click on "Practical Internet Exercises." There you will find the following Internet research exercises that you can perform to learn more about the topics covered in this chapter.

PRACTICAL INTERNET EXERCISE 12–1   LEGAL PERSPECTIVE—Contract Damages and
                                        Contract Theory

PRACTICAL INTERNET EXERCISE 12–2   MANAGEMENT PERSPECTIVE—The Duty to Mitigate

BEFORE THE TEST

Go to this text's Web site at **www.cengage.com/blaw/fbl**, select "Chapter 12," and click on "Interactive Quizzes." You will find a number of interactive questions relating to this chapter.

Glossary

A

abandoned property ■ Property with which the owner has voluntarily parted, with no intention of recovering it.

acceleration clause ■ A clause that allows a payee or other holder of a time instrument to demand payment of the entire amount due, with interest, if a certain event occurs, such as a default in the payment of an installment when due.

acceptance ■ In contract law, a voluntary act by the offeree that shows assent, or agreement, to the terms of an offer; may consist of words or conduct. In negotiable instruments law, the drawee's signed agreement to pay a draft when it is presented.

acceptor ■ A drawee that is legally obligated to pay an instrument when it is presented later for payment.

accession ■ Occurs when an individual adds value to personal property by the use of either labor or materials. In some situations, a person may acquire ownership rights in another's property through accession.

accommodation party ■ A person who signs an instrument for the purpose of lending her or his name as credit to another party on the instrument.

accord and satisfaction ■ A common means of settling a disputed claim, whereby a debtor offers to pay a lesser amount than the creditor purports is owed. The creditor's acceptance of the offer creates an accord (agreement), and when the accord is executed, satisfaction occurs.

accredited investors ■ In the context of securities offerings, "sophisticated" investors, such as banks, insurance companies, investment companies, the issuer's executive officers and directors, and persons whose income or net worth exceeds certain limits.

act of state doctrine ■ A doctrine providing that the judicial branch of one country will not examine the validity of public acts committed by a recognized foreign government within its own territory.

actionable ■ Capable of serving as the basis of a lawsuit. An actionable claim can be pursued in a lawsuit or other court action.

actual malice ■ The deliberate intent to cause harm, which exists when a person makes a statement either knowing that it is false or showing a reckless disregard for whether it is true. In defamation law, a statement made about a public figure normally must be made with actual malice for the plaintiff to recover damages.

actus reus ■ A guilty (prohibited) act. The commission of a prohibited act is one of the two essential elements required for criminal liability, the other element being the intent to commit a crime.

adhesion contract ■ A "standard-form" contract, such as that between a large retailer and a consumer, in which the stronger party dictates the terms.

adjudicate ■ The act of rendering a judicial decision. In an administrative process, the proceeding in which an administrative law judge hears and decides on issues that arise when an administrative agency charges a person or a firm with violating a law or regulation enforced by the agency.

administrative agency ■ A federal or state government agency established to perform a specific function. Administrative agencies are authorized by legislative acts to make and enforce rules in order to administer and enforce the acts.

administrative law ■ The body of law created by administrative agencies (in the form of rules, regulations, orders, and decisions) in order to carry out their duties and responsibilities.

administrative process ■ The procedure used by administrative agencies in the administration of law.

administrator ■ One who is appointed by a court to handle the probate (disposition) of a person's estate if that person dies intestate (without a valid will) or if the executor named in the will cannot serve.

adverse possession ■ The acquisition of title to real property by occupying it openly, without the consent of the owner, for a period of time specified by a state statute. The occupation must be actual, open, notorious, exclusive, and in opposition to all others, including the owner.

affirmative action ■ Job-hiring policies that give special consideration to members of protected classes in an effort to overcome present effects of past discrimination.

after-acquired property ■ Property that is acquired by the debtor after the execution of a security agreement.

agency ■ A relationship between two parties in which one party (the agent) agrees to represent or act for the other (the principal).

agent ■ A person who agrees to represent or act for another, called the principal.

agreement ■ A meeting of two or more minds in regard to the terms of a contract; usually broken down into two events—an offer by one party to form a contract and an acceptance of the offer by the person to whom the offer is made.

alien corporation ■ A designation in the United States for a corporation formed in another country but doing business in the United States.

alienation ■ The process of transferring land out of one's possession (thus "alienating" the land from oneself).

allonge ■ A piece of paper firmly attached to a negotiable instrument, on which transferees can make indorsements if there is no room left on the instrument itself.

alternative dispute resolution (ADR) ■ The resolution of disputes in ways other than those involved in the traditional judicial process. Negotiation, mediation, and arbitration are forms of ADR.

answer ■ Procedurally, a defendant's response to the plaintiff's complaint.

anticipatory repudiation ■ An assertion or action by a party indicating that he or she will not perform an obligation that the party is contractually obligated to perform at a future time.

apparent authority ■ Authority that is only apparent, not real. In agency law, a person may be deemed to have had the power to act as an agent for another party if the other party's manifestations to a third party led the third party to believe that an agency existed when, in fact, it did not.

appraisal right ■ The right of a dissenting shareholder, who objects to an extraordinary transaction of the corporation (such as a merger or a consolidation), to have his or her shares appraised and to be paid the fair value of those shares by the corporation.

appropriation ■ In tort law, the use by one person of another person's name, likeness, or other identifying characteristic without permission and for the benefit of the user.

arbitration ■ The settling of a dispute by submitting it to a disinterested third party (other than a court), who renders a decision that is (most often) legally binding.

arbitration clause ■ A clause in a contract that provides that, in the event of a dispute, the parties will submit the dispute to arbitration rather than litigate the dispute in court.

arson ■ The intentional burning of another's dwelling. Some statutes have expanded this to include any real property regardless of ownership and the destruction of property by other means—for example, by explosion.

articles of incorporation ■ The document filed with the appropriate governmental agency, usually the secretary of state, when a business is incorporated. State statutes usually prescribe what kind of information must be contained in the articles of incorporation.

articles of organization ■ The document filed with a designated state official by which a limited liability company is formed.

articles of partnership ■ A written agreement that sets forth each partner's rights and obligations with respect to the partnership.

artisan's lien ■ A possessory lien given to a person who has made improvements and added value to another person's personal property as security for payment for services performed.

assault ■ Any word or action intended to make another person fearful of immediate physical harm; a reasonably believable threat.

assignee ■ A party to whom the rights under a contract are transferred, or assigned.

assignment ■ The act of transferring to another all or part of one's rights arising under a contract.

assignor ■ A party who transfers (assigns) his or her rights under a contract to another party (called the *assignee*).

assumption of risk ■ A doctrine under which a plaintiff may not recover for injuries or damage suffered from risks he or she knows of and has voluntarily assumed.

attachment ■ In a secured transaction, the process by which a secured creditor's interest "attaches" to the property of another (collateral) and the creditor's security interest becomes enforceable. In the context of judicial liens, a court-ordered seizure and taking into custody of property prior to the securing of a judgment for a past-due debt.

automatic stay ■ In bankruptcy proceedings, the suspension of virtually all litigation and other action by creditors against the debtor or the debtor's property. The stay is effective the moment the debtor files a petition in bankruptcy.

award ■ In litigation, the amount of monetary compensation awarded to a plaintiff in a civil lawsuit as damages. In the context of alternative dispute resolution, the decision rendered by an arbitrator.

backdating ■ The practice of marketing a document with a date that precedes the actual date. Persons who backdate stock options are picking a date when the stock was trading at a lower price than the date of the options grant.

bailee ■ One to whom goods are entrusted by a bailor.

bailment ■ A situation in which the personal property of one person (a bailor) is entrusted to another (a bailee), who is obligated to return the bailed property to the bailor or dispose of it as directed.

bailor ■ One who entrusts goods to a bailee.

bankruptcy court ■ A federal court of limited jurisdiction that handles only bankruptcy proceedings, which are governed by federal bankruptcy law.

battery ■ The unprivileged, intentional touching of another.

bearer ■ A person in possession of an instrument payable to bearer or indorsed in blank.

bearer instrument ■ Any instrument that is not payable to a specific person, including instruments payable to the bearer or to "cash."

bequest ■ A gift of personal property by will (from the verb *to bequeath*).

beyond a reasonable doubt ■ The standard of proof used in criminal cases. If there is any reasonable doubt that a criminal defendant committed the crime with which she or he has been charged, then the verdict must be "not guilty."

bilateral contract ■ A type of contract that arises when a promise is given in exchange for a return promise.

bilateral mistake ■ A mistake that occurs when both parties to a contract are mistaken about the same material fact and the mistake is one that a reasonable person would make; either party can rescind the contract.

Bill of Rights ■ The first ten amendments to the U.S. Constitution.

binder ■ A written, temporary insurance policy.

binding authority ■ Any source of law that a court must follow when deciding a case.

blank indorsement ■ An indorsement that specifies no particular indorsee and can consist of a mere signature. An order instrument that is indorsed in blank becomes a bearer instrument.

blue laws ■ State or local laws that prohibit the performance of certain types of commercial activities on Sunday.

blue sky laws ■ State laws that regulate the offering and sale of securities.

bona fide occupational qualification (BFOQ) ■ Identifiable characteristics reasonably necessary to the normal operation of a particular business. These characteristics can include gender, national origin, and religion, but not race.

bond ■ A certificate that evidences a corporate (or government) debt. It is a security that involves no ownership interest in the issuing entity.

bond indenture ■ A contract between the issuer of a bond and the bondholder.

bounty payment ■ A reward (payment) given to a person or persons who perform a certain service, such as informing legal authorities of illegal actions.

breach ■ The failure to perform a legal obligation.

breach of contract ■ The failure, without legal excuse, of a promisor to perform the obligations of a contract.

brief ■ A formal legal document prepared by a party's attorney and submitted to an appellate court when a case is appealed, which outlines the facts and issues of the case that are in dispute.

browse-wrap terms ■ Terms and conditions of use that are presented to an Internet user at the time certain products, such as software, are being downloaded but that need not be agreed to (by clicking "I agree," for example) before the user is able to install or use the product.

burglary ■ The unlawful entry or breaking into a building with the intent to commit a felony (or any crime, in some states).

business ethics ■ Ethics in a business context; a consensus as to what constitutes right or wrong behavior in the world of business and the application of moral principles to situations that arise in a business setting.

business invitee ■ A person, such as a customer or a client, who is invited onto business premises by the owner of those premises for business purposes.

business judgment rule ■ A rule that immunizes corporate management from liability for actions that result in corporate losses or damages if the actions are undertaken in good faith and are within both the power of the corporation and the authority of management to make.

business necessity ■ A defense to allegations of employment discrimination in which the employer demonstrates that an employment practice that discriminates against members of a protected class is related to job performance.

business tort ■ Wrongful interference with another's business rights.

business trust ■ A form of business organization in which investors (trust beneficiaries) transfer cash or property to trustees in exchange for trust certificates that represent their investment shares. The certificate holders share in the trust's profits but have limited liability.

bylaws ■ A set of governing rules adopted by a corporation or other association.

case law ■ The rules of law announced in court decisions. Case law includes the aggregate of reported cases that interpret judicial precedents, statutes, regulations, and constitutional provisions.

cashier's check ■ A check drawn by a bank on itself.

categorical imperative ■ A concept developed by the philosopher Immanuel Kant as an ethical guideline for behavior. In deciding whether an action is right or wrong, or desirable or undesirable, a person should evaluate the action in terms of what would happen if everybody else in the same situation, or category, acted the same way.

causation in fact ■ An act or omission without which an event would not have occurred.

certificate of deposit (CD) ■ A note issued by a bank in which the bank acknowledges the receipt of funds from a party and promises to repay that amount, with interest, to the party on a certain date.

certificate of limited partnership ■ The basic document filed with a designated state official by which a limited partnership is formed.

certification mark ■ A mark used by one or more persons, other than the owner, to certify the region, materials, mode of manufacture, quality, or other characteristic of specific goods or services.

certified check ■ A check that has been accepted in writing by the bank on which it is drawn. Essentially, the bank, by certifying (accepting) the check, promises to pay the check at the time the check is presented.

charitable trust ■ A trust in which the property held by the trustee must be used for a charitable purpose, such as the advancement of health, education, or religion.

chattel ■ All forms of personal property.

check ■ A draft drawn by a drawer ordering the drawee bank or financial institution to pay a certain amount of money to the holder on demand.

choice-of-language clause ■ A clause in a contract designating the official language by which the contract will be interpreted in the event of a future disagreement over the contract's terms.

choice-of-law clause ■ A clause in a contract designating the law (such as the law of a particular state or nation) that will govern the contract.

citation ■ A reference to a publication in which a legal authority—such as a statute or a court decision—or other source can be found.

civil law ■ The branch of law dealing with the definition and enforcement of all private or public rights, as opposed to criminal matters.

civil law system ■ A system of law derived from that of the Roman Empire and based on a code rather than case law; the predominant system of law in the nations of continental Europe and the nations that were once their colonies.

clearinghouse ■ A system or place where banks exchange checks and drafts drawn on each other and settle daily balances.

click-on agreement ■ An agreement that arises when a buyer, engaging in a transaction on a computer, indicates assent to be bound by the terms of an offer by clicking on a button that says, for example, "I agree"; sometimes referred to as a *click-on license* or a *click-wrap agreement*.

close corporation ■ A corporation whose shareholders are limited to a small group of persons, often including only family members.

closed shop ■ A firm that requires union membership by its workers as a condition of employment. The closed shop was made illegal by the Labor-Management Relations Act of 1947.

codicil ■ A written supplement or modification to a will. A codicil must be executed with the same formalities as a will.

collateral ■ Under Article 9 of the UCC, the property subject to a security interest, including accounts and chattel paper that have been sold.

collateral promise ■ A secondary promise that is ancillary (subsidiary) to a principal transaction or primary contractual relationship, such as a promise made by one person to pay the debts of another if the latter fails to perform. A collateral promise normally must be in writing to be enforceable.

collecting bank ■ Any bank handling an item for collection, except the payor bank.

collective mark ■ A mark used by members of a cooperative, association, union, or other organization to certify the region, materials, mode of manufacture, quality, or other characteristic of specific goods or services.

comity ■ The principle by which one nation defers to and gives effect to the laws and judicial decrees of another nation. This recognition is based primarily on respect.

commerce clause ■ The provision in Article I, Section 8, of the U.S. Constitution that gives Congress the power to regulate interstate commerce.

commercial impracticability ■ A doctrine under which a party may be excused from performing a contract when (1) a contingency occurs, (2) the contingency's occurrence makes performance impracticable, and (3) the nonoccurrence of the contingency was a basic assumption on which the contract was made.

commingle ■ To put funds or goods together into one mass so that they are so mixed that they no longer have separate identities. In corporate law, if personal and corporate interests are commingled to the extent that the corporation has no separate identity, a court may "pierce the corporate veil" and expose the shareholders to personal liability.

common law ■ The body of law developed from custom or judicial decisions in English and U.S. courts, not attributable to a legislature.

common stock ■ Shares of ownership in a corporation that give the owner of the stock a proportionate interest in the corporation with regard to control, earnings, and net assets. Shares of common stock are lowest in priority with respect to payment of dividends and distribution of the corporation's assets on dissolution.

community property ■ A form of concurrent ownership of property in which each spouse technically owns an undivided one-half interest in property acquired during the marriage.

comparative negligence ■ A rule followed by most states in tort cases that reduces the plaintiff's recovery in proportion to the plaintiff's degree of fault, rather than barring recovery completely.

compensatory damages ■ A monetary award equivalent to the actual value of injuries or damage sustained by the aggrieved party.

complaint ■ The pleading made by a plaintiff alleging wrongdoing on the part of the defendant; the document that, when filed with a court, initiates a lawsuit.

computer crime ■ Any act that is directed against computers and computer parts, that uses computers as instruments of crime, or that involves computers and constitutes abuse.

concurrent conditions ■ Conditions that must occur or be performed at the same time; they are mutually dependent. No obligations arise until these conditions are simultaneously performed.

concurrent ownership ■ Joint ownership.

condemnation ■ The process of taking private property for public use through the government's power of eminent domain.

condition ■ A qualification, provision, or clause in a contractual agreement, the occurrence or nonoccurrence of which creates, suspends, or terminates the obligations of the contracting parties.

condition precedent ■ In a contractual agreement, a condition that must be met before a party's promise becomes absolute.

condition subsequent ■ A condition in a contract that, if not fulfilled, operates to terminate a party's absolute promise to perform.

confession of judgment ■ The act or agreement of a debtor in permitting a judgment to be entered against him or her by a creditor, for an agreed sum, without the institution of legal proceedings.

confiscation ■ A government's taking of a privately owned business or personal property without a proper public purpose or an award of just compensation.

conforming goods ■ Goods that conform to contract specifications.

confusion ■ The mixing together of goods belonging to two or more owners so that the separately owned goods cannot be identified.

consent ■ Voluntary agreement to a proposition or an act of another; a concurrence of wills.

consequential damages ■ Special damages that compensate for a loss that does not directly or immediately result from the breach (for example, lost profits). For the plaintiff to collect consequential damages, they must have been reasonably foreseeable at the time the breach or injury occurred.

consideration ■ Generally, the value given in return for a promise; involves two elements—the giving of something of legally sufficient value and a bargained-for exchange. The consideration must result in a detriment to the promisee or a benefit to the promisor.

consignment ■ A transaction in which an owner of goods (the consignor) delivers the goods to another (the consignee) for the consignee to sell. The consignee pays the consignor only for the goods that are sold by the consignee.

consolidation ■ A contractual and statutory process in which two or more corporations join to become a completely new corporation. The original corporations cease to exist, and the new corporation acquires all their assets and liabilities.

constitutional law ■ The body of law derived from the U.S. Constitution and the constitutions of the various states.

constructive delivery ■ An act equivalent to the actual, physical delivery of property that cannot be physically delivered because of difficulty or impossibility. For example, the transfer of a key to a safe constructively delivers the contents of the safe.

constructive discharge ■ A termination of employment brought about by making the employee's working conditions so intolerable that the employee reasonably feels compelled to leave.

constructive eviction ■ A form of eviction that occurs when a landlord fails to perform adequately any of the duties (such as providing heat in the winter) required by the lease, thereby making the tenant's further use and enjoyment of the property exceedingly difficult or impossible.

constructive trust ■ An equitable trust that is imposed in the interests of fairness and justice when someone wrongfully holds legal title to property. A court may require the owner to hold the property in trust for the person or persons who should rightfully own the property.

consumer-debtor ■ An individual whose debts are primarily consumer debts (debts for purchases made primarily for personal, family, or household use).

continuation statement ■ A statement that, if filed within six months prior to the expiration date of the original financing statement, continues the perfection of the original security interest for another five years. The perfection of a security interest can be continued in the same manner indefinitely.

contract ■ An agreement that can be enforced in court; formed by two or more competent parties who agree, for consideration, to perform or to refrain from performing some legal act now or in the future.

contractual capacity ■ The threshold mental capacity required by the law for a party who enters into a contract to be bound by that contract.

contributory negligence ■ A rule in tort law that completely bars the plaintiff from recovering any damages if the damage suffered is partly the plaintiff's own fault; used in a minority of states.

conversion ■ Wrongfully taking or retaining possession of an individual's personal property and placing it in the service of another.

conveyance ■ The transfer of title to land from one person to another by deed; a document (such as a deed) by which an interest in land is transferred from one person to another.

"cooling-off" laws ■ Laws that allow buyers a period of time, such as three days, in which to cancel door-to-door sales contracts.

copyright ■ The exclusive right of an author or originator of a literary or artistic production (including computer programs) to publish, print, or sell that production for a statutory period of time.

corporate governance ■ A set of policies or procedures affecting the way a corporation is directed or controlled.

corporate social responsibility ■ The idea that corporations can and should act ethically and be accountable to society for their actions.

corporation ■ A legal entity formed in compliance with statutory requirements that is distinct from its shareholder-owners.

correspondent bank ■ A bank in which another bank has an account (and vice versa) for the purpose of facilitating fund transfers.

cost-benefit analysis ■ A decision-making technique that involves weighing the costs of a given action against the benefits of that action.

co-surety ■ A joint surety; a person who assumes liability jointly with another surety for the payment of an obligation.

counterclaim ■ A claim made by a defendant in a civil lawsuit against the plaintiff. In effect, the defendant is suing the plaintiff.

counteroffer ■ An offeree's response to an offer in which the offeree rejects the original offer and at the same time makes a new offer.

course of dealing ■ Prior conduct between the parties to a contract that establishes a common basis for their understanding.

covenant not to compete ■ A contractual promise of one party to refrain from conducting business similar to that of another party for a certain period of time and within a specified geographic area. Courts commonly enforce such covenants if they are reasonable in terms of time and geographic area and are part of, or supplemental to, a contract for the sale of a business or an employment contract.

covenant not to sue ■ An agreement to substitute a contractual obligation for some other type of legal action based on a valid claim.

cover ■ Under the UCC, a remedy that allows the buyer or lessee, on the seller's or lessor's breach, to purchase goods from another seller or lessor and substitute them for the goods due under the contract. If the cost of cover exceeds the cost of the contract goods, the buyer or lessee can recover the difference, plus incidental and consequential damages.

cram-down provision ■ A provision of the Bankruptcy Code that allows a court to confirm a debtor's Chapter 11 reorganization plan even though only one class of creditors has accepted it.

creditors' composition agreement ■ An agreement formed between a debtor and his or her creditors in which the creditors agree to accept a lesser sum than that owed by the debtor in full satisfaction of the debt.

crime ■ A wrong against society proclaimed in a statute and, if committed, punishable by society through fines and/or imprisonment—and, in some cases, death.

criminal law ■ Law that defines and governs actions that constitute crimes. Generally, criminal law has to do with wrongful actions committed against society for which society demands redress.

cross-collateralization ■ The use of an asset that is not the subject of a loan to collateralize that loan.

cure ■ The right of a party who tenders nonconforming performance to correct that performance within the contract period [UCC 2–508(1)].

cyber crime ■ A crime that occurs online, in the virtual community of the Internet, as opposed to the physical world.

cyber mark ■ A trademark in cyberspace.

cyber tort ■ A tort committed in cyberspace.

cyberlaw ■ An informal term used to refer to all laws governing electronic communications and transactions, particularly those conducted via the Internet.

cybernotary ■ A legally recognized authority that can certify the validity of digital signatures.

cybersquatting ■ The act of registering a domain name that is the same as, or confusingly similar to, the trademark of another and then offering to sell that domain name back to the trademark owner.

cyberterrorist ■ A hacker whose purpose is to exploit a target computer for a serious impact, such as corrupting a program to sabotage a business.

damages ■ Money sought as a remedy for a breach of contract or a tortious action.

debtor ■ Under Article 9 of the UCC, any party who owes payment or performance of a secured obligation, whether or not the party actually owns or has rights in the collateral.

debtor in possession (DIP) ■ In Chapter 11 bankruptcy proceedings, a debtor who is allowed to continue in possession of the estate in property (the business) and to continue business operations.

deed ■ A document by which title to property (usually real property) is passed.

defalcation ■ Embezzlement; the misappropriation of funds by a party, such as a corporate officer or public official, in a fiduciary relationship with another.

defamation ■ Anything published or publicly spoken that causes injury to another's good name, reputation, or character.

default ■ Failure to observe a promise or discharge an obligation; commonly used to refer to failure to pay a debt when it is due.

default judgment ■ A judgment entered by a court against a defendant who has failed to appear in court to answer or defend against the plaintiff's claim.

defendant ■ One against whom a lawsuit is brought; the accused person in a criminal proceeding.

defense ■ A reason offered and alleged by a defendant in an action or suit as to why the plaintiff should not recover or establish what she or he seeks.

deficiency judgment ■ A judgment against a debtor for the amount of a debt remaining unpaid after the collateral has been repossessed and sold.

delegatee ■ A party to whom contractual obligations are transferred, or delegated.

delegation of duties ■ The act of transferring to another all or part of one's duties arising under a contract.

delegator ■ A party who transfers (delegates) her or his obligations under a contract to another party (called the *delegatee*).

depositary bank ■ The first bank to receive a check for payment.

deposition ■ The testimony of a party to a lawsuit or a witness taken under oath before a trial.

destination contract ■ A contract for the sale of goods in which the seller is required or authorized to ship the goods by carrier and tender delivery of the goods at a particular destination. The seller assumes liability for any losses or damage to the goods until they are tendered at the destination specified in the contract.

devise ■ As a noun, a gift of real property by will; as a verb, to make a gift of real property by will.

devisee ■ One designated in a will to receive a gift of real property.

digital cash ■ Funds contained on computer software, in the form of secure programs stored on microchips and on other computer devices.

disaffirmance ■ The legal avoidance, or setting aside, of a contractual obligation.

discharge ■ The termination of an obligation. In contract law, discharge occurs when the parties have fully performed their contractual obligations or when other events occur that release the parties from performance. In bankruptcy proceedings, discharge is the

extinction of the debtor's dischargeable debts, thereby relieving the debtor of the obligation to pay the debts.

disclosed principal ■ A principal whose identity is known to a third party at the time the agent makes a contract with the third party.

discovery ■ A phase in the litigation process during which the opposing parties may obtain information from each other and from third parties prior to trial.

dishonor ■ A negotiable instrument is dishonored when payment or acceptance of the instrument, whichever is required, is refused even though the instrument is presented in a timely and proper manner.

disparagement of property ■ An economically injurious falsehood made about another's product or property; a general term for torts that are more specifically referred to as slander of quality or slander of title.

disparate-impact discrimination ■ A form of employment discrimination that results from certain employer practices or procedures that, although not discriminatory on their face, have a discriminatory effect.

disparate-treatment discrimination ■ A form of employment discrimination that results when an employer intentionally discriminates against employees who are members of protected classes.

dissociation ■ The severance of the relationship between a partner and a partnership when the partner ceases to be associated with the carrying on of the partnership business.

dissolution ■ The formal disbanding of a partnership or a corporation. It can take place by (1) acts of the partners or, in a corporation, acts of the shareholders and board of directors; (2) the subsequent illegality of the firm's business; (3) the expiration of a time period stated in a partnership agreement or a certificate of incorporation; or (4) judicial decree.

distributed network ■ A network that can be used by persons located (distributed) around the country or the globe to share computer files.

distribution agreement ■ A contract between a seller and a distributor of the seller's products setting out the terms and conditions of the distributorship.

diversity of citizenship ■ Under Article III, Section 2, of the U.S. Constitution, a basis for federal district court jurisdiction over a lawsuit between (1) citizens of different states, (2) a foreign country and citizens of a state or of different states, or (3) citizens of a state.

dividend ■ A distribution to corporate shareholders of corporate profits or income, disbursed in proportion to the number of shares held.

docket ■ The list of cases entered on a court's calendar and thus scheduled to be heard by the court.

document of title ■ A paper exchanged in the regular course of business that evidences the right to possession of goods (for example, a bill of lading or a warehouse receipt).

domain name ■ The last part of an Internet address, such as "westlaw.edu." The top level (the part of the name to the right of the period) indicates the type of entity that operates the site ("edu" is an abbreviation for "educational"). The second level (the part of the name to the left of the period) is chosen by the entity.

domestic corporation ■ In a given state, a corporation that does business in, and is organized under the law of, that state.

dominion ■ Ownership rights in property, including the right to possess and control the property.

double jeopardy ■ A situation occurring when a person is tried twice for the same criminal offense; prohibited by the Fifth Amendment to the Constitution.

draft ■ Any instrument drawn on a drawee that orders the drawee to pay a certain sum of money, usually to a third party (the payee), on demand or at a definite future time.

dram shop act ■ A state statute that imposes liability on the owners of bars and taverns, as well as those who serve alcoholic drinks to the public, for injuries resulting from accidents caused by intoxicated persons when the sellers or servers of alcoholic drinks contributed to the intoxication.

drawee ■ The party that is ordered to pay a draft or check. With a check, a bank or a financial institution is always the drawee.

drawer ■ The party that initiates a draft (such as a check), thereby ordering the drawee to pay.

due diligence ■ A required standard of care that certain professionals, such as accountants, must meet to avoid liability for securities violations.

due process clause ■ The provisions in the Fifth and Fourteenth Amendments to the Constitution that guarantee that no person shall be deprived of life, liberty, or property without due process of law. Similar clauses are found in most state constitutions.

dumping ■ The selling of goods in a foreign country at a price below the price charged for the same goods in the domestic market.

duress ■ Unlawful pressure brought to bear on a person, causing the person to perform an act that she or he would not otherwise perform.

duty of care ■ The duty of all persons, as established by tort law, to exercise a reasonable amount of care in their dealings with others. Failure to exercise due care, which is normally determined by the reasonable person standard, constitutes the tort of negligence.

e-agent ■ A computer program that by electronic or other automated means can independently initiate an action or respond to electronic messages or data without review by an individual.

easement ■ A nonpossessory right to use another's property in a manner established by either express or implied agreement.

e-contract ■ A contract that is formed electronically.

e-evidence ■ Evidence that consists of computer-generated or electronically recorded information, including e-mail, voice mail, spreadsheets, word-processing documents, and other data.

electronic fund transfer (EFT) ■ A transfer of funds with the use of an electronic terminal, a telephone, a computer, or magnetic tape.

emancipation ■ In regard to minors, the act of being freed from parental control; occurs when a child's parent or legal guardian relinquishes the legal right to exercise control over the child or when a minor leaves home to support himself or herself.

embezzlement ■ The fraudulent appropriation of funds or other property by a person to whom the funds or property has been entrusted.

eminent domain ■ The power of a government to take land from private citizens for public use on the payment of just compensation.

e-money ■ Prepaid funds recorded on a computer or a card (such as a smart card or a stored-value card).

employment at will ■ A common law doctrine under which either party may terminate an employment relationship at any time for any reason, unless a contract specifies otherwise.

employment contract ■ A contract between an employer and an employee in which the terms and conditions of employment are stated.

employment discrimination ■ Treating employees or job applicants unequally on the basis of race, color, national origin, religion, gender, age, or disability; prohibited by federal statutes.

enabling legislation ■ A statute enacted by Congress that authorizes the creation of an administrative agency and specifies the name, composition, purpose, and powers of the agency being created.

entrapment ■ In criminal law, a defense in which the defendant claims that he or she was induced by a public official—usually an undercover agent or police officer—to commit a crime that he or she would otherwise not have committed.

entrepreneur ■ One who initiates and assumes the financial risk of a new business enterprise and undertakes to provide or control its management.

entrustment rule ■ The transfer of goods to a merchant who deals in goods of that kind and who may transfer those goods and all rights to them to a buyer in the ordinary course of business [UCC 2–403(2)].

e-signature ■ As defined by the Uniform Electronic Transactions Act, "an electronic sound, symbol, or process attached to or logically associated with a record and executed or adopted by a person with the intent to sign the record."

establishment clause ■ The provision in the First Amendment to the Constitution that prohibits the government from establishing any state-sponsored religion or enacting any law that promotes religion or favors one religion over another.

estate in property ■ In bankruptcy proceedings, all of the debtor's interests in property currently held, wherever located, together with certain jointly owned property, property transferred in transactions voidable by the trustee, proceeds and profits from the property of the estate, and certain property interests to which the debtor becomes entitled within 180 days after filing for bankruptcy.

estopped ■ Barred, impeded, or precluded.

estray statute ■ A statute defining finders' rights in property when the true owners are unknown.

ethical reasoning ■ A reasoning process in which an individual links his or her moral convictions or ethical standards to the particular situation at hand.

ethics ■ Moral principles and values applied to social behavior.

eviction ■ A landlord's act of depriving a tenant of possession of the leased premises.

exclusionary rule ■ In criminal procedure, a rule under which any evidence that is obtained in violation of the accused's constitutional rights guaranteed by the Fourth, Fifth, and Sixth Amendments, as well as any evidence derived from illegally obtained evidence, will not be admissible in court.

exclusive distributorship ■ A distributorship in which the seller and the distributor of the seller's products agree that the distributor will distribute only the seller's products.

exclusive jurisdiction ■ Jurisdiction that exists when a case can be heard only in a particular court or type of court.

exculpatory clause ■ A clause that releases a contractual party from liability in the event of monetary or physical injury, no matter who is at fault.

executed contract ■ A contract that has been completely performed by both parties.

execution ■ An action to carry into effect the directions in a court decree or judgment.

executive agency ■ An administrative agency within the executive branch of government. At the federal level, executive agencies are those within the cabinet departments.

executor ■ A person appointed by a testator in a will to see that her or his will is administered appropriately.

executory contract ■ A contract that has not as yet been fully performed.

export ■ The goods and services that domestic firms sell to buyers located in other countries.

express contract ■ A contract in which the terms of the agreement are stated in words, oral or written.

express warranty ■ A seller's or lessor's oral or written promise or affirmation of fact, ancillary to an underlying sales or lease agreement, as to the quality, description, or performance of the goods being sold or leased.

expropriation ■ The seizure by a government of a privately owned business or personal property for a proper public purpose and with just compensation.

extension clause ■ A clause in a time instrument that allows the instrument's date of maturity to be extended into the future.

family limited liability partnership (FLLP) ■ A type of limited liability partnership owned by family members or fiduciaries of family members.

federal question ■ A question that pertains to the U.S. Constitution, acts of Congress, or treaties. A federal question provides a basis for federal jurisdiction.

Federal Reserve System ■ A network of twelve district banks and related branches located around the country and headed by the Federal Reserve Board of Governors. Most banks in the United States have Federal Reserve accounts.

fee simple ■ An absolute form of property ownership entitling the property owner to use, possess, or dispose of the property as he or she chooses during his or her lifetime. On death, the interest in the property descends to the owner's heirs.

fee simple absolute ■ An ownership interest in land in which the owner has the greatest possible aggregation of rights, privileges, and power. Ownership in fee simple absolute is limited absolutely to a person and her or his heirs.

felony ■ A crime—such as arson, murder, rape, or robbery—that carries the most severe sanctions, ranging from one year in a state or federal prison to the death penalty.

fictitious payee ■ A payee on a negotiable instrument whom the maker or drawer does not intend to have an interest in the instrument. Indorsements by fictitious payees are treated as authorized indorsements under Article 3 of the UCC.

fiduciary ■ As a noun, a person having a duty created by his or her undertaking to act primarily for another's benefit in matters connected with the undertaking. As an adjective, a relationship founded on trust and confidence.

filtering software ■ A computer program that is designed to block access to certain Web sites based on their content. The software blocks the retrieval of a site whose URL or key words are on a list within the program.

financing statement ■ A document prepared by a secured creditor and filed with the appropriate state or local official, to give notice to the public that the creditor has a security interest in collateral belonging to the debtor named in the statement. Financing statement's must contain the names and addresses of both the debtor and the secured party and must describe the collateral.

firm offer ■ An offer (by a merchant) that is irrevocable without the necessity of consideration for a stated period of time or, if no definite period is stated, for a reasonable time (neither period to exceed three months). A firm offer by a merchant must be in writing and must be signed by the offeror.

fixed-term tenancy ■ A type of tenancy under which property is leased for a specified period of time, such as a month, a year, or a period of years; also called a *tenancy for years.*

fixture ■ A thing that was once personal property but has become attached to real property in such a way that it takes on the characteristics of real property and becomes part of that real property.

floating lien ■ A security interest in proceeds, after-acquired property, or collateral subject to future advances by the secured party (or all three); a security interest in collateral that is retained even when the collateral changes in character, classification, or location.

forbearance ■ The act of refraining from an action that one has a legal right to undertake.

force majeure **clause** ■ A provision in a contract stipulating that certain unforeseen events—such as war, political upheavals, or acts of God—will excuse a party from liability for nonperformance of contractual obligations.

foreign corporation ■ In a given state, a corporation that does business in the state without being incorporated therein.

foreign exchange market ■ A worldwide system in which foreign currencies are bought and sold.

forgery ■ The fraudulent making or altering of any writing in a way that changes the legal rights and liabilities of another.

formal contract ■ A contract that by law requires a specific form, such as being executed under seal, for its validity.

forum-selection clause ■ A provision in a contract designating the court, jurisdiction, or tribunal that will decide any disputes arising under the contract.

franchise ■ Any arrangement in which the owner of a trademark, trade name, or copyright licenses another to use that trademark, trade name, or copyright in the selling of goods or services.

franchisee ■ One receiving a license to use another's (the franchisor's) trademark, trade name, or copyright in the sale of goods and services.

franchisor ■ One licensing another (the franchisee) to use the owner's trademark, trade name, or copyright in the selling of goods or services.

fraudulent misrepresentation ■ Any misrepresentation, either by misstatement or by omission of a material fact, knowingly made with the intention of deceiving another and on which a reasonable person would and does rely to his or her detriment.

free exercise clause ■ The provision in the First Amendment to the Constitution that prohibits the government from interfering with people's religious practices or forms of worship.

free-writing prospectus ■ Any type of written, electronic, or graphic offer that describes the issuing corporation or its securities and includes a legend indicating that the investor may obtain the prospectus at the SEC's Web site.

frustration of purpose ■ A court-created doctrine under which a party to a contract will be relieved of her or his duty to perform when the objective purpose for performance no longer exists (due to reasons beyond that party's control).

fungible goods ■ Goods that are alike by physical nature, by agreement, or by trade usage (for example, wheat, oil, and wine that are identical in type and quality). When owners of fungible goods hold the goods as tenants in common, title and risk can pass without actually separating the goods being sold from the mass of fungible goods.

garnishment ■ A legal process used by a creditor to collect a debt by seizing property of the debtor (such as wages) that is being held by a third party (such as the debtor's employer).

general partner ■ In a limited partnership, a partner who assumes responsibility for the management of the partnership and liability for all partnership debts.

generally accepted accounting principles (GAAP) ■ The conventions, rules, and procedures that define accepted accounting practices at a particular time. The source of the principles is the Financial Accounting Standards Board.

generally accepted auditing standards (GAAS) ■ Standards concerning an auditor's professional qualities and the judgment exercised by him or her in the performance of an audit and report. The source of the standards is the American Institute of Certified Public Accountants.

gift ■ Any voluntary transfer of property made without consideration, past or present.

gift *causa mortis* ■ A gift made in contemplation of death. If the donor does not die of that ailment, the gift is revoked.

gift *inter vivos* ■ A gift made during one's lifetime and not in contemplation of imminent death, in contrast to a gift *causa mortis*.

good faith purchaser ■ A purchaser who buys without notice of any circumstance that would cause a person of ordinary prudence to inquire as to whether the seller has valid title to the goods being sold.

good Samaritan statute ■ A state statute stipulating that persons who provide emergency services to, or rescue, someone in peril cannot be sued for negligence, unless they act recklessly, thereby causing further harm.

grand jury ■ A group of citizens called to decide, after hearing the state's evidence, whether a reasonable basis (probable cause) exists for believing that a crime has been committed and that a trial ought to be held.

guarantor ■ A person who agrees to satisfy the debt of another (the debtor) only after the principal debtor defaults. Thus, a guarantor's liability is secondary.

hacker ■ A person who uses one computer to break into another. Professional computer programmers refer to such persons as "crackers."

holder ■ Any person in possession of an instrument drawn, issued, or indorsed to him or her, to his or her order, to bearer, or in blank.

holder in due course (HDC) ■ A holder who acquires a negotiable instrument for value; in good faith; and without notice that the instrument is overdue, that it has been dishonored, that any person has a defense against it or a claim to it, or that the instrument contains unauthorized signatures, has been altered, or is so irregular or incomplete as to call into question its authenticity.

holding company ■ A company whose business activity is holding shares in another company.

holographic will ■ A will written entirely in the signer's handwriting and usually not witnessed.

homestead exemption ■ A law permitting a debtor to retain the family home, either in its entirety or up to a specified dollar amount, free from the claims of unsecured creditors or trustees in bankruptcy.

hot-cargo agreement ■ An agreement in which employers voluntarily agree with unions not to handle, use, or deal in other employers' goods that were not produced by union employees; a type of secondary boycott explicitly prohibited by the Labor-Management Reporting and Disclosure Act of 1959.

I-9 verification ■ All employers must verify the employment eligibility and identity of any worker hired in the United States. To comply with the law, employers must complete an I-9 Employment Eligibility Verification Form for all new hires within three business days.

I-551 Alien Registration Receipt ■ A document that provides proof that a foreign-born individual is lawfully admitted for permanent residence in the United States; commonly referred to as a "green card." Persons seeking employment can prove to prospective employers that they are legally within the U.S. by showing this receipt.

identification ■ In a sale of goods, the express designation of the goods provided for in the contract.

identity theft ■ The act of stealing another's identifying information—such as a name, date of birth, or Social Security number—and using that information to access the victim's financial resources.

implied warranty ■ A warranty that arises by law because of the circumstances of a sale, rather than by the seller's express promise.

implied warranty of fitness for a particular purpose ■ A warranty that goods sold or leased are fit for a particular purpose. The warranty arises when any seller or lessor knows the particular purpose for which a buyer or lessee will use the goods and knows that the buyer or lessee is relying on the skill and judgment of the seller or lessor to select suitable goods.

implied warranty of habitability ■ An implied promise by a landlord that rented residential premises are fit for human habitation—that is, in a condition that is safe and suitable for people to live there.

implied warranty of merchantability ■ A warranty that goods being sold or leased are reasonably fit for the general purpose for which they are sold or leased, are properly packaged and labeled, and are of proper quality. The warranty automatically arises in every sale or lease of goods made by a merchant who deals in goods of the kind sold or leased.

implied-in-fact contract ■ A contract formed in whole or in part from the conduct of the parties (as opposed to an express contract).

impossibility of performance ■ A doctrine under which a party to a contract is relieved of her or his duty to perform when performance becomes objectively impossible or totally impracticable (through no fault of either party).

imposter ■ One who, by use of the mails, Internet, telephone, or personal appearance, induces a maker or drawer to issue an instrument in the name of an impersonated payee. Indorsements by imposters are treated as authorized indorsements under Article 3 of the UCC.

incidental beneficiary ■ A third party who incidentally benefits from a contract but whose benefit was not the reason the contract was formed. An incidental beneficiary has no rights in a contract and cannot sue to have the contract enforced.

incidental damages ■ Damages awarded to compensate for reasonable expenses that are directly incurred because of a breach of contract—such as the cost of obtaining performance from another source.

independent contractor ■ One who works for, and receives payment from, an employer but whose working conditions and methods are not controlled by the employer. An independent contractor is not an employee but may be an agent.

independent regulatory agency ■ An administrative agency that is not considered part of the government's executive branch and is not subject to the authority of the president. Independent agency officials cannot be removed without cause.

indictment ■ A charge by a grand jury that a named person has committed a crime.

indorsee ■ The person to whom a negotiable instrument is transferred by indorsement.

indorsement ■ A signature placed on an instrument for the purpose of transferring one's ownership rights in the instrument.

indorser ■ A person who transfers an instrument by signing (indorsing) it and delivering it to another person.

informal contract ■ A contract that does not require a specified form or formality to be valid.

information ■ A formal accusation or complaint (without an indictment) issued in certain types of actions (usually criminal actions involving lesser crimes) by a government prosecutor.

information return ■ A tax return submitted by a partnership that only reports the income and losses earned by the business. The partnership as an entity does not pay taxes on the income received by the partnership. A partner's profit from the partnership (whether distributed or not) is taxed as individual income to the individual partner.

inside director ■ A person on the board of directors who is also an officer of the corporation.

insider trading ■ The purchase or sale of securities on the basis of *inside information* (information that has not been made available to the public).

insolvent ■ Under the UCC, a term describing a person who ceases to pay "his [or her] debts in the ordinary course of business or cannot pay his [or her] debts as they become due or is insolvent within the meaning of federal bankruptcy law" [UCC 1–201(23)].

installment contract ■ Under the UCC, a contract that requires or authorizes delivery in two or more separate lots to be accepted and paid for separately.

insurable interest ■ In regard to the sale or lease of goods, a property interest in the goods that is sufficiently substantial to permit a party to insure against damage to the goods. In the context of insurance, an interest either in a person's life or well-being that is sufficiently substantial to justify insuring against injury to (or death of) the person.

insurance ■ A contract in which, for a stipulated consideration, one party agrees to compensate the other for loss on a specific subject by a specified peril.

intangible property ■ Property that cannot be seen or touched but exists only conceptually, such as corporate stocks and bonds, patents and copyrights, and ordinary contract rights. Article 2 of the UCC does not govern intangible property.

intellectual property ■ Property resulting from intellectual, creative processes.

intended beneficiary ■ A third party for whose benefit a contract is formed. An intended beneficiary can sue the promisor if such a contract is breached.

intentional tort ■ A wrongful act knowingly committed.

inter vivos **trust** ■ A trust created by the grantor (settlor) and effective during the grantor's lifetime; a trust not established by a will.

intermediary bank ■ Any bank to which an item is transferred in the course of collection, except the depositary or payor bank.

international law ■ The law that governs relations among nations. National laws, customs, treaties, and international conferences and organizations are generally considered to be the most important sources of international law.

international organization ■ In international law, a term that generally refers to an organization composed mainly of nations and usually established by treaty. The United States is a member of more than one hundred multilateral and bilateral organizations, including at least twenty through the United Nations.

interrogatories ■ A series of written questions for which written answers are prepared by a party to a lawsuit, usually with the assistance of the party's attorney, and then signed under oath.

intestacy laws ■ State statutes that specify how property will be distributed when a person dies intestate (without a valid will); also called *statutes of descent and distribution.*

intestate ■ As a noun, one who has died without having created a valid will; as an adjective, the state of having died without a will.

investment company ■ A company that acts on behalf of many smaller shareholders/owners by buying a large portfolio of securities and professionally managing that portfolio.

investment contract ■ In securities law, a transaction in which a person invests in a common enterprise reasonably expecting profits that are derived primarily from the efforts of others.

joint and several liability ■ In partnership law, a doctrine under which a plaintiff may sue, and collect a judgment from, all of the partners together (jointly) or one or more of the partners separately (severally, or individually). This is true even if one of the partners sued did not participate in, ratify, or know about whatever it was that gave rise to the cause of action.

joint tenancy ■ The joint ownership of property by two or more co-owners in which each co-owner owns an undivided portion of the property. On the death of one of the joint tenants, his or her interest automatically passes to the surviving joint tenant(s).

judicial review ■ The process by which a court decides on the constitutionality of legislative enactments and actions of the executive branch.

junior lienholder ■ A party that holds a lien that is subordinate to one or more other liens on the same property.

jurisdiction ■ The authority of a court to hear and decide a specific case.

jurisprudence ■ The science or philosophy of law.

justiciable controversy ■ A controversy that is not hypothetical or academic but real and substantial; a requirement that must be satisfied before a court will hear a case.

larceny ■ The wrongful taking and carrying away of another person's personal property with the intent to permanently deprive the owner of the property. Some states classify larceny as either grand or petit, depending on the property's value.

law ■ A body of enforceable rules governing relationships among individuals and between individuals and their society.

lease ■ Under Article 2A of the UCC, a transfer of the right to possess and use goods for a period of time in exchange for payment.

lease agreement ■ In regard to the lease of goods, an agreement in which one person (the lessor) agrees to transfer the right to the possession and use of property to another person (the lessee) in exchange for rental payments.

leasehold estate ■ An estate in realty held by a tenant under a lease. In every leasehold estate, the tenant has a qualified right to possess and/or use the land.

legacy ■ A gift of personal property under a will.

legatee ■ One designated in a will to receive a gift of personal property.

lessee ■ A person who acquires the right to the possession and use of another's goods in exchange for rental payments.

lessor ■ A person who transfers the right to the possession and use of goods to another in exchange for rental payments.

letter of credit ■ A written instrument, usually issued by a bank on behalf of a customer or other person, in which the issuer promises to honor drafts or other demands for payment by third persons in accordance with the terms of the instrument.

levy ■ The obtaining of funds by legal process through the seizure and sale of nonsecured property, usually done after a writ of execution has been issued.

libel ■ Defamation in writing or other form having the quality of permanence (such as a digital recording).

license ■ A revocable right or privilege of a person to come onto another person's land. In the context of intellectual property law, an agreement permitting the use of a trademark, copyright, patent, or trade secret for certain limited purposes.

lien ■ An encumbrance on a property to satisfy a debt or protect a claim for payment of a debt.

life estate ■ An interest in land that exists only for the duration of the life of some person, usually the holder of the estate.

limited liability company (LLC) ■ A hybrid form of business enterprise that offers the limited liability of a corporation and the tax advantages of a partnership.

limited liability limited partnership (LLLP) ■ A type of limited partnership in which the liability of all of the partners, including general partners, is limited to the amount of their investments.

limited liability partnership (LLP) ■ A hybrid form of business organization that is used mainly by professionals who normally do business in a partnership. Like a partnership, an LLP is a pass-through entity for tax purposes, but the personal liability of the partners is limited.

limited partner ■ In a limited partnership, a partner who contributes capital to the partnership but has no right to participate in the management and operation of the business. The limited partner assumes no liability for partnership debts beyond the capital contributed.

limited partnership ■ A partnership consisting of one or more general partners (who manage the business and are liable to the full extent of their personal assets for debts of the partnership) and one or more limited partners (who contribute only assets and are liable only up to the extent of their contributions).

liquidated damages ■ An amount, stipulated in a contract, that the parties to the contract believe to be a reasonable estimation of the damages that will occur in the event of a breach.

liquidated debt ■ A debt for which the amount has been ascertained, fixed, agreed on, settled, or exactly determined. If the amount of the debt is in dispute, the debt is considered unliquidated.

liquidation ■ The sale of all of the nonexempt assets of a debtor and the distribution of the proceeds to the debtor's creditors. Chapter 7 of the Bankruptcy Code provides for liquidation bankruptcy proceedings.

litigation ■ The process of resolving a dispute through the court system.

long arm statute ■ A state statute that permits a state to obtain personal jurisdiction over nonresident defendants. A defendant must have certain "minimum contacts" with that state for the statute to apply.

lost property ■ Property with which the owner has involuntarily parted and then cannot find or recover.

M

mailbox rule ■ A rule providing that an acceptance of an offer becomes effective on dispatch (on being placed in an official mailbox), if mail is, expressly or impliedly, an authorized means of communication of acceptance to the offeror.

maker ■ One who promises to pay a fixed amount of money to the holder of a promissory note or a certificate of deposit (CD).

malpractice ■ Professional misconduct or unreasonable lack of skill. The failure of a professional to use the degree of care common to the average reputable members of the profession or to apply the skills and learning the professional claims to possess, resulting in injury, loss, or damage to those relying on the professional.

market-share liability ■ A theory of sharing liability among all firms that manufactured and distributed a particular product during a certain period of time. This form of liability sharing is used only in some jurisdictions and only when the true source of the harmful product in unidentifiable.

mechanic's lien ■ A statutory lien on the real property of another, created to ensure payment for work performed and materials furnished in the repair or improvement of real property, such as a building.

mediation ■ A method of settling disputes outside of court by using the services of a neutral third party, who acts as a communicating agent between the parties and assists them in negotiating a settlement.

member ■ The term used to designate a person who has an ownership interest in a limited liability company.

mens rea ■ Mental state, or intent. A wrongful mental state is as necessary as a wrongful act to establish criminal liability. What constitutes a mental state varies according to the wrongful action. Thus, for murder, the *mens rea* is the intent to take a life.

merchant ■ A person who is engaged in the purchase and sale of goods. Under the UCC, a person who deals in goods of the kind involved in the sales contract or who holds herself or himself out as having skill or knowledge peculiar to the practices or goods being purchased or sold [UCC 2–104].

merger ■ A contractual and statutory process in which one corporation (the surviving corporation) acquires all of the assets and liabilities of another corporation (the merged corporation). The shareholders of the merged corporation either are paid for their shares or receive shares in the surviving corporation.

meta tag ■ A key word in a document that can serve as an index reference to the document. On the Web, search engines return results based, in part, on the tags in Web documents.

minimum wage ■ The lowest wage, either by government regulation or union contract, that an employer may pay an hourly worker.

mirror image rule ■ A common law rule that requires that the terms of the offeree's acceptance adhere exactly to the terms of the offeror's offer for a valid contract to be formed.

misdemeanor ■ A lesser crime than a felony, punishable by a fine or incarceration in jail for up to one year.

mislaid property ■ Property with which the owner has voluntarily parted and then cannot find or recover.

mitigation of damages ■ A rule requiring a plaintiff to do whatever is reasonable to minimize the damages caused by the defendant.

money laundering ■ Falsely reporting income that has been obtained through criminal activity as income obtained through a legitimate business enterprise—in effect, "laundering" the "dirty money."

moral minimum ■ The minimum degree of ethical behavior expected of a business firm, which is usually defined as compliance with the law.

mortgage ■ A written instrument giving a creditor an interest in (lien on) the debtor's real property as security for payment of a debt.

mortgagee ■ Under a mortgage agreement, the creditor who takes a security interest in the debtor's property.

mortgagor ■ Under a mortgage agreement, the debtor who gives the creditor a security interest in the debtor's property in return for a mortgage loan.

motion for a directed verdict ■ In a jury trial, a motion for the judge to take the decision out of the hands of the jury and to direct a verdict for the party who filed the motion on the ground that the other party has not produced sufficient evidence to support her or his claim.

motion for a new trial ■ A motion asserting that the trial was so fundamentally flawed (because of error, newly discovered evidence, prejudice, or another reason) that a new trial is necessary to prevent a miscarriage of justice.

motion for judgment n.o.v. ■ A motion requesting the court to grant judgment in favor of the party making the motion on the ground that the jury's verdict against him or her was unreasonable and erroneous.

motion for judgment on the pleadings ■ A motion by either party to a lawsuit at the close of the pleadings requesting the court to decide the issue solely on the pleadings without proceeding to trial. The motion will be granted only if no facts are in dispute.

motion for summary judgment ■ A motion requesting the court to enter a judgment without proceeding to trial. The motion can be based on evidence outside the pleadings and will be granted only if no facts are in dispute.

motion to dismiss ■ A pleading in which a defendant asserts that the plaintiff's claim fails to state a cause of action (that is, has no basis in law) or that there are other grounds on which a suit should be dismissed. Although the defendant normally is the party requesting a dismissal, either the plaintiff or the court can also make a motion to dismiss the case.

mutual fund ■ A specific type of investment company that continually buys or sells to investors shares of ownership in a portfolio.

national law ■ Law that pertains to a particular nation (as opposed to international law).

necessaries ■ Necessities required for life, such as food, shelter, clothing, and medical attention; may include whatever is believed to be necessary to maintain a person's standard of living or financial and social status.

negligence ■ The failure to exercise the standard of care that a reasonable person would exercise in similar circumstances.

negligence *per se* ■ An action or failure to act in violation of a statutory requirement.

negotiable instrument ■ A signed writing (record) that contains an unconditional promise or order to pay an exact sum on demand or at an exact future time to a specific person or order, or to bearer.

negotiation ■ A process in which parties attempt to settle their dispute informally, with or without attorneys to represent them. In the context of negotiable instruments, the transfer of an instrument in such form that the transferee (the person to whom the instrument is transferred) becomes a holder.

nominal damages ■ A small monetary award (often one dollar) granted to a plaintiff when no actual damage was suffered.

nonpossessory interest ■ In the context of real property, an interest in land that does not include any right to possess the property.

normal trade relations (NTR) status ■ A status granted in an international treaty by a provision stating that the citizens of the contracting nations may enjoy the privileges accorded by either party to citizens of its NTR nations. Generally, this status is designed to establish equality of international treatment.

notary public ■ A public official authorized to attest to the authenticity of signatures.

novation ■ The substitution, by agreement, of a new contract for an old one, with the rights under the old one being terminated. Typically, novation involves the substitution of a new person who is responsible for the contract and the removal of an original party's rights and duties under the contract.

nuncupative will ■ An oral will (often called a *deathbed will*) made before witnesses; usually limited to transfers of personal property.

objective theory of contracts ■ A theory under which the intent to form a contract will be judged by outward, objective facts (what the party said when entering into the contract, how the party acted or appeared, and the circumstances surrounding the transaction) as interpreted by a reasonable person, rather than by the party's own secret, subjective intentions.

obligee ■ One to whom an obligation is owed.

obligor ■ One who owes an obligation to another.

offer ■ A promise or commitment to perform or refrain from performing some specified act in the future.

offeree ■ A person to whom an offer is made.

offeror ■ A person who makes an offer.

online dispute resolution (ODR) ■ The resolution of disputes with the assistance of organizations that offer dispute-resolution services via the Internet.

operating agreement ■ In a limited liability company, an agreement in which the members set forth the details of how the business will be managed and operated. State statutes typically give the members wide latitude in deciding for themselves the rules that will govern their organization.

option contract ■ A contract under which the offeror cannot revoke the offer for a stipulated time period. During this period, the offeree can accept or reject the offer without fear that the offer will be made to another person. The offeree must give consideration for the option (the irrevocable offer) to be enforceable.

order for relief ■ A court's grant of assistance to a complainant. In bankruptcy proceedings, the order relieves the debtor of the immediate obligation to pay the debts listed in the bankruptcy petition.

order instrument ■ A negotiable instrument that is payable "to the order of an identified person" or "to an identified person or order."

ordinance ■ A regulation enacted by a city or county legislative body that becomes part of that state's statutory law.

output contract ■ An agreement in which a seller agrees to sell and a buyer agrees to buy all or up to a stated amount of what the seller produces.

outside director ■ A person on the board of directors who does not hold a management position at the corporation.

overdraft ■ A check that is paid by the bank when the checking account on which the check is written contains insufficient funds to cover the check.

parol evidence rule ■ A rule under which a court will not receive into evidence the parties' prior negotiations, prior agreements, or contemporaneous oral agreements if that evidence contradicts or varies the terms of the parties' written contract.

parent-subsidiary merger ■ A merger of companies in which one company (the parent corporation) owns most of the stock of the other (the subsidiary corporation). A parent-subsidiary merger (short-form merger) can use a simplified procedure when the parent corporation owns at least 90 percent of the outstanding shares of each class of stock of the subsidiary corporation.

partially disclosed principal ■ A principal whose identity is unknown by a third party, but the third party knows that the agent is or may be acting for a principal at the time the agent and the third party form a contract.

partnering agreement ■ An agreement between a seller and a buyer who frequently do business with each other concerning the terms and conditions that will apply to all subsequently formed electronic contracts.

partnership ■ An agreement by two or more persons to carry on, as co-owners, a business for profit.

pass-through entity ■ A business entity that has no tax liability. The entity's income is passed through to the owners, and the owners pay taxes on the income.

past consideration ■ An act that takes place before the contract is made and that ordinarily, by itself, cannot be consideration for a later promise to pay for the act.

patent ■ A government grant that gives an inventor the exclusive right or privilege to make, use, or sell his or her invention for a limited time period.

payee ■ A person to whom an instrument is made payable.

payor bank ■ The bank on which a check is drawn (the drawee bank).

peer-to-peer (P2P) networking ■ The sharing of resources (such as files, hard drives, and processing styles) among multiple computers without necessarily requiring a central network server.

penalty ■ A contractual clause that states that a certain amount of monetary damages will be paid in the event of a future default or breach of contract. The damages are a punishment for a default and not a measure of compensation for the contract's breach. The agreement as to the penalty amount will not be enforced, and recovery will be limited to actual damages.

per capita ■ A Latin term meaning "per person." In the law governing estate distribution, a method of distributing the property of an intestate's estate so that each heir in a certain class (such as grandchildren) receives an equal share.

per stirpes ■ A Latin term meaning "by the roots." In estate law, a method of distributing an intestate's estate so that each heir in a certain class (such as grandchildren) takes the share to which her or his deceased ancestor (such as a mother or father) would have been entitled.

perfection ■ The legal process by which secured parties protect themselves against the claims of third parties who may wish to have their debts satisfied out of the same collateral; usually accomplished by filing a financing statement with the appropriate government official.

performance ■ In contract law, the fulfillment of one's duties arising under a contract with another; the normal way of discharging one's contractual obligations.

periodic tenancy ■ A lease interest in land for an indefinite period involving payment of rent at fixed intervals, such as week to week, month to month, or year to year.

personal defenses ■ Defenses that can be used to avoid payment to an ordinary holder of a negotiable instrument but not a holder in due course (HDC) or a holder with the rights of an HDC.

personal property ■ Property that is movable; any property that is not real property.

persuasive authority ■ Any legal authority or source of law that a court may look to for guidance but on which it need not rely in making its decision. Persuasive authorities include cases from other jurisdictions and secondary sources of law.

petition in bankruptcy ■ The document that is filed with a bankruptcy court to initiate bankruptcy proceedings. The official forms required for a petition in bankruptcy must be completed accurately, sworn to under oath, and signed by the debtor.

petty offense ■ In criminal law, the least serious kind of criminal offense, such as a traffic or building-code violation.

piercing the corporate veil ■ An action in which a court disregards the corporate entity and holds the shareholders personally liable for corporate debts and obligations. ■

plaintiff ■ One who initiates a lawsuit.

plea bargaining ■ The process by which a criminal defendant and the prosecutor in a criminal case work out a mutually satisfactory disposition of the case, subject to court approval; usually involves the defendant's pleading guilty to a lesser offense in return for a lighter sentence.

pleadings ■ Statements made by the plaintiff and the defendant in a lawsuit that detail the facts, charges, and defenses involved in the litigation. The complaint and answer are part of the pleadings.

pledge ■ A common law security device (retained in Article 9 of the UCC) in which personal property is transferred into the possession of the creditor as security for the payment of a debt and retained by the creditor until the debt is paid.

policy ■ In insurance law, a contract between the insurer and the insured in which, for a stipulated consideration, the insurer agrees to compensate the insured for loss on a specific subject by a specified peril.

power of attorney ■ A written document, which is usually notarized, authorizing another to act as one's agent; can be special (permitting the agent to do specified acts only) or general (permitting the agent to transact all business for the principal).

precedent ■ A court decision that furnishes an example or authority for deciding subsequent cases involving identical or similar facts.

predatory behavior ■ Business behavior that is undertaken with the intention of unlawfully driving competitors out of the market.

predominant-factor test ■ A test courts use to determine whether a contract is primarily for the sale of goods or for the sale of services.

preemption ■ A doctrine under which certain federal laws preempt, or take precedence over, conflicting state or local laws.

preemptive rights ■ Rights held by shareholders that entitle them to purchase newly issued shares of a corporation's stock, equal in percentage to shares already held, before the stock is offered to any outside buyers. Preemptive rights enable shareholders to maintain their proportionate ownership and voice in the corporation.

preference ■ In bankruptcy proceedings, property transfers or payments made by the debtor that favor (give preference to) one creditor over others. The bankruptcy trustee is allowed to recover payments made both voluntarily and involuntarily to one creditor in preference over another.

preferred creditor ■ In the context of bankruptcy, a creditor who has received a preferential transfer from a debtor.

preferred stock ■ Classes of stock that have priority over common stock as to both payment of dividends and distribution of assets on the corporation's dissolution.

premium ■ In insurance law, the price paid by the insured for insurance protection for a specified period of time.

prenuptial agreement ■ An agreement made before marriage that defines each partner's ownership rights in the other partner's property. Prenuptial agreements must be in writing to be enforceable.

presentment ■ The act of presenting an instrument to the party liable on the instrument to collect payment. Presentment also occurs when a person presents an instrument to a drawee for a required acceptance.

presentment warranties ■ Implied warranties, made by any person who presents an instrument for payment or acceptance, that (1) the person obtaining payment or acceptance is entitled to enforce the instrument or is authorized to obtain payment or acceptance on behalf of a person who is entitled to enforce the instrument, (2) the instrument has not been altered, and (3) the person obtaining payment or acceptance has no knowledge that the signature of the drawer of the instrument is unauthorized.

***prima facie* case** ■ A case in which the plaintiff has produced sufficient evidence of his or her claim that the case can go to a jury; a case in which the evidence compels a decision for the plaintiff if the defendant produces no affirmative defense or evidence to disprove the plaintiff's assertion.

primary source of law ■ A document that establishes the law on a particular issue, such as a constitution, a statute, an administrative rule, or a court decision.

principal ■ In agency law, a person who agrees to have another, called the agent, act on her or his behalf.

principle of rights ■ The principle that human beings have certain fundamental rights (to life, freedom, and the pursuit of happiness, for example). Those who adhere to this "rights theory" believe that a key factor in determining whether a business decision is ethical is how that decision affects the rights of various groups. These groups include the firm's owners, its employees, the consumers of its products or services, its suppliers, the community in which it does business, and society as a whole.

private equity capital ■ A financing method by which a company sells equity in an existing business to a private or institutional investor.

privilege ■ A legal right, exemption, or immunity granted to a person or a class of persons. In the context of defamation, an absolute privilege immunizes the person making the statements from a lawsuit, regardless of whether the statements were malicious.

privity of contract ■ The relationship that exists between the promisor and the promisee of a contract.

probable cause ■ Reasonable grounds for believing that a person should be arrested or searched.

probate ■ The process of proving and validating a will and settling all matters pertaining to an estate.

probate court ■ A state court of limited jurisdiction that conducts proceedings relating to the settlement of a deceased person's estate.

procedural law ■ Law that establishes the methods of enforcing the rights established by substantive law.

proceeds ■ Under Article 9 of the UCC, whatever is received when collateral is sold or otherwise disposed of, such as by exchange.

product liability ■ The legal liability of manufacturers, sellers, and lessors of goods to consumers, users, and bystanders for injuries or damages that are caused by the goods.

profit ■ In real property law, the right to enter onto and remove things from the property of another (for example, the right to enter onto a person's land and remove sand and gravel).

promise ■ An assertion that something either will or will not happen in the future.

promisee ■ A person to whom a promise is made.

promisor ■ A person who makes a promise.

promissory estoppel ■ A doctrine that applies when a promisor makes a clear and definite promise on which the promisee justifiably relies. Such a promise is binding if justice will be better served by the enforcement of the promise.

promissory note ■ A written promise made by one person (the maker) to pay a fixed amount of money to another person (the payee or a subsequent holder) on demand or on a specified date.

property ■ Legally protected rights and interests in anything with an ascertainable value that is subject to ownership.

prospectus ■ A written document, required by securities laws, that describes the security being sold, the financial operations of the issuing corporation, and the investment or risk attaching to the security. It is designed to provide sufficient information to enable investors to evaluate the risk involved in purchasing the security.

protected class ■ A group of persons protected by specific laws because of the group's defining characteristics. Under laws prohibiting employment discrimination, these characteristics include race, color, religion, national origin, gender, age, and disability.

proximate cause ■ Legal cause; exists when the connection between an act and an injury is strong enough to justify imposing liability.

proxy ■ In corporation law, a written agreement between a stockholder and another under which the shareholder authorizes the other to vote the stockholder's shares in a certain manner.

puffery ■ A salesperson's often exaggerated claims concerning the quality of property offered for sale. Such claims involve opinions rather than facts and are not considered to be legally binding promises or warranties.

punitive damages ■ Monetary damages that may be awarded to a plaintiff to punish the defendant and deter future similar conduct.

purchase-money security interest (PMSI) ■ A security interest that arises when a seller or lender extends credit for part or all of the purchase price of goods purchased by a buyer.

qualified indorsement ■ An indorsement on a negotiable instrument in which the indorser disclaims any contract liability on the instrument. The notation "without recourse" is commonly used to create a qualified indorsement.

quasi contract ■ A fictional contract imposed on the parties by a court in the interests of fairness and justice; usually imposed to avoid the unjust enrichment of one party at the expense of another.

question of fact ■ In a lawsuit, an issue that involves only disputed facts, and not what the law is on a given point. Questions of fact are decided by the jury in a jury trial (by the judge if there is no jury).

question of law ■ In a lawsuit, an issue involving the application or interpretation of a law. Only a judge, not a jury, can rule on questions of law.

quitclaim deed ■ A deed intended to pass any title, interest, or claim that the grantor may have in the property without warranting that such title is valid. A quitclaim deed offers the least amount of protection against defects in the title.

quorum ■ The number of members of a decision making body that must be present before business may be transacted.

quota ■ A set limit on the amount of goods that can be imported.

R

ratification ■ The act of accepting and giving legal force to an obligation that previously was not enforceable.

reaffirmation agreement ■ An agreement between a debtor and a creditor in which the debtor voluntarily agrees to pay, or reaffirm, a debt dischargeable in bankruptcy. To be enforceable, the agreement must be made before the debtor is granted a discharge.

real property ■ Land and everything attached to it, such as trees and buildings.

reasonable person standard ■ The standard of behavior expected of a hypothetical "reasonable person"; the standard against which negligence is measured and that must be observed to avoid liability for negligence.

record ■ According to the Uniform Electronic Transactions Act, information that is either inscribed on a tangible medium or stored in an electronic or other medium and is retrievable.

recording statutes ■ Statutes that allow deeds, mortgages, and other real property transactions to be recorded so as to provide notice to future purchasers or creditors of an existing claim on the property.

red herring prospectus ■ A preliminary prospectus that can be distributed to potential investors after the registration statement (for a securities offering) has been filed with the Securities and Exchange Commission. The name derives from the red legend printed across the prospectus stating that the registration has been filed but has not become effective.

reformation ■ A court-ordered correction of a written contract so that it reflects the true intentions of the parties.

Regulation E ■ A set of rules issued by the Federal Reserve System's Board of Governors to protect users of elecronic fund transfer systems.

release ■ A contract in which one party forfeits the right to pursue a legal claim against the other party.

remedy ■ The relief given to an innocent party to enforce a right or compensate for the violation of a right.

replevin ■ An action to recover identified goods in the hands of a party who is wrongfully withholding them from the other party. Under the UCC, this remedy is usually available only if the buyer or lessee is unable to cover.

reply ■ Procedurally, a plaintiff's response to a defendant's answer.

requirements contract ■ An agreement in which a buyer agrees to purchase and the seller agrees to sell all or up to a stated amount of what the buyer needs or requires.

res ipsa loquitur ■ A doctrine under which negligence may be inferred simply because an event occurred, if it is the type of event that would not occur in the absence of negligence. Literally, the term means "the facts speak for themselves."

rescission ■ A remedy whereby a contract is canceled and the parties are returned to the positions they occupied before the contract was made; may be effected through the mutual consent of the parties, by the parties' conduct, or by court decree.

respondeat superior ■ Latin for "let the master respond." A doctrine under which a principal or an employer is held liable for the wrongful acts committed by agents or employees while acting within the course and scope of their agency or employment.

restitution ■ An equitable remedy under which a person is restored to his or her original position prior to loss or injury, or placed in the position he or she would have been in had the breach not occurred.

restrictive indorsement ■ Any indorsement on a negotiable instrument that requires the indorsee to comply with certain instructions regarding the funds involved. A restrictive indorsement does not prohibit the further negotiation of the instrument.

resulting trust ■ An implied trust arising from the conduct of the parties. A trust in which a party holds the actual legal title to another's property but only for that person's benefit.

retained earnings ■ The portion of a corporation's profits that has not been paid out as dividends to shareholders.

revocation ■ In contract law, the withdrawal of an offer by an offeror. Unless the offer is irrevocable, it can be revoked at any time prior to acceptance without liability.

right of contribution ■ The right of a co-surety who pays more than her or his proportionate share on a debtor's default to recover the excess paid from other co-sureties.

right of reimbursement ■ The legal right of a person to be restored, repaid, or indemnified for costs, expenses, or losses incurred or expended on behalf of another.

right of subrogation ■ The right of a person to stand in the place of (be substituted for) another, giving the substituted party the same legal rights that the original party had.

right-to-work law ■ A state law providing that employees may not be required to join a union as a condition of retaining employment.

risk ■ A prediction concerning potential loss based on known and unknown factors.

risk management ■ Planning that is undertaken to protect one's interest should some event threaten to undermine its security. In the context of insurance, risk management involves transferring certain risks from the insured to the insurance company.

robbery ■ The act of forcefully and unlawfully taking personal property of any value from another. Force or intimidation is usually necessary for an act of theft to be considered robbery.

rule of four ■ A rule of the United States Supreme Court under which the Court will not issue a writ of *certiorari* unless at least four justices approve of the decision to issue the writ.

S

S corporation ■ A close business corporation that has met certain requirements set out in the Internal Revenue Code and thus qualifies for special income tax treatment. Essentially, an S corporation is taxed the same as a partnership, but its owners enjoy the privilege of limited liability.

sale ■ The passing of title to property from the seller to the buyer for a price.

sale on approval ■ A type of conditional sale in which the buyer may take the goods on a trial basis. The sale becomes absolute only when the buyer approves of (or is satisfied with) the goods being sold.

sale or return ■ A type of conditional sale in which title and possession pass from the seller to the buyer, but the buyer retains the option to return the goods during a specified period even though the goods conform to the contract.

sales contract ■ A contract for the sale of goods under which the ownership of goods is transferred from a seller to a buyer for a price.

scienter ■ Knowledge by the misrepresenting party that material facts have been falsely represented or omitted with an intent to deceive.

search warrant ■ An order granted by a public authority, such as a judge, that authorizes law enforcement personnel to search a particular premise or property.

seasonably ■ Within a specified time period or, if no period is specified, within a reasonable time.

SEC Rule 10b-5 ■ A rule of the Securities and Exchange Commission that makes it unlawful, in connection with the purchase or sale of any security, to make any untrue statement of a material fact or to omit a material fact if such omission causes the statement to be misleading.

secondary boycott ■ A union's refusal to work for, purchase from, or handle the products of a secondary employer, with whom the union has no dispute, in order to force that employer to stop doing business with the primary employer, with whom the union has a labor dispute.

secondary source of law ■ A publication that summarizes or interprets the law, such as a legal encyclopedia, a legal treatise, or an article in a law review.

secured party ■ A lender, seller, or any other person in whose favor there is a security interest, including a person to whom accounts or chattel paper have been sold.

secured transaction ■ Any transaction in which the payment of a debt is guaranteed, or secured, by personal property owned by the debtor or in which the debtor has a legal interest.

securities ■ Generally, stock certificates, bonds, notes, debentures, warrants, or other documents given as evidence of an ownership interest in a corporation or as a promise of repayment by a corporation.

security ■ Generally, a stock certificate, bond, note, debenture, warrant, or other document or record evidencing an ownership interest in a corporation or a promise to repay a corporation's debt.

security agreement ■ An agreement that creates or provides for a security interest between the debtor and a secured party.

security interest ■ Any interest in personal property or fixtures that secures payment or performance of an obligation.

self-defense ■ The legally recognized privilege to protect oneself or one's property against injury by another. The privilege of self-defense usually applies only to acts that are reasonably necessary to protect oneself, one's property, or another person.

self-incrimination ■ The giving of testimony that may subject the testifier to criminal prosecution. The Fifth Amendment to the Constitution protects against self-incrimination by providing that no person "shall be compelled in any criminal case to be a witness against himself."

seniority system ■ In regard to employment relationships, a system in which those who have worked longest for the employer are first in line for promotions, salary increases, and other benefits. They are also the last to be laid off if the workforce must be reduced.

service mark ■ A mark used in the sale or the advertising of services to distinguish the services of one person from those of others. Titles, character names, and other distinctive features of radio and television programs may be registered as service marks.

sexual harassment ■ In the employment context, the demanding of sexual favors in return for job promotions or other benefits, or language or conduct that is so sexually offensive that it creates a hostile working environment.

shareholder's derivative suit ■ A suit brought by a shareholder to enforce a corporate cause of action against a third person.

shelter principle ■ The principle that the holder of a negotiable instrument who cannot qualify as a holder in due course (HDC), but who derives his or her title through an HDC, acquires the rights of an HDC.

shipment contract ■ A contract for the sale of goods in which the seller is required or authorized to ship the goods by carrier. The seller assumes liability for any losses or damage to the goods until they are delivered to the carrier.

short-form (parent-subsidiary) merger ■ A merger of companies in which one company (the parent corporation) owns at least 90 percent of the outstanding shares of each class of stock of the other corporation (the subsidiary corporation). The merger can be accomplished without the approval of the shareholders of either corporation.

shrink-wrap agreement ■ An agreement whose terms are expressed in a document located inside a box in which goods (usually software) are packaged; sometimes called a *shrink-wrap license.*

signature ■ Under the UCC, "any symbol executed or adopted by a party with a present intention to authenticate a writing."

slander ■ Defamation in oral form.

slander of quality (trade libel) ■ The publication of false information about another's product, alleging that it is not what its seller claims.

slander of title ■ The publication of a statement that denies or casts doubt on another's legal ownership of any property, causing financial loss to that property's owner.

small claims court ■ A special court in which parties may litigate small claims (such as $5,000 or less). Attorneys are not required in small claims courts and, in some states, are not allowed to represent the parties.

smart card ■ A card containing a microprocessor that permits storage of funds via security programming, can communicate with other computers, and does not require online authorization for fund transfers.

sole proprietorship ■ The simplest form of business organization, in which the owner is the business. The owner reports business income on his or her personal income tax return and is legally responsible for all debts and obligations incurred by the business.

sovereign immunity ■ A doctrine that immunizes foreign nations from the jurisdiction of U.S. courts when certain conditions are satisfied.

spam ■ Bulk, unsolicited ("junk") e-mail.

special indorsement ■ An indorsement on an instrument that indicates the specific person to whom the indorser intends to make the instrument payable; that is, it names the indorsee.

special warranty deed ■ A deed in which the grantor warrants only that the grantor or seller held good title during his or her ownership of the property and does not warrant that there were no defects of title when the property was held by previous owners.

specific performance ■ An equitable remedy requiring exactly the performance that was specified; usually granted only when monetary damages would be an inadequate remedy and the subject matter of the contract is unique.

spendthrift trust ■ A trust created to protect the beneficiary from spending all the funds to which she or he is entitled. Only a certain portion of the total amount is given to the beneficiary at any one time, and most states prohibit creditors from attaching assets of the trust.

stale check ■ A check, other than a certified check, that is presented for payment more than six months after its date.

standing to sue ■ The requirement that an individual must have a sufficient stake in a controversy before he or she can bring a lawsuit. The plaintiff must demonstrate that he or she has been either injured or threatened with injury.

stare decisis ■ A common law doctrine under which judges are obligated to follow the precedents established in prior decisions.

Statute of Frauds ■ A state statute under which certain types of contracts must be in writing to be enforceable.

statute of limitations ■ A federal or state statute setting the maximum time period during which a certain action can be brought or certain rights enforced.

statutory law ■ The body of law enacted by legislative bodies (as opposed to constitutional law, administrative law, or case law).

stock ■ An equity (ownership) interest in a corporation, measured in units of shares.

stock certificate ■ A certificate issued by a corporation evidencing the ownership of a specified number of shares in the corporation.

stock options ■ An agreement that grants the owner the option to buy a given number of shares of stock, usually within a set time period.

stock warrant ■ A certificate that grants the owner the option to buy a given number of shares of stock, usually within a set time period.

stop-payment order ■ An order by a bank customer to his or her bank not to pay or certify a certain check.

stored-value card ■ A card bearing a magnetic strip that holds magnetically encoded data, providing access to stored funds.

strict liability ■ Liability regardless of fault. In tort law, strict liability is imposed on a manufacturer or seller that introduces into commerce a good that is unreasonably dangerous when in a defective condition.

sublease ■ A lease executed by the lessee of real estate to a third person, conveying the same interest that the lessee enjoys but for a shorter term than that held by the lessee.

substantive law ■ Law that defines, describes, regulates, and creates legal rights and obligations.

summary jury trial (SJT) ■ A method of settling disputes, used in many federal courts, in which a trial is held, but the jury's verdict is not binding. The verdict acts only as a guide to both sides in reaching an agreement during the mandatory negotiations that immediately follow the summary jury trial.

summons ■ A document informing a defendant that a legal action has been commenced against him or her and that the defendant must appear in court on a certain date to answer the plaintiff's complaint.

surety ■ A person, such as a cosigner on a note, who agrees to be primarily responsible for the debt of another.

suretyship ■ An express contract in which a third party to a debtor-creditor relationship (the surety) promises to be primarily responsible for the debtor's obligation.

symbolic speech ■ Nonverbal expressions of beliefs. Symbolic speech, which includes gestures, movements, and articles of clothing, is given substantial protection by the courts.

takeover ■ The acquisition of control over a corporation through the purchase of a substantial number of the voting shares of the corporation.

taking ■ The taking of private property by the government for public use. The government may not take private property for public use without "just compensation."

tangible property ■ Property that has physical existence and can be distinguished by the senses of touch or sight. A car is tangible property; a patent right is intangible property.

target corporation ■ The corporation to be acquired in a corporate takeover; a corporation whose shareholders receive a tender offer.

tariff ■ A tax on imported goods.

tenancy at sufferance ■ A type of tenancy under which a tenant who, after rightfully being in possession of leased premises, continues (wrongfully) to occupy the property after the lease has terminated. The tenant has no rights to possess the property and occupies it only because the person entitled to evict the tenant has not done so.

tenancy at will ■ A type of tenancy that either party can terminate without notice; usually arises when a tenant who has been under a tenancy for years retains possession, with the landlord's consent, after the tenancy for years has terminated.

tenancy in common ■ Co-ownership of property in which each party owns an undivided interest that passes to her or his heirs at death.

tender ■ An unconditional offer to perform an obligation by a person who is ready, willing, and able to do so.

tender of delivery ■ Under the Uniform Commercial Code, a seller's or lessor's act of placing conforming goods at the disposal of the buyer or lessee and giving the buyer or lessor whatever notification is reasonably necessary to enable the buyer or lessee to take delivery.

tender offer ■ An offer to purchase made by one company directly to the shareholders of another (target) company; sometimes referred to as a *takeover bid.*

testamentary trust ■ A trust that is created by will and therefore does not take effect until the death of the testator.

testate ■ Having left a will at death.

testator ■ One who makes and executes a will.

third party beneficiary ■ One for whose benefit a promise is made in a contract but who is not a party to the contract.

tippee ■ A person who receives inside information.

tombstone ad ■ An advertisement, historically in a format resembling a tombstone, of a securities offering. The ad tells potential investors where and how they may obtain a prospectus.

tort ■ A civil wrong not arising from a breach of contract; a breach of a legal duty that proximately causes harm or injury to another.

tortfeasor ■ One who commits a tort.

Totten trust ■ A trust created by the deposit of a person's own funds in his or her own name as a trustee for another. It is a tentative trust, revocable at will until the depositor dies or completes the gift in his or her lifetime by some unequivocal act or declaration.

trade dress ■ The image and overall appearance of a product—for example, the distinctive decor, menu, layout, and style of service of a particular restaurant. Basically, trade dress is subject to the same protection as trademarks.

trade libel ■ The publication of false information about another's product, alleging it is not what its seller claims; also referred to as *slander of quality.*

trade name ■ A term that is used to indicate part or all of a business's name and that is directly related to the business's reputation and goodwill. Trade names are protected under the common law (and under trademark law, if the name is the same as the firm's trademarked product).

trade secrets ■ Information or processes that give a business an advantage over competitors that do not know the information or processes.

trademark ■ A distinctive mark, motto, device, or emblem that a manufacturer stamps, prints, or otherwise affixes to the goods it produces so that they may be identified on the market and their origins made known. Once a trademark is established (under the common law or through registration), the owner is entitled to its exclusive use.

transfer warranties ■ Implied warranties, made by any person who transfers an instrument for consideration to subsequent transferees and holders who take the instrument in good faith, that (1) the transferor is entitled to enforce the instrument; (2) all signatures are authentic and authorized; (3) the instrument has not been altered; (4) the instrument is not subject to a defense or claim of any party that can be asserted against the transferor; and (5) the transferor has no knowledge of any insolvency proceedings against the maker, the acceptor, or the drawer of the instrument.

traveler's check ■ A check that is payable on demand, drawn on or payable through a financial institution (bank), and designated as a traveler's check.

treaty ■ An agreement formed between two or more independent nations.

trespass to land ■ The entry onto, above, or below the surface of land owned by another without the owner's permission or legal authorization.

trespass to personal property ■ The unlawful taking or harming of another's personal property; interference with another's right to the exclusive possession of his or her personal property.

trust ■ An arrangement in which title to property is held by one person (a trustee) for the benefit of another (a beneficiary).

trust indorsement ■ An indorsement for the benefit of the indorser or a third person; also known as an *agency indorsement.* The indorsement results in legal title vesting in the original indorsee.

U.S. trustee ■ A government official who performs certain administrative tasks that a bankruptcy judge would otherwise have to perform.

ultra vires ■ A Latin term meaning "beyond the powers"; in corporate law, acts of a corporation that are beyond its express and implied powers to undertake.

unconscionable contract (or unconscionable clause) ■ A contract or clause that is void on the basis of public policy because one party, as a result of disproportionate bargaining power, is forced to accept terms that are unfairly burdensome and that unfairly benefit the dominating party.

underwriter ■ In insurance law, the insurer, or the one assuming a risk in return for the payment of a premium.

undisclosed principal ■ A principal whose identity is unknown by a third person, and the third person has no knowledge that the agent is acting for a principal at the time the agent and the third person form a contract.

unenforceable contract ■ A valid contract rendered unenforceable by some statute or law.

uniform law ■ A model law created by the National Conference of Commissioners on Uniform State Laws and/or the American Law Institute for the states to consider adopting. If the state adopts the law, it becomes statutory law in that state. Each state has the option of adopting or rejecting all or part of a uniform law.

unilateral contract ■ A contract that results when an offer can only be accepted by the offeree's performance.

unilateral mistake ■ A mistake that occurs when only one party to a contract is mistaken about a material fact.

union shop ■ A firm that requires all workers, once employed, to become union members within a specified period of time as a condition of their continued employment.

universal defenses ■ Defenses that are valid against all holders of a negotiable instrument, including holders in due course (HDCs) and holders with the rights of HDCs.

unreasonably dangerous product ■ In product liability law, a product that is defective to the point of threatening a consumer's health and safety. A product will be considered unreasonably dangerous if it is dangerous beyond the expectation of the ordinary consumer or if a less dangerous alternative was economically feasible for the manufacturer, but the manufacturer failed to produce it.

usage of trade ■ Any practice or method of dealing having such regularity of observance in a place, vocation, or trade as to justify an expectation that it will be observed with respect to the transaction in question.

usury ■ Charging an illegal rate of interest.

utilitarianism ■ An approach to ethical reasoning that evaluates behavior in light of the consequences of that behavior for those who will be affected by it, rather than on the basis of any absolute ethical or moral values. In utilitarian reasoning, a "good" decision is one that results in the greatest good for the greatest number of people affected by the decision.

valid contract ■ A contract that results when the elements necessary for contract formation (agreement, consideration, legal purpose, and contractual capacity) are present.

venture capital ■ Capital (funds and other assets) provided by professional, outside investors (*venture capitalists*, usually groups of wealthy investors and investment banks) to start new business ventures.

venue ■ The geographic district in which a legal action is tried and from which the jury is selected.

vesting ■ The creation of an absolute or unconditional right or power.

vicarious liability ■ Legal responsibility placed on one person for the acts of another; indirect liability imposed on a supervisory party (such as an employer) for the actions of a subordinate (such as an employee) because of the relationship between the two parties.

void contract ■ A contract having no legal force or binding effect.

voidable contract ■ A contract that may be legally avoided (canceled, or annulled) at the option of one or both of the parties.

voir dire ■ An old French phrase meaning "to speak the truth." In legal terms, it refers to the process in which the attorneys question prospective jurors to learn about their backgrounds, attitudes, biases, and other characteristics that may affect their ability to serve as impartial jurors.

warranty deed ■ A deed in which the grantor assures (warrants to) the grantee that the grantor has title to the property conveyed in the deed, that there are no encumbrances on the property other than what the grantor has represented, and that the grantee will enjoy quiet possession of the property; a deed that provides the greatest amount of protection for the grantee.

watered stock ■ Shares of stock issued by a corporation for which the corporation receives, as payment, less than the stated value of the shares.

whistleblowing ■ An employee's disclosure to government authorities, upper-level managers, or the press that the employer is engaged in unsafe or illegal activities.

white-collar crime ■ Nonviolent crime committed by individuals or corporations to obtain a personal or business advantage.

will ■ An instrument directing what is to be done with the testator's property on his or her death, made by the testator and revocable during his or her lifetime. No interests in the testator's property pass until the testator dies.

will substitutes ■ Various documents that attempt to dispose of an estate in the same or similar manner as a will, such as trusts or life insurance plans.

winding up ■ The second of two stages in the termination of a partnership or corporation. Once the firm is dissolved, it continues to exist legally until the process of winding up all business affairs (collecting and distributing the firm's assets) is complete.

workers' compensation laws ■ State statutes establishing an administrative procedure for compensating workers' injuries that arise out of—or in the course of—their employment, regardless of fault.

working papers ■ The various documents used and developed by an accountant during an audit, such as notes and computations, that make up the work product of an accountant's services to a client.

workout ■ An out-of-court agreement between a debtor and creditors in which the parties work out a payment plan or schedule under which the debtor's debts can be discharged.

writ of attachment ■ A court's order, issued prior to a trial to collect a debt, directing the sheriff or other public officer to seize nonexempt property of the debtor. If the creditor prevails at trial, the seized property can be sold to satisfy the judgment.

writ of *certiorari* ■ A writ from a higher court asking the lower court for the record of a case.

writ of execution ■ A court's order, issued after a judgment has been entered against a debtor, directing the sheriff to seize (levy) and sell any of the debtor's nonexempt real or personal property. The proceeds of the sale are used to pay off the judgment, accrued interest, and costs of the sale; any surplus is paid to the debtor.

wrongful discharge ■ An employer's termination of an employee's employment in violation of the law.

APPENDIX A
How to Brief Cases and Analyze Case Problems

How to Brief Cases

To fully understand the law with respect to business, you need to be able to read and understand court decisions. To make this task easier, you can use a method of case analysis that is called *briefing*. There is a fairly standard procedure that you can follow when you "brief" any court case. You must first read the case opinion carefully. When you feel you understand the case, you can prepare a brief of it.

Although the format of the brief may vary, typically it will present the essentials of the case under headings such as those listed below.

1 Citation. Give the full citation for the case, including the name of the case, the date it was decided, and the court that decided it.

2 Facts. Briefly indicate (a) the reasons for the lawsuit; (b) the identity and arguments of the plaintiff(s) and defendant(s), respectively; and (c) the lower court's decision—if appropriate.

3 Issue. Concisely phrase, in the form of a question, the essential issue before the court. (If more than one issue is involved, you may have two—or even more—questions here.)

4 Decision. Indicate here—with a "yes" or "no," if possible—the court's answer to the question (or questions) in the *Issue* section above.

5 Reason. Summarize as briefly as possible the reasons given by the court for its decision (or decisions) and the case or statutory law relied on by the court in arriving at its decision.

An Example of a Brief Sample Court Case

As an example of the format used in briefing cases, we present here a briefed version of the sample court case that was presented in Exhibit 1A–3 on pages 31 and 32.

BERGER v. CITY OF SEATTLE
United States Court of Appeals,
Ninth Circuit, 2008.
512 F.3d 582.

FACTS The Seattle Center is an entertainment "zone" in downtown Seattle, Washington, that attracts nearly ten million tourists each year. The center encompasses theaters, arenas, museums, exhibition halls, conference rooms, outdoor stadiums, and restaurants, and features street performers. Under the authority of the city, the center's director issued rules in 2002 to address safety concerns and other matters. Among other things, street performers were required

to obtain permits and wear badges. After members of the public filed numerous complaints of threatening behavior by street performer and balloon artist Michael Berger, Seattle Center staff cited Berger for several rules violations. He filed a suit in a federal district court against the city and others, alleging, in part, that the rules violated his free speech rights under the First Amendment to the U.S. Constitution. The court issued a judgment in the plaintiff's favor. The city appealed to the U.S. Court of Appeals for the Ninth Circuit.

ISSUE Did the rules issued by the Seattle Center under the city's authority meet the requirements for valid restrictions on speech under the First Amendment?

DECISION Yes. The U.S. Court of Appeals for the Ninth Circuit reversed the decision of the lower court and remanded the case for further proceedings. "Such content neutral and narrowly tailored rules * * * must be upheld."

REASON The court concluded first that the rules requiring permits and badges were "content neutral." Time, place, and manner restrictions do not violate the First Amendment if they burden all expression equally and do not allow officials to treat different messages differently. In this case, the rules met this test and thus did not discriminate based on content. The court also concluded that the rules were "narrowly tailored" to "promote a substantial government interest that would be achieved less effectively" otherwise. With the rules, the city was trying to "reduce territorial disputes among performers, deter patron harassment, and facilitate the identification and apprehension of offending performers." This was pursuant to the valid governmental objective of protecting the safety and convenience of the other performers and the public generally. The public's complaints about Berger and others showed that unregulated street performances posed a threat to these interests. The court was "satisfied that the city's permit scheme was designed to further valid governmental objectives."

Review of Sample Court Case

Here, we provide a review of the briefed version to indicate the kind of information that is contained in each section.

CITATION The name of the case is *Berger v. City of Seattle*. Berger is the plaintiff; the City of Seattle is the defendant. The U.S. Court of Appeals for the Ninth Circuit decided this case in 2008. The citation states that this case can be found in volume 512 of the *Federal Reporter, Third Series*, on page 582.

FACTS The *Facts* section identifies the plaintiff and the defendant, describes the events leading up to this suit, the allegations made by the plaintiff in the initial suit, and (because this case is an appellate court decision) the lower court's ruling and the party appealing. The party appealing's argument on appeal is also sometimes included here.

ISSUE The *Issue* section presents the central issue (or issues) decided by the court. In this case, the U.S. Court of Appeals for the Ninth Circuit considered whether certain rules imposed on street performers by local government authorities satisfied the requirements for valid restrictions on speech under the First Amendment to the U.S. Constitution.

DECISION The *Decision* section includes the court's decision on the issues before it. The decision reflects the opinion of the judge or justice hearing the case. Decisions by appellate courts are frequently phrased in reference to the lower court's decision. In other words, the appellate court may "affirm" the lower court's ruling or "reverse" it. Here, the court determined that Seattle's rules were "content neutral" and "narrowly tailored" to "promote a substantial government interest that would otherwise be achieved less effectively." The court found in favor of the city and reversed the lower court's ruling in the plaintiff's (Berger's) favor.

REASON The *Reason* section includes references to the relevant laws and legal principles that the court applied in coming to its conclusion in the case. The relevant law in the *Berger* case included the requirements under the First Amendment for evaluating the purpose and effect of government regulation with respect to expression. This section also explains the court's application of the law to the facts in this case.

Analyzing Case Problems

In addition to learning how to brief cases, students of business law and the legal environment also find it helpful to know how to analyze case problems. Part of the study of business law and the legal environment usually involves analyzing case problems, such as those included in this text at the end of each chapter.

For each case problem in this book, we provide the relevant background and facts of the lawsuit and the issue before the court. When you are assigned one of these problems, your job will be to determine how the court should decide the issue, and why. In other words, you will need to engage in legal analysis and reasoning. Here, we offer some suggestions on how to make this task less daunting. We begin by presenting a sample problem:

> While Janet Lawson, a famous pianist, was shopping in Quality Market, she slipped and fell on a wet floor in one of the aisles. The floor had recently been mopped by one of the store's employees, but there were no signs warning customers that the floor in that area was wet. As a result of the fall, Lawson injured her right arm and was unable to perform piano concerts for the next six months. Had she been able to perform the scheduled concerts, she would have earned approximately $60,000 over that period of time. Lawson sued Quality Market for this amount, plus another $10,000 in medical expenses. She claimed

that the store's failure to warn customers of the wet floor constituted negligence and therefore the market was liable for her injuries. Will the court agree with Lawson? Discuss.

Understand the Facts

This may sound obvious, but before you can analyze or apply the relevant law to a specific set of facts, you must clearly understand those facts. In other words, you should read through the case problem carefully—more than once, if necessary—to make sure you understand the identity of the plaintiff(s) and defendant(s) in the case and the progression of events that led to the lawsuit.

In the sample case problem just given, the identity of the parties is fairly obvious. Janet Lawson is the one bringing the suit; therefore, she is the plaintiff. Quality Market, against whom she is bringing the suit, is the defendant. Some of the case problems you may work on have multiple plaintiffs or defendants. Often, it is helpful to use abbreviations for the parties. To indicate a reference to a plaintiff, for example, the *pi* symbol—π—is often used, and a defendant is denoted by a *delta*—Δ—a triangle.

The events leading to the lawsuit are also fairly straightforward. Lawson slipped and fell on a wet floor, and she contends that Quality Market should be liable for her injuries because it was negligent in not posting a sign warning customers of the wet floor.

When you are working on case problems, realize that the facts should be accepted as they are given. For example, in our sample problem, it should be accepted that the floor was wet and that there was no sign. In other words, avoid making conjectures, such as "Maybe the floor wasn't too wet," or "Maybe an employee was getting a sign to put up," or "Maybe someone stole the sign." Questioning the facts as they are presented only adds confusion to your analysis.

Legal Analysis and Reasoning

Once you understand the facts given in the case problem, you can begin to analyze the case. Recall from Chapter 1 that the IRAC method is a helpful tool to use in the legal analysis and reasoning process. IRAC is an acronym for Issue, Rule, Application, Conclusion. Applying this method to our sample problem would involve the following steps:

1 First, you need to decide what legal **issue** is involved in the case. In our sample case, the basic issue is whether Quality Market's failure to warn customers of the wet floor constituted negligence. As discussed in Chapter 4 negligence is a *tort*—a civil wrong. In a tort lawsuit, the plaintiff seeks to be compensated for another's wrongful act. A defendant will be deemed negligent if he or she breached a duty of care owed to the plaintiff and the breach of that duty caused the plaintiff to suffer harm.

2 Once you have identified the issue, the next step is to determine what **rule of law** applies to the issue. To make this determination, you will want to review carefully the text of the chapter in which the relevant rule of law for the problem appears. Our sample case problem involves the tort of negligence, which is covered in Chapter 4. The applicable rule of law is the tort law principle that business owners owe a duty to exercise reasonable care to protect their customers (*business invitees*). Reasonable care, in this

context, includes either removing—or warning customers of—*foreseeable* risks about which the owner *knew* or *should have known*. Business owners need not warn customers of "open and obvious" risks, however. If a business owner breaches this duty of care (fails to exercise the appropriate degree of care toward customers), and the breach of duty causes a customer to be injured, the business owner will be liable to the customer for the customer's injuries.

3 The next—and usually the most difficult—step in analyzing case problems is the **application** of the relevant rule of law to the specific facts of the case you are studying. In our sample problem, applying the tort law principle just discussed presents few difficulties. An employee of the store had mopped the floor in the aisle where Lawson slipped and fell, but no sign was present indicating that the floor was wet. That a customer might fall on a wet floor is clearly a foreseeable risk. Therefore, the failure to warn customers about the wet floor was a breach of the duty of care owed by the business owner to the store's customers.

4 Once you have completed Step 3 in the IRAC method, you should be ready to draw your **conclusion.** In our sample problem, Quality Market is liable to Lawson for her injuries, because the market's breach of its duty of care caused Lawson's injuries.

The fact patterns in the case problems presented in this text are not always as simple as those presented in our sample problem. Often, for example, a case has more than one plaintiff or defendant. A case may also involve more than one issue and have more than one applicable rule of law. Furthermore, in some case problems the facts may indicate that the general rule of law should not apply. For example, suppose that a store employee advised Lawson not to walk on the floor in the aisle because it was wet, but Lawson decided to walk on it anyway. This fact could alter the outcome of the case because the store could then raise the defense of *assumption of risk* (see Chapter 4). Nonetheless, a careful review of the chapter should always provide you with the knowledge you need to analyze the problem thoroughly and arrive at accurate conclusions.

APPENDIX B
The Constitution of the United States

PREAMBLE

We the People of the United States, in Order to form a more perfect Union, establish Justice, insure domestic Tranquility, provide for the common defence, promote the general Welfare, and secure the Blessings of Liberty to ourselves and our Posterity, do ordain and establish this Constitution for the United States of America.

ARTICLE I

Section 1. All legislative Powers herein granted shall be vested in a Congress of the United States, which shall consist of a Senate and House of Representatives.

Section 2. The House of Representatives shall be composed of Members chosen every second Year by the People of the several States, and the Electors in each State shall have the Qualifications requisite for Electors of the most numerous Branch of the State Legislature.

No Person shall be a Representative who shall not have attained to the Age of twenty five Years, and been seven Years a Citizen of the United States, and who shall not, when elected, be an Inhabitant of that State in which he shall be chosen.

Representatives and direct Taxes shall be apportioned among the several States which may be included within this Union, according to their respective Numbers, which shall be determined by adding to the whole Number of free Persons, including those bound to Service for a Term of Years, and excluding Indians not taxed, three fifths of all other Persons. The actual Enumeration shall be made within three Years after the first Meeting of the Congress of the United States, and within every subsequent Term of ten Years, in such Manner as they shall by Law direct. The Number of Representatives shall not exceed one for every thirty Thousand, but each State shall have at Least one Representative; and until such enumeration shall be made, the State of New Hampshire shall be entitled to chuse three, Massachusetts eight, Rhode Island and Providence Plantations one, Connecticut five, New York six, New Jersey four, Pennsylvania eight, Delaware one, Maryland six, Virginia ten, North Carolina five, South Carolina five, and Georgia three.

When vacancies happen in the Representation from any State, the Executive Authority thereof shall issue Writs of Election to fill such Vacancies.

The House of Representatives shall chuse their Speaker and other Officers; and shall have the sole Power of Impeachment.

Section 3. The Senate of the United States shall be composed of two Senators from each State, chosen by the Legislature thereof, for six Years; and each Senator shall have one Vote.

Immediately after they shall be assembled in Consequence of the first Election, they shall be divided as equally as may be into three Classes. The Seats of the Senators of the first Class shall be vacated at the Expiration of the second Year, of the second Class at the Expiration of the fourth Year, and of the third Class at the Expiration of the sixth Year, so that one third may be chosen every second Year; and if Vacancies happen by Resignation, or otherwise, during the Recess of the Legislature of any State, the Executive thereof may make temporary Appointments until the next Meeting of the Legislature, which shall then fill such Vacancies.

No Person shall be a Senator who shall not have attained to the Age of thirty Years, and been nine Years a Citizen of the United States, and who shall not, when elected, be an Inhabitant of that State for which he shall be chosen.

The Vice President of the United States shall be President of the Senate, but shall have no Vote, unless they be equally divided.

The Senate shall chuse their other Officers, and also a President pro tempore, in the Absence of the Vice President, or when he shall exercise the Office of President of the United States.

The Senate shall have the sole Power to try all Impeachments. When sitting for that Purpose, they shall be on Oath or Affirmation. When the President of the United States is tried, the Chief Justice shall preside: And no Person shall be convicted without the Concurrence of two thirds of the Members present.

Judgment in Cases of Impeachment shall not extend further than to removal from Office, and disqualification to hold and enjoy any Office of honor, Trust, or Profit under the United States: but the Party convicted shall nevertheless be liable and subject to Indictment, Trial, Judgment, and Punishment, according to Law.

Section 4. The Times, Places and Manner of holding Elections for Senators and Representatives, shall be prescribed in each State by the Legislature thereof; but the Congress may at any time by Law make or alter such Regulations, except as to the Places of chusing Senators.

The Congress shall assemble at least once in every Year, and such Meeting shall be on the first Monday in December, unless they shall by Law appoint a different Day.

Section 5. Each House shall be the Judge of the Elections, Returns, and Qualifications of its own Members, and a Majority of each shall constitute a Quorum to do Business; but a smaller Number may adjourn from day to day, and may be authorized to compel the Attendance of absent Members, in such Manner, and under such Penalties as each House may provide.

Each House may determine the Rules of its Proceedings, punish its Members for disorderly Behavior, and, with the Concurrence of two thirds, expel a Member.

Each House shall keep a Journal of its Proceedings, and from time to time publish the same, excepting such Parts as may in their Judgment require Secrecy; and the Yeas and Nays of the Members of either House on any question shall, at the Desire of one fifth of those Present, be entered on the Journal.

Neither House, during the Session of Congress, shall, without the Consent of the other, adjourn for more than three days, nor to any other Place than that in which the two Houses shall be sitting.

Section 6.   The Senators and Representatives shall receive a Compensation for their Services, to be ascertained by Law, and paid out of the Treasury of the United States. They shall in all Cases, except Treason, Felony and Breach of the Peace, be privileged from Arrest during their Attendance at the Session of their respective Houses, and in going to and returning from the same; and for any Speech or Debate in either House, they shall not be questioned in any other Place.

No Senator or Representative shall, during the Time for which he was elected, be appointed to any civil Office under the Authority of the United States, which shall have been created, or the Emoluments whereof shall have been increased during such time; and no Person holding any Office under the United States, shall be a Member of either House during his Continuance in Office.

Section 7.   All Bills for raising Revenue shall originate in the House of Representatives; but the Senate may propose or concur with Amendments as on other Bills.

Every Bill which shall have passed the House of Representatives and the Senate, shall, before it become a Law, be presented to the President of the United States; If he approve he shall sign it, but if not he shall return it, with his Objections to the House in which it shall have originated, who shall enter the Objections at large on their Journal, and proceed to reconsider it. If after such Reconsideration two thirds of that House shall agree to pass the Bill, it shall be sent together with the Objections, to the other House, by which it shall likewise be reconsidered, and if approved by two thirds of that House, it shall become a Law. But in all such Cases the Votes of both Houses shall be determined by Yeas and Nays, and the Names of the Persons voting for and against the Bill shall be entered on the Journal of each House respectively. If any Bill shall not be returned by the President within ten Days (Sundays excepted) after it shall have been presented to him, the Same shall be a Law, in like Manner as if he had signed it, unless the Congress by their Adjournment prevent its Return in which Case it shall not be a Law.

Every Order, Resolution, or Vote, to which the Concurrence of the Senate and House of Representatives may be necessary (except on a question of Adjournment) shall be presented to the President of the United States; and before the Same shall take Effect, shall be approved by him, or being disapproved by him, shall be repassed by two thirds of the Senate and House of Representatives, according to the Rules and Limitations prescribed in the Case of a Bill.

Section 8.   The Congress shall have Power To lay and collect Taxes, Duties, Imposts and Excises, to pay the Debts and provide for the common Defence and general Welfare of the United States; but all Duties, Imposts and Excises shall be uniform throughout the United States;

To borrow Money on the credit of the United States;

To regulate Commerce with foreign Nations, and among the several States, and with the Indian Tribes;

To establish an uniform Rule of Naturalization, and uniform Laws on the subject of Bankruptcies throughout the United States;

To coin Money, regulate the Value thereof, and of foreign Coin, and fix the Standard of Weights and Measures;

To provide for the Punishment of counterfeiting the Securities and current Coin of the United States;

To establish Post Offices and post Roads;

To promote the Progress of Science and useful Arts, by securing for limited Times to Authors and Inventors the exclusive Right to their respective Writings and Discoveries;

To constitute Tribunals inferior to the supreme Court;

To define and punish Piracies and Felonies committed on the high Seas, and Offenses against the Law of Nations;

To declare War, grant Letters of Marque and Reprisal, and make Rules concerning Captures on Land and Water;

To raise and support Armies, but no Appropriation of Money to that Use shall be for a longer Term than two Years;

To provide and maintain a Navy;

To make Rules for the Government and Regulation of the land and naval Forces;

To provide for calling forth the Militia to execute the Laws of the Union, suppress Insurrections and repel Invasions;

To provide for organizing, arming, and disciplining, the Militia, and for governing such Part of them as may be employed in the Service of the United States, reserving to the States respectively, the Appointment of the Officers, and the Authority of training the Militia according to the discipline prescribed by Congress;

To exercise exclusive Legislation in all Cases whatsoever, over such District (not exceeding ten Miles square) as may, by Cession of particular States, and the Acceptance of Congress, become the Seat of the Government of the United States, and to exercise like Authority over all Places purchased by the Consent of the Legislature of the State in which the Same shall be, for the Erection of Forts, Magazines, Arsenals, dock-Yards, and other needful Buildings;—And

To make all Laws which shall be necessary and proper for carrying into Execution the foregoing Powers, and all other Powers vested by this Constitution in the Government of the United States, or in any Department or Officer thereof.

Section 9.   The Migration or Importation of such Persons as any of the States now existing shall think proper to admit, shall not be prohibited by the Congress prior to the Year one thousand eight hundred and eight, but a Tax or duty may be imposed on such Importation, not exceeding ten dollars for each Person.

The privilege of the Writ of Habeas Corpus shall not be suspended, unless when in Cases of Rebellion or Invasion the public Safety may require it.

No Bill of Attainder or ex post facto Law shall be passed.

No Capitation, or other direct, Tax shall be laid, unless in Proportion to the Census or Enumeration herein before directed to be taken.

No Tax or Duty shall be laid on Articles exported from any State.

No Preference shall be given by any Regulation of Commerce or Revenue to the Ports of one State over those of another: nor shall

Vessels bound to, or from, one State be obliged to enter, clear, or pay Duties in another.

No Money shall be drawn from the Treasury, but in Consequence of Appropriations made by Law; and a regular Statement and Account of the Receipts and Expenditures of all public Money shall be published from time to time.

No Title of Nobility shall be granted by the United States: And no Person holding any Office of Profit or Trust under them, shall, without the Consent of the Congress, accept of any present, Emolument, Office, or Title, of any kind whatever, from any King, Prince, or foreign State.

Section 10. No State shall enter into any Treaty, Alliance, or Confederation; grant Letters of Marque and Reprisal; coin Money; emit Bills of Credit; make any Thing but gold and silver Coin a Tender in Payment of Debts; pass any Bill of Attainder, ex post facto Law, or Law impairing the Obligation of Contracts, or grant any Title of Nobility.

No State shall, without the Consent of the Congress, lay any Imposts or Duties on Imports or Exports, except what may be absolutely necessary for executing its inspection Laws: and the net Produce of all Duties and Imposts, laid by any State on Imports or Exports, shall be for the Use of the Treasury of the United States; and all such Laws shall be subject to the Revision and Controul of the Congress.

No State shall, without the Consent of Congress, lay any Duty of Tonnage, keep Troops, or Ships of War in time of Peace, enter into any Agreement or Compact with another State, or with a foreign Power, or engage in War, unless actually invaded, or in such imminent Danger as will not admit of delay.

ARTICLE II

Section 1. The executive Power shall be vested in a President of the United States of America. He shall hold his Office during the Term of four Years, and, together with the Vice President, chosen for the same Term, be elected, as follows:

Each State shall appoint, in such Manner as the Legislature thereof may direct, a Number of Electors, equal to the whole Number of Senators and Representatives to which the State may be entitled in the Congress; but no Senator or Representative, or Person holding an Office of Trust or Profit under the United States, shall be appointed an Elector.

The Electors shall meet in their respective States, and vote by Ballot for two Persons, of whom one at least shall not be an Inhabitant of the same State with themselves. And they shall make a List of all the Persons voted for, and of the Number of Votes for each; which List they shall sign and certify, and transmit sealed to the Seat of the Government of the United States, directed to the President of the Senate. The President of the Senate shall, in the Presence of the Senate and House of Representatives, open all the Certificates, and the Votes shall then be counted. The Person having the greatest Number of Votes shall be the President, if such Number be a Majority of the whole Number of Electors appointed; and if there be more than one who have such Majority, and have an equal Number of Votes, then the House of Representatives shall immediately chuse by Ballot one of them for President; and if no Person have a Majority, then from the five highest on the List the said House shall in like Manner chuse the President. But in chusing the President, the Votes shall be taken by States, the

Representation from each State having one Vote; A quorum for this Purpose shall consist of a Member or Members from two thirds of the States, and a Majority of all the States shall be necessary to a Choice. In every Case, after the Choice of the President, the Person having the greater Number of Votes of the Electors shall be the Vice President. But if there should remain two or more who have equal Votes, the Senate shall chuse from them by Ballot the Vice President.

The Congress may determine the Time of chusing the Electors, and the Day on which they shall give their Votes; which Day shall be the same throughout the United States.

No person except a natural born Citizen, or a Citizen of the United States, at the time of the Adoption of this Constitution, shall be eligible to the Office of President; neither shall any Person be eligible to that Office who shall not have attained to the Age of thirty five Years, and been fourteen Years a Resident within the United States.

In Case of the Removal of the President from Office, or of his Death, Resignation or Inability to discharge the Powers and Duties of the said Office, the same shall devolve on the Vice President, and the Congress may by Law provide for the Case of Removal, Death, Resignation or Inability, both of the President and Vice President, declaring what Officer shall then act as President, and such Officer shall act accordingly, until the Disability be removed, or a President shall be elected.

The President shall, at stated Times, receive for his Services, a Compensation, which shall neither be increased nor diminished during the Period for which he shall have been elected, and he shall not receive within that Period any other Emolument from the United States, or any of them.

Before he enter on the Execution of his Office, he shall take the following Oath or Affirmation: "I do solemnly swear (or affirm) that I will faithfully execute the Office of President of the United States, and will to the best of my Ability, preserve, protect and defend the Constitution of the United States."

Section 2. The President shall be Commander in Chief of the Army and Navy of the United States, and of the Militia of the several States, when called into the actual Service of the United States; he may require the Opinion, in writing, of the principal Officer in each of the executive Departments, upon any Subject relating to the Duties of their respective Offices, and he shall have Power to grant Reprieves and Pardons for Offenses against the United States, except in Cases of Impeachment.

He shall have Power, by and with the Advice and Consent of the Senate to make Treaties, provided two thirds of the Senators present concur; and he shall nominate, and by and with the Advice and Consent of the Senate, shall appoint Ambassadors, other public Ministers and Consuls, Judges of the supreme Court, and all other Officers of the United States, whose Appointments are not herein otherwise provided for, and which shall be established by Law; but the Congress may by Law vest the Appointment of such inferior Officers, as they think proper, in the President alone, in the Courts of Law, or in the Heads of Departments.

The President shall have Power to fill up all Vacancies that may happen during the Recess of the Senate, by granting Commissions which shall expire at the End of their next Session.

Section 3. He shall from time to time give to the Congress Information of the State of the Union, and recommend to their

Consideration such Measures as he shall judge necessary and expedient; he may, on extraordinary Occasions, convene both Houses, or either of them, and in Case of Disagreement between them, with Respect to the Time of Adjournment, he may adjourn them to such Time as he shall think proper; he shall receive Ambassadors and other public Ministers; he shall take Care that the Laws be faithfully executed, and shall Commission all the Officers of the United States.

Section 4.   The President, Vice President and all civil Officers of the United States, shall be removed from Office on Impeachment for, and Conviction of, Treason, Bribery, or other high Crimes and Misdemeanors.

ARTICLE III

Section 1.   The judicial Power of the United States, shall be vested in one supreme Court, and in such inferior Courts as the Congress may from time to time ordain and establish. The Judges, both of the supreme and inferior Courts, shall hold their Offices during good Behaviour, and shall, at stated Times, receive for their Services a Compensation, which shall not be diminished during their Continuance in Office.

Section 2.   The judicial Power shall extend to all Cases, in Law and Equity, arising under this Constitution, the Laws of the United States, and Treaties made, or which shall be made, under their Authority;—to all Cases affecting Ambassadors, other public Ministers and Consuls;—to all Cases of admiralty and maritime Jurisdiction;—to Controversies to which the United States shall be a Party;—to Controversies between two or more States;—between a State and Citizens of another State;—between Citizens of different States;—between Citizens of the same State claiming Lands under Grants of different States, and between a State, or the Citizens thereof, and foreign States, Citizens or Subjects.

In all Cases affecting Ambassadors, other public Ministers and Consuls, and those in which a State shall be a Party, the supreme Court shall have original Jurisdiction. In all the other Cases before mentioned, the supreme Court shall have appellate Jurisdiction, both as to Law and Fact, with such Exceptions, and under such Regulations as the Congress shall make.

The Trial of all Crimes, except in Cases of Impeachment, shall be by Jury; and such Trial shall be held in the State where the said Crimes shall have been committed; but when not committed within any State, the Trial shall be at such Place or Places as the Congress may by Law have directed.

Section 3.   Treason against the United States, shall consist only in levying War against them, or, in adhering to their Enemies, giving them Aid and Comfort. No Person shall be convicted of Treason unless on the Testimony of two Witnesses to the same overt Act, or on Confession in open Court.

The Congress shall have Power to declare the Punishment of Treason, but no Attainder of Treason shall work Corruption of Blood, or Forfeiture except during the Life of the Person attainted.

ARTICLE IV

Section 1.   Full Faith and Credit shall be given in each State to the public Acts, Records, and judicial Proceedings of every other State. And the Congress may by general Laws prescribe the Manner in which such Acts, Records and Proceedings shall be proved, and the Effect thereof.

Section 2.   The Citizens of each State shall be entitled to all Privileges and Immunities of Citizens in the several States.

A Person charged in any State with Treason, Felony, or other Crime, who shall flee from Justice, and be found in another State, shall on Demand of the executive Authority of the State from which he fled, be delivered up, to be removed to the State having Jurisdiction of the Crime.

No Person held to Service or Labour in one State, under the Laws thereof, escaping into another, shall, in Consequence of any Law or Regulation therein, be discharged from such Service or Labour, but shall be delivered up on Claim of the Party to whom such Service or Labour may be due.

Section 3.   New States may be admitted by the Congress into this Union; but no new State shall be formed or erected within the Jurisdiction of any other State; nor any State be formed by the Junction of two or more States, or Parts of States, without the Consent of the Legislatures of the States concerned as well as of the Congress.

The Congress shall have Power to dispose of and make all needful Rules and Regulations respecting the Territory or other Property belonging to the United States; and nothing in this Constitution shall be so construed as to Prejudice any Claims of the United States, or of any particular State.

Section 4.   The United States shall guarantee to every State in this Union a Republican Form of Government, and shall protect each of them against Invasion; and on Application of the Legislature, or of the Executive (when the Legislature cannot be convened) against domestic Violence.

ARTICLE V

The Congress, whenever two thirds of both Houses shall deem it necessary, shall propose Amendments to this Constitution, or, on the Application of the Legislatures of two thirds of the several States, shall call a Convention for proposing Amendments, which, in either Case, shall be valid to all Intents and Purposes, as part of this Constitution, when ratified by the Legislatures of three fourths of the several States, or by Conventions in three fourths thereof, as the one or the other Mode of Ratification may be proposed by the Congress; Provided that no Amendment which may be made prior to the Year One thousand eight hundred and eight shall in any Manner affect the first and fourth Clauses in the Ninth Section of the first Article; and that no State, without its Consent, shall be deprived of its equal Suffrage in the Senate.

ARTICLE VI

All Debts contracted and Engagements entered into, before the Adoption of this Constitution shall be as valid against the United States under this Constitution, as under the Confederation.

This Constitution, and the Laws of the United States which shall be made in Pursuance thereof; and all Treaties made, or which shall be made, under the Authority of the United States, shall be the supreme Law of the Land; and the Judges in every State shall be bound thereby, any Thing in the Constitution or Laws of any State to the Contrary notwithstanding.

The Senators and Representatives before mentioned, and the Members of the several State Legislatures, and all executive and judicial Officers, both of the United States and of the several States, shall be bound by Oath or Affirmation, to support this Constitution; but no religious Test shall ever be required as a Qualification to any Office or public Trust under the United States.

ARTICLE VII

The Ratification of the Conventions of nine States shall be sufficient for the Establishment of this Constitution between the States so ratifying the Same.

AMENDMENT I [1791]

Congress shall make no law respecting an establishment of religion, or prohibiting the free exercise thereof; or abridging the freedom of speech, or of the press; or the right of the people peaceably to assembly, and to petition the Government for a redress of grievances.

AMENDMENT II [1791]

A well regulated Militia, being necessary to the security of a free State, the right of the people to keep and bear Arms, shall not be infringed.

AMENDMENT III [1791]

No Soldier shall, in time of peace be quartered in any house, without the consent of the Owner, nor in time of war, but in a manner to be prescribed by law.

AMENDMENT IV [1791]

The right of the people to be secure in their persons, houses, papers, and effects, against unreasonable searches and seizures, shall not be violated, and no Warrants shall issue, but upon probable cause, supported by Oath or affirmation, and particularly describing the place to be searched, and the persons or things to be seized.

AMENDMENT V [1791]

No person shall be held to answer for a capital, or otherwise infamous crime, unless on a presentment or indictment of a Grand Jury, except in cases arising in the land or naval forces, or in the Militia, when in actual service in time of War or public danger; nor shall any person be subject for the same offence to be twice put in jeopardy of life or limb; nor shall be compelled in any criminal case to be a witness against himself, nor be deprived of life, liberty, or property, without due process of law; nor shall private property be taken for public use, without just compensation.

AMENDMENT VI [1791]

In all criminal prosecutions, the accused shall enjoy the right to a speedy and public trial, by an impartial jury of the State and district wherein the crime shall have been committed, which district shall have been previously ascertained by law, and to be informed of the nature and cause of the accusation; to be confronted with the witnesses against him; to have compulsory process for obtaining witnesses in his favor, and to have the Assistance of Counsel for his defence.

AMENDMENT VII [1791]

In Suits at common law, where the value in controversy shall exceed twenty dollars, the right of trial by jury shall be preserved, and no fact tried by jury, shall be otherwise re-examined in any Court of the United States, than according to the rules of the common law.

AMENDMENT VIII [1791]

Excessive bail shall not be required, nor excessive fines imposed, nor cruel and unusual punishments inflicted.

AMENDMENT IX [1791]

The enumeration in the Constitution, of certain rights, shall not be construed to deny or disparage others retained by the people.

AMENDMENT X [1791]

The powers not delegated to the United States by the Constitution, nor prohibited by it to the States, are reserved to the States respectively, or to the people.

AMENDMENT XI [1798]

The Judicial power of the United States shall not be construed to extend to any suit in law or equity, commenced or prosecuted against one of the United States by Citizens of another State, or by Citizens or Subjects of any Foreign State.

AMENDMENT XII [1804]

The Electors shall meet in their respective states, and vote by ballot for President and Vice-President, one of whom, at least, shall not be an inhabitant of the same state with themselves; they shall name in their ballots the person voted for as President, and in distinct ballots the person voted for as Vice-President, and they shall make distinct lists of all persons voted for as President, and of all persons voted for as Vice-President, and of the number of votes for each, which lists they shall sign and certify, and transmit sealed to the seat of the government of the United States, directed to the President of the Senate;—The President of the Senate shall, in the presence of the Senate and House of Representatives, open all the certificates and the votes shall then be counted;—The person having the greatest number of votes for President, shall be the President, if such number be a majority of the whole number of Electors appointed; and if no person have such majority, then from the persons having the highest numbers not exceeding three on the list of those voted for as President, the House of Representatives shall choose immediately, by ballot, the President. But in choosing the President, the votes shall be taken by states, the representation from each state having one vote; a quorum for this purpose shall consist of a member or members from two-thirds of the states, and a majority of all states shall be necessary to a choice. And if the House of Representatives shall not choose a President whenever the right of choice shall devolve upon them, before the fourth day of March next following, then the Vice-President shall act as President, as in the case of the death or other constitutional disability of the President.—The person having the greatest number of votes as Vice-President, shall be the Vice-President, if such number be a majority of the whole number of Electors appointed, and if no person have a majority, then from the two highest numbers on the list, the Senate shall choose the Vice-President; a quorum for the purpose shall consist of two-thirds of the whole number of Senators, and a majority of the whole number shall be necessary to a choice. But no person constitutionally ineligible to the office of President shall be eligible to that of Vice-President of the United States.

Amendment XIII [1865]

Section 1. Neither slavery nor involuntary servitude, except as a punishment for crime whereof the party shall have been duly convicted, shall exist within the United States, or any place subject to their jurisdiction.

Section 2. Congress shall have power to enforce this article by appropriate legislation.

Amendment XIV [1868]

Section 1. All persons born or naturalized in the United States, and subject to the jurisdiction thereof, are citizens of the United States and of the State wherein they reside. No State shall make or enforce any law which shall abridge the privileges or immunities of citizens of the United States; nor shall any State deprive any person of life, liberty, or property, without due process of law; nor deny to any person within its jurisdiction the equal protection of the laws.

Section 2. Representatives shall be apportioned among the several States according to their respective numbers, counting the whole number of persons in each State, excluding Indians not taxed. But when the right to vote at any election for the choice of electors for President and Vice President of the United States, Representatives in Congress, the Executive and Judicial officers of a State, or the members of the Legislature thereof, is denied to any of the male inhabitants of such State, being twenty-one years of age, and citizens of the United States, or in any way abridged, except for participation in rebellion, or other crime, the basis of representation therein shall be reduced in the proportion which the number of such male citizens shall bear to the whole number of male citizens twenty-one years of age in such State.

Section 3. No person shall be a Senator or Representative in Congress, or elector of President and Vice President, or hold any office, civil or military, under the United States, or under any State, who having previously taken an oath, as a member of Congress, or as an officer of the United States, or as a member of any State legislature, or as an executive or judicial officer of any State, to support the Constitution of the United States, shall have engaged in insurrection or rebellion against the same, or given aid or comfort to the enemies thereof. But Congress may by a vote of two-thirds of each House, remove such disability.

Section 4. The validity of the public debt of the United States, authorized by law, including debts incurred for payment of pensions and bounties for services in suppressing insurrection or rebellion, shall not be questioned. But neither the United States nor any State shall assume or pay any debt or obligation incurred in aid of insurrection or rebellion against the United States, or any claim for the loss or emancipation of any slave; but all such debts, obligations and claims shall be held illegal and void.

Section 5. The Congress shall have power to enforce, by appropriate legislation, the provisions of this article.

Amendment XV [1870]

Section 1. The right of citizens of the United States to vote shall not be denied or abridged by the United States or by any State on account of race, color, or previous condition of servitude.

Section 2. The Congress shall have power to enforce this article by appropriate legislation.

Amendment XVI [1913]

The Congress shall have power to lay and collect taxes on incomes, from whatever source derived, without apportionment among the several States, and without regard to any census or enumeration.

Amendment XVII [1913]

Section 1. The Senate of the United States shall be composed of two Senators from each State, elected by the people thereof, for six years; and each Senator shall have one vote. The electors in each State shall have the qualifications requisite for electors of the most numerous branch of the State legislatures.

Section 2. When vacancies happen in the representation of any State in the Senate, the executive authority of such State shall issue writs of election to fill such vacancies: *Provided,* That the legislature of any State may empower the executive thereof to make temporary appointments until the people fill the vacancies by election as the legislature may direct.

Section 3. This amendment shall not be so construed as to affect the election or term of any Senator chosen before it becomes valid as part of the Constitution.

Amendment XVIII [1919]

Section 1. After one year from the ratification of this article the manufacture, sale, or transportation of intoxicating liquors within, the importation thereof into, or the exportation thereof from the United States and all territory subject to the jurisdiction thereof for beverage purposes is hereby prohibited.

Section 2. The Congress and the several States shall have concurrent power to enforce this article by appropriate legislation.

Section 3. This article shall be inoperative unless it shall have been ratified as an amendment to the Constitution by the legislatures of the several States, as provided in the Constitution, within seven years from the date of the submission hereof to the States by the Congress.

Amendment XIX [1920]

Section 1. The right of citizens of the United States to vote shall not be denied or abridged by the United States or by any State on account of sex.

Section 2. Congress shall have power to enforce this article by appropriate legislation.

Amendment XX [1933]

Section 1. The terms of the President and Vice President shall end at noon on the 20th day of January, and the terms of Senators and Representatives at noon on the 3d day of January, of the years in which such terms would have ended if this article had not been ratified; and the terms of their successors shall then begin.

Section 2. The Congress shall assemble at least once in every year, and such meeting shall begin at noon on the 3d day of January, unless they shall by law appoint a different day.

Section 3. If, at the time fixed for the beginning of the term of the President, the President elect shall have died, the Vice President elect shall become President. If the President shall not have been chosen before the time fixed for the beginning of his term, or if the President elect shall have failed to qualify, then the Vice President elect shall act as President until a President shall have qualified; and the Congress may by law provide for the case wherein neither a President elect nor a Vice President elect shall have qualified, declaring who shall then act as President, or the manner in which one who is to act shall be selected, and such person shall act accordingly until a President or Vice President shall have qualified.

Section 4. The Congress may by law provide for the case of the death of any of the persons from whom the House of Representatives may choose a President whenever the right of choice shall have devolved upon them, and for the case of the death of any of the persons from whom the Senate may choose a Vice President whenever the right of choice shall have devolved upon them.

Section 5. Sections 1 and 2 shall take effect on the 15th day of October following the ratification of this article.

Section 6. This article shall be inoperative unless it shall have been ratified as an amendment to the Constitution by the legislatures of three-fourths of the several States within seven years from the date of its submission.

AMENDMENT XXI [1933]

Section 1. The eighteenth article of amendment to the Constitution of the United States is hereby repealed.

Section 2. The transportation or importation into any State, Territory, or possession of the United States for delivery or use therein of intoxicating liquors, in violation of the laws thereof, is hereby prohibited.

Section 3. This article shall be inoperative unless it shall have been ratified as an amendment to the Constitution by conventions in the several States, as provided in the Constitution, within seven years from the date of the submission hereof to the States by the Congress.

AMENDMENT XXII [1951]

Section 1. No person shall be elected to the office of the President more than twice, and no person who has held the office of President, or acted as President, for more than two years of a term to which some other person was elected President shall be elected to the office of President more than once. But this Article shall not apply to any person holding the office of President when this Article was proposed by the Congress, and shall not prevent any person who may be holding the office of President, or acting as President, during the term within which this Article becomes operative from holding the office of President or acting as President during the remainder of such term.

Section 2. This article shall be inoperative unless it shall have been ratified as an amendment to the Constitution by the legislatures of three-fourths of the several States within seven years from the date of its submission to the States by the Congress.

AMENDMENT XXIII [1961]

Section 1. The District constituting the seat of Government of the United States shall appoint in such manner as the Congress may direct:

A number of electors of President and Vice President equal to the whole number of Senators and Representatives in Congress to which the District would be entitled if it were a State, but in no event more than the least populous state; they shall be in addition to those appointed by the states, but they shall be considered, for the purposes of the election of President and Vice President, to be electors appointed by a state; and they shall meet in the District and perform such duties as provided by the twelfth article of amendment.

Section 2. The Congress shall have power to enforce this article by appropriate legislation.

AMENDMENT XXIV [1964]

Section 1. The right of citizens of the United States to vote in any primary or other election for President or Vice President, for electors for President or Vice President, or for Senator or Representative in Congress, shall not be denied or abridged by the United States, or any State by reason of failure to pay any poll tax or other tax.

Section 2. The Congress shall have power to enforce this article by appropriate legislation.

AMENDMENT XXV [1967]

Section 1. In case of the removal of the President from office or of his death or resignation, the Vice President shall become President.

Section 2. Whenever there is a vacancy in the office of the Vice President, the President shall nominate a Vice President who shall take office upon confirmation by a majority vote of both Houses of Congress.

Section 3. Whenever the President transmits to the President pro tempore of the Senate and the Speaker of the House of Representatives his written declaration that he is unable to discharge the powers and duties of his office, and until he transmits to them a written declaration to the contrary, such powers and duties shall be discharged by the Vice President as Acting President.

Section 4. Whenever the Vice President and a majority of either the principal officers of the executive departments or of such other body as Congress may by law provide, transmit to the President pro tempore of the Senate and the Speaker of the House of Representatives their written declaration that the President is unable to discharge the powers and duties of his office, the Vice President shall immediately assume the powers and duties of the office as Acting President.

Thereafter, when the President transmits to the President pro tempore of the Senate and the Speaker of the House of Representatives his written declaration that no inability exists, he shall resume the powers and duties of his office unless the Vice President and a majority of either the principal officers of the executive department or of such other body as Congress may by law provide, transmit within four days to the President pro tempore of the Senate and the Speaker of the House of Representatives their written declaration that the President is unable to discharge the powers and duties of his office. Thereupon Congress shall decide the issue, assembling within forty-eight hours for that purpose if not in session. If the Congress, within twenty-one days after receipt of the latter written declaration, or, if Congress is not in session, within twenty-one days after Congress is required to assemble, determines by two-thirds vote of both Houses that the President is unable to discharge the powers and duties of his office, the Vice President shall continue to discharge the same as Acting President; otherwise, the President shall resume the powers and duties of his office.

Amendment XXVI [1971]

Section 1. The right of citizens of the United States, who are eighteen years of age or older, to vote shall not be denied or abridged by the United States or by any State on account of age.

Section 2. The Congress shall have power to enforce this article by appropriate legislation.

Amendment XXVII [1992]

No law, varying the compensation for the services of the Senators and Representatives, shall take effect, until an election of Representatives shall have intervened.

APPENDIX D
The Sarbanes-Oxley Act of 2002 (Excerpts and Explanatory Comments)

Note: The author's explanatory comments appear in italics following the excerpt from each section.

SECTION 302

Corporate responsibility for financial reports[1]

(a) Regulations required

The Commission shall, by rule, require, for each company filing periodic reports under section 13(a) or 15(d) of the Securities Exchange Act of 1934 (15 U.S.C. 78m, 78o(d)), that the principal executive officer or officers and the principal financial officer or officers, or persons performing similar functions, certify in each annual or quarterly report filed or submitted under either such section of such Act that—

(1) the signing officer has reviewed the report;

(2) based on the officer's knowledge, the report does not contain any untrue statement of a material fact or omit to state a material fact necessary in order to make the statements made, in light of the circumstances under which such statements were made, not misleading;

(3) based on such officer's knowledge, the financial statements, and other financial information included in the report, fairly present in all material respects the financial condition and results of operations of the issuer as of, and for, the periods presented in the report;

(4) the signing officers—

(A) are responsible for establishing and maintaining internal controls;

(B) have designed such internal controls to ensure that material information relating to the issuer and its consolidated subsidiaries is made known to such officers by others within those entities, particularly during the period in which the periodic reports are being prepared;

(C) have evaluated the effectiveness of the issuer's internal controls as of a date within 90 days prior to the report; and

(D) have presented in the report their conclusions about the effectiveness of their internal controls based on their evaluation as of that date;

(5) the signing officers have disclosed to the issuer's auditors and the audit committee of the board of directors (or persons fulfilling the equivalent function)—

(A) all significant deficiencies in the design or operation of internal controls which could adversely affect the issuer's ability to record, process, summarize, and report financial data and have identified for the issuer's auditors any material weaknesses in internal controls; and

(B) any fraud, whether or not material, that involves management or other employees who have a significant role in the issuer's internal controls; and

(6) the signing officers have indicated in the report whether or not there were significant changes in internal controls or in other factors that could significantly affect internal controls subsequent to the date of their evaluation, including any corrective actions with regard to significant deficiencies and material weaknesses.

(b) Foreign reincorporations have no effect

Nothing in this section shall be interpreted or applied in any way to allow any issuer to lessen the legal force of the statement required under this section, by an issuer having reincorporated or having engaged in any other transaction that resulted in the transfer of the corporate domicile or offices of the issuer from inside the United States to outside of the United States.

(c) Deadline

The rules required by subsection (a) of this section shall be effective not later than 30 days after July 30, 2002.

* * * *

EXPLANATORY COMMENTS: *Section 302 requires the chief executive officer (CEO) and chief financial officer (CFO) of each public company to certify that they have reviewed the company's quarterly and annual reports to be filed with the Securities and Exchange Commission (SEC). The CEO and CFO must certify that, based on their knowledge, the reports do not contain any untrue statement of a material fact or any half-truth that would make the report misleading, and that the information contained in the reports fairly presents the company's financial condition.*

In addition, this section also requires the CEO and CFO to certify that they have created and designed an internal control system for their company and have recently evaluated that system to ensure that it is effectively providing them with relevant and accurate financial information. If the signing officers have found any significant deficiencies or weaknesses in the company's system or have discovered any evidence of fraud, they must have reported the situation, and any corrective actions they have taken, to the auditors and the audit committee.

---

1. This section of the Sarbanes-Oxley Act is codified at 15 U.S.C. Section 7241.

SECTION 306

Insider trades during pension fund blackout periods[2]

(a) Prohibition of insider trading during pension fund blackout periods

(1) In general

Except to the extent otherwise provided by rule of the Commission pursuant to paragraph (3), it shall be unlawful for any director or executive officer of an issuer of any equity security (other than an exempted security), directly or indirectly, to purchase, sell, or otherwise acquire or transfer any equity security of the issuer (other than an exempted security) during any blackout period with respect to such equity security if such director or officer acquires such equity security in connection with his or her service or employment as a director or executive officer.

(2) Remedy

(A) In general

Any profit realized by a director or executive officer referred to in paragraph (1) from any purchase, sale, or other acquisition or transfer in violation of this subsection shall inure to and be recoverable by the issuer, irrespective of any intention on the part of such director or executive officer in entering into the transaction.

(B) Actions to recover profits

An action to recover profits in accordance with this subsection may be instituted at law or in equity in any court of competent jurisdiction by the issuer, or by the owner of any security of the issuer in the name and in behalf of the issuer if the issuer fails or refuses to bring such action within 60 days after the date of request, or fails diligently to prosecute the action thereafter, except that no such suit shall be brought more than 2 years after the date on which such profit was realized.

(3) Rulemaking authorized

The Commission shall, in consultation with the Secretary of Labor, issue rules to clarify the application of this subsection and to prevent evasion thereof. Such rules shall provide for the application of the requirements of paragraph (1) with respect to entities treated as a single employer with respect to an issuer under section 414(b), (c), (m), or (o) of Title 26 to the extent necessary to clarify the application of such requirements and to prevent evasion thereof. Such rules may also provide for appropriate exceptions from the requirements of this subsection, including exceptions for purchases pursuant to an automatic dividend reinvestment program or purchases or sales made pursuant to an advance election.

(4) Blackout period

For purposes of this subsection, the term "blackout period", with respect to the equity securities of any issuer—

(A) means any period of more than 3 consecutive business days during which the ability of not fewer than 50 percent of the participants or beneficiaries under all individual account plans maintained by the issuer to purchase, sell, or otherwise acquire

or transfer an interest in any equity of such issuer held in such an individual account plan is temporarily suspended by the issuer or by a fiduciary of the plan; and

(B) does not include, under regulations which shall be prescribed by the Commission—

(i) a regularly scheduled period in which the participants and beneficiaries may not purchase, sell, or otherwise acquire or transfer an interest in any equity of such issuer, if such period is—

(I) incorporated into the individual account plan; and

(II) timely disclosed to employees before becoming participants under the individual account plan or as a subsequent amendment to the plan; or

(ii) any suspension described in subparagraph (A) that is imposed solely in connection with persons becoming participants or beneficiaries, or ceasing to be participants or beneficiaries, in an individual account plan by reason of a corporate merger, acquisition, divestiture, or similar transaction involving the plan or plan sponsor.

(5) Individual account plan

For purposes of this subsection, the term "individual account plan" has the meaning provided in section 1002(34) of Title 29, except that such term shall not include a one-participant retirement plan (within the meaning of section 1021(i)(8)(B) of Title 29).

(6) Notice to directors, executive officers, and the Commission

In any case in which a director or executive officer is subject to the requirements of this subsection in connection with a blackout period (as defined in paragraph (4)) with respect to any equity securities, the issuer of such equity securities shall timely notify such director or officer and the Securities and Exchange Commission of such blackout period.

*   *   *   *

EXPLANATORY COMMENTS: *Corporate pension funds typically prohibit employees from trading shares of the corporation during periods when the pension fund is undergoing significant change. Prior to 2002, however, these blackout periods did not affect the corporation's executives, who frequently received shares of the corporate stock as part of their compensation. During the collapse of Enron, for example, its pension plan was scheduled to change administrators at a time when Enron's stock price was falling. Enron's employees therefore could not sell their shares while the price was dropping, but its executives could and did sell their stock, consequently avoiding some of the losses. Section 306 was Congress's solution to the basic unfairness of this situation. This section of the act required the SEC to issue rules that prohibit any director or executive officer from trading during pension fund blackout periods. (The SEC later issued these rules, entitled Regulation Blackout Trading Restriction, or Reg BTR.) Section 306 also provided shareholders with a right to file a shareholder's derivative suit against officers and directors who have profited from trading during these blackout periods (provided that the corporation has failed to bring a suit). The officer or director can be forced to return to the corporation any profits received, regardless of whether the director or officer acted with bad intent.*

---

2. Codified at 15 U.S.C. Section 7244.

SECTION 402

Periodical and other reports[3]

* * * *

(i) Accuracy of financial reports

Each financial report that contains financial statements, and that is required to be prepared in accordance with (or reconciled to) generally accepted accounting principles under this chapter and filed with the Commission shall reflect all material correcting adjustments that have been identified by a registered public accounting firm in accordance with generally accepted accounting principles and the rules and regulations of the Commission.

(j) Off-balance sheet transactions

Not later than 180 days after July 30, 2002, the Commission shall issue final rules providing that each annual and quarterly financial report required to be filed with the Commission shall disclose all material off-balance sheet transactions, arrangements, obligations (including contingent obligations), and other relationships of the issuer with unconsolidated entities or other persons, that may have a material current or future effect on financial condition, changes in financial condition, results of operations, liquidity, capital expenditures, capital resources, or significant components of revenues or expenses.

(k) Prohibition on personal loans to executives

(1) In general

It shall be unlawful for any issuer (as defined in section 7201 of this title), directly or indirectly, including through any subsidiary, to extend or maintain credit, to arrange for the extension of credit, or to renew an extension of credit, in the form of a personal loan to or for any director or executive officer (or equivalent thereof) of that issuer. An extension of credit maintained by the issuer on July 30, 2002, shall not be subject to the provisions of this subsection, provided that there is no material modification to any term of any such extension of credit or any renewal of any such extension of credit on or after July 30, 2002.

(2) Limitation

Paragraph (1) does not preclude any home improvement and manufactured home loans (as that term is defined in section 1464 of Title 12), consumer credit (as defined in section 1602 of this title), or any extension of credit under an open end credit plan (as defined in section 1602 of this title), or a charge card (as defined in section 1637(c)(4)(e) of this title), or any extension of credit by a broker or dealer registered under section 78o of this title to an employee of that broker or dealer to buy, trade, or carry securities, that is permitted under rules or regulations of the Board of Governors of the Federal Reserve System pursuant to section 78g of this title (other than an extension of credit that would be used to purchase the stock of that issuer), that is—

(A) made or provided in the ordinary course of the consumer credit business of such issuer;

(B) of a type that is generally made available by such issuer to the public; and

(C) made by such issuer on market terms, or terms that are no more favorable than those offered by the issuer to the general public for such extensions of credit.

(3) Rule of construction for certain loans

Paragraph (1) does not apply to any loan made or maintained by an insured depository institution (as defined in section 1813 of Title 12), if the loan is subject to the insider lending restrictions of section 375b of Title 12.

(l) Real time issuer disclosures

Each issuer reporting under subsection (a) of this section or section 78o(d) of this title shall disclose to the public on a rapid and current basis such additional information concerning material changes in the financial condition or operations of the issuer, in plain English, which may include trend and qualitative information and graphic presentations, as the Commission determines, by rule, is necessary or useful for the protection of investors and in the public interest.

EXPLANATORY COMMENTS: *Corporate executives during the Enron era typically received extremely large salaries, significant bonuses, and abundant stock options, even when the companies for which they worked were suffering. Executives were also routinely given personal loans from corporate funds, many of which were never paid back. The average large company during that period loaned almost $1 million a year to top executives, and some companies, including Tyco International and Adelphia Communications Corporation, loaned hundreds of millions of dollars to their executives every year. Section 402 amended the 1934 Securities Exchange Act to prohibit public companies from making personal loans to executive officers and directors. There are a few exceptions to this prohibition, such as home-improvement loans made in the ordinary course of business. Note also that while loans are forbidden, outright gifts are not. A corporation is free to give gifts to its executives, including cash, provided that these gifts are disclosed on its financial reports. The idea is that corporate directors will be deterred from making substantial gifts to their executives by the disclosure requirement—particularly if the corporation's financial condition is questionable—because making such gifts could be perceived as abusing their authority.*

SECTION 403

Directors, officers, and principal stockholders[4]

(a) Disclosures required

(1) Directors, officers, and principal stockholders required to file

Every person who is directly or indirectly the beneficial owner of more than 10 percent of any class of any equity security (other than an exempted security) which is registered pursuant to section 78l of this title, or who is a director or an officer of the issuer of such security, shall file the statements required by this subsection with the Commission (and, if such security is registered on a national securities exchange, also with the exchange).

(2) Time of filing

The statements required by this subsection shall be filed—

---

3. This section of the Sarbanes-Oxley Act amended some of the provisions of the 1934 Securities Exchange Act and added the paragraphs reproduced here at 15 U.S.C. Section 78m.

4. This section of the Sarbanes-Oxley Act amended the disclosure provisions of the 1934 Securities Exchange Act, at 15 U.S.C. Section 78p.

(A) at the time of the registration of such security on a national securities exchange or by the effective date of a registration statement filed pursuant to section 78l(g) of this title;

(B) within 10 days after he or she becomes such beneficial owner, director, or officer;

(C) if there has been a change in such ownership, or if such person shall have purchased or sold a security-based swap agreement (as defined in section 206(b) of the Gramm-Leach-Bliley Act (15 U.S.C. 78c note)) involving such equity security, before the end of the second business day following the day on which the subject transaction has been executed, or at such other time as the Commission shall establish, by rule, in any case in which the Commission determines that such 2-day period is not feasible.

(3) Contents of statements

A statement filed—

(A) under subparagraph (A) or (B) of paragraph (2) shall contain a statement of the amount of all equity securities of such issuer of which the filing person is the beneficial owner; and

(B) under subparagraph (C) of such paragraph shall indicate ownership by the filing person at the date of filing, any such changes in such ownership, and such purchases and sales of the security-based swap agreements as have occurred since the most recent such filing under such subparagraph.

(4) Electronic filing and availability

Beginning not later than 1 year after July 30, 2002—

(A) a statement filed under subparagraph (C) of paragraph (2) shall be filed electronically;

(B) the Commission shall provide each such statement on a publicly accessible Internet site not later than the end of the business day following that filing; and

(C) the issuer (if the issuer maintains a corporate website) shall provide that statement on that corporate website, not later than the end of the business day following that filing.

*   *   *   *

EXPLANATORY COMMENTS: *This section dramatically shortens the time period provided in the Securities Exchange Act of 1934 for disclosing transactions by insiders. The prior law stated that most transactions had to be reported within ten days of the beginning of the following month, although certain transactions did not have to be reported until the following fiscal year (within the first forty-five days). Because some of the insider trading that occurred during the Enron fiasco did not have to be disclosed (and was therefore not discovered) until long after the transactions, Congress added this section to reduce the time period for making disclosures. Under Section 403, most transactions by insiders must be electronically filed with the SEC within two business days. Also, any company that maintains a Web site must post these SEC filings on its site by the end of the next business day. Congress enacted this section in the belief that if insiders are required to file reports of their transactions promptly with the SEC, companies will do more to police themselves and prevent insider trading.*

SECTION 404

Management assessment of internal controls[5]

(a) Rules required

The Commission shall prescribe rules requiring each annual report required by section 78m(a) or 78o(d) of this title to contain an internal control report, which shall—

(1) state the responsibility of management for establishing and maintaining an adequate internal control structure and procedures for financial reporting; and

(2) contain an assessment, as of the end of the most recent fiscal year of the issuer, of the effectiveness of the internal control structure and procedures of the issuer for financial reporting.

(b) Internal control evaluation and reporting

With respect to the internal control assessment required by subsection (a) of this section, each registered public accounting firm that prepares or issues the audit report for the issuer shall attest to, and report on, the assessment made by the management of the issuer. An attestation made under this subsection shall be made in accordance with standards for attestation engagements issued or adopted by the Board. Any such attestation shall not be the subject of a separate engagement.

*   *   *   *

EXPLANATORY COMMENTS: *This section was enacted to prevent corporate executives from claiming they were ignorant of significant errors in their companies' financial reports. For instance, several CEOs testified before Congress that they simply had no idea that the corporations' financial statements were off by billions of dollars. Congress therefore passed Section 404, which requires each annual report to contain a description and assessment of the company's internal control structure and financial reporting procedures. The section also requires that an audit be conducted of the internal control assessment, as well as the financial statements contained in the report. This section goes hand in hand with Section 302 (which, as discussed previously, requires various certifications attesting to the accuracy of the information in financial reports).*

Section 404 has been one of the more controversial and expensive provisions in the Sarbanes-Oxley Act because it requires companies to assess their own internal financial controls to make sure that their financial statements are reliable and accurate. A corporation might need to set up a disclosure committee and a coordinator, establish codes of conduct for accounting and financial personnel, create documentation procedures, provide training, and outline the individuals who are responsible for performing each of the procedures. Companies that were already well managed have not experienced substantial difficulty complying with this section. Other companies, however, have spent millions of dollars setting up, documenting, and evaluating their internal financial control systems. Although initially creating the internal financial control system is a one-time-only expense, the costs of maintaining and evaluating it are ongoing. Some corporations that spent considerable sums complying with Section 404 have been able to offset these costs by discovering and correcting inefficiencies or frauds within their systems. Nevertheless, it is unlikely that any corporation will find compliance with this section to be inexpensive.

---

5. Codified at 15 U.S.C. Section 7262.

SECTION 802(a)

Destruction, alteration, or falsification of records in Federal investigations and bankruptcy[6]

Whoever knowingly alters, destroys, mutilates, conceals, covers up, falsifies, or makes a false entry in any record, document, or tangible object with the intent to impede, obstruct, or influence the investigation or proper administration of any matter within the jurisdiction of any department or agency of the United States or any case filed under title 11, or in relation to or contemplation of any such matter or case, shall be fined under this title, imprisoned not more than 20 years, or both.

Destruction of corporate audit records[7]

(a) (1) Any accountant who conducts an audit of an issuer of securities to which section 10A(a) of the Securities Exchange Act of 1934 (15 U.S.C. 78j-1(a)) applies, shall maintain all audit or review workpapers for a period of 5 years from the end of the fiscal period in which the audit or review was concluded.

(2) The Securities and Exchange Commission shall promulgate, within 180 days, after adequate notice and an opportunity for comment, such rules and regulations, as are reasonably necessary, relating to the retention of relevant records such as workpapers, documents that form the basis of an audit or review, memoranda, correspondence, communications, other documents, and records (including electronic records) which are created, sent, or received in connection with an audit or review and contain conclusions, opinions, analyses, or financial data relating to such an audit or review, which is conducted by any accountant who conducts an audit of an issuer of securities to which section 10A(a) of the Securities Exchange Act of 1934 (15 U.S.C. 78j-1(a)) applies. The Commission may, from time to time, amend or supplement the rules and regulations that it is required to promulgate under this section, after adequate notice and an opportunity for comment, in order to ensure that such rules and regulations adequately comport with the purposes of this section.

(b) Whoever knowingly and willfully violates subsection (a)(1), or any rule or regulation promulgated by the Securities and Exchange Commission under subsection (a)(2), shall be fined under this title, imprisoned not more than 10 years, or both.

(c) Nothing in this section shall be deemed to diminish or relieve any person of any other duty or obligation imposed by Federal or State law or regulation to maintain, or refrain from destroying, any document.

* * * *

EXPLANATORY COMMENTS: *Section 802(a) enacted two new statutes that punish those who alter or destroy documents. The first statute is not specifically limited to securities fraud cases. It provides that anyone who alters, destroys, or falsifies records in federal investigations or bankruptcy may be criminally prosecuted and sentenced to a fine or to up to twenty years in prison, or both. The second statute requires auditors of public companies to keep all audit or review working papers for five years but expressly allows the SEC to amend or supplement these requirements as it sees fit. The SEC has, in fact,*

amended this section by issuing a rule that requires auditors who audit reporting companies to retain working papers for seven years from the conclusion of the review. Section 802(a) further provides that anyone who knowingly and willfully violates this statute is subject to criminal prosecution and can be sentenced to a fine, imprisoned for up to ten years, or both if convicted.

This portion of the Sarbanes-Oxley Act implicitly recognizes that persons who are under investigation often are tempted to respond by destroying or falsifying documents that might prove their complicity in wrongdoing. The severity of the punishment should provide a strong incentive for these individuals to resist the temptation.

SECTION 804

Time limitations on the commencement of civil actions arising under Acts of Congress[8]

(a) Except as otherwise provided by law, a civil action arising under an Act of Congress enacted after the date of the enactment of this section may not be commenced later than 4 years after the cause of action accrues.

(b) Notwithstanding subsection (a), a private right of action that involves a claim of fraud, deceit, manipulation, or contrivance in contravention of a regulatory requirement concerning the securities laws, as defined in section 3(a)(47) of the Securities Exchange Act of 1934 (15 U.S.C. 78c(a)(47)), may be brought not later than the earlier of—

(1) 2 years after the discovery of the facts constituting the violation; or

(2) 5 years after such violation.

* * * *

EXPLANATORY COMMENTS: *Prior to the enactment of this section, Section 10(b) of the Securities Exchange Act of 1934 had no express statute of limitations. The courts generally required plaintiffs to have filed suit within one year from the date that they should (using due diligence) have discovered that a fraud had been committed but no later than three years after the fraud occurred. Section 804 extends this period by specifying that plaintiffs must file a lawsuit within two years after they discover (or should have discovered) a fraud but no later than five years after the fraud's occurrence. This provision has prevented the courts from dismissing numerous securities fraud lawsuits.*

SECTION 806

Civil action to protect against retaliation in fraud cases[9]

(a) Whistleblower protection for employees of publicly traded companies.—

No company with a class of securities registered under section 12 of the Securities Exchange Act of 1934 (15 U.S.C. 78l), or that is required to file reports under section 15(d) of the Securities Exchange Act of 1934 (15 U.S.C. 78o(d)), or any officer, employee, contractor, subcontractor, or agent of such company, may discharge, demote, suspend, threaten, harass, or in any other manner discriminate against an

---

6. Codified at 15 U.S.C. Section 1519.
7. Codified at 15 U.S.C. Section 1520.

8. Codified at 28 U.S.C. Section 1658.
9. Codified at 18 U.S.C. Section 1514A.

employee in the terms and conditions of employment because of any lawful act done by the employee—

(1) to provide information, cause information to be provided, or otherwise assist in an investigation regarding any conduct which the employee reasonably believes constitutes a violation of section 1341, 1343, 1344, or 1348, any rule or regulation of the Securities and Exchange Commission, or any provision of Federal law relating to fraud against shareholders, when the information or assistance is provided to or the investigation is conducted by—

(A) a Federal regulatory or law enforcement agency;

(B) any Member of Congress or any committee of Congress; or

(C) a person with supervisory authority over the employee (or such other person working for the employer who has the authority to investigate, discover, or terminate misconduct); or

(2) to file, cause to be filed, testify, participate in, or otherwise assist in a proceeding filed or about to be filed (with any knowledge of the employer) relating to an alleged violation of section 1341, 1343, 1344, or 1348, any rule or regulation of the Securities and Exchange Commission, or any provision of Federal law relating to fraud against shareholders.

(b) Enforcement action.—

(1) In general.—A person who alleges discharge or other discrimination by any person in violation of subsection (a) may seek relief under subsection (c), by—

(A) filing a complaint with the Secretary of Labor; or

(B) if the Secretary has not issued a final decision within 180 days of the filing of the complaint and there is no showing that such delay is due to the bad faith of the claimant, bringing an action at law or equity for de novo review in the appropriate district court of the United States, which shall have jurisdiction over such an action without regard to the amount in controversy.

(2) Procedure.—

(A) In general.—An action under paragraph (1)(A) shall be governed under the rules and procedures set forth in section 42121(b) of title 49, United States Code.

(B) Exception.—Notification made under section 42121(b)(1) of title 49, United States Code, shall be made to the person named in the complaint and to the employer.

(C) Burdens of proof.—An action brought under paragraph (1)(B) shall be governed by the legal burdens of proof set forth in section 42121(b) of title 49, United States Code.

(D) Statute of limitations.—An action under paragraph (1) shall be commenced not later than 90 days after the date on which the violation occurs.

(c) Remedies.—

(1) In general.—An employee prevailing in any action under subsection (b)(1) shall be entitled to all relief necessary to make the employee whole.

(2) Compensatory damages.—Relief for any action under paragraph (1) shall include—

(A) reinstatement with the same seniority status that the employee would have had, but for the discrimination;

(B) the amount of back pay, with interest; and

(C) compensation for any special damages sustained as a result of the discrimination, including litigation costs, expert witness fees, and reasonable attorney fees.

(d) Rights retained by employee.—Nothing in this section shall be deemed to diminish the rights, privileges, or remedies of any employee under any Federal or State law, or under any collective bargaining agreement.

EXPLANATORY COMMENTS: *Section 806 is one of several provisions that were included in the Sarbanes-Oxley Act to encourage and protect whistleblowers—that is, employees who report their employer's alleged violations of securities law to the authorities. This section applies to employees, agents, and independent contractors who work for publicly traded companies or testify about such a company during an investigation. It sets up an administrative procedure at the U.S. Department of Labor for individuals who claim that their employer retaliated against them (fired or demoted them, for example) for blowing the whistle on the employer's wrongful conduct. It also allows the award of civil damages—including back pay, reinstatement, special damages, attorneys' fees, and court costs—to employees who prove that they suffered retaliation. Since this provision was enacted, whistleblowers have filed numerous complaints with the U.S. Department of Labor under this section.*

SECTION 807

Securities fraud[10]

Whoever knowingly executes, or attempts to execute, a scheme or artifice—

(1) to defraud any person in connection with any security of an issuer with a class of securities registered under section 12 of the Securities Exchange Act of 1934 (15 U.S.C. 78l) or that is required to file reports under section 15(d) of the Securities Exchange Act of 1934 (15 U.S.C. 78o(d)); or

(2) to obtain, by means of false or fraudulent pretenses, representations, or promises, any money or property in connection with the purchase or sale of any security of an issuer with a class of securities registered under section 12 of the Securities Exchange Act of 1934 (15 U.S.C. 78l) or that is required to file reports under section 15(d) of the Securities Exchange Act of 1934 (15 U.S.C. 78o(d)); shall be fined under this title, or imprisoned not more than 25 years, or both.

* * * *

EXPLANATORY COMMENTS: *Section 807 adds a new provision to the federal criminal code that addresses securities fraud. Prior to 2002, federal securities law had already made it a crime—under Section 10(b) of the Securities Exchange Act of 1934 and SEC Rule 10b-5, both of which are discussed in Chapter 27—to intentionally defraud someone in connection with a purchase or sale of securities, but the offense was not listed in the federal criminal code. Also, paragraph 2 of Section 807 goes beyond what is prohibited under securities law by making it a crime to obtain by means of false or fraudulent pretenses any money or property from the purchase or sale of securities. This new provision allows violators to be punished by up to twenty-five years in prison, a fine, or both.*

---

10. Codified at 18 U.S.C. Section 1348.

SECTION 906

Failure of corporate officers to certify financial reports[11]

(a) Certification of periodic financial reports.—Each periodic report containing financial statements filed by an issuer with the Securities Exchange Commission pursuant to section 13(a) or 15(d) of the Securities Exchange Act of 1934 (15 U.S.C. 78m(a) or 78o(d)) shall be accompanied by a written statement by the chief executive officer and chief financial officer (or equivalent thereof) of the issuer.

(b) Content.—The statement required under subsection (a) shall certify that the periodic report containing the financial statements fully complies with the requirements of section 13(a) or 15(d) of the Securities Exchange Act of 1934 (15 U.S.C. 78m or 78o(d)) and that information contained in the periodic report fairly presents, in all material respects, the financial condition and results of operations of the issuer.

(c) Criminal penalties.—Whoever—

(1) certifies any statement as set forth in subsections (a) and (b) of this section knowing that the periodic report accompanying the statement does not comport with all the requirements set forth in this section shall be fined not more than $1,000,000 or imprisoned not more than 10 years, or both; or

(2) willfully certifies any statement as set forth in subsections (a) and (b) of this section knowing that the periodic report accompanying the statement does not comport with all the requirements set forth in this section shall be fined not more than $5,000,000, or imprisoned not more than 20 years, or both.

EXPLANATORY COMMENTS: *As previously discussed, under Section 302 a corporation's CEO and CFO are required to certify that they believe the quarterly and annual reports their company files with the SEC are accurate and fairly present the company's financial condition. Section 906 adds "teeth" to these requirements by authorizing criminal penalties for those officers who intentionally certify inaccurate SEC filings. Knowing violations of the requirements are punishable by a fine of up to $1 million, ten years' imprisonment, or both. Willful violators may be fined up to $5 million, sentenced to up to twenty years' imprisonment, or both. Although the difference between a knowing and a willful violation is not entirely clear, the section is obviously intended to remind corporate officers of the serious consequences of certifying inaccurate reports to the SEC.*

---

11. Codified at 18 U.S.C. Section 1350.

APPENDIX E
Sample Answers for End-of-Chapter Hypothetical Questions with Sample Answers

1.2A Hypothetical Question with Sample Answer

1. The U.S. Constitution—The U.S. Constitution is the supreme law of the land. A law in violation of the Constitution, no matter what its source, will be declared unconstitutional and will not be enforced.
2. The federal statute—Under the U.S. Constitution, when there is a conflict between federal law and state law, federal law prevails.
3. The state statute—State statutes are enacted by state legislatures. Areas not covered by state statutory law are governed by state case law.
4. The U.S. Constitution—State constitutions are supreme within their respective borders unless they conflict with the U.S. Constitution, which is the supreme law of the land.
5. The federal administrative regulation—Under the U.S. Constitution, when there is a conflict between federal law and state law, federal law prevails.

2.2A Hypothetical Question with Sample Answer

Marya can bring suit in all three courts. The trucking firm did business in Florida, and the accident occurred there. Thus, the state of Florida would have jurisdiction over the defendant. Because the firm was headquartered in Georgia and had its principal place of business in that state, Marya could also sue in a Georgia court. Finally, because the amount in controversy exceeds $75,000, the suit could be brought in federal court on the basis of diversity of citizenship.

3.2A Hypothetical Question with Sample Answer

This question essentially asks whether good behavior can ever be unethical. The answer to this question depends on which approach to ethical reasoning you are using. Under the outcome-based approach of utilitarianism, it is simply not possible for selfish motives to be unethical if they result in good conduct. A good outcome is moral regardless of the nature of the action itself or the reason for the action. Under a duty-based approach, motive would be more relevant in assessing whether a firm's conduct was ethical. You would need to analyze the firm's conduct in terms of religious truths or to determine whether human beings were being treated with the inherent dignity that they deserve. Although a good motive would not justify a bad act to a religious ethicist, in this situation the actions were good and the motive was questionable (because the firm was simply seeking to increase its profit). Nevertheless, unless one's religion prohibited making a profit, the firm's actions would likely not be considered unethical. Applying Kantian ethics would require you to evaluate the firm's actions in light of what would happen if everyone in society acted that way (categorical imperative). Here, because the conduct was good, it would be positive for soci-ety if every firm acted that way. Hence, the profit-seeking motive would be irrelevant in a Kantian analysis. In a debate between motive and conduct, then, conduct is almost always given greater weight in evaluating ethics.

4.2A Hypothetical Question with Sample Answer

The correct answer is (2). The *Restatement (Second) of Torts* defines negligence as "conduct that falls below the standard established by law for the protection of others against unreasonable risk of harm." The standard established by law is that of a reasonable person acting with due care in the circumstances. Mary was well aware that the medication she took would make her drowsy, and her failure to observe due care (that is, refrain from driving) under the circumstances was negligent. Answer (1) is incorrect because Mary had no reason to believe the golf club was defective, and she could not have prevented the injury by the exercise of due care.

5.2A Hypothetical Question with Sample Answer

1. Making a photocopy of an article in a scholarly journal "for purposes such as . . . scholarship, or research, is not an infringement of copyright" under Section 107 of the Copyright Act.
2. This is an example of trademark infringement. Whenever a trademark is copied to a substantial degree or used in its entirety by one who is not entitled to its use, the trademark has been infringed.
3. This is the most likely example of copyright infringement. Generally, determining whether the reproduction of copyrighted material constitutes copyright infringement is made on a case-by-case basis under the "fair use" doctrine, as expressed in Section 107 of the Copyright Act. Courts look at such factors as the "purpose and character" of a use, such as whether it is "of a commercial nature;" "the amount and substantiality of the portion used in relation to the copyrighted work as a whole;" and "the effect of the use on the potential market" for the copied work. In this question, the DVD store owner is copying copyright-protected works in their entirety for commercial purposes, thereby affecting the market for the works.
4. Recording a television program "for purposes such as . . . teaching . . . is not an infringement of copyright" under Section 107 of the Copyright Act.

6.2A Hypothetical Question with Sample Answer

1. Sarah has wrongfully taken and carried away the personal property of another with the intent to permanently deprive the owner of such property. She has committed the crime of larceny.

2. Sarah has unlawfully and forcibly taken the personal property of another. She has committed the crime of robbery.

3. Sarah has broken and entered a dwelling with the intent to commit a felony. She has committed the crime of burglary. (Most states have dispensed with the requirement that the act take place at night.)

Note the basic differences: Burglary requires breaking and entering into a building without the use of force against a person. Robbery does not involve any breaking and entering, but force is required. Larceny is the taking of personal property without force and without breaking and entering into a building. Generally, because force is used, robbery is considered the most serious of these crimes and carries the most severe penalties. Larceny involves no force or threat to human life; therefore, it carries the least severe penalty of the three. Burglary, because it involves breaking and entering, frequently where people live, carries a lesser penalty than robbery but a greater penalty than larceny.

7.2A HYPOTHETICAL QUESTION WITH SAMPLE ANSWER

According to the question, Janine was apparently unconscious or otherwise unable to agree to a contract for the nursing services she received while she was in the hospital. As you read in the chapter, however, sometimes the law will create a fictional contract in order to prevent one party from unjustly receiving a benefit at the expense of another. This is known as a quasi contract and provides a basis for Nursing Services to recover the value of the services it provided while Janine was in the hospital. As for the at-home services that were provided to Janine, because Janine was aware that those services were being provided for her, Nursing Services can recover for those services under an implied-in-fact contract. Under this type of contract, the conduct of the parties creates and defines the terms. Janine's acceptance of the services constitutes her agreement to form a contract, and she will probably be required to pay Nursing Services in full.

8.2A HYPOTHETICAL QUESTION WITH SAMPLE ANSWER

1. Death of either the offeror or the offeree prior to acceptance automatically terminates a revocable offer. The basic legal reason is that the offer is personal to the parties and cannot be passed on to others, not even to the estate of the deceased. This rule applies even if the other party is unaware of the death. Thus, Cherneck's offer terminates on Cherneck's death, and Bollow's later acceptance does not constitute a contract.

2. An offer is automatically terminated by the destruction of the specific subject matter of the offer prior to acceptance. Thus, Bollow's acceptance after the fire does not constitute a contract.

3. When the offer is irrevocable, under an option contract, death of the offeror does not terminate the option contract, and the offeree can accept the offer to sell the equipment, binding the offeror's estate to performance. Performance is not personal to Cherneck, as the estate can transfer title to the equipment. Knowledge of the death is immaterial to the offeree's right of acceptance. Thus, Bollow can hold Cherneck's estate to a contract for the purchase of the equipment.

4. When the offer is irrevocable, under an option contract, death of the offeree also does not terminate the offer. Because the option is a

separate contract, the contract survives and passes to the offeree's estate, which can exercise the option by acceptance within the option period. Thus, acceptance by Bollow's estate binds Cherneck to a contract for the sale of the equipment.

9.2A HYPOTHETICAL QUESTION WITH SAMPLE ANSWER

Contracts in restraint of trade are usually illegal and unenforceable. An exception to this rule applies to a covenant not to compete that is ancillary to certain types of business contracts in which some fair protection is deemed appropriate (such as in the sale of a business). The covenant, however, must be reasonable in terms of time and area to be legally enforceable. If either term is excessive, the court can declare that the restraint goes beyond what is necessary for reasonable protection. In this event, the court can either declare the covenant illegal or it can reform the covenant to make the terms of time and area reasonable and then enforce it. Suppose the court declares the covenant illegal and unenforceable. Because the covenant is ancillary and severable from the primary contract, the primary contract is not affected by such a ruling. In the case of Hotel Lux, the primary contract concerns employment; the covenant is ancillary and desirable for the protection of the hotel. The time period of one year may be considered reasonable for a chef with an international reputation. The reasonableness of the three-state area restriction may be questioned, however. If it is found to be reasonable, the covenant probably will be enforced. If it is not found to be reasonable, the court could declare the entire covenant illegal, allowing Perlee to be employed by any restaurant or hotel, including one in direct competition with Hotel Lux. Alternatively, the court could reform the covenant, making its terms reasonable for protecting Hotel Lux's normal customer market area.

10.2A HYPOTHETICAL QUESTION WITH SAMPLE ANSWER

In this situation, Gemma becomes what is known as a *guarantor* on the loan. That is, she guarantees the hardware store that she will pay for the mower if her brother fails to do so. This kind of collateral promise, in which the guarantor states that he or she will become responsible *only* if the primary party does not perform, must be in writing to be enforceable. There is an exception, however. If the main purpose in accepting secondary liability is to secure a personal benefit — for example, if Gemma's brother bought the mower for her — the contract need not be in writing. The assumption is that a court can infer from the circumstances of the case whether the main purpose was to secure a personal benefit and thus, in effect, to answer for the guarantor's own debt.

11.3A. HYPOTHETICAL QUESTION WITH SAMPLE ANSWER

As a general rule any right(s) flowing from a contract can be assigned. There are, however, exceptions, such as when the contract expressly and specifically prohibits or limits the right of assignment. Because of the principle of freedom of contract, this type of prohibition is enforced — unless it is deemed contrary to public policy. For example, courts have held that a prohibition clause against assignment that restrains the alienation of property is invalid by virtue of being against public policy. Authorities differ on how a case like Aron's should be decided. Some courts would enforce the prohibition completely, holding that Aron's assignment to Erica is completely ineffective without the landlord's consent. Others would permit the assignment to be effective, with the landlord's remedies limited to the normal contract remedies ensuing from Aron's breach.

12.2A Hypothetical Question with Sample Answer

Generally, the equitable remedy of specific performance will be granted only if two criteria are met: monetary damages (under the circumstances) must be inadequate as a remedy, and the subject matter of the contract must be unique.

1. In the sale of land, the buyer's contract is for a specific piece of real property. The land under contract is unique, because no two pieces of real property have the same legal description. In addition, monetary damages would not compensate a buyer adequately, as the same land cannot be purchased elsewhere. Specific performance is an appropriate remedy.

2. The basic criteria for specific performance do not apply well to personal service contracts. If the identical service contracted for is readily available from others, the service is not unique and monetary damages for nonperformance are adequate. If, however, the services are so personal that only the contracted party can perform them, the contract meets the test of uniqueness; but the courts will refuse to decree specific performance based on either of two theories. First, the enforcement of specific performance requires involuntary servitude (prohibited by the Thirteenth Amendment to the U. S. Constitution). Second, it is impractical to attempt to force meaningful performance by someone against his or her will. In the case of Marita and Horace, specific performance is not an appropriate remedy.

3. A rare coin is unique, and monetary damages for breach are inadequate, as Juan cannot obtain a substantially identical substitute in the market. This is a typical case where specific performance is an appropriate remedy.

4. The key fact for consideration here is that this is a closely held corporation. Therefore, the stock is not available in the market, and the shares become unique. The uniqueness of these shares is enhanced by the fact that if Cary sells his 4 percent of the shares to De Valle, De Valle will have a controlling voice in the corporation. Because of this, monetary damages for De Valle are totally inadequate as a remedy. Specific performance is an appropriate remedy.

13.2A Hypothetical Question with Sample Answer

Anne has entered into an enforceable contract to subscribe to *E-Commerce Weekly*. In this problem, the offer to deliver, via e-mail, the newsletter was presented by the offeror with a statement of how to accept—by clicking on the "SUBSCRIBE" button. Consideration was in the promise to deliver the newsletter and at the price that the subscriber agreed to pay. The offeree had an opportunity to read the terms of the subscription agreement before making the contract. Whether or not she actually read those terms does not matter.

14.2A Hypothetical Question with Sample Answer

The entire answer falls under UCC 2–206(1)(b), because the situation deals with a buyer's order to buy goods for prompt shipment. The law is that such an order or offer invites acceptance by

a prompt *promise* to ship conforming goods. If the promise (acceptance) is sent by a medium reasonable under the circumstances, the acceptance is effective when sent. Therefore, a contract was formed on October 8, and it required Fulsom to ship one hundred model Color-X television sets. Fulsom's shipment is nonconforming, and Salinger is correct in claiming that Fulsom is in breach. Fulsom's claim would be valid if Fulsom had not sent its promise of shipment. The Code provides that shipment of nonconforming goods constitutes an acceptance *unless* the seller seasonably notifies the buyer that such shipment is sent only as an accommodation. Thus, had a contract not been formed on October 8, the nonconforming shipment on the 28th would not be treated as an acceptance, and no contract would be in existence to breach.

15.2A Hypothetical Question with Sample Answer

1. In a destination contract, the risk of loss passes to the buyer when the goods are tendered to the buyer at the specified destination—in this case, San Francisco.

2. In a shipment contract, if the seller is required or authorized to ship goods by carrier, but the contract specifies no locale, the risk of loss passes to the buyer when the goods are duly delivered to the carrier.

3. If the seller is a merchant, risk of loss to goods held by the seller passes to the buyer when the buyer actually takes physical possession of the goods. If the seller is not a merchant, the risk of loss to goods held by the seller passes to the buyer on tender of delivery.

4. When a bailee is holding goods for a person who has contracted to sell them and the goods are to be delivered without being moved, risk of loss passes to the buyer when (1) the buyer receives a negotiable document of title for the goods, (2) the bailee acknowledges the buyer's right to possess the goods, or (3) the buyer receives a nonnegotiable document of title and has had a reasonable time to present the document to the bailee and demand the goods. (If the bailee refuses to honor the document, the risk of loss remains with the seller.) If the goods are to be delivered by being moved, but the contract does not specify whether it is a destination or a shipment contract, it is presumed to be a shipment contract. If no locale is specified in the contract, risk of loss passes to the buyer when the seller delivers the goods to the carrier.

16.2A Hypothetical Question with Sample Answer

No. Cummings had not breached the sales contract because the C.O.D. shipment had deprived him of his absolute right, in the absence of agreement, to inspect the goods before accepting them. Had Cummings requested or agreed to the C.O.D. method of shipment, the result would have been different. Because he had not agreed to the C.O.D. shipment, he was fully within his rights to refuse to accept the goods because he could not inspect them prior to acceptance. In this case, it was the seller who had breached the contract by shipping the goods C.O.D. without Cummings's consent.

17.2A Hypothetical Question with Sample Answer

Yes. To disclaim the implied warranty of fitness for a particular purpose, the disclaimer must be in writing and be conspicuous. Although the implied warranty of merchantability can be disclaimed orally, if the disclaimer is in writing it must be conspicuously written. This means that the disclaimer must—either by different color or type size or some other technique—stand out from the context in which it is printed so as to readily alert the reader of the document of the disclaimer. In this case, the disclaimer was printed in the same size and color of type as the rest of the contract and was not conspicuous. If this was the only warranty disclaimer, it is not effective and Tandy can recover.

18.2A HYPOTHETICAL QUESTION WITH SAMPLE ANSWER

No. Material alteration of a negotiable instrument may be a real defense against payment on the instrument. As against a holder in due course, the raising of the amount (material alteration) is only a defense as to the altered amount, and the HDC can recover according to the original tenor of the instrument [UCC 3–407(b)]. In this case, however, Williams materially contributed to the alteration by his negligence in writing the check in pencil. Thus, the defense of material alteration was not available to him, and Williams is liable to Boz for the $10,000 [UCC 3–406]. If Williams had written the check in ink, and Stein had altered the amount in such a clever fashion that Boz could take the check without notice and become an HDC, then Williams would have a real defense against paying $10,000. In the latter case, Boz, as an HDC, could collect only $1,000, the original amount of the check.

19.2A HYPOTHETICAL QUESTION WITH SAMPLE ANSWER

Under the Home Mortgage Disclosure Act (HMDA) and the Community Reinvestment Act of 1977, which were passed to prevent discrimination in lending practices, a bank is required to define its market area. This area must be established contiguous to the bank's branch offices. It must be mapped using the existing boundaries of the counties or the standard metropolitan areas (SMAs) in which the offices are located. A bank must delineate the community served, and annually review this delineation. The issue here is how a successful Internet-only bank could delineate its community. Does an Internet bank have a physically limited market area or serve a physically distinct community? Will the Federal Reserve Board, the government agency charged with enforcing this law, allow a bank to describe its market area as a "cybercommunity"?

20.2A HYPOTHETICAL QUESTION WITH SAMPLE ANSWER

Mendez has a security interest in Arabian Knight and is a perfected secured party. He has met all the necessary criteria listed under UCC 9–203 to be a secured creditor. Mendez has given value of $5,000 and has taken possession of the collateral, Arabian Knight, owned by Marsh (who has rights in the collateral). Thus, he has a security interest even though Marsh did not sign a security agreement. Once a security interest attaches, a transfer of possession of the collateral to the secured party can perfect the party's security interest without a filing [UCC 9–310(b)(6); 9–313]. Thus, a security interest was created and perfected at the time Marsh transferred Arabian Knight to Mendez as security for the loan.

21.2A. HYPOTHETICAL QUESTION WITH SAMPLE ANSWER

The Bankruptcy Code establishes a payment priority of claims from the debtor's estate. Each class of debt in this priority list must be fully paid before the next class in priority is entitled to any of the proceeds. If insufficient funds remain to pay an entire class, the proceeds are distributed on a pro rata basis to each creditor within that class. The order of priority for claims listed in this problem is as follows:

1. Administrative bankruptcy costs (Martinez)—$500.
2. Claims for back wages, limited to $4,300 per claimant, provided wages were earned within ninety days of petition (Kohak)—$4,300.
3. Taxes and penalties due and owing (Micanopa County)—$1,000.
4. General creditors, $10,000 (First Bank of Sunny Acres—$5,000; Calvin—$2,500; balance of Kohak wages owed—$2,500).

Because the amount remaining after paying (a), (b), and (c) is only $1,200, the general creditors will share on a pro rata basis. First Bank of Sunny Acres will receive $600 ($5,000/$10,000 × $1,200 = $600), and Calvin and Kohak will each receive $300 ($2,500/$10,000 × $1,200 = $300).

22.2A HYPOTHETICAL QUESTION WITH SAMPLE ANSWER

Agency is usually a consensual relationship in that the principal and agent agree that the agent will have the authority to act for the principal, binding the principal to any contract with a third party. If no agency in fact exists, the purported agent's contracts with third parties are not binding on the principal. In this case, no agency by agreement was created. Brown may claim that an agency by estoppel was created; however, this argument will fail. Agency by estoppel is applicable only when a *principal* causes a third person to believe that another person is the principal's agent. Then the third party's actions in dealing with the agent are in reliance upon the principal's words or actions and the third party's reasonable belief that the agent has authority. This is said to estop the principal from claiming that in fact no agency existed. Acts and declarations of the *agent*, however, do not in and of themselves create an agency by estoppel, because such actions should not reasonably lead a third person to believe that the purported agent has authority. In this case, Wade's declarations and allegations alone led Brown to believe that Wade was an agent. Gett's actions were not involved. It is not reasonable to believe that someone is an agent solely because he or she is a friend of the principal. Therefore, Brown cannot hold Gett liable unless Gett ratifies Wade's contract—which is unlikely, as Wade has disappeared with the rare coin.

23.2A HYPOTHETICAL QUESTION WITH SAMPLE ANSWER

The Occupational Safety and Health Act (OSHA) requires employers to provide safe working conditions for employees. The act prohibits employers from discharging or discriminating against any employee who refuses to work when the employee believes in good faith that he or she will risk death or great bodily harm by undertaking the employment activity. Denton and Carlo had sufficient reason to believe that the maintenance job required of them by their employer involved great risk, and therefore, under OSHA, their discharge was wrongful. Denton and Carlo can turn to the Occupational Safety and Health Administration, which is part of the U.S. Department of Labor, for assistance.

24.2A. QUESTION WITH SAMPLE ANSWER

1. A limited partner's interest is assignable. In fact, assignment allows the assignee to become a substituted limited partner with the consent of the remaining partners. The assignment, however, does not dissolve the limited partnership.

2. Bankruptcy of the limited partnership itself causes dissolution, but bankruptcy of one of the limited partners does not dissolve the partnership unless it causes the bankruptcy of the firm.
3. The retirement, death, or insanity of a general partner dissolves the partnership unless the business can be continued by the remaining general partners. Because Dorinda was the only general partner, her death dissolves the limited partnership.

25.2A Hypothetical Question with Sample Answer

It could be argued that Kora exceeded his authority when he cosigned the note on behalf of the corporation. The board of directors of a corporation delegates the authority to transact all ordinary business of the corporation to the president. If cosigning a note for a personal loan is not "ordinary business of the corporation," then the board, as principal, must ratify the act. There is no indication in the question that the board did so in this case.

26.2A Hypothetical Question with Sample Answer

Directors are personally answerable to the corporation and the shareholders for breach of their duty to exercise reasonable care in conducting the affairs of the corporation. Reasonable care is defined as being the degree of care that a reasonably prudent person would use in the conduct of personal business affairs. When directors delegate the running of the corporate affairs to officers, the directors are expected to use reasonable care in the selection and supervision of such officers. Failure to do so will make the directors liable for negligence or mismanagement. A director who dissents to an action by the board is not personally liable for losses resulting from that action. Unless the dissent is entered into the board meeting minutes, however, the director is presumed to have assented. Therefore, the first issue in the case of Starboard, Inc., is whether the board members failed to use reasonable care in the selection of the president, Tyson. If so, and particularly if the board failed to provide a reasonable amount of supervision (and openly embezzled funds indicate that failure), the directors will be personally liable. This liability will include Ellsworth unless she can prove that she dissented and that she tried to reasonably supervise Tyson. Considering the facts in this case, it is questionable that Ellsworth could prove this.

27.2A Hypothetical Question with Sample Answer

No. Under federal securities law, a stock split is exempt from registration requirements. This is because no *sale* of stock is involved. The existing shares are merely being split, and no consideration is received by the corporation for the additional shares created.

28.3A Hypothetical Question with Sample Answer

For Curtis to recover against the hotel, he must first prove that a bailment relationship was created between himself and the hotel as to the car or the fur coat, or both. For a bailment to exist, there must be a delivery of the personal property that gives the bailee exclusive possession of the property, and the bailee must knowingly accept the bailed property. If either element is lacking, there is no bailment relationship and no liability on the part of the bailee hotel. The facts clearly indicate that the bailee hotel took exclusive possession and control of Curtis's car, and it knowingly accepted the car when the attendant took the car from Curtis and parked it in the underground guarded garage, retaining the keys. Thus, a bailment was created as to the car, and, because a mutual benefit bailment was created, the hotel owes Curtis the duty to exercise reasonable care over the property and to return the bailed car at the end of the bailment. Failure to return the car creates a presumption of negligence (lack of reasonable care), and unless the hotel can rebut this presumption, the hotel is liable to Curtis for the loss of the car. As to the fur coat, the hotel neither knew nor expected that the trunk contained an expensive fur coat. Thus, although the hotel knowingly took exclusive possession of the car, the hotel did not do so with the fur coat. (But for a regular coat and other items likely to be in the car, the hotel would be liable.) Because no bailment of the expensive fur coat was created, the hotel has no liability for its loss.

29.2A Hypothetical Question with Sample Answer

Wiley understandably wants a general warranty deed, as this type of deed will give him the most extensive protection against any defects of title claimed against the property transferred. The general warranty would have Gemma warranting the following covenants:
1. Covenant of seisin and right to convey—a warranty that the seller has good title and power to convey.
2. Covenant against encumbrances—a guaranty by the seller that, unless stated, there are no outstanding encumbrances or liens against the property conveyed.
3. Covenant of quiet possession—a warranty that the grantee's possession will not be disturbed by others claiming a prior legal right. Gemma, however, is conveying only ten feet along a property line that may not even be accurately surveyed. Gemma therefore does not wish to make these warranties. Consequently, she is offering a quitclaim deed, which does not convey any warranties but conveys only whatever interest, if any, the grantor owns. Although title is passed by the quitclaim deed, the quality of the title is not warranted. Because Wiley really needs the property, it appears that he has three choices: he can accept the quitclaim deed; he can increase his offer price to obtain the general warranty deed he wants; or he can offer to have a title search made, which should satisfy both parties.

30.2A Hypothetical Question with Sample Answer

1. In most states, for a will to be valid, it must be in writing, signed by the testator, and witnessed (attested to) according to the statutes of the state. In some states the testator is also required to publish (declare) that the document is his or her last will and testament. (Such is not required under the Uniform Probate Code.) In the case of Benjamin, the will is unquestionably written (typewritten) and signed by the testator. The only problem is with the witnesses. Some states require three witnesses, and some invalidate a will if a named beneficiary is also a witness. The Uniform Probate Code provides that a will is valid even if attested to by an interested witness. Therefore, whether the will is valid depends on the state laws dealing with witness qualifications.
2. If the will is declared invalid, Benjamin's estate will pass in accordance with the state's intestacy laws. These statutes provide for distribution of an estate when there is no valid will. The intent of the statutes is to distribute the estate in the way that the deceased person would have wished. Generally, the estate is divided between a surviving spouse and all surviving children. Because Benjamin is a widower, if his only surviving child is Edward, the entire estate

will go to Edward, and Benjamin's grandchildren, Perry and Paul, will receive nothing from the estate.

3. If the will is valid, the estate will be divided between Benjamin's two children, Patricia and Edward. Should either or both predecease Benjamin, leaving children (Benjamin's grandchildren), the grandchildren take *per stirpes* the share that would have gone to their parent. In this case Edward, as a surviving child of Benjamin, would receive one-half of the estate, and Perry and Paul, as grandchildren, would each receive *per stirpes* one-fourth of the estate (one-half of the share that would have gone to their deceased mother, Patricia).

31.2A HYPOTHETICAL QUESTION WITH SAMPLE ANSWER

Assuming that the circuit court has abandoned the *Ultramares* rule, it is likely that the accounting firm of Goldman, Walters, Johnson & Co. will be held liable to Happydays State Bank for negligent preparation of financial statements. This hypothetical scenario is partially derived from *Citizens State Bank v. Timm, Schmidt & Co.* In *Citizens State Bank* the Supreme Court of Wisconsin enunciated various policy reasons for holding accountants liable to third parties even in the absence of privity. The court suggested that this potential liability would make accountants more careful in the preparation of financial statements. Moreover, in some situations the accountants may be the only solvent defendants, and hence, unless liability is imposed on accountants, third parties who reasonably rely on financial statements may go unprotected. The court further asserted that accountants, rather than third parties, are in better positions to spread the risks. If third parties such as banks have to absorb the costs of bad loans made as a result of negligently prepared financial statements, then the cost of credit to the public in general will increase.

In contrast, the court suggests that accountants are in a better position to spread the risk by purchasing liability insurance.

32.2A HYPOTHETICAL QUESTION WITH SAMPLE ANSWER

Each system has its advantages and its disadvantages. In a common law system, the courts independently develop the rules governing certain areas of law, such as torts and contracts. This judge-made law exists in addition to the laws passed by a legislature. Judges must follow precedential decisions in their jurisdictions, but courts may modify or even overturn precedents when deemed necessary. Also, if there is no case law to guide a court, the court may create a new rule of law. In a civil law system, the only official source of law is a statutory code. Courts are required to interpret the code and apply the rules to individual cases, but courts may not depart from the code and develop their own laws. In theory, the law code will set forth all the principles needed for the legal system. Common law and civil law systems are not wholly distinct. For example, the United States has a common law system, but crimes are defined by statute as in civil law systems. Civil law systems may allow considerable room for judges to develop law: law codes cannot be so precise as to address every contested issue, so the judiciary must interpret the codes. There are also significant differences among common law countries. The judges of different common law nations have produced differing common law principles. The roles of judges and lawyers under the different systems should be taken into account. Among other factors that should be considered in establishing a business law system and in deciding what regulations to impose are the goals that the system and its regulations are intended to achieve and the expectations of those to whom both will apply, including foreign and domestic investors.

index